Web Services: A Java™ Developer's Guide Using E-Speak

Y0-CGM-026

ISBN 0-13-062338-5

90000

9 780130 623386

Hewlett-Packard® Professional Books

OPERATING SYSTEMS

Diercks	MPE/iX System Administration Handbook
Fernandez	Configuring CDE: The Common Desktop Environment
Lund	Integrating UNIX and PC Network Operating Systems
Madell	Disk and File Management Tasks on HP-UX
Poniatowski	HP-UX 11i System Administration Handbook and Toolkit
Poniatowski	HP-UX 11.x System Administration Handbook and Toolkit
Poniatowski	HP-UX 11.x System Administration "How To" Book
Poniatowski	HP-UX System Administration Handbook and Toolkit
Poniatowski	Learning the HP-UX Operating System
Poniatowski	UNIX User's Handbook, Second Edition
Rehman	HP Certified, HP-UX System Administration
Roberts	UNIX and Windows 2000 Interoperability Guide
Sauers, Weygant	HP-UX Tuning and Performance
Stone, Symons	UNIX Fault Management
Weygant	Clusters for High Availability: A Primer of HP Solutions, Second Edition
Wong	HP-UX 11i Security

ONLINE/INTERNET

Amor	The E-business (R)evolution: Living and Working in an Interconnected World
Greenberg, Lakeland	A Methodology for Developing and Deploying Internet and Intranet Solutions
Greenberg, Lakeland	Building Professional Web Sites with the Right Tools
Klein	Building Enhanced HTML Help with DHTML and CSS
Werry, Mowbray	Online Communities: Commerce, Community Action, and the Virtual University

NETWORKING/COMMUNICATIONS

Blommers	OpenView Network Node Manager: Designing and Implementing an Enterprise Solution
Blommers	Practical Planning for Network Growth
Bruce, Dempsey	Security in Distributed Computing: Did You Lock the Door?
Lucke	Designing and Implementing Computer Workgroups

ENTERPRISE

Blommers	Architecting Enterprise Solutions with UNIX Networking
Cook	Building Enterprise Information Architectures
Missbach/Hoffmann	SAP Hardware Solutions: Servers, Storage, and Networks for mySAP.com
Pipkin	Halting the Hacker: A Practical Guide to Computer Security
Pipkin	Information Security: Protecting the Global Enterprise
Thornburgh	Fibre Channel for Mass Storage
Thornburgh, Schoenborn	Storage Area Networks: Designing and Implementing a Mass Storage System
Todman	Designing a Data Warehouse: Supporting Customer Relationship Management

PROGRAMMING

IMAGE PROCESSING

OTHER TITLES OF INTEREST

Library of Congress Cataloging-in-Publication Data

A catalog record for this book can be obtained from the Library of Congress.

Editorial/Production Supervision: Carol Wheelan
Acquisitions Editor: Jill Harry
Marketing Manager: Dan DePasquale
Manufacturing Buyer: Maura Zaldivar
Cover Design: Talar Boorujy
Cover Design Direction: Jerry Votta
Interior Series Design: Gail Cocker-Bogusz
Publisher, Hewlett-Packard Books: Patricia Pekary

© 2002 by Hewlett-Packard Company
Published by Prentice Hall PTR
Prentice-Hall, Inc.
Upper Saddle River, NJ 07458

Prentice Hall books are widely used by corporations and government agencies for training, marketing, and resale.

The publisher offers discounts on this book when ordered in bulk quantities. For more information, contact Corporate Sales Department, phone: 800-382-3419; fax: 201-236-7141; email: corpsales@prenhall.com. Or write Corporate Sales Department, Prentice Hall PTR, One Lake Street, Upper Saddle River, NJ 07458.

Product and company names mentioned herein are the trademarks or registered trademarks of their respective owners.

Printed in the United States of America

10 9 8 7 6 5 4 3 2 1

ISBN 0-13-062338-5

Pearson Education LTD.
Pearson Education Australia PTY, Limited
Pearson Education Singapore, Pte. Ltd.
Pearson Education North Asia Ltd.
Pearson Education Canada, Ltd.
Pearson Educación de Mexico, S.A. de C.V.
Pearson Education—Japan
Pearson Education Malaysia, Pte. Ltd.
Pearson Education, Upper Saddle River, New Jersey

Web Services: A Java™ Developer's Guide Using E-Speak

Naresh Apte
Toral Mehta

Hewlett-Packard Company
www.hp.com/hpbooks

Prentice Hall PTR
Upper Saddle River, New Jersey 07458
www.phptr.com

CONTENTS

FOREWORD

Most inventions or phenomena that have a fundamental impact on society are judged to be so only after the fact. It is only rarely that an invention that truly changes the world is recognized for its potential before it is actually put down on paper or, as in the case of software, before the idea is committed to code. In spite of this, I have no trepidation in repeating what I have consistently said since I first publicly shared my vision for "e-services" in 1996: e-services will have an impact on society that will surpass that of the Web. Now this is not to imply that e-services and the Web are competing with each other in any way — e-services build on and leverage the Web just as the Web built on and leveraged the Internet.

E-services was the marketing term for the concepts that my small team[1] and I had developed in a project we had started in 1995 and had impertinently called "Client-Utility." The term Client-Utility was to help contrast with "Client-Server." The idea with which we started was simple: abstract away IT resources, collect them in a virtual pool, and mediate requests to these resources. The mediation was bidirectional, in that the model was natively peer-to-peer from its very inception.

In 1998 my team and I were given the opportunity to start a new HP division, the E-Speak Operation, to productize our work. The charter that we largely defined for ourselves was to put HP back on the map as a pioneer that would gently open the world to an explosive new economy of e-services (later to be termed "web services") — a world where individuals and companies, small and large, all over the world could painlessly and quickly convert their ideas and assets into electroni-

---

[1] The renegade team consisted of Alan Karp, now at HP Labs, and Bill Rozas, now at Transmeta, and was later joined by Arindam Banerji, now also at HP Labs.

cally distributable services that could be discovered and used by other individuals and companies; a world where the barriers for profitable participation in this new internet-service economy would be sufficiently lowered for it to be inclusive and pervasive. In other words, to do for electronically distributable services what the Web had done for electronically distributable data. In fact, my oft-stated goal in this endeavor was to allow anyone to go from an idea to an operational service in 20 minutes or less. While not there yet, we will get there.

We succeeded in our charter as evinced by a number of analyst reports. And from my personal point of view, the ferocity with which IBM (WebSphere), Microsoft (.NET), Sun (SunOne), Oracle (Dynamic Web Services), and every major ISV, and in fact every major IT company, are throwing themselves at the Web services vision, gives me great confidence that our ideas of service-based computing will indeed become a pervasive reality. It gives me great satisfaction that HP's crusade is not a lonely one.

Let me step back and share with you a couple of the mechanisms we added as we moved from our original IT-centric vision of Client-Utility to our service-based computing vision embodied in e-services. These mechanisms are covered in more detail in this book. The first one was to add intelligence in the mediator for functionality like automatic fail-over, security, auditing, management, and brokering to find the *best* provider of a service request. The second came when we looked at our work from the point of view of what was happening with the Web. We decided to make not just IT but everything on the Web accessible as a mediated resource. While not particularly insightful by itself, it nevertheless pushed us in the direction of adopting http as the default transport protocol and the Document Exchange Model through the use of XML (and what later became SOAP) as the default messaging protocol. And from there it was a seemingly short but architecturally deep step of providing the underlying mechanisms that enabled capabilities to be added on-the-fly, as e-services themselves. The longevity of the Web can be ascribed to it being simple, open, and extensible. For e-Speak to enable our vision of e-services, it had to similarly be simple, open, and dynamically extensible. But making something simple is hard work. Making it dynamically extensible is even harder.

These motivations drove us to what will perhaps be the longest-lasting legacy of our work — we defined the fundamental, atomic constructs, the primordial soup, if you will, on top of which could be built all of the traditional capabilities required of an e-services platform. These constructs are embodied in the e-Speak engine. The e-Speak engine therefore can be reasonably accurately regarded as the operating system for e-services.

The voracious appetite in the industry today for "everything web services" has some excesses, no question, but it is not hype. The best part is that while the impact is revolutionary the technology can be applied in an evolutionary manner. It is apparent that when appropriately applied, presenting business assets or even content as web services will surely lead to organizations and business interactions that are evolvable and responsive.

This book will take you through the concepts that we developed early on around service-based computing. While it discusses the nitty-grittys of the e-Speak software, it also delves into the details of nontechnical aspects of service-based computing. Concepts such as a service ecosystem and service lifecycle are important foundations that are independent of any technology used to facilitate service-based computing. Naresh and Toral have done an excellent job in keeping the right balance between the two angles to make the book appropriate for both the technical developers as well as business managers. Whether you want to use the e-Speak software suite to create your e-service or just like to understand the e-service concepts, this book will provide you most of what you need.

Welcome to the world of e-services and web services!

Rajiv Gupta
HP Labs
Hewlett-Packard Company

PREFACE

Disruptive technologies are chasms in the way the world works. Internet- and intranet-based service economies are a fundamentally different way of exposing a company's assets to its consumers and partners. A company's assets are also expanded to include more than the physical finished goods inventory. In this new world, a company's business process is also an asset and thereby a revenue-generating vehicle.

The problem with disruptive technologies is the lack of solution-focused information that the victims of such chaos can hold onto and learn how to ride the wave with. The idea for this book was really a realization that the paradigm of Internet- and intranet-based services truly was a disruptive idea at the intersection of business and high tech.

The Spark
For Naresh, the spark for the book came while working with a group of developers and IT managers on a Hewlett-Packard Company (HP) project; Naresh saw a gaping hole between a representative set of expected users and the e-Speak technology. He discovered that the technical documentation providing in-depth information at the application programming interface (API) level or design level was not doing justice to business managers or even developers. They needed to be acclimated and welcomed into the world of Internet and intranet service-based economies as well as supported in the process of designing, developing, and deploying e-Speak-based e-services and web services.

The spark usually begins as a vague, somewhat ethereal reality in the artist's mind.

It's only the artist who can conceptualize the spark's existence. For Naresh, a tabla (Indian drums) artist himself, the book was just that — a spark of what could be. As he mustered support for this spark, it started to take shape. "We'll explain the concepts in an onion fashion," he said. The spark now had form, shape, and size as he and Toral worked on its proposal. To Naresh, being a part of and watching the spark leave his mind to appear as words on paper was a very fulfilling experience. The ability to connect with people all over the world (literally from Stamford, Connecticut to Pune, India) rallying around the spark will be remembered.

Moonlighting

For Toral, helping Naresh materialize the spark was a stimulating and very rewarding experience. A program manager by profession, she generally dealt with software from the outside — managing its lifecycle. Writing this book gave her a view from the inside; it gave her a chance to see the inner workings of software and, in the end, she could confidently say she knew what made e-Speak tick.

Jumping into the world of interface definitions and mailboxes was not the only highlight of writing this book for Toral. Also a freelance writer, she was used to having a creative license but she quickly learned how to funnel that creativity within the confines of technology offering. Her ability to harness the strong support of many others by relentlessly selling the spark was a pleasant and very memorable experience, as well.

We hope this book provides you the tool you need to fit e-service and web service technologies in your road maps because they are expected to be the next Chapter of the Internet.

Naresh Apte   Toral Mehta
Sunnyvale, CA   Milpitas, CA
July 2001   July 2001

ACKNOWLEDGMENTS

Writing this book has truly been a rewarding experience for us. The idea of writing a book was simply that — an idea. There were many people who helped turn that idea into a reality; without these people and their support, guidance, and — most of all — patience, this book would have remained simply an idea.

We managed to harness the extreme excitement and support of a few people who made valuable contributions to the content in the book. We hope that they are proud of the result of their hard work. Scott Williams helped to develop the competitive analysis chapters while developing Hewlett-Packard Company's (HP's) Web Services Tool Strategy and preparing for the arrival of his new baby — Devin Stewart Williams. Pramod Waingankar tapped his expertise in e-marketplaces and e-commerce and contributed his time and efforts to the case-study chapter while balancing his work as Director of Product Management at Enamics, Inc. Tom Dewan, a technical writing guru, provided not only his writing talent to the Introduction but also provided valuable guidance to us first-time authors. Meera Bavadekar used her programming talents to code an example for us and managed to infuse some of the book fever in her mother, Mrs. Date, who developed the http://www.insidewebservices.com Web site for the book. Kristin Brennan and Joseph McGonnell, marketing managers within the HP's Web Services Operation, guided the development of the future of the e-Speak chapter. Lastly, Kannan Govindarajan managed to juggle being an e-Speak architect, Massachusetts Institute of Technology MBA student, and official Prentice Hall technical reviewer of the content in this book.

As is the case with learning any new technology or product, there were times when we got stuck or just did not know what we were doing. Several e-Speak engineers came to the rescue at various times to bail us out. We want to thank this emergency crew for its time and efforts: Ernest Mak, Don McKee, Doug Myers, Palani Nachimuthu, Shawn Saeed, Shamik Sharma, Shankar Umamaheshwaran, Young Wang, and Ilan Zgor.

So, what's a book without a topic? That is just what HP's e-Speak inventors and former executive management Rajiv Gupta (General Manager) and Arindam Banerji (R & D Lab Manager) provided us. They, along with Alan Karp and Bill Rozas, co-invented the e-Speak technology behind HP's e-service/web service vision. It was not only their invention but their support as sponsors that gave us the pleasure of delving into the vision and the e-Speak technology we present here.

Last, but not least, we want to thank our very experienced and fantastic publishing team. They answered questions, juggled around our many schedule slips, and showed us what it takes to publish a book — all with extreme patience and understanding. Our special thanks to our editor, Jill Harry (Prentice Hall Executive Editor), for taking two writers and turning them into authors. We also want to thank Jeffrey Pepper (Prentice Hall), Susan Wright (HP Press), Pat Pekary (HP Press), and Jim Markham (Development Editor) for their support and guidance through both the HP and Prentice Hall processes.

Special thanks go to our family and friends. We disappeared from many lives while undertaking this project but they remained supportive and encouraging throughout. We especially want to acknowledge the patience and understanding of Pratima Mehta (Toral's mother) who momentarily lost her daughter in this project but nonetheless provided us some Indian delicacies and snacks for those long working sessions. Special mention and gratitude to Shilpa Apte, who not only provided her friendship and made sure we stayed on track, but also coded several e-Speak examples, provided the formula to clear and crisp images, and methodically went through the entire manuscript with a fine-tooth comb!

INTRODUCTION

I t is not surprising that one of the most quoted business writers today is Charles Darwin. In the field of business-to-business e-commerce and, most recently, mobile commerce, evolution is not simply a metaphor; it is a reality. Many businesses have failed to meet expectations — or simply failed — because they could not adapt their existing products and services to a new, more dynamic Internet environment. As IT departments are viewed more and more favorably as business differentiators, compared with cost-of-sales, it behooves business application developers to turn current IT assets into collections of e-services or web services that take full advantage of the speed, flexibility, and instant global reach of the Internet.

A number of obstacles exist, however in achieving an services-based business model. Currently, a typical business-to-business transaction involves:

- Multiple standards: One of the reasons this transaction is so time-consuming is that there is not a common standard for presenting and negotiating information. Each paper supplier uses a different method for pricing paper, establishing delivery times, and negotiating contracts. The procurement department of the company must read and evaluate each proposal individually. The lack of standards makes it difficult to automate this process.

- Entrenched processes and services: Business transactions that require a great deal of human intervention are difficult to maintain and evolve. Changes in prices, products, and deadlines can mean starting negotiations over from square one. Simply trying to fine tune human processes to meet changing needs is a short-term and costly solution.

■ Lack of an online directory: There are number of Web site search engines and listings; however, there is no global and well-populated depot to search for e-services and web services that fit a company's business needs.

■ Static, point-to-point negotiating: For example, suppose that a printing company wants to buy a large quantity of paper. The procurement department uses personal contacts, industry directories, and so on, to develop a list of potential suppliers. They contact each supplier, describe their needs, and solicit proposals. Typically, after some negotiation, the printing company finds a supplier and buys its paper.

In summary, if we look at these characteristics of a typical business transaction, none of them even remotely take advantage of the speed, flexibility, and openness of the Internet. The problem is even more acute in the mobile space in which the operating environment is not yet mature. In the mobile environment, even the basic communication technology is also not standardized across the world. The problem becomes finding a relatively quick and economical way to adapt current business processes to a new paradigm. In the world of services, the ability of different resources to interact with each other is at the core of the new world order. This interaction is based on standards and is driven by dynamism made possible by the network that connects these services together.

Welcome to the Evolution

Service-based interaction provides a different way of transacting business "over the Web." In this case, the resources providing a service need not have prior knowledge of each other's existence and can adapt to the ever-changing landscape of services. In many ways, the services behave like human beings or the companies they represent — except that the services operate in a digital world. Some of the benefits that the service-based solutions bring are:

- Open and standards-based solutions: This level of speed and automation is possible because the businesses can easily *wrap* their current services through standardized interactions. Businesses in this environment communicate with each other using a standard *grammar*.

- Flexible, constantly evolving "services": The end result is that businesses can locate and use services much more easily. These services become genuine e-services as flexible and adaptable as the Internet itself. This can even be used to create complex services — a collection of simple individual services brought together just in time to meet a particular need.

- Dynamic, automated partnering and negotiating: By eliminating human intervention, a business can locate partners and negotiate with them much more quickly.

As always, the problem does not end at the idea but at the implementation or solution. This book introduces a toolkit for creating and using e-services: e-Speak A.03.11 from Hewlett-Packard Company (HP).

E-Speak — A New Grammar for Business-to-Business Transactions

E-Speak is an open source software that makes the service-centric computing vision real. It is a critical part of HP's NetAction software suite that aims at taking the pain out of the search for and interaction between a service and its potential users. The services themselves can be any set of functionality, ranging from a file service to an order fulfillment service.

Through the implementation of service features, e-Speak makes it easy for businesses to collaborate with each other. It enables businesses to establish many-to-many business relationships, provides the flexibility to add new members quickly and easily, provides a single software interface, and enables applications and data to be treated as e-services and web services. It enables companies to extend their business-to-business or business-to-consumer offerings to create ecosystems of services quickly and easily. Organizations such as ecosystem creators, IT departments involved in supply chain initiatives, and software developers and system integrators creating solutions for businesses can use this software to fulfill their needs better, compared with conventional methods.

This book discusses both the service vision and the e-Speak software that implements that vision. The software is available on the accompanying CD but can also be obtained via the `http://www.e-speak.net/` open source web site. While the software includes installation directions, in Appendix A, we include a set of quick start instructions to get you started.

Recently, several companies, including Microsoft and IBM, have announced initiatives similar to HP's service vision. As is common with emerging technologies, much of the work on these initiatives will eventually converge into a common standard that is adopted industry-wide. The current convergence point appears to be around the concept of web service, which, in terms of functionality and features, is similar to an e-service. The discussion around e-services is thus pertinent to the web services, as well. Wherever applicable, we have compared and contrasted between the e-services and web services.

E-Speak is not the only software that facilitates creation of the ecosystem of services. However, it is the only software to date that implements all aspects of the e-service or web service vision. In that sense, it should be treated as the reference implementation of that vision. The future of this version of e-Speak, as well as software from other vendors, is likely to solidify the reference implementation features by making it more robust, interoperable, and better integrated with a certain business area. However, this only emphasizes the need for a clearer understanding of the reference implementation.

Using this Book

This book is designed to get you using e-Speak quickly and easily. By the end of this book, we hope to have provided a good, basic understanding of the product and the ability to develop your own e-Speak services. In general, each chapter has two parts — one that provides a conceptual framework for some service feature and another that provides a code-level example of how e-Speak can be used to implement it. While the second part is aimed at the developers, the first part would be useful for developers as well as business and technical managers. The managers can use this discussion as a gauge to test the readiness of the existing systems, as well as new ones under development, for participating in service-based architectures and economies. Although the service-based environment is not prevalent yet, it will soon be a reality with industry giants such as HP, Microsoft, and IBM rallying behind it. Thus, it is essential to assess the readiness of the current and future application landscape for an organization. An extensive background in the web services or e-services is not necessary in using this book. However, for the code-level discussion, basic understanding of Java or distributed computing is essential.

The discussion in the book is supported by code for working examples that explains and demonstrates the concept well. Each chapter builds on the one before, so that, by the end of the book, you have gone through the development of a complete, working service. We have chosen the travel industry as our primary example; however, you will find the concepts in the book easily applicable to your own projects. The companion CD includes all the source code in the book. The book ends with two case studies that provide step-by-step design for the solution. A chapter each is also devoted to competitive analysis and to discussion of the future direction of the e-Speak technology.

The book has the following chapters.

Chapter 1, "The Web Service Phenomenon," introduces the service vision. The discussion includes identification of roles in a service-based ecosystem.

Chapter 2, "E-speak Overview," introduces e-Speak components, terms, and concepts. Each concept is discussed at the feature level and its positioning in the e-Speak software suite.

Chapter 3, "A Simple E-Speak Service," teaches you how to write your first e-Speak application. The concept of dynamic discovery is also introduced in this chapter.

Chapter 4, "Understanding Client-Service Interactions," discusses how the e-Speak engine, clients, and services communicate with each other. For a complex inter-component interaction, this chapter provides the basics of how conversations between these components are facilitated at the technology level.

Chapter 5, "Vocabularies and Contracts," shows how services are described to the rest of the e-Speak environment (vocabularies) and the rules services use to interact with each other (contracts).

Chapter 6, "Advanced Service Interactions," discusses the e-Speak event model and "service composition." Events provide an asynchronous communication channel and are an important vehicle for real-world business transactions. Service composition allows several granular services to be composed together to create a complex service. The example in this chapter is out-of-band data transfer technique that can be used to blend an e-Speak communication channel with other bulk data transfer mechanisms, such as hypertext transfer protocol (HTTP).

Chapter 7, "Multicore Environment," demonstrates how several e-Speak engines can work together in a distributed computing environment. Such an environment can cater to the needs of various solution components that are deployed across organizational or geographical boundaries.

Chapter 8, "Security," explains e-Speak's security philosophy and how attribute-based security can achieve two main aspects of security: authentication and authorization.

Chapter 9, "Firewall Traversal," describes how clients and services can communicate with each other from behind their respective firewalls.

Chapter 10, "Persistence," discusses techniques to make all the components in a solution persistent. The minimal set of components in a solution includes a service, the e-Speak service engine, and at least one client. Making a component persistent makes recovery from an abnormal termination transparent to the entity at the other end of a communication channel.

Chapter 11, "Service Registries," discusses the importance of the services registry in a services-based economy and, in particular, focuses on the e-Speak registry, E-Services Village.

Chapter 12, "Case Studies," discusses two case studies. The first case study is based on the supply chain area and the second case study looks at the mobile solutions using e-Speak.

Chapter 13, "E-services and Web Services," looks at the difference between the two industry terms *e-services* and *web services*.

Chapter 14, "Comparable Technologies," looks at the comparable technologies from other vendors in the e-service and web service space. The comparison is based on features rather than on stability and maturity of the platform. All the technology offerings are in the early development stage and will be undergoing changes in the future that make them more mature.

Chapter 15, "Competitive Landscape," looks at the competitive landscape in the e-service and web service space. A special focus on recognized leaders, Microsoft and IBM, is presented in this chapter.

Chapter 16, "Future of E-services and Web Services at HP," shows the direction in which e-Speak and related technologies are headed. As we discussed earlier, the industry is at the beginning of technology convergence. This convergence is shaping the product offerings from several vendors.

In addition, we have also included several appendices that help in running the examples or expand on certain concepts. A glossary at the end also provides a quick reference for many of the terms used in the book. The index provides an easy reference to relevant terms.

Conventions

Throughout the book, we have used different types of fonts to indicate different types of information:

- ▪ `Code segments, classes, methods, and variables use this font.` The code segments are also indented so that they stand out from rest of the text. Each code segment is also associated with a file name to indicate the file to which the code belongs. This should help in locating the relevant code snippet in the accompanying CD.

- ▪ *New terms or e-Speak-specific words are in this form.* This denotes a new term or an emphasis on some word.

- ▪ *File names are in this font.* Different types of files used in this book include class files, data files, and configuration files. The file names are used throughout the text and in particular in a code segment.

Examples are included and discussed in many of the chapters. The companion CD includes the code associated with these examples. The working directory on the CD for each example is located on the chapter title page for each chapter under the section headings. Each of the examples provides a complete business situation and design and solution for that situation.

We have also used "Note" sections in the book to emphasize a related point in a discussion. These notes provide information that is useful to the discussion in which they appear but are not directly related to it. The notes include information such as industry anecdotes, history, a specific e-Speak feature or "gotchas." An example of a note is below:

> **Note**
>
> This is an example of a note. Notes highlight a point that is related to the text around them.

For More Information

After reading this book, you may want to get some more information about the book in particular or about the e-Speak technology and its evolution. We would also like your comments and suggestions. Your feedback will be valuable for us to improve future editions of this book, as well as other works. Suggestions specific to the e-Speak platform are also welcome. We will communicate those to the e-Speak team at HP. To reach the authors or to get more information about the book, visit our Web site at http://www.insidewebservices.com.

If you would like more information on HP's e-Speak technology, you can visit http://www.hp.com/go/espeak and http://www.e-speak.net (HP's open source site). These sites include downloadable versions of all the e-Speak product manuals and information about the e-Speak developer's program.

We enjoyed working on this book and hope that you find it useful in a journey toward a service-based business environment of the future. To know more about it, let's enter the world of services.

Web Services

PART
One

IN THIS PART

The Web Service Phenomenon

Chapter 1

THE WEB SERVICE
PHENOMENON

The e-service or web service phenomenon is about dynamic business interactions blurring the boundaries between businesses, partners, and customers. A
complex web of services makes the Web work, rather than working for the Web. E-
Speak makes this vision tangible by providing a services-development paradigm.
In the broader view of the world, e-Speak is all about services and the ecosystems
they reside in. These ecosystems themselves reside on the Internet.

1.1   The Information Age and the Internet

In the beginning, there were no computers. People had to do calculations using
an abacus or later by hand. Scribes would spend a lifetime creating aesthetically
pleasing copies of the Bible. Even news was spread via the town crier. Then one
fine day, somebody said, "Let there be computers." And computers were born.[1]
People looked at computers and said, "This is good." Initially, computers were
used for processing heavy scientific calculations. As technology advanced, allowing computers to increase in affordability, they gained in popularity — slowly at first,
eventually picking up speed as people discovered more ways that computers could
make tasks more efficient.

---

[1] That wasn't exactly how computers were born. We have glossed over a lot of significant inventions
that led us to computers, but that's fine for this discussion.

However, there was still one problem with computers. They could not talk to each other. People had to carry clunky media (disks) to take their stuff from one computer to another until one day when somebody said, "Let there be networking to connect these computers." So computer networks were born. They were rather slow initially, but learned to be quite fast soon. This helped in luring more people into the computer fiefdom — also known as the Digital Age.

Now the problem was that computers spoke some really bizarre languages that only a select few demigods called *programmers* could understand. That made it hard for normal people to interact with it. There were several attempts (such as COBOL and fourth-generation languages) to make computers human-friendly. All such attempts had only limited success.

Eventually, computers were primary vehicles for not only creating information but also for sharing information. Behind the doors of the physics offices at the European Organization for Nuclear Research (CERN), someone said, "Let there be a web of computers, and let it be world wide so that we can share documents easily." This *web of computers* also had one characteristic not present in earlier computer networks. They used a rather simple protocol to communicate with each other and provided a simple language for human beings to get things done. For a lot of people, this gave birth to a new medium of interaction called the *World Wide Web* (WWW). The World Wide Web (after going through a period called *World Wide Wait*) became quite a powerful means of information exchange. The WWW brought digital information exchange to the general public. Email, commonly used in universities and government agencies, became a common means of communicating. People created pleasing *Web sites* that published information about themselves and the products they wanted to sell. The ease with which different kinds of information could be exchanged using the WWW translated into several new businesses, and dot.com phenomena developed. Suddenly, the consumers and the companies they buy products from found a new way to reach each other. Companies deployed a very low-cost infrastructure based on *the Web* to communicate with each other and exchange information about parts, orders, and design changes.

The WWW made sharing and information simply a matter of loading the pages with some special tags on a sophisticated computer called a *Web server* that is attached to a network. However, the simplicity led to another problem — information overload. Tons of Web sites sprang up with varying levels of information quality and freshness. Making the Web work for you was not really very easy.

1.1.1 Trip-Planning Experience

Imagine that you are trying to go to New York from San Francisco via airplane. You will need an airline ticket, a hotel, and maybe some sightseeing information. You can always go to a travel agency and get everything arranged for you (for a small fee, of course). But if you are lawfully employed, taxpaying citizens of the world like the authors of this book, you might want to save some money by doing this all yourself. So you turn to the Web and click, click. Then you click some more. After about half an hour of click-clicking and keying in your personal data some 50 times, you get fed up and finally take the deal that you think is best.

This is very inconvenient but it does work with a little time and patience. However, now suppose that your project slipped schedule and you need to postpone the trip. Now you need to change travel dates and hotel and tour booking, and because of all this, cancel the jazz festival completely. You go to the Web sites to make that change and — lo and behold — the fares are not the same anymore, are they? You are left with repeating the whole process again, as depicted in Figure 1.1.

You are left thinking it would be great if *the Web could work for me*. You tell the Web what to do and it returns the results with the same confidence as doing it yourself. Not a bad proposition — an age (*Service Age*) in which the Web takes your instructions and works for you.

1.1.2 I Am Interested, Tell Me More

Before we let out the secret that e-Speak is about, making the interactions with the Web easier, we first look at what was difficult in the above trip-planning experience. Among the firsts are the ease of use. Yes, the Web made information exchange very easy but resulted in information overload. Because it is so easy for everybody to publish content for the Web, almost everybody did, and as a result, Web users found that there was no easy way to wade through all of that and get to the *right* content. Secondly, there was no central place you could go to get a job done. For

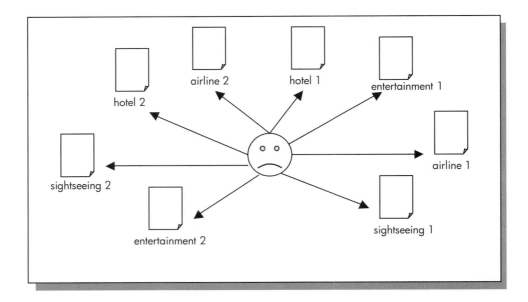

Figure 1.1. Frenzied Web interaction.

hotels you had to go to various hotel sites, for sightseeing to a few more, and the jazz festival was at a site you did not even know existed until now.

Formally, in an ideal Web environment:

- There should be some known, trustworthy spots on the Web for you where you can go and ask for whatever you want.

- You should be able to express what you want in a meaningful way to the computer (and the Web).

- The choices you get back should be based on your expression/whim/mood at that moment, not on some general profile information years ago. Also, the results returned should be relevant for you and what you are looking for. No information that just happens to have the right keywords should make its way to you.

- The Web sites you find may never have seen you before but they should be able to serve you in a customized way as much as possible.

▊ Finally, when you change your mind, you should be able to repeat the whole process in a painless manner.

All these features are helpful in making the Web work for you, rather than you working on the Web. Of course, some of these are present in the world today to a varying degree of functionality and success. What would be desirable is to make them available on a consistent basis. Once that happens, an experience such as trip reservation and planning, as described above, would be a more pleasant experience from a user point of view.

How can we make the Web work for you? E-Speak presents one approach. But before we talk about the details of e-Speak, it is first important to understand how e-Speak views the world. Rather than a client-server or a server-centric architecture view, e-Speak views the world as a web of services fulfilling needs of each other and eventually those of the users or clients that use these services.

1.2   The Web of Services

In today's Web-centric world, it is convenient to think of entities or resources that are connected to each other through some mechanism — by means of a *hyperlink* in most simple form. The primary purpose of the WWW is to make it easy to share information among interested parties. The pages, together with the hyperlinks, create a *web* of information. Any visitor to a page can jump to another by following the hyperlinks or by explicitly providing the Uniform Resource Locator (URL) for the page of interest. This is the state of most of the World Wide Web (WWW) as we know it today. This infrastructure is what also facilitates the e-commerce applications today for companies that want to reach their customers over the Internet.

We can extend the concept of the Web to include not only pages, but more active components of the Internet — namely, the *services*. A *web of services* is similar to the web of pages in a lot of ways. For example, they will be connected to each other through some mechanism, and their users will be able to go from one service to the other using these links. However, the service web that e-Speak envisions is also very different from the web of pages. It is these differences that distinguish the web of services from the web of pages. The principle differences are in the form of service interactions. We can classify these interactions in three different categories:

1. User-to-Service interaction

2. Service-to-Service interaction

3. Service Deployer-to-Service Deployer interaction

1.2.1   User-to-Service Interaction

We have been talking about the *services* until now without any specific definition for that word. Although we all have some notion of what a service is, a formal definition will be useful for the rest of the book. It must be noted that the definition we give below is not expected to be something that will be all-encompassing but rather a working description of the notion of service that will be used in this book.

> **Service:** *A service is an active program or a software component in a given environment that provides and manages access to a resource that is essential for the function of other entities in the environment.*

Figure 1.2 depicts a service. It is important to note that the notion of *resource* is rather broad in this definition. A resource could be a piece of hardware, such as a hard disk, or software, such as a math library. It could also be some data in a database or some information, such as a news item. This definition is somewhat simplistic yet very powerful. It is simplistic because it tries to be as broad as possible and specifies very few specific characteristics or restrictions on qualifying entities. A service need only be a program or a library function to qualify. The key, however, is in provision and management of a resource. *Provision* means that it has to make the resource available to other entities, and *management* denotes controlling and granting the access rights. You can see that this automatically mandates *interaction* with other entities in its environment. Thus, a program or a software component that does not interact with other entities will not qualify as a service. An equally important aspect is *controlling* a resource that is desirable by other entities in the service environment. Any resource that is useful only internally to the program does not help in making that program a service.

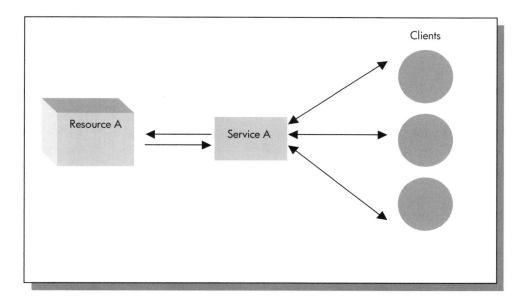

Figure 1.2. Resource access via a service.

As can be noted from this definition, a service is an active component, whereas a Web page is a static, one-time representation of some information. One can interact with a service (to access a certain resource that the service manages), and the service responds back with a response (rejecting or providing access to the resource). One could argue that a page can do something similar but, in fact, it is the Common Gateway Interface (CGI) program or the servlet behind the page that will be responding to the request. The page provides the means for communication between the user and the program or the servlet. It is the CGI program or the servlet that is acting as a *service* in this case.

The interactions with active components as services are richer, compared with the passive components, such as Web pages. A service can show a high level of dynamism while catering to the user. Due to this a high degree of customization, flexibility can be achieved, thus giving a better user experience. So far, we have been delivering the services through a series of Web pages. So how is this dynamism exhibited today?

Most of the initial Web content was on static Web pages. When the CGI technology was invented, it became possible to connect programs to the Web pages. These programs could be used to process user input (such as a login or an order status information request) and render a complete Web page dynamically. This dynamically generated page would contain information specific to the user request. With the advent of style sheets and Java/Active Server Pages (JSP and ASP) technologies, most of the Web pages can be expressed in terms of the overall style, with the connected program *filling in* the specifics.

It can be noticed that there are a lot of standards on the presentation aspect — the browsers, presentation language Hypertext Markup Language (HTML) and style sheets. However, we are missing on the standards on the actual *interactions* these presentation technologies are supposed to facilitate. How should access to a resource be provided? How should the user and the service agree on describing a resource and describing the *usage* of that resource?

In a service-centric world, the emphasis is put on answering such questions. The presentation is a final-stage consideration when it is time to deliver the resource to the user on a specific medium. In a web of services, the user is thus free to choose the appropriate medium of delivery at a specific time. This, coupled with presentation-level flexibility, can produce a highly customized user experience.

The emphasis on the *description* of various entities also opens up quite interesting possibilities in discovering services for a user or creating a new business partnership to enhance a service offering of a business. As long as the user and a collection of similar services agree on the *terms of description*, the user can, in theory, choose any service to accomplish a task. The choice could be based on a variety of criteria such as past experience, third-party rating, or even user's whim at that moment. Regardless of which service is chosen, it is possible for the users to express their tasks in a consistent, previously agreed-on manner. From a cognizant user's perspective, this means that there is now a choice about which service to choose based on certain criteria — the description of the *service class*. Such a user can choose any service after due diligence. On the other hand, from an nonconscious user's standpoint, it doesn't matter which service serves your request so long as you can describe your needs well and the service is capable of understanding your description and acting on it to fulfill your request. Imagine buying a car. One can do all the necessary research about car dealers, provide the *descrip-*

tion of the car, float a request for quote to all the "qualified" dealers, and choose the dealer that has the best price. On the other hand, one can also just find the nearest dealer and buy the car so long as the price sounds reasonable. Between the two scenarios, the users did not agree on the best way to choose a service, but in either case, they could reach a service that could fulfill their need. There is only one fundamental thing the users and the dealers needed to agree on — the description of a car. There is one more aspect to the user-to-service interaction — *discovery*. We already discussed the description for a class of services. Discovery of a service means choosing, either deliberately or accidentally, a specific service from a class of services, using a specific description. *Intelligent matchmaking* like this can ease the pain in finding and interacting with the *right* service.

To extend the idea further, imagine now a task that is so complex that no single service can do it — such as the trip-planning task we described earlier. In such a case, to accomplish the task, we will have to choose a *set* of right services and interact with them individually. As we will see in the next section, a service-to-service interaction mechanism can help solve this problem effectively. Such a *composition* of services will create a seamless experience for the user.

In the e-Speak vision of the services, the user-to-service interaction is thus characterized by:

☐ Service description
☐ Service discovery
☐ A high degree of customized experience
☐ Service composition to accomplish higher level tasks from services acting as basic building blocks

You will notice that e-Speak's vision describes a *special* class of services. The services from this class are highly interoperable in offering their services. Such services are called *e-services*.

> **E-service:** *An e-service is a service that abides by a specific framework to offer its services. The framework provides the means to describe and discover the service, audit its service offering, and integrate the e-service with other e-services to offer higher level e-services.*

The industry has adopted the term web services for this class of services. This book concentrates on the service-centric computing, including both e-services and web services. As a result, both the terms *web service* and *e-service* point to this class of services for our discussion and we have used these terms interchangeably in the rest of the book except in Chapter 13.

1.2.2   Service-to-Service Interaction

A user of a service can expect a significantly different experience while interacting with it, as we saw earlier. We also mentioned that the e-services are highly interactive components and communicate with other e-services. Such interactions could be either to use the service offered by an e-service or to collaborate together to form a higher level service that can be used to add complementary or additional value. In either case, the interacting services should have an experience at least similar in nature to the service-to-user interactions we described previously. Should the interaction be richer than that?

Let's look at the service-to-service interactions more closely. By the definition, a service is an active software component. Thus, the service-to-service interaction inherently implies at least two software objects communicating with each other. Such an interaction is different from either the Web page interaction or the service-to-user interaction. Compared with a set of Web pages joined together by hyperlinks, a service-to-service interaction is very dynamic in nature. In the Web page realm, the hyperlinks (or the connections) are either purely static or (maybe) somewhat dynamic. In the service world, the connections formed are determined and bound on the fly, based on the requirements. Take the trip-planning example from the previous section. In that case, a *trip-planning service* can decide which airline reservation service to collaborate with dynamically, based on the user's preferences, which could include using a specific airline, lowest price, shortest travel time, or the destination itself. Note that this search can result in finding airlines or airline reservation services that the trip-planning service may not be aware of until that moment! It is this level of dynamism that differentiates a service-to-service interaction from the usual "Web page"-like interaction. E-Speak is designed to support such dynamism.

The other aspect of service-to-service interaction is the notion of *dialog* between the two interacting services. A service can have a dialog, a bidirectional communication, with other services. In the passive Web page world the absence of such a dialog is near total. A Web page can redirect you to another Web page, either automatically or via a hyperlink without giving any prior indication to the other page. Also very rarely is there any communication between two pages.

Note

There are a few examples of unidirectional communications between Web pages. A Web page, while redirecting the user to the other Web page, can communicate information regarding itself to the Web server or the Web page being loaded. The server or the page can use this information to present the page information differently or to maintain a log. Various business models have been built around such a capability. One such business model is revenue sharing. When a Web portal redirects the user (automatically or by conscious user choice) to another company's Web page selling a product, the Web portal is compensated monetarily for the redirection. A product company may have such an arrangement with several portals, and vice versa. In such a case, for each redirection, a context for redirecting the page must be communicated to the product company's Web server or Web page. This context is then used to determine the revenue-sharing amount for each portal and the participating product companies.

The possibility of bidirectional communication can help in creating a more customized and richer set of interactions. As we will see later in this book, such interactions make it possible to *introspect* a service to understand its description, information-sharing format, and workflow sequences. Based on this knowledge, one can qualify (or disqualify) a service or amend its own workflow to accommodate (or abide by) the other service's workflow. Again, this is an aspect of the dynamic behavior that is absent in the web of pages. It should be noted that such a level of dynamism is also not typically exhibited in the service-to-user interaction. A user usually has a specific behavioral pattern, and this pattern is difficult to change to accommodate a found service. In fact, in most cases, systems are designed to accommodate this behavior pattern. In the e-Speak world, as well, the same principle follows. It is summarized in the e-Speak motto: *To make the Web work for you and not make you work on the Web.*

1.2.3   Service Deployer-to-Service Deployer Interaction

A rich interaction pattern between a service and its users or other services can create an environment that can also influence the interaction between the service deployers. In the current state of the Web, the relationship between various service deployers is rather static — at least in the electronic world. Service deployers enter into an alliance to connect each other's services. The agreement to form this alliance happens in the paper world or from the electronic world's perspective — *offline.*

After an alliance is formed, a team of engineers gets to work to build the electronic bridges between the two companies forming the alliance. The electronic bridges built are usually in the form of a Virtual Private Network (VPN) or a collection of Web pages secured through some mechanism, such as digital certificates from either side. Whatever the form of these bridges is, veteran programmers can tell you that it takes some significant effort to build them, and the maintenance of them is even more cumbersome. In the meantime, the executives at each company are busy forming new alliances to expand the business or severing the ones that do not live up to the expectations. This activity between the business managers and technologists in a company creates a *constant state of flux* in which the electronic bridges are constantly being built or torn down — each of which is a labor-intensive endeavor.

The problem lies in the fact that the *semi-dynamic* technology-level solutions cannot live up to the expectations of *hyper-dynamic* world of business alliances. The efforts required to build or tear down electronic linkages between two or more companies comes in the way of rapidly forming lucrative alliances or pulling down unprofitable ones. Currently, the technology folks are trying hard to keep up with the business people on this issue.

If, however, it is possible, to find dynamically a collection of services suitable for the task you want to accomplish on the fly, as we discussed earlier, it should also be possible to form the alliances (or break them, as the case may be) at the same pace. The e-Speak infrastructure is designed to make this possible.   Whereas e-Speak provides the description of a service to find it, it has the *terms of use* and other constructs to communicate the modalities of the service being offered. These e-Speak constructs, although termed a *contract*, are somewhat rudimentary and are not quite as powerful as a contract in the real world. However, it is possible to devise such instruments of business operation using them. It must also be noted that the legal system around contract formation in the digital world is not fully developed as yet, and without that, the effectiveness of even a sophisticated implementation will also be limited. However, the e-Speak implementation is a step in the right direction, and as we mentioned earlier, it is possible to create a more advanced mechanism for contract formation using it.

Equipped with the dynamic discovery and contract formation on the fly, one can imagine a very different world. In such an environment, it would be possible to offer a service and reach customers you didn't even know existed. Also, from a customer's point of view, it would be possible to describe what they want and find a set of services that fulfill it. The discovered and eventually selected services will vary every time, based on the parameters the customer provides, such as location, rating, and preferences. For the chosen set of services, one could retrieve the terms of use and other quality-of-service aspects and make a decision on which service to use. In fact, instead of going through the whole process, we could delegate that task to another service we trust!

As you can see from the description above, the service-oriented world like this means a large variety of service providers. Each of the service providers by themselves are providing only a small piece of functionality — a functionality that is their core competency. However, when they are together, connected through the mechanisms described by e-Speak, they can create a very powerful service-providing environment. E-Speak calls such an environment an *ecosystem*.

1.3   The Ecosystem

An ecosystem, as we saw earlier, is a collection of related services. This collection, as a whole, provides a set of services in a specific domain. Using the example we discussed earlier, a *Travel Industry ecosystem* would cater to the traveling needs of a certain set of customers or a *Medical ecosystem* would provide services related to medicine — including services such as medical advice, sale of prescription and nonprescription drugs, and archiving of medical history. But an ecosystem is not just a collection of services. As the name implies, it is an *orderly* group. Just like a biological ecosystem, an ecosystem of services can have a hierarchy among its citizens, and it provides a set of rules and regulations that every member must abide by. However, in this case, the hierarchy is not in the sense of food chain or power, but one with the notion of higher and lower level services. A hierarchical view of the ecosystem helps in defining service composition — bringing together lower level services to create higher level services. In the Travel Industry ecosystem, for example, the airlines, cab services, and hotels can be thought of as lower level member services in that ecosystem. A higher level service aggregates these services to create a tour package that consists of traveling by a certain airline, going to points of interest using a specific cab service, and staying at a specific hotel. The *tour package service* can either have static relationships with certain entities or can put together a package unique to the set of requirements provided.

The regulatory aspect of the ecosystem is essential for smoother interoperability between the members of the ecosystem. In that respect, an ecosystem can be thought of as having two separate classes of services.

■ Regulatory class services — These are services that ensure interoperability among the members of the ecosystem and enforce standards and regulations required for that purpose. Some examples of this are standards-setting services, service-rating services, and monitoring and dispute-settlement services.

■ Member class services — These are the services that use the standards and rules set by the regulatory class services to offer a certain service that is within the domain of the ecosystem.

Together, these two layers of services provide a complete ecosystem that can sustain itself and provide useful services to its users. Among these classes, there are several roles that different entities will play to make an ecosystem successful.

1.3.1   Roles of Ecosystem Citizens

The complexity of an ecosystem can vary significantly as can the necessity for various roles. The discussion below provides a general view of an ecosystem and corresponding roles. The exact nature and types of the roles are dependent on a specific ecosystem. Figure 1.3 shows the relationship between various roles in an ecosystem.

Ecosystem Host

This entity is responsible for providing the necessary infrastructure for an ecosystem to function. The host's role is mainly to facilitate the general functioning of the ecosystem. An example of an ecosystem host would be the New York Stock Exchange (NYSE). It provides the means for the stock traders to buy or sell stocks and to provide data about those transactions, such as bid/ask prices and the Dow Jones Industrial Average (DJIA) — an index expressing the market's general sentiments about the top 30 companies listed at NYSE. The host also has policies for granting or revoking membership to interested parties. The NYSE, for example, has certain policies in place to let a trader firm trade any shares using its facilities.

Governing Body

A governing body, as the name suggests, provides policies in an ecosystem that form the framework for transactions in the ecosystem. It is important to distinguish between the roles of the ecosystem host and the ecosystem governing body. The governing body is a more passive entity — one that sets the policies but does not look into operational or day-to-day functioning of the ecosystem. It also does not facilitate interactions in the ecosystem. That responsibility is on the ecosystem host. For trading of company shares and other financial securities, the Securities and Exchange Commission (SEC) acts as the governing body.

Because the governing body is not associated with a specific ecosystem host, it is possible for multiple hosts to host an ecosystem that follows the guidelines provided by the governing body. For example, the NASDAQ provides an alternative stock trading facility to the NYSE. The two rival infrastructures are separate from each other; however, they both follow SEC guidelines. The companies listed on either of these two exchanges are expected to abide by SEC guidelines and to follow the day-to-day operational policies set by the respective ecosystem hosts. We will discuss a similar scenario in Chapter 5.

In the service world, a governing body will most likely be a consortium. A consortium is a group of interested parties that work together to develop a specification for a certain task. Consortiums typically are a group of partners, competitors, common-interest parties, or legislature people; they determine certain guidelines, rules, maybe even interaction patterns and quality-of-service levels. The specification developed by a consortium is not necessarily binding to the members of the consortium, nor is a membership necessarily required to accept a specification. If a specification provided by a consortium is widely accepted, it becomes a *standard* for performing that task. Consortiums can deal with any topic you might imagine. Some examples of consortium are:

- Consortiums of similar functions coming together to actualize economies of scale or to streamline their business process (for example, RosettaNet)
- Consortiums of groups trying to solve a certain societal problem
- Consortiums of technology pioneers (for example, W3C or Universal Description, Discovery, and Integration [UDDI])

E-Speak supports vocabularies and contracts to allow groups such as consortiums (discussed in Chapter 5), standards-setting bodies, or other governing third parties to apply these concepts to the network of services and clients that have decided to participate together in a service-based ecosystem. We introduce the ecosystem players in Figure 1.3.

Ecosystem Monitor

An ecosystem monitor entity monitors the interactions between ecosystem members and ensures that the members of the ecosystem are following the interaction guidelines set by the ecosystem host and the governing body. Based on this, the ecosystem monitor can recommend changes in the functioning of a specific member entity or the ecosystem as a whole. There can be several monitoring entities

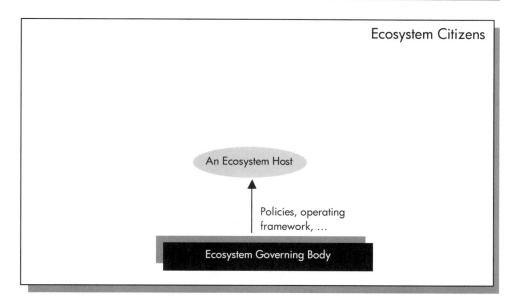

Figure 1.3. Introducing the ecosystem players.

in a given ecosystem. Also a specific monitoring entity may concentrate on only certain aspects in an ecosystem. For example, in the financial securities world, various independent auditing firms act as monitoring entities that audit the accounting and other financial business practices of companies to ensure compliance.

The monitors can also provide metadata about an ecosystem and its members, based on their observations. One example of such metadata is *service rating*. A service rating can provide a relative or absolute standing of a service's offering, based on a variety of parameters, such as price of the service and usage satisfaction. The users of the service can then judge whether to use the service or not, based on this rating.

Ecosystem Arbitrator

It is possible in an ecosystem that the members get involved in a dispute for several reasons, including noncompliance with guidelines, unsatisfactory quality of service, breach of contract, or fraud. An ecosystem arbitrator acts as the mediator between the parties involved to resolve the issue. The governing body may provide guidelines for such arbitration, as well. In some cases, the ecosystem host or the governing body itself may act as the arbitrator. An example of this is the Internal Revenue Service (IRS) in the Tax ecosystem. However, the arbitrator must be noted as a separate role in an ecosystem.

Member/Service Directories

A directory in an ecosystem is a useful tool to locate a certain participating entity or a member of the ecosystem. Because it is possible that the number of the ecosystem members could be huge, the directories are an important means to get information about them. For the stock markets, several such directories, such as ValueLine, are available that provide a variety of data about listed companies and their financials. In service-based ecosystems, such directories provide specifics about the registered services. Earlier in the chapter, we described how services can be discovered and used on the fly. The service directories have a crucial role in *effective discovery of services* mechanism. In Chapter 11, we discuss the default service directory that e-Speak provides.

Note

The role of a service directory and its importance in an ecosystem are widely accepted in the industry. As a result, standards are emerging to formalize creation of service directories. An example of this is UDDI. It is an industry-wide initiative to create a platform-independent open framework for building service directories.

Ecosystem Members/Services

The ecosystem member entities are the very reason why an ecosystem exists. These form the second tier of the ecosystem — the *member class services*. The entities in this category use the ecosystem infrastructure provided by the ecosystem host and interact with each other to fulfill their needs. The ecosystem members must abide by the rules provided by the governing body, and they are subject to audits from the monitoring entities. Figure 1.4 diagrams the relationships of these additional ecosystem citizens.

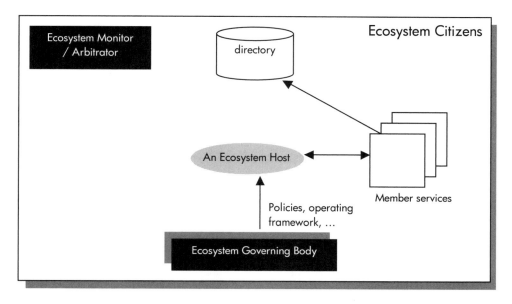

Figure 1.4. Relationships of ecosystem players.

In the service-based ecosystem, a further characterization of the member services is necessary. There are three main roles that can be identified for launch and use of a service:

1. Service Provider

2. Service Deployer

3. Service User

Service Provider

A service provider's role is to provide the core functionality for offering the service. For example, a service provider for the *Order Status service* will provide the means to query the order database using several fields from the database and related conditions and will extract the order status information from the database in some format. Usually, a service provider will need to cater to needs of several interested entities and may not have the expertise or reason to pay close attention to needs of a specific entity or its operational environment. That is the responsibility of the *service deployer* (see the following).

We use the term *business logic* in this book to refer to the core functionality provided by the service provider. For example, the business logic provided by a stock broker service is the functionality to buy or sell stock with potential buyers or sellers, based on user-specified criteria (such as limit price) at the stock exchange.

Service Deployer

As mentioned earlier, a service provider is generally agnostic to the operational environment of the user of the service. A service deployer, on the other hand, is very sensitive to the operational environment and can do the best job of creating a user-friendly service experience. A service deployer works with the service provider to bring the service's business logic to a certain ecosystem and corresponding operational environment. For example, Enterprise Resource Planning (ERP) system vendors, such as SAP, provide an operational environment to streamline the business processes for a company. The core for the business processes is in the form of the business process analyst team in the company, and the vendor's professional services team helps in bringing those processes to the ERP platform.

A clear separation between the service provider and service deployer ensures optimal use of competencies. A service provider with the core competency in providing business logic can cater to several interested parties and platforms. On the other hand, the service deployer can help several service providers to provide their service to a specific ecosystem and its operational environment.

E-Speak's architecture is based on this clear separation. In several examples we will discuss in subsequent chapters, this architecture has been used.

Service User

A service user uses the service offered by the service provider to fulfill its needs. There are several resources available in a service-based ecosystem at the disposal of the service user to ensure ease of use and quality of service.   The service provider and the service deployer are mainly responsible for the ease of use and the regulatory class services ensure that a certain quality of service is maintained. The service user uses the appropriate service directories and the monitor ratings to choose a service that is most suitable for its needs. Any disputes regarding the service delivery between a user and provider can be resolved by the arbitrator.

Note

A user is not necessarily just a *user* in the web service architecture. Because it is possible to compose several lower level services to create a higher level service, a user of a service can be another service itself! Thus, for all practical purposes, the distinction between a service and a service user is notional. An entity can be a service provider in one interaction and a service user in the other.

Figure 1.5 depicts the complete ecosystem with all its citizens.

1.3.2   Fostering Ecosystem Loyalty

For an ecosystem to be successful, it is necessary to have the right mix of all of the aforementioned roles. Only that would ensure that the ecosystem is scalable, sustainable, and can cater to a growing user base. There are also two other factors that influence the subscription to an ecosystem.

Confidence: An ecosystem will be widely adopted if potential service providers and service users feel confident about the ecosystem environment. The ecosystem environment includes not only the existing members and the composition and credibility of the host and the governing body, but also the operating processes that the ecosystem employs. The existing and potential members should feel confident that the ecosystem provides a trusted environment for their business process and

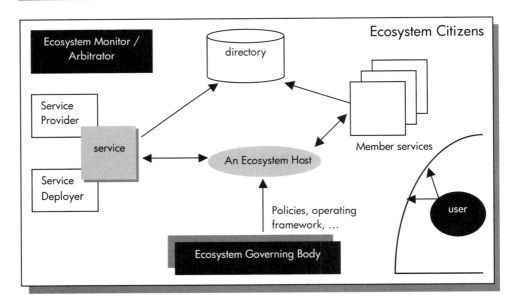

Figure 1.5. The complete ecosystem.

for dispute resolution. This trust or the confidence in the ecosystem comes from adoption of appropriate business standards and effective functioning of ecosystem-monitoring entities.

Note

Having trust in an ecosystem does not necessarily imply the same trust assumptions for individual members of the ecosystem. In a dynamic business environment, it is likely that you may not even be aware of the existence of the entity you *discover*, much less its trustworthiness. The importance of trust in the overall ecosystem environment is more underscored, due to that.

Security: The wide variety of roles in an ecosystem also raises an important question — What are some of the security measures required in an ecosystem to make it a safe environment for the business transactions to take place? This concern comes from the fact that an ecosystem is an open environment that facilitates intercompany transactions and, thus, carries sensitive data about business dealings. Before you send a quote for a certain product to a potential customer or a product specification to a potential vendor, you want to be assured that it will not fall into the wrong hands and that even if it did, they will be able to read it.

There are several security aspects that the ecosystem host and/or the governing body need to address — first, independently, to address each of them thoroughly, then, collectively, to maintain consistency. These security aspects range from encryption of data on the wire and authenticity of an individual entity to security enforcement infrastructure of the ecosystem as a whole. Chapter 8 discusses the mechanisms that e-Speak uses to address the security, as well as the trust assumptions.

1.3.3   Service Lifecycle

Bringing services to life is an interesting task for business IT managers of the ecosystem participants. It requires not only the operational resources, such as time, talent, and funding, but also the strategic (both horizontal and vertical) partnerships of other ecosystem members. It is an all-encompassing activity that is very akin to the efforts required in building a product or software. From a business manager's perspective, it is useful to recognize the similarity. Following a lifecycle approach to launching a service can greatly assist in planning; however, recognizing the nuances is also important. The standard lifecycle is depicted in Figure 1.6.

Strategic planning: Appropriate business relationships are formed in this phase. Should a consortium to foster co-opetition be desired, the discussions and negotiations with competitors and partners must happen here. Having a clear vision of what the consortium should provide will help guide the discussions. The consortium then needs to work to develop the framework for services to participate together in.

Requirements: The requirements for the service will be gleaned from the consortium decisions, as well as the target market. It is important to notice that some of what the service does (or the minimum that the service does) will be strongly influenced and governed by an ecosystem and its monitor, so taking these into consideration will be very important during the service planning.

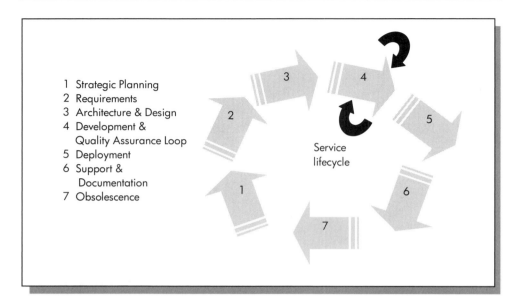

1 Strategic Planning
2 Requirements
3 Architecture & Design
4 Development &
   Quality Assurance Loop
5 Deployment
6 Support &
   Documentation
7 Obsolescence

Service
lifecycle

Figure 1.6. Service lifecycle.

Architecture and design: Catering to an "unfamiliar" audience will be important. Because of the dynamic discovery capabilities of a service-centric architecture, you will find a whole host of users (hopefully!) who may or may not be familiar with your name. Accounting for unfamiliarity will promote use of your service and perhaps allow for repeat business and a superior service rating.

The usual distributing computing design issues still exist.   Internet latency and instability must be designed for in the service so that reliability and speed can be forced and handled in the complex web of computers.

Development and quality assurance loop: The standard software development processes follow in this phase for the service. The later chapters of this book discuss the development of services based on the e-Speak technology. However, the chapters also discuss service programming basics that are applicable toward using other platforms. However, the quality assurance must take into account any requirements placed on the service by the ecosystem in terms of system engineering metrics. Ensuring that it is "fast enough," as defined by the ecosystem, stays "alive" long enough again, as defined by the ecosystem, and so on, is essential in this phase.

<u>Deployment</u>: The deployment of a service or the "opening" of the service doors really is activating it in the ecosystem environment. The ecosystem dependencies need to be thought out; thus, deployment needs to be orchestrated such that all prior ecosystem dependencies are fulfilled.

<u>Support and service documentation</u>:   The complexities and frustrations of distributed computing — separation of the requestor and the doer — are enhanced in a service-centric environment. The service support model must be not only one of effective documentation and help desks but also of reactive and after-the-fact resolution. The kinds of questions that need to be addressed by a comprehensive support model are:

- How do I use this service?
- What do I do if the service does not perform its task?
- How do I report data discrepancy?
- What is my liability protection for bad service implementations?

<u>Obsolescence</u>: A service's offering becomes outdated over its life. It is important to recognize this and to plan for improved offerings via future enhanced services.

1.3.4   New and Improved Trip-Planning Experience

Earlier in this book, we discussed the problems of working with the Web. Figure 1.1 depicts the complicated and tedious task of trying to pull together something such as a trip. Ecosystems of services help to put a rational face to the complexity and simplify the experience for the user. Now, planning a trip from San Francisco to New York is simply a matter of finding the right Travel Industry ecosystem and using a trip-planning service. This service transforms your trip criteria into a travel itinerary that includes everything from airline tickets to the most appropriate jazz concert reservations. The choice of airline or hotel would be based on *your* preferences, restrictions, and criteria. If your travel plans must change, you need only let the trip-planning service know, and it can do everything all over for you. Note that the resultant set of lower level services, such as airlines, and hotels, could be completely different from the original itinerary yet still satisfy your original trip wishes. The final result is that ecosystems and services *make the Web work for you*. Figure 1.7 shows this new and improved way of getting work done.

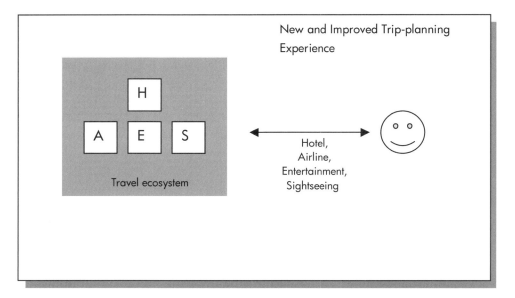

Figure 1.7. Making the Web work for you.

1.3.5   Ecosystem Enablers

Creating an ecosystem can be a very complex task. As we discussed earlier, there are several roles that must be fulfilled by relevant entities to populate the ecosystem environment and make it sustainable. The most crucial role, the governing body, needs to identify the processes and policies for the functional aspects, whereas the ecosystem host needs to deal with the operational environment to facilitate the processes and implement the policies.

Several tools (software, hardware, professional services) are available in the market to address a single aspect of ecosystem creation. However, a holistic approach makes it easier to build such ecosystems. Such an approach provides a framework for different areas in ecosystem creation. Because the idea of service-based computing and ecosystem of service is now adopted as the future of distributed computing, there are a few initiatives in the works from leading companies such as Microsoft, IBM, Sun Microsystems, and HP.

However, other industry initiatives are rallying behind the concept of a *web service*. At the conceptual level, a web service and an e-service are not that different. However, the foundations they are built on and the underlying technologies are where they differ. Web services are built on interoperability and standards-based initiatives, whereas e-Speak (also a visionary in this space) had to focus on providing a complete solution to realize the vision because there was not much available in the market.

E-Speak is focused on providing a whole solution to foster the ability of deploying e-Speak-based services in an ecosystem. In that light, it addresses everything from service description to service discovery and, to some extent, high-level business interaction on the wire — all within a highly secured environment. Web services are focused on ensuring an interoperable environment based on the exchange of a specific electronic document formatted in a particular way *(an XML document)* is produced. To some extent, web services are agnostic of the technology, as long as the exposed endpoints (the web services in the ecosystem) can understand the XML document carrying the information.

Conceptually, e-services and web services support the concept of making the Web work for you. Exposing business assets in such a way that they can be dynamically registered, discovered, and invoked through a series of programmatic constructs (e-Speak Java Application Programming Interface (APIs) or web service electronic documents) is at the heart of the service economy. We discuss the current technological nuances that differentiate the two industry terms in Chapter 13. In the near future, these terms are likely to converge into one common meaning and technology.

In the next chapter, we look at the e-Speak architecture and how it supports a service-centric economy.

E-Speak Overview

- The E-Speak Service Engine
- Service Registry
- Service Framework Specification

Chapter 2

E-SPEAK OVERVIEW

In Chapter 1, we built the foundations of web services and how web services *make the Web work for you*. Web service concepts are at the heart of the e-Speak framework. E-Speak is a reference implementation of the service-centric computing vision. In this chapter, we discuss how the e-Speak architecture enables service-centric computing and ecosystem creation.

Figure 1.6 describes the service lifecycle. This lifecycle considered the stages a service goes through in its lifetime. Let's consider a different time span and a narrower scope of simply *creating and using* a service. The steps involved in that are shown in Figure 2.1.

As shown in the figure, the first step is to create and deploy the service in an ecosystem. Both the service provider and service deployer are involved in creating and deploying a service. The service provider manages the implementation of the business-level decisions such as the service's business logic, market, and pricing. The service deployer manages the implementation of the transactional framework of the service, based on the operational requirements set by the ecosystem's governing body.

A deployed service is functionally ready to be *discovered* and *used* by service users; however, it must be *registered* and *advertised* first with the ecosystem. This is done during the *Service Registration* and *Service Advertisement* steps. More complex services (made up of other, simpler services) may need to be composed prior to being invoked by the service users. After the composition, the complex service is *fully formed* and usable. Users can interact with discovered services to

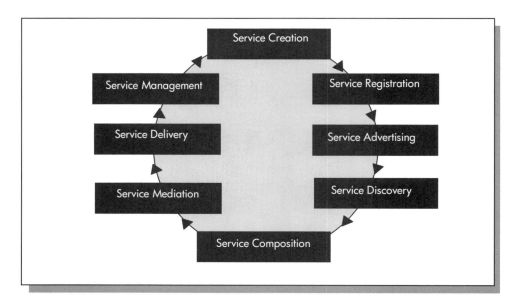

Figure 2.1. Steps in service deployment.

accomplish the specific task for which they were chosen. This interaction with the services can be direct or brokered through a mediator.

A mediator is desired for transactions between a service and its clients. It plays the role of a *trusted third party* in a dynamic interaction environment. The mediator can log and monitor the interaction. It can also create a *persistent* interaction experience for the service or the client by shielding them from failures on either side. In a fully trusted environment, direct interaction between a service and client is possible.

Note

There is a cost associated with the mediator's benefits. The added step in the interaction sequence may result in lower throughput. A service user may experience slower response during a mediated transaction versus a direct transaction.

The e-Speak architecture consists of components that are aimed at facilitating all the stages in service creation and use, as explained before. It consists of three components:

1. Service engine

2. Service registry

3. Service modeling framework

In subsequent sections, we discuss the role of each of these components. As is true with any emerging technology, the e-Speak technology is undergoing significant changes. Thus, wherever applicable, we have provided the most recent developments in these components. Chapter 16 presents the evolving roadmap of the e-Speak technology.

2.1 The E-Speak Service Engine

The e-Speak service engine is the software component of the e-Speak architecture. It provides the development and deployment environment for the services. The engine consists of:

- Logical Machine: a platform abstraction for service runtime environment
- Resource: A component-based representation of a service
- Interaction Mechanisms: The application programming interfaces (APIs) for service discovery and invocation

Figure 2.2 depicts the relationship among these components.

2.1.1 E-Speak Logical Machine

The e-Speak service engine[1] provides functionality that is analogous to the kernel of an operating system (OS). A computer OS manages a set of hardware resources. It provides the necessary abstractions for the underlying devices, such

---

[1] Throughout the book, you will find the e-Speak service engine referred to as the *e-Speak service engine*, the *service engine*, the *core*, or the *engine*.

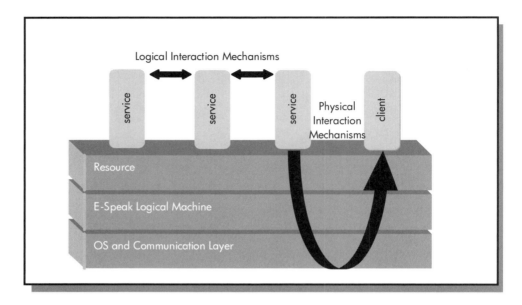

Figure 2.2. The e-Speak service engine architecture.

as a disk, memory, CPU, or file. To a programmer, all these physical entities appear as *resources* that are available via software APIs. The programmer need not worry about the specifics of how a hardware device functions. The software APIs provided by the OS shield the programmers from those details. Besides providing these abstractions for the physical devices, the OS manages proper initialization, access control and security around them. An e-Speak engine provides similar functionality for services. Figure 2.3 draws the analogy between the OS and e-Speak.

As shown in Figure 2.3, a service is analogous to a physical resource. It provides a functionality that is desired by a service client. The e-Speak engine mediates the interaction between the service and its clients to provide similar abstractions, access control, and security mechanisms for the services as the OS does to the devices of a computer. The core set of abstractions provided by the e-Speak engine includes a resource, resource namespaces, resource mailboxes, resource security, resource description, and resource management.

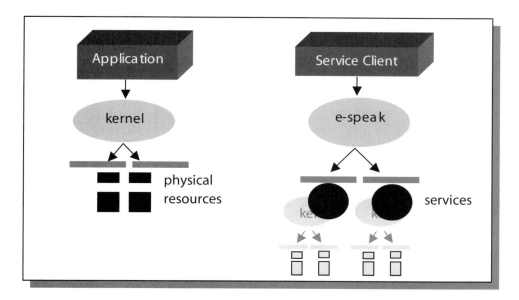

Figure 2.3. Analogy between e-Speak engine and operating system.

A Resource

A *resource* is a fundamental abstraction provided in the service engine. An e-Speak resource is a *whole* entity that is *addressable* by other entities in its environment. A resource should have all the necessary pieces contained in itself to provide the required functionality. The addressability refers to a unique identity (or a name) for the resource. This identity uniquely refers to one and only one resource in the e-Speak infrastructure. The address of a resource is in the form of a Uniform Resource Locator (URL): `es://...`

Resources composed in this fashion can be registered, advertised, discovered, and interacted with. A service comprises one or more resources. At the finest granularity, a service is a single resource. More complex services consist of several services (which, in turn, consist of several resources). A simple service resource can be thought of as a service with finest granularity whereas a higher level service comprises a collection of resources. Figure 2.4 depicts this hierarchy. E-Speak manages the metadata surrounding a resource. In the same manner that a Dewey decimal library card contains information about the author, publisher, and location of a book in the library, the service engine catalogs attributes, description, and location information about a resource. Throughout the book, we use the word *service* to describe an e-Speak registered resource of the appropriate granularity.

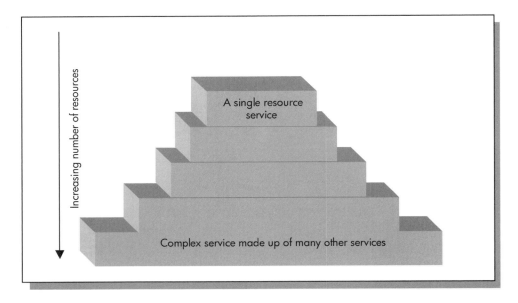

Figure 2.4. Service-resource relationship.

Although most of the resources registered with a service engine are resources outside the engine, there are some resources that are handled and managed by the engine itself. These resources are built-in resources and are called *core-managed resources*. The name frames, explained next, are an example of core-managed resources.

Resource Namespaces

The resources registered with the e-Speak engine are referred to using their *names*. The identity (or the name) of a resource is unique. However, e-Speak does not require globally unique names. Instead, the e-Speak standard stipulates a local (or private) unique naming scheme. This concept is best explained using name-spaces.

A namespace is a *set* of names. The interpretation of the word *set* is mathe-matical. This means that there are no duplicate entries allowed in a namespace set. In the e-Speak service engine, the namespaces are maintained using core-managed resources called *name frames*. A name frame, being a resource itself, can be maintained in another name frame. Thus, e-Speak has a hierarchy of name frames, with the root of hierarchy called *Root* name frame. Name frames are used extensively when searching a specific resource registered with an engine.

The namespaces spare the service deployers and users from creating and using globally unique names for the registered resources. A name is always qualified us-ing the name frame it is contained within. Because the name frame has a globally unique identifier, the *qualified* name also becomes globally unique. Thus, a service deployer can name the service anything, so long as it is unique within the pertinent nameframe. Similarly, a user can create a local reference (alias) to a discovered service.

Resource Mailboxes

E-Speak uses the concept of mailboxes to facilitate interaction between a resource and the service engine. Each resource has an *Outbox* and an *Inbox*. Any mes-sage sent *to* the resource, such as a service request, is delivered to its Inbox, whereas any message originating *from* the resource, such as a response to a ser-vice request, is stored in the Outbox. This message is then picked up by the service engine for further processing.

Note

The mailbox based architecture does not imply any messaging happening between the resource and the service engine. Only the interfaces for communication are defined in terms of mailboxes.

A typical interaction between a service and a service user involves a request mes-sage sent from the Outbox of a service user to the Inbox of the service and a response message sent from the Outbox of the service to the Inbox of the service user. We elaborate on the mailbox architecture in Chapter 4 to illustrate how a service and its client communicate with each other.

Resource Security

An e-Speak registered resource must be secured from unauthorized access and usage. To enforce security, access control policies must be defined for each resource. Under the e-Speak infrastructure, each resource is treated with the strictest access permissions. Each resource must relax this security by specifically granting access to other resources.

Beyond access control, the communication between a service and an authenticated client must also happen in a secure environment. E-Speak architecture defines Session Layer Security (SLS) on top of the Simple Public Key Infrastructure (SPKI). The messages between the two communicating parties are encrypted using the keys provided by SPKI.

Note

In a mediated interaction, the service engine acts as a midpoint between the communicating parties. As a result, there is no TCP connection between the two endpoints. Thus, TCP-based security protocols, such as Secured Socket Layer (SSL) and Transport Layer Security (TLS), are not appropriate for end-to-end security in this case.

E-Speak also maintains a separate environment for each resource, called a *protection domain*. A protection domain can be used to keep data specific to the resource, such as memory usage and references to other resources in the system. A protection domain is analogous to a home directory associated with a login account in an OS.

Resource Description

For a resource to be discoverable, it must be described using certain attributes. To be effective, this description must have information about the functionality the resource provides, as well as quality of service metrics. As described in Chapter 1, an ecosystem governing body typically defines the description attributes so that all services within a certain class can be described consistently. E-Speak provides the mechanisms called *vocabularies* and *contracts* for this purpose. We discuss these constructs in detail in Chapter 5.

Resource Management

An e-Speak resource is managed by the service engine. This resource management is at the service interaction level. Thus, although the engine does not manage memory and disk usage, it mediates a resource's interaction with other entities in the ecosystem. An e-Speak-mediated communication is called an *in-band* communication.

Using the mediated communication channel, the service engine can monitor a resource's interaction with other entities. This monitoring can be used to assess a service's compliance with the appropriate performance standards. An ecosystem monitor, as discussed in Section 1.3, can use this monitoring functionality. The monitoring also enforces the security policies of the service deployer to protect a service from malicious access by unauthorized entities.

The e-Speak management architecture consists of the following components:

- A set of core-managed resources that manage resource metadata and the functional management of the e-Speak platform.

- A repository containing resource metadata. The metadata for a resource is created during its registration and used during the discovery.

- An e-Speak logical machine that routes service requests between a service and its clients in the form of messages.

2.1.2   Resource Interaction Architecture

The resource architecture of the service engine is similar to the *component* architecture in Java or Common Object Request Broker Architecture (CORBA). The component architecture is the base for contemporary distributed computing technologies. These technologies are used to implement systems based on *tiered* or *peer-to-peer* architectures. In the tiered architecture, different tiers have different responsibilities to provide a set of functionality. Figure 2.5 shows the tiered architecture.

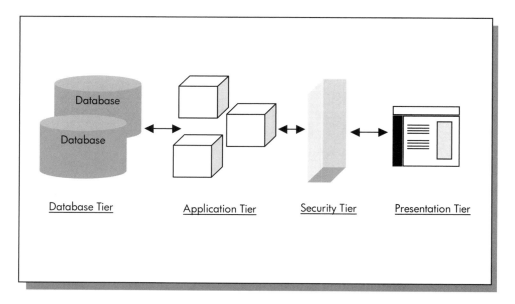

Figure 2.5. Tiered architecture.

In the peer-to-peer architecture, there is no hierarchy among entities, as in the tiered architecture. Instead, each entity is a stand-alone entity that provides a specific service or performs a specific task. Each entity is also responsible for its own security, communication, and management needs. Figure 2.6 shows peer-to-peer architecture.

In both the tiered and peer-to-peer architectures, a certain entity or a certain tier is a self-contained unit. It contains all the necessary features to accomplish its responsibility. This *architectural unit* makes the component in a component architecture. Formally, a component has the following characteristics:

◻ It has a well-defined build-time and runtime interface for interaction.

◻ It can be thought of as an independent entity, compared with other components of the architecture. It can be built, deployed, and undeployed without

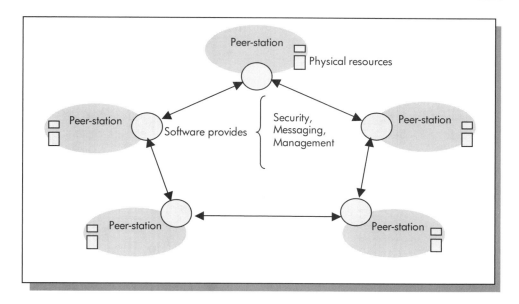

Figure 2.6. Peer-to-peer architecture.

affecting other components in the architecture (however, this might affect the *functioning* of the system).

■ It is *individually addressable* in the system. This means that it can be approached and communicated with by other entities in its ecosystem. The addressability of a component separates it from other software modules that are merely results of functional decomposition.

An e-Speak resource has all the characteristics mentioned above. E-Speak has an Interface Definition Language (IDL) that is used to define the interface of a resource. The resource users use this interface, as defined by the IDL, to communicate with the resource. In subsequent chapters, we explain how a resource and its interface can be used programmatically to create a service. We also discuss how to use these characteristics to register and discover a service in e-Speak. The ability to register and discover differentiates a service from a component.

2.1.3   Resource Interaction Mechanisms

Though we have drawn similarities between a service and a component, they differ in a fundamental way. A component is tied to the languages or frameworks that define it. Java and CORBA are good examples of such architectures. This restricts a programmer as to how a component can be created and deployed in a system. It also poses interoperability issues. If there are multiple standards on how to build a component, software must be written to bridge the gap between the two standards to ensure interoperability. A service, on the other hand, is not tied to any specific language or platform. A COBOL program can be, conceptually, turned into a service. This helps immensely in addressing interoperability and marrying legacy systems — developed using decades-old technology — with state-of-the-art technologies.

The other difference between a component and a service is related to the type of functionality they are supposed to address. An interaction with a component is typically synchronous (blocking). Under the synchronous interaction paradigm, the client of a component is blocked until it gets a response back from the component. However, there are several examples of business-level interactions that are asynchronous. To model them using synchronous interaction-based components is not difficult but forces awkward design. A service with an asynchronous communication model can be used in this scenario to fulfill that task without such difficulties.

E-Speak's notion of a service encompasses both the interaction patterns described above. It provides Java-based APIs for synchronous interactions, whereas XML is used to facilitate asynchronous interactions. Using the e-Speak classification, a component-based architecture for an e-Speak solution is based on the Network Object Model (NOM), while the asynchronous interaction is based on Document Exchange Model (DEM). The NOM approach is generally a good fit for tightly coupled systems, whereas DEM is better suited for loosely coupled systems.

One advantage of using a DEM in the context of services that could be spread around the world is that it scales much better than synchronous method calls. Synchronous method calls can work very well in small Local Area Network (LAN) environments and sometimes behind the firewall within larger organizations. However, when a synchronous method call goes out over the Internet, the IP packets that contain that method call are routed potentially around the world through a number of routers, firewalls, bridges, and so on. The end result is that a remote method call that could take 1 millisecond (1/1000th of a second) to invoke on a local LAN could take 30 seconds or more to complete over the Internet. There are outages and "stale" data (such as IP addresses that are no longer valid) that do occur on the Internet, which would cause synchronous method calls to fail altogether.

Another reason for using a DEM is that many of the transports developed for the Internet were designed to transport messages (electronic documents) over large distances over unreliable networks. Some protocols, such as the Simple Mail Transport Protocol (SMTP), allow for ways to send documents into a *holding bin* — such as someone's email inbox — for later retrieval and processing. What this means is that a client can send an electronic document along to a web service using Internet transports, and that document will eventually make its way to the service for processing. If the web service expects to get a large number of documents from a large number of clients, it can make itself accessible only via a queuing mechanism — such as a message queue or an email server and SMTP — thereby allowing the web service to process the documents it receives when it has time to process them.

One of the other primary benefits to using the document exchange technologies is that businesses are very familiar with the concept of transacting business through the exchange of documents. Therefore, when business process analysts are defining business-to-businesses transactions that will occur using services, they can easily understand the concept of exchanging documents, securing documents, and guaranteeing their delivery, to name a few. Because the DEM is so familiar to businesses, web services tools can be built that allow users to model web services solutions as exchanges of business documents. This behavior is a natural extension of what business process modelers are used to doing in the nondigital world.

Table 2.1 summarizes the differences between the two interaction mechanisms. Chapter 13 discusses the DEM further in the context of web services.

The current implementation of the e-Speak engine primarily facilitates the NOM architecture. It provides a subset of that functionality in the DEM modules. The subsequent versions of e-Speak, however, will emphasize the DEM functionality

Table 2.1. Comparison of Service Interaction Mechanisms

NOM Interactions	DEM Interactions
Supports tightly coupled architecture	Supports loosely coupled architecture
Suitable for programmatic interaction	Suitable for document-based interaction
Objects have *state* and behavior	Documents do not contain any state information
Mostly suitable for short-lived interactions	Mostly suitable for long-lived interactions
IDL defines interaction interface	Document schemas and metadata define interaction interface
Code-level method binding	Agreement on document semantics rather than interfaces
Uses technology-specific protocols	Uses language-independent protocols
Works best in intranet environment	Can work in both intranet and Internet environment

based on XML more than the NOM features, due to the advantages of the DEM model, as previously described. We have used mostly the NOM-based approach in the book to demonstrate maximum e-Speak functionality. However, as the e-Speak DEM model evolves, these examples could be implemented using that model, as well. We show one such transformation later in the book.

Despite the differences in the two interaction mechanisms, e-Speak provides the same set of abstractions for both. The concept of a resource, for example, stays the same, regardless of the interaction mechanism it uses. The description, security, and management abstractions are also identical between the two interaction mechanisms. This interaction-agnostic approach is very useful. It allows for resources based on different mechanisms to interoperate. For example, the developer is free to choose the best interaction mechanism suitable for the client, irrespective of the service's interaction mechanism.

Although it is conceptually possible to be interaction-agnostic, the current e-Speak version has some limitations. These limitations prevent us from creating a truly interoperable environment. Nonetheless, it provides good insights into the eventual solution.

2.1.4   Multicore Interactions

As discussed earlier, an e-Speak logical machine is responsible for managing the resources registered in it. It also mediates the interaction between a resource (or a service) and its user. Technically, every resource in a large system could be registered with the same e-Speak engine. However, a separation between the *resource categories* is a much more manageable option. Thus, in a Travel Industry ecosystem, we could think of one service engine hosting all the hotel services, another hosting the airline services, and yet another the travel companies.

In an environment where several engines (cores) exist, a core-to-core interaction must be facilitated. From a logical machine standpoint, a logical machine-to-logical machine communication path is required. E-Speak provides two core-managed resources for this purpose — Connection Manager and Remote Resource Manager.

Connection Manager

The Connection Manager is responsible for initiating, managing, and closing a remote core connection as required. Each service engine instance has its dedicated instance of the Connection Manager. The URL of a Connection Manager is of the form `es://<server>/CORE/ConnectionManager`, where `<server>` denotes the IP address where the engine is instantiated and the port number it is listening on. Given a host name and port number, a Connection Manager can negotiate with its remote counterpart on that location to establish a connection between the two engines.

Remote Resource Manager

The Remote Resource Manager is responsible for importing and exporting resources from a remote service engine. The Remote Resource Manager requires an established Connection Manager connection with the remote engine. On a service engine, it is located at `es://<server>/CORE/RemoteResourceManager`.

In most cases, during the import and export of resources, only the resource metadata is exchanged between the two Remote Resource Managers. This is analogous to the *call-by-reference* programming paradigm. In this case, there is only one resource, regardless of the number of engines that hold the data about it. Certain core-managed resources are exchanged *by value*. In this case, a local copy of the resources exists on each engine that participates in the resource exchange.

When a service client searches for a suitable service based on its search criteria, the local as well as remote resources are examined for their eligibility. This eligibility is based on the metadata about the locally or remotely registered resources. E-Speak provides an *advertising service* that provides scalability in this service lookup. The multicore interactions using the advertising service are discussed in more detail in Chapter 7.

2.2   Service Registry

As services propagate and the *web of services* discussed in Chapter 1 develops, the need for large-scale service registries increases, as well. Such registries enable Internet-scale service ecosystems. Service deployers can advertise or register their services in such a registry for discovery by service users. Service users can discover services to fulfill their particular need by querying the registry. Figure 2.7 depicts the relationship between ecosystem citizens and a service registry.

E-Speak provides one such global registry at `http://www.eservicesvillage.com`. This registry, called *E-services Village* (ESV), is based on the e-Speak technology. It is a portal for e-Speak services. It provides the tools needed for registering, finding, and using e-Speak services. It enables ecosystem creation by providing:

■ Ability to customize e-Speak constructs, such as vocabularies and contracts

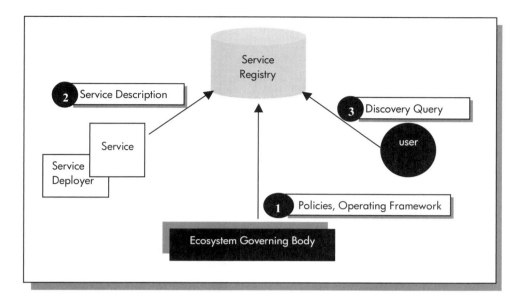

Figure 2.7. Ecosystem citizens and registries.

- Secure portal account management
- Codeless Service Registration
- Logging and service monitoring
- Robust searching capabilities (keyword search, browse and advanced search)
- Support for multiple types of services, such as engine-hosted, ESV-mediated, firewall-protected, or XML-based)

ESV will provide support for the new emerging industry standard, Universal Description Discovery Integration (UDDI), discussed in Chapter 14. Providing complete UDDI support ensures compatibility and interoperability with other services being deployed industry-wide.

2.2.1   Private Registries

Internet-wide ecosystems provide a public registry to allow external entities to discover and invoke services available for broad consumption. However, business entities may decide to deploy isolated registries for greater control over participation and data protection. Such private registries may choose whether to roll up into the Internet-wide ecosystem. An analogy of this paradigm is seen on the Internet today. The public Internet is generally reachable at some level but corporate *intranets* or *virtual private networks* (VPNs) are protected stand-alone nets that provide complete access control and data privacy.

2.3   Service Framework Specification

The e-Speak engine provides a means to create and deploy a service, as we discussed earlier. However, a service deployment tool, such as the engine, is only a partial answer to making the service-centric computing vision a reality. The engine solves the technical problem of describing and deploying services. We also need to look at these services with a broader perspective in which the viewpoint of the business analysts must also be considered. The business process and the technology viewpoints, together, are required to create a complete picture of the service strategy for a company. In other words, to increase the adoption of service-oriented design, a more holistic approach is necessary.

2.3.1   Current Business Environment

The current business environment consists of several incompatible software platforms and business models. These software platforms and business models are designed to optimize the local environment in which they operate. For example, implementation of an Enterprise Resource Planning (ERP) system for a company is based on the business practices of that company. Companies may buy an off-the-shelf product or custom build a solution themselves to automate a business process. Such a locally optimized approach in software implementation is normally very effective. However, in the big picture (participating in an ecosystem), this poses several problems, such as:

- Technical lock-in to proprietary platforms

- Business model lock-in to platform capabilities

- Difficulty in interoperability (between two or more such software platforms), due to incompatibility

- Cost of creating the one-off cross-platform adapters

An ecosystem, by definition, is a very collaborative environment. The ability to interact with discovered services is essential for proper functioning of an ecosystem. Thus, the problems mentioned here are the main hindrances in creating an ecosystem consisting of entities with internally focused software solutions. To address these issues, we need a *service framework*.   A service framework can provide guidelines for service design, creation, and deployment that will ensure seamless interaction between entities within an ecosystem.

2.3.2   Service Framework Elements

It must be noted that there are no existing *standardized* frameworks available today that can provide solutions to all the problems discussed earlier. However, the e-service vision does provide some guidance about what such a framework should consist of. The goal of the framework should be to provide a blueprint for the creation, deployment, and dynamic discovery of e-services on the Internet. Currently, there are several proposed standards that address some or part of the service framework. Chapter 15 discusses these. A service framework should:

- Be based on standards for expressing business and technical abstractions

- Support multiple transport protocols and ensure interoperability across any hardware and software platforms

- Support multiple XML business schemas (for example, RosettaNet, CommerceNet, BizTalk)

- Provide a uniform service and service interaction model across several software platforms and across all service complexities

- Allow interactions over a synchronous (Network Object) or an asynchronous (Document Exchange) Model

- Define messaging, addressability, and context communication between services

🔲 Define specifications for major business processes (for example, negotiation and contract formation)

🔲 Incorporate multiple interaction security standards

It can be seen that a service framework is an all-encompassing specification that defines the service's environment. The issues it addresses can range from how a stateful service should differ in behavior from a stateless service to how to ensure business-level integrity in a contract formation transaction. Figure 2.8 shows a specification stack for such a service framework. This stack includes both the technology and business-level interactions with a service.

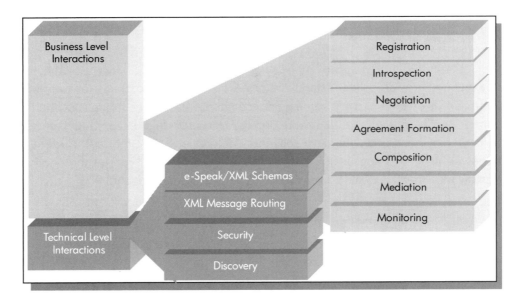

Figure 2.8. Service Framework Specification stack.

Although there are no established frameworks, e-Speak developed Service Framework Specification (SFS) as a preliminary answer to this problem. The work in this area, like the preliminary work on ESV, will evolve to encompass emerging industry standards. Chapter 13 discusses features of SFS vis-à-vis some of the competing service frameworks.

Although the e-Speak architecture provides the necessary components to realize the web services vision, it needs to be complemented by standard software components, such as those for fault tolerance, high availability, and persistence.

Web Service Development

PART Two

IN THIS PART

A Simple E-Speak Service

Chapter 3

A SIMPLE E-SPEAK SERVICE

Open up any computer science or programmers' book and you will see that it starts with the age-old, time-tested *Hello World* example. A few lines of code that print *Hello World* on the screen, right? In keeping with that tradition, let us take you through Hello World, as well — with a slight twist. These days, software makers everywhere are trying to personalize and customize everything. Gone are the days when generic, one-size-fits-all was the way to go. So, rather than saying *Hello!* to the world in general but to no one in particular, our e-Speak service prints out a customized greeting when it is invoked by the client. Figure 3.1 depicts the *Hello World* environment and the corresponding interaction patterns. On one side are the steps the service component goes through to offer the *Hello World* service; on the other side are the steps a typical client of such a service goes through to use it.

3.1 Interfaces and the ESIDL Compiler

Let's start with defining the interface for the *Hello World* service. Why are we starting with the *interface*, you ask? In the distributed systems world, the first place to start while developing a distributed component is the interface. The interface allows other components in a distributed system to talk to the business logic of a specific component. These other components will use this *published* interface to communicate with the component. In other words, an interface defines all the functionality of a distributed component that is visible to the other components.

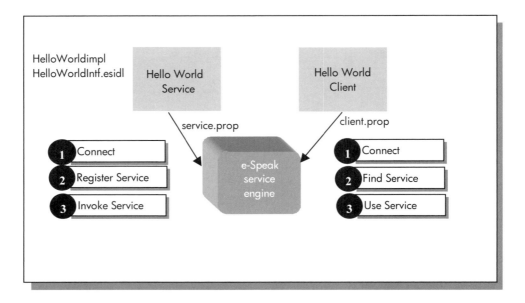

Figure 3.1. Hello World service delivery and interactions.

Figure 3.2 illustrates the process of communicating via the distributed architecture.

In this example, Hello World's interface will expose a simple method called `greet` that provides the greeting functionality. Our client will use this method to interact with the Hello World service. We have put this interface in *HelloWorldIntf.esidl*. The extension *.esidl* denotes that this is a file defining an interface, using the e-Speak interface definition language (ESIDL). ESIDL is an e-Speak-specific IDL to describe an interface. Structurally, it is similar to the Java-RMI IDL. These IDL files must have the extension *esidl* for the ESIDL compiler to recognize them as e-Speak IDL files.

All service interfaces in e-Speak must extend the `ESService` class, and each interface method must throw the exception `ESInvocationException`. `ESService` is an abstract class that represents any service within the e-Speak world. In a similar fashion, the class `ESInvocationException` is also a top-level class in e-Speak for any exception handling.

Here is the interface for the Hello World service in the file *HelloWorldIntf.esidl*:

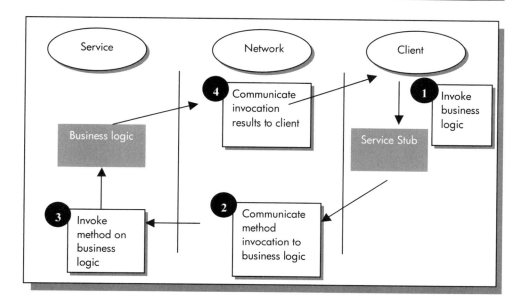

Figure 3.2. Distributed component architecture.

HelloWorldIntf.esidl

```
public interface HelloWorldIntf extends ESService
{
public void greet (String s) throws ESInvocationException;
}
```

Note that the client will need this IDL file to create the necessary stubs from us-ing e-Speak's ESIDL compiler. Recall that a stub is a client-side representation of the interface. The ESIDL compiler, like any other IDL compiler, creates the nec-essary stubs for the remote method calls. For each method, it generates code that sends and receives multiple messages between two or more communicating components.

3.2   The Greeting Service

Having described the `HelloWorldIntf` interface that other components can use to communicate with it, we are ready to develop the greeting service based on that interface. This entails *implementing* the methods described in the interface `HelloWorldIntf` in the business logic of the service. The specification for the implementation is also provided by the interface itself. For example, in this case, to implement the `HelloWorldIntf` interface, we need to create a method called `greet`, which accepts one `String` parameter and returns `void`.

Okay, Java experts go ahead and create your own `greet` function. Here is an example implementation of the `HelloWorldIntf` — the `HelloWorldImpl` class. You will notice that there is nothing *e-Speaky* about this implementation. All we did was ensure that we adhered to the specifications of the `HelloWorldIntf` interface.

HelloWorldImpl.java

```
class HelloWorldImpl implements HelloWorldIntf
{
    public void greet(String name)
    {
        System.out.println("Hello " + name + "!");
        System.out.println("Welcome to E-Speak!");
    }
}
```

3.3   Deploying a Service

By implementing the interface, we have developed the *business logic* of the service. However, until this logic is *deployed*, it cannot be accessed. Let's create the `HelloWorldService` class that will do exactly that. The first thing we need to do in the deploying class is establish connection with the e-Speak service engine. This is done using the `ESConnection` object. The `ESConnection` object uses a configuration file (specified as an argument) to set the context for connection with the e-Speak engine. This configuration file specifies appropriate connection parameters. You will notice that our configuration file, *Service.prop*, contains few simple entries. It contains the minimal set of connection properties.

service.prop

```
# where service engine is running
hostname = localhost
# port the engine listens on
portnumber = 2950
# group name this engine belongs to
community = null
```

Appendix E has information on all the properties and their values or defaults.

Note

If your configuration file is not located in the current working directory, you will need to specify the relative path for it when using it as an argument to ESConnection.

Here is code from the HelloWorldService class.

HelloWorldService.java

```
ESConnection Connection = null;
Connection = new ESConnection("Service.prop");
System.out.println("Connected to E-Speak");
```

At this point, the service is connected to the engine. Several methods from the ESConnection class can be used now to get security or account information or to set context for the current connection. For example, getConfiguration can provide all the configuration information associated with the connection environment. setContexts is an alternative way to set the context of the connection, based on the configuration properties. The Javadoc for the ESConnection class, which is part of the installation package, provides a complete listing of all the methods.

Note that, at this point, while the `HelloWorldService` is connected to the engine, the engine has no information about this service other than certain connection-related parameters. It's a bit like meeting someone at a party and not giving out your name or phone number. Not very useful because you cannot be contacted (maybe that was purposeful!). But in this example, we want to tell others more about this Hello World service so they can use it. For this purpose, we need to *describe* this service, using certain attributes (name-value pairs). This is analogous to describing a person with certain characteristics or describing a car using its features. Such attributes, characteristics, and features help in general when describing and finding an entity — in this case, a service. E-Speak takes care of this by providing the `ESServiceDescription` and the `ESServiceElement` classes. These classes allow us to provide the engine with certain attributes that describe the service.

In this example, we have defined the Hello World service with only one simple attribute — `Name`. An `ESServiceDescription` object stores the service description attributes.

HelloWorldService.java

```
ESServiceDescription Description = null;
Description = new ESServiceDescription();
Description.addAttribute("Name", "myGreetingService");
```

The `ESServiceElement` is a container class that keeps the context for the service being registered. It contains the information about connection with the engine and the service description. The class implementing the service logic is designated using the `setImplementation` method.

HelloWorldService.java

```
ESServiceElement myServiceElement = null;
myServiceElement = new ESServiceElement(Connection,Description);
myServiceElement.setImplementation(new HelloWorldImpl());
```

The last step to bring the service truly online with e-Speak is to register and start it. The `register` method stores the service element information in the e-Speak repository so that other e-Speak clients are able to discover the service. The method `start` allows the service to receive requests from client applications that find it.

HelloWorldService.java

```
myServiceElement.register();
myServiceElement.start();
```

Let's take this opportunity to recap what we have done so far. We created

1. Hello World's interface (*HelloWorldIntf.esidl*)

2. Hello World's implementation (*HelloWorldImpl.class*)

3. Hello World's service deployer (*HelloWorldService.class*)

3.4   The Service Client

The doors of our "service" are now open for business. All we need are some customers or service users. But unlike a Web site, access to this service is programmatic, not click-through. What does this mean to a potential customer (or service consumer)? It needs to develop a program (client) that can connect to the service engine and communicate with the registered service. This is the `HelloWorldClient` class. The very first part to ensuring that the client can communicate with service, in this case, `HelloWorldService`, is to compile the service's IDL file. To run the ESIDL compiler for the Hello World service, we would issue the following command:

```
java net.espeak.util.esidl.IDLCompiler  HelloWorldIntf.esidl
```

Of course, when you write your own interface file, you will replace *HelloWorld-Intf.esidl* with your own ESIDL file name. Let's look at what the ESIDL compiler has done with the interface file. Looking at the working directory, you will see that the following files were created:

▪ *HelloWorldIntf.java*:
defines the interface class.

▪ *HelloWorldStub.java*:
includes code for service object communication, routing of business logic invocation through e-Speak service engine, and handling messaging

▪ *HelloWorldIntfMessageRegistry.java*:
includes code for instantiating and initializing the message handlers

Feel free to look at these files if you are especially curious or adventurous. You will find details on how each remote procedure call from the interface results in the exchange of messages. Normally, you won't need to make any changes in these files. You should effect any changes via the ESIDL file, rather than modifying the generated files. The client will need these files to communicate with the service over the wire.

Now we are ready to develop the `HelloWorldClient`. Just like the service, the client also needs to establish and maintain a connection with the engine. Note, in this case, that this is the same engine to which Hello World service is connected.

HelloWorldClient.java

```
ESConnection Connection = new ESConnection("Client.prop");
System.out.println("Connected to espeak!");
```

As in the case of the service, we need to create a connection configuration file — *Client.prop*, in this case.

Client.prop

```
hostname = localhost
portnumber = 2950
community = null
```

You will notice that these entries look exactly the same as the *Service.prop* file. That is what we mean by using the same e-Speak service engine. However, the client is not yet ready to invoke the service's `greet` method. This is because the communication channel between the client and the service has not been fully established. To establish an end-to-end connection between service and client, the client needs to retrieve the *handle* for the Hello World service from the engine's repository. This is accomplished by querying the engine's repository using the service's description attributes and its interface. The engine will perform a search based on this query and return the handle to the client.

The `ESServiceFinder` object creates the context for such a query, and the `ESQuery` object contains the formatted search query. In this case, the client program is looking for a service that implements the `HelloWorldIntf` interface and has a specific value (`myGreetingService`) for the attribute `Name`. `ESServiceFinder`'s `find` method returns the handle to any service matching the search criteria.

HelloWorldClient.java

```
ESServiceFinder Finder = null;
Finder = new ESServiceFinder(Connection,"HelloWorldIntf");
ESQuery Query = new ESQuery("Name == 'myGreetingService'" );
HelloWorldIntf Result =  (HelloWorldIntf)Finder.find(Query);
```

The curious programmer will notice that the result of the find has been typecast to `HelloWorldIntf`. Due to this typecasting, the client can programmatically invoke the `HelloWorldIntf` method (`greet`) using the handle.

HelloWorldClient.java

```
System.out.println("Service Found! Contacting ...");
myResult.greet(name);
```

3.5   In Action

Are you ready to see this new and improved Hello World in action? First start up the e-Speak engine in one window using the following command from the e-Speak installation *config* directory:

```
c:/> ..\bin\espeak -i core.ini
```

You will always start the engine from within the $\backslash e$-$speak\backslash config$ directory. Figure 3.3 is a screen shot of what you can expect when you start your e-Speak service engine.

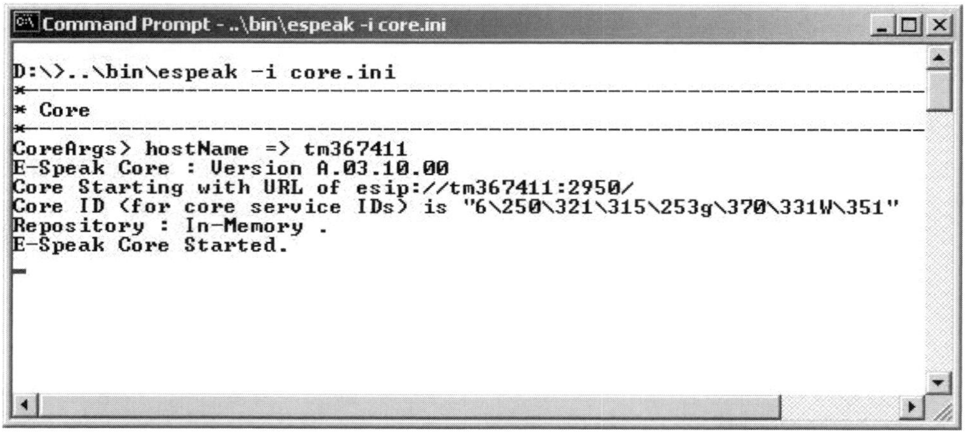

Figure 3.3. Starting the e-Speak service engine.

Figure 3.4. Starting the Hello World service.

Then, in another window, start up the Hello World service, as in Figure 3.4. Did you notice that there is a -D option to set the system property espeak_home? This

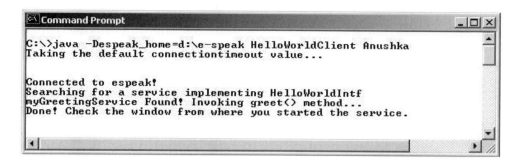

Figure 3.5. Starting the Hello World client.

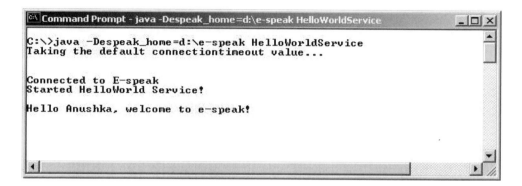

Figure 3.6. Hello World service results.

variable is already set in your system environment during the e-Speak installation. However, the folks designing Java have removed the capability to access the system properties directly in a Java program for security reasons. Thanks to this, you have to set this variable explicitly whenever you run services or clients via the JVM (later on, you will see that even using e-Speak's management desktop, the -D will be required). However, in starting the engine itself in Figure 3.3, we did not use this option. This is because the e-Speak utility *espeak.exe* is a regular Windows application and *does* have access to the system properties. Finally, in a third window, start up the HelloWorld client, as shown in Figure 3.5.

The way the service was coded, the greeting happens on the service side and is not visible to the client. So make sure to check your results on the service window.

You should see output similar to Figure 3.6.

And there you have it! A few classes with a few lines of e-Speak and Java code, and you've created, deployed, and used your own service.

So, did you see a pattern in what we did? We

- Defined a problem space
- Developed an interface for service providers to adhere to
- Coded the service logic
- Deployed the service and
- Developed a client to find or discover the service

The rest of our examples will follow the same style — introducing a few more cool things each time (read "more complexity"!). Take our next example, for instance. Isn't it really boring to have the service do something over there in service land, with the client getting back nothing but `void`? How would the client know whether anything happened at all? What would be more interesting and useful is if the service does something and sends the results to the client. There are cases when this unidirectional communication is useful; for example, initiating a process that kicks off a chain of events such as the backup process for computers or a Web crawler that gets initiated to search the Web for specific news items or information.

One comment might be appropriate here. What we are showing here are some basics — some simple ways to get a concept to work in the real world. There are, of course, multiple ways of doing something in e-Speak, as in any other software. If your interest is piqued further, take a look at e-Speak's manuals.

Understanding Client-Service Interactions

- ■ Communicating Results to the Client
  example working directory:
  \Examples\Ex02BidirectionalDataFlow

- ■ A Service's Many Clients
  example working directory:
  \Examples\Ex03SingleInstance

- ■ Problems with Single-Instance Service Deployment

- ■ Effective Service Architectures
  example working directory:
  \Examples\Ex04DedicatedInstance

- ■ Where Do You Stand?

Chapter 4

UNDERSTANDING CLIENT-SERVICE INTERACTIONS

In the previous chapter, we looked at how a simple service, such as Hello World, can be written. We saw how basic client and service interactions occur. We allowed the service to display the service processing results on the service side — ignoring the client's need for access to the results. In this chapter, we show you how to send results back to the client. The service results can be both primitive and user-defined data elements. Communicating data between classes (services and clients) in e-Speak is close to the usual programming paradigms. The client sends data to the service through method parameters, and the service returns any result back as a return value. However, there is some extra work needed on the programmer's part. We must probe further to understand how this extra work translates into data elements being communicated between a service and its clients.

These service and client interactions also help us in designing e-Speak-based applications that have some desirable qualities — flexibility, scalability, and robustness, to name a few. The metrics of these qualities are plenty; no matter how many we try to address, there will be a few we miss because, just like the authors of this book, the experts in performance analysis are busy writing books defining newer metrics! As a result, rather than giving you some benchmarking-style examples, we talk about the inner workings of the e-Speak platform. Armed with that information and using the corresponding examples in this book you can design your own benchmark programs to test the scalability and robustness of your service.

4.1 Communicating Results to the Client

In Chapter 3, the Hello World service printed a greeting message in the service process window when invoked by the client. The greeting included a string passed from the client to the service. After the greeting was printed, the service returned only the success or failure of the invocation. However, a service that does its own thing, only to return success or failure, is a good learning tool but not very practical. For all *practical* purposes, the client would need more than limited, one-way access to the service. Typically, the client would expect the results to make their way across the wire to the client process. The real beauty of invoking a service is to have a task remotely accomplished for you and the results returned to you, whether it be a reservation, e-tickets for your favorite concert, or a doctor's appointment. Ideally, the Hello World service would have printed the greeting in the client's process window and *not* in the service's process window. So, how do results (either primitive or user-defined data elements) make their way around in e-Speak? E-Speak, together with Java, provides a solution to this problem. E-Speak provides a custom serialization mechanism that is similar to Java's serialization.

4.1.1 Serialization and ESSerialization

First, let's talk a little about serialization for those of you who have not seen it in a while. Serialization allows distributed systems to send data through different computer architectures and still survive the journey. Serialization encodes objects into a stream of bytes. It also supports the reconstruction of these objects at their final destination. Serialization allows for components of a distributed architecture to understand clearly and accurately the objects by another component, even if the receiving component is installed on an architecture that is incompatible with that of the sender. *Object serialization* is the Java way to accomplish this task. It entails writing your object using the `writeObject` method to an output stream and rebuilding your object on the other side by reading from an input stream, using the `readObject` method.

E-Speak has created its own serialization mechanism — ESSerialization. You
might wonder why, if Java already provides one, do we need another type. It is
faster, for one thing. E-Speak serialization relies on explicit provision of how to
handle the data across the wire. On the other hand, Java serialization relies on
introspection to derive the serialization code. Secondly, e-Speak's serialization will
work across different languages and platforms because it does not depend on the
Java architecture. This feature helps in providing language independence — a
desired characteristic for an e-service, because it allows developers to work in the
language of their choice.

4.1.2   The User Data Service

Imagine that a system administrator (SA) wants to build a service that can gauge
the state and health of your PC. Of course, the SA would not want any service to
delve into the depths of a customer's hardware for security reasons. The information gathered from the PC can be combined with a PC problem-solution knowledge
database and — *voilà* — you have a quick *self-service* helpdesk that can take some
of the load off of the shrinking IT departments.

In this next example, we develop the basic skeleton of this *self-service* helpdesk.
This involves creating a service that gathers some data from the system for an authenticated client. The SA will develop a service, UserDataService, that provides
an authenticated user several pieces of information from different sources (*ini* file,
system parameters, system statistics). And yes, this time, the data does make its
way back to the client and does not get stuck in the service.

Take a look at the *UserDataIntf.esidl*. It looks fairly similar to the Hello World
interface. Take a second look! There is a very small but significant difference.
The discerning reader will notice that the User Data Service's IDL interface lists
methods that return *something else*, as compared with the greet() method's void.
If you didn't notice, it's okay; it was a trick question. Besides, the reason we have
written this book is to point out these things. The return type SystemStoreData, in
this case, is the container class object that communicates data between the client
and service. Figure 4.1 explains how container class objects facilitate client and
service interactions.

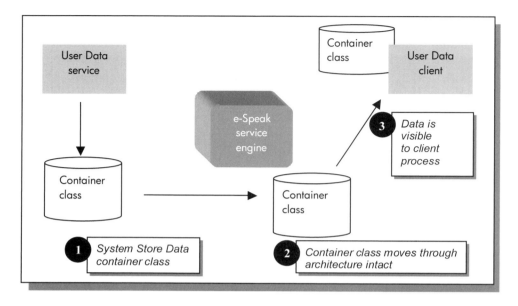

Figure 4.1. Container classes and the e-Speak architecture.

4.1.3   The Container Class

The SA has to use a small trick to get the desired data from the service class (UserDataService) to the client class (UserDataClient). As is true in any Java application, parameters used in methods defined in an ESIDL interface are always *passed by value*, and only *one* data type can be returned. Hence, to communicate multiple data elements, the SA would need to package them into a single object — (a *container class*). You'll see that the retrieve() method returns an object of type StoreSystemData. This mechanism is closest to the regular programming paradigm that we are all familiar with. E-Speak also supports an event-based model that can be useful. We discuss this in Chapter 6.

The container class acts as a mechanism to communicate between the service and the client. This object needs to implement the Esserializable interface and define the sendObject() and receiveObject() methods for the class. This will allow the container class (StoreSystemData) to move through the distributed computing jungle. The sendObject() method writes the system data properties to the

MessageOutputStream (a subclass of DataOutputStream), and receiveObject() reconstructs it on the client side by reading it from the MessageInputStream (a subclass of DataInputStream). In essence, the two methods sendObject() and receiveObject() define on-the-wire protocol to communicate data between two entities. In this example, we have used a very simple on-the-wire format, but it is possible to create a more complex format based on needs. The implementation of some standard, well-known protocol such as the Simple Object Access Protocol (SOAP) will also be contained within these two methods. In such a scenario, these method will use corresponding XML tags. Here is our implementation of these methods from the SystemStoreData container:

SystemStoreData.java

```
public void sendObject(MessageOutputStream out)
   throws IOException
{

   out.writeObject(prop1);
   out.writeObject(prop2);
   out.writeObject(prop3);
   out.writeObject(prop4);
   out.writeObject(prop5);


}

public Object receiveObject(MessageInputStream in)
   throws IOException
{
   StoreSystemData  rtnObj = new StoreSystemData();
   String prop1;
   prop1 = (String) in.readObject();
   rtnObj.prop1 = prop1;

   String prop2;
   prop2 = (String) in.readObject();
   rtnObj.prop2 = prop2;
```

```
String prop3;
prop3 = (String) in.readObject();
rtnObj.prop3 = prop3;

String prop4;
prop4 = (String) in.readObject();
rtnObj.prop4 = prop4;

String prop5;
prop5 = (String) in.readObject();
rtnObj.prop5 = prop5;


return rtnObj;
}
```

The `UserDataImpl` class completes the implementation of `UserDataIntf`. It constructs the container class that was created in conjunction with the interface as
follows:

UserDataImpl.java

```
StoreSystemData stData = null;
stData = new StoreSystemData(System.getProperty("user.name"),
sysDate,sysTime,connTimeOut,version);
```

As long as the container classes implement the `ESSerializable` interface, user-
defined elements can be treated as any other fundamental data types and can be
reliably passed to the client.

So, now we are ready to write a client to access the User Data service. All the
same e-Speak-related activities are still required. However, there is a difference in
using the service because it requires simple authentication. The client will need to
provide the service with the right credentials in order to receive the data. This is a
very easy way to include the minimal level of security in your e-Speak application.

Simply replace the hard-coded constants with a user-database implementation, and you have an authentication solution.

In our example, the `login` method of the `UserDataImpl` class does the login-password authentication. It will check whether the client has given the appropriate credentials before attempting to retrieve the system data from the service and print it. All these tasks are taken care of by the implementation that is backed by e-Speak's object serialization.

UserDataImpl.java

```
UserDataIntf Result =  (UserDataIntf)Finder.find(Query);
if (Result.login(name,password))
{
    System.out.println();
    StoreSystemData sysData;
    sysData = Result.retrieveData();
    sysData.printResult();
}

else
{
    System.out.println("Wrong Login/Password");
}
```

4.1.4   In Action

You first need to start the engine, as shown in Figure 3.3. Then start the User Data service as in Figure 4.2.

Now, start the client and type in the user login (`admin`) and password (`qc453fg`). Depending on how you coded the implementation, you could use the hard-coded password or feel free to try something more elaborate. You will notice in Figure 4.3 that your system's data is printed to the client process screen and not the service process screen as in Hello World!

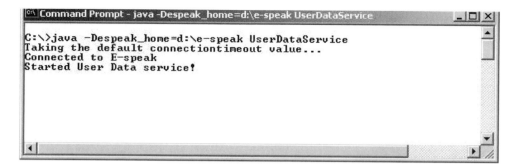

Figure 4.2. Starting the User Data service.

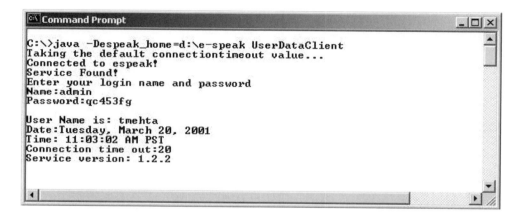

Figure 4.3. The User Data service client with results.

4.2   A Service's Many Clients

It was an interesting exercise to see how we can send rather complicated data back to a "single" client. However, in the real world, services must handle multiple clients. A service architect should anticipate several concurrent clients contending for use of the service at the same time. The obvious choice in such a scenario is to share the service resources among the clients in a transparent manner. Sharing of service resources poses some interesting problems, including quality of service and even privacy. In this section, we will look at these two issues more closely. The subsequent section delves into the details on how to circumvent these issues.

Let's say that you set up an Order Status service for the regional Porsche distributor to handle the many inquiries from the newly rich dot.com'ers or other local Porsche dealers regarding their orders. Naturally, the *nouveau riche* dot.com'ers have a very different profile from a car dealer. As individuals, their expectations from the service are quite different from those of dealerships. We walk you through this example and show you how two different clients (BigCo Motor Company and independent Porsche buyer, Scott) run into some problems sharing the Order Status service resources.

Because *XML* is the form *du jour* of communication, assume that the local Porsche dealer, BigCo, wants to communicate with the Order Status service, using XML. The beauty of XML is that it presents the data in a manner that can programmatically feed into backend supply chain systems of the car dealership. Scott, however, sticks to plain text so he can visually process the information. Providing options for data presentation makes your service very user-friendly and accommodating. This is also a fairly common requirement. A good service architecture should take into account its user base and provide options that make incorporating the service into the user's environment much simpler.

We provide a rather straightforward Order Status service implementation. Look at the files *CheckOrderStatusIntf.esidl*, *CheckOrderStatusService.java*, and *Check-OrderStatusImpl.java*. Notice that the Order Status service interface is not doing anything radically outside normal programming boundaries. In fact, it is simpler than the User Data service because the `getData` method returns a string buffer type (standard data type in Java); hence, no *ESSerialization* or container classes are needed. The class `CheckOrderStatusService` takes an argument `-d` (stands for *delay*). Using this argument, we can introduce additional processing time, if required, to simulate processing time consumption to a desired level during a service method invocation. The constructor for class `CheckOrderStatusImpl` uses this parameter while implementing the `getData` method.

CheckOrderStatusImpl.java

```
public StringBuffer getData(int choice, String choiceDetails)
    throws ESInvocationException;
{
...
```

```
//
// If the user has set any delay, introduce it here.
//

if (processingDelay > 0)
{
    for (int i=0; i< processingDelay; i++)
    for (int j=0; j< processingDelay; j++)
    // Do nothing
}
...
}
```

We will be using this delay parameter during our experiments on the Order Status service.

You will see that the order information (clients, orders, and so on) is all stored in a database that the distributor has — *orderDB.mdb*. Appendix B has the Data Source Name (DSN) entry information. User authentication and order status data is extracted from this company database. The necessary code to deal with the database is in the `DatabaseWrapper` class. This wrapper class hides the details of dealing with a database through the Java Database Connectivity-Open Database Connectivity (JDBC-ODBC) bridge from the rest of the classes in the service. Both the database schemas (for all databases used in this book) and wrapper class description are available in Appendix C. We will be using this wrapper class in subsequent examples, as well, so it is packaged as part of the `Shared` package. The code for simple authentication and the database wrapper class are included on the example CD. You can modify these to add more advanced features or simply use them as is for your work.

4.2.1   The Order Status Service

Take a moment to understand the business logic (`CheckOrderStatusImpl`) that constructs the Structured Query Language (SQL) query, extracts the order status information from the database, and presents it either in XML or text format (this is

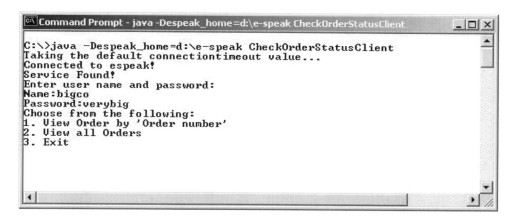

Figure 4.4. BigCo login for Order Status service.

plain Java application programming and outside the scope of this book). We are going to run two tests to highlight the problems with multiple clients (BigCo and Scott) accessing the Order Status service.

Test 1: Checking Client Context

Start the Order Status service as follows:

```
c:\>java -Despeak_home=d:\e-speak CheckOrderStatusService
```

Start the client and login as BigCo (user login: `bigco`, password: `verybig`), as shown in Figure 4.4. Choose option 2 to see all of BigCo's open orders. BigCo is registered within the service's database as a user that prefers order status information in XML format. Figure 4.5 shows BigCo's open orders in XML format.

In the service window, a message appears that indicates the customer for which the order status request was completed. For example:

```
Completed Order Status query for THE BIG COMPANY:
```

Without quitting from BigCo's client session, start a new client instance in a separate window and login as Scott (user login: `scott`, password: `scottymn`). Follow

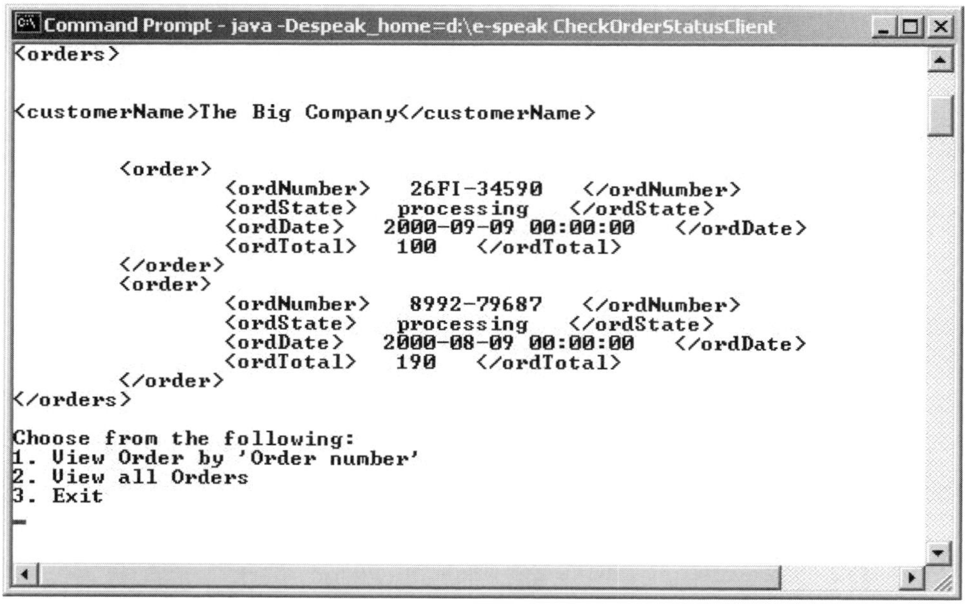

```
Command Prompt - java -Despeak_home=d:\e-speak CheckOrderStatusClient    _ □ X
<orders>


<customerName>The Big Company</customerName>


        <order>
                <ordNumber>    26FI-34590    </ordNumber>
                <ordState>    processing    </ordState>
                <ordDate>    2000-09-09 00:00:00    </ordDate>
                <ordTotal>    100    </ordTotal>
        </order>
        <order>
                <ordNumber>    8992-79687    </ordNumber>
                <ordState>    processing    </ordState>
                <ordDate>    2000-08-09 00:00:00    </ordDate>
                <ordTotal>    190    </ordTotal>
        </order>
</orders>

Choose from the following:
1. View Order by 'Order number'
2. View all Orders
3. Exit
```

Figure 4.5. BigCo XML results.

through the same action sequence as BigCo to get the order status information for Scott. Again, you will see a message in the service window that reflects the completion of Scott's query:

```
Completed Order Status query for SCOTT BAUMANN:
```

Because Scott is an individual user, the order status information appears in text format. Now go back to the client instance for BigCo and request order status information again. What do you see? Information for Scott's orders! Even in the service window, you see that the query was run for the user scott and not bigco. It seems as though the Order Status service is confused and has lost the user context information while processing client requests. Let's do another test.

Test 2: Client Timeout

In this test, we introduce the processing delay. In our example, extracting order status data and sending it to the client is a task that is completed in a few milliseconds. However, in reality, such a query (and many queries of a similar nature) can take a very long time. Even if the processing time is short, a single instance of a service serving multiple clients will soon be overloaded. As a result, a single client instance will experience some latency in response. To simulate either scenario, we use the processing delay option when starting the service. To perform this test, start the service with the -d option as follows. Of course, you could choose any valid Java integer value as a delay factor.

```
C:>java -Despeak_home=d:\e-speak CheckOrderStatusService
    -d 900000
```

You will see a message in the service window confirming the introduction of this delay factor. Now start the client sessions for BigCo and Scott simultaneously and issue order status requests from both these clients in quick succession. After some time you will see an error, as shown in Figure 4.6 in one or both client windows. If both the clients successfully complete the request, it means that you are running the examples on an exceptionally faster computer, compared with that of the authors, and you should try an even higher delay factor. No matter how fast your computer is, ultimately, a large enough delay factor would force the timeout error, as depicted in Figure 4.6. The quality of the service can degrade as the service gets overloaded, causing its clients to timeout.

4.2.2   Test Analysis

We do realize that we have orchestrated these tests to exaggerate the problems that a poor service architecture can cause. However, the discussion that follows provides service architecture options for more rational scenarios. We simply wanted to show the problems as a backdrop to the solution discussion that follows.

The first test uncovered the fact that, when a single service processes requests from several clients, the service does not have any implicit way of pairing requests

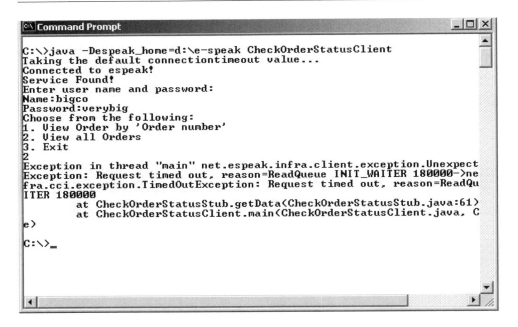

Figure 4.6. Client exception caused by request timeouts.

and clients together. E-Speak will facilitate the communication between the service and the client but it will not handle such a pairing — namely, *the context*. It will simply queue up messages targeted for a service. We see later on why this is, architecturally, and how it can be handled. The second test introduced a delay of 900,000 units. On our hardware, this was a sufficient amount of simulated service processing time to demonstrate the timeout effect the second client could experience. Again, e-Speak acts as a funnel for requests and although it handles the security and dispatching of requests, it does nothing by default to ensure that service levels are achieved and timeouts are prevented. The service needs to be designed in such a manner as to handle this.

The next section discusses how the current architecture causes these problems and how potential solutions can avoid them.

4.3   Problems with Single-Instance Service Deployment

There are two main problems with deploying a service that uses a single instance to serve multiple clients, as we saw in the previous example, when both BigCo and Scott tried to access the Order Status service concurrently. What we were faced with was problems of quality of service with respect to performance (scalability) and data accuracy/privacy (client context). These are fairly large issues that need to be addressed in a robust service architecture. We talk about these problems in greater detail, then show you how you can overcome them in a simple manner. But first, a quick peek at the service engine to learn more about *mailboxes*.

4.3.1   Mailboxes

When a service deployer registers a service with the e-Speak service engine, a *handler* gets assigned for the service which is called the *Inbox*. An Inbox is a basic infrastructure resource of the service engine that provides a communication channel from the engine to the service and is analogous to a mailbox. By the same token, when a client connects to the service engine, it also receives a mailbox — an *Outbox*. The Outbox, like the Inbox, is also connected to the engine, and messages are picked up from the Outbox and moved to the appropriate service Inbox for processing. Any messages for the service in a client's Outbox are delivered via the Inbox. Note that this is a one-way communication channel. The reverse channel is formed by the client's *Inbox* and the service's *Outbox*. Together, these four mailboxes provide a bidirectional communication channel between a client and a service. Figure 4.7 depicts this. A client request and associated service response are, in fact, *messages* traveling through such a bidirectional channel. The problem is that an Inbox stores messages serially until the resource associated with it (service or client) is able to process them. We can now explore how this characteristic of the mailboxes contributes to the problems at hand.

4.3.2   Client Context

In a multiclient scenario, the messages from various clients will be intermingled — queued in the order in which they are received. When a service processes

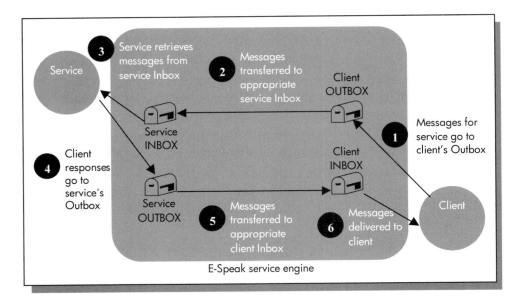

Figure 4.7. E-Speak's mailbox architecture.

the incoming messages from its Inbox, it does so in a First-In-First-Out (FIFO) fashion. This means that two successive messages in a service's Inbox could be from two different clients. It follows then that the context changes between two such messages. If a service's business logic fails to anticipate that (as does the Order Status service), it could lead to an out-of-context response. In the Order Status service, the business logic maintained the context in a rather trivial way — by preserving the login credentials and format preferences for the last authenticated client.

In the earlier Test 1, BigCo was the last client that logged in successfully. Thus, when Scott (who logged in before BigCo) requested order status, he received order status information for BigCo in XML format. Note that both the serialized message queuing and the business logic are responsible for this breach of data integrity.

4.3.3   Scalability

As is true with all customers, clients of a service would expect the service to respond within a certain time frame. In e-Speak, this is specified by the connection timeout parameter. Typically, a simple service would respond within the client's tolerance boundary. If the service fails to respond within this boundary, the client will timeout. Combine a long serial queue with significant processing time per message, and you have the perfect recipe for a timeout!

In Test 2, the delay factor simulated nontrivial processing time to process a request in the Order Status service. This forced the clients to wait for response, due not only to processing time but also to queuing time, depending on their place in the queue. Hence, the client timeout.

4.4   **Effective Service Architectures**

We showed you two potential problems with the current architecture of the Order Status service. Alternative service architectures could solve one or both of these problems; any one of them can be implemented, depending on the requirements placed on your service by the user base.   However, data privacy has to be solved, regardless, because there are legal and financial implications to the service provider. We discuss a few architectural options to solve these problems. Finally, we provide code based on a service architecture that solves both problems quite well.

If your service processing time really is not an issue and you are interested in only protecting the data that moves between service and client, you could design a *user context token-based service architecture*. This particular service architecture would require the client to send a "user token" with each request made to the service. This token would identify "who" the request is coming from, thus ensuring that appropriate data is processed and returned to the requestor. Figure 4.8 illustrates the interaction pattern that would be followed. The service engine will treat the token as any data that gets passed back and forth (you've seen something similar in previous examples, where authentication was passed back to the service), which means that the *processing* of the token needs to happen at the service level. This would require changes to the interface and the implementation to handle the token processing.

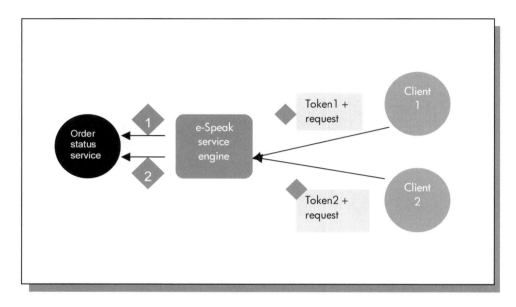

Figure 4.8. User context token-based service architecture.

The user context token-based solution might work in some cases, where the service is doing something so trivial that the likelihood of a client timeout is low and the number of clients expected is also very low. However, this is not going to be the typical scenario. Service processing time will most likely be an issue and, of course, we hope that the number of clients is, in fact, numerous (especially if clients are also money-paying consumers!). Another potential architecture would be simply to start *n* instances of the service. Clients would then be associated with a specific instance and would be allowed to access only that instance. Figure 4.9 depicts this scenario.

Here we have a solution that does solve both the privacy and the timeout problem of the Order Status service. However, you can see how this is clearly inefficient because the service is idle unless a specific client is active. It also will be limited by the hardware's ability to handle *n* services. It can be easily seen how a massive hardware landscape would be needed to work around the inherent inefficiency built

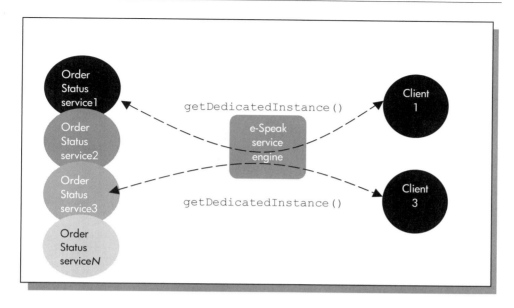

Figure 4.9. Client-specific service architecture.

into this solution. However, like the user context token-based service architecture, this solution does have its place in a limited service deployment where response time is of great importance but the number of clients is limited.

Ideally, we would want to remove the inefficiency — have services spawn only when necessary and not have them associated with a particular client. This can be accomplished by putting a front-end service to handle requests for *access to* the service. We call this front-end service the `Dispatcher` service, and its main job is to handle requests for a service and return a new handle to a newly spawned child service. Figure 4.10 depicts this particular architecture.

With this architecture, clients receive an immediate response because there is no competition for service resources, and the client's data is protected because the client credentials are separated from each other and kept only at the corresponding dedicated instance. This solution is also more efficient because we spawn an instance only when necessary. We have actually provided this architecture solution in example 4. The main difference here is that the client no longer *finds* the Order Status service. Instead, it queries for and receives access to the `Dispatcher`

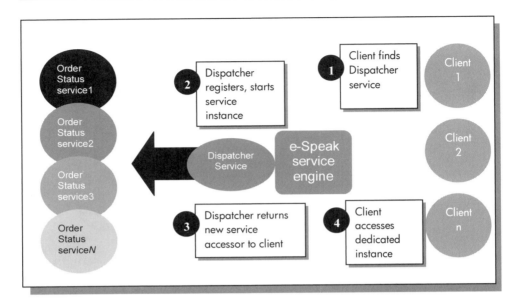

Figure 4.10. Dynamically allocated service architecture.

service. Compare the `OrderStatusClient` from example 3 and example 4. In example 4, the client queries the e-Speak service engine for the `Dispatcher` service and not the Order Status service directly.

CheckOrderStatusClient.java

```
String interfaceName = DispatcherIntf.class.getName();
ESServiceFinder Finder = new ESServiceFinder
        (Connection,interfaceName);
ESQuery Query = new ESQuery("Name == 'dispatcherService'" );
DispatcherIntf dispatcher =  (DispatcherIntf)Finder.find(Query);
System.out.println("Dispatcher Service Found!");
```

The client now has access to the `Dispatcher` service. Take a look at *Dispatcher-Intf.esidl*. You will see the only method it defines is the `getDedicatedInstance` method. The client then calls that method to provide a handle to a dedicated instance of the Order Status service. A look at the implementation of this interface will show you that it simply registers and starts an instance of the Order Status service with the service engine and returns the service handle to the client. This solution does rid us of the inefficiency of having spawned services, regardless of whether they are used; it is also limited by the hardware's ability to handle *n* instances of the service.

4.4.1   In Action

To run the Check Order Status service using the dynamically allocated service architecture requires us to run the Dispatcher service as the mediator. The Dispatcher service will manage the Order Status service instances for the various clients. After starting the engine, we need to start the `Dispatcher` service. To do so, run the following command:

```
C:\>java -Despeak_home=d:\e-speak DispatcherService
```

A message stating that the Dispatcher service was started will be displayed on a successful start of the service. Then start the Order Status client which will search for the `Dispatcher` service and subsequently the Order Status service.

```
C:\>java -Despeak_home=d:\e-speak CheckOrderStatusClient
```

After the client successfully starts and locates the `Dispatcher` service, you will notice in the Dispatcher window that it started a *dedicated instance* of the Check Order Status service.

4.4.2   Summary

It seems that the *dynamically allocated service architecture* suits a wide range of problem sets: services that do have a nontrivial processing time, a sizable expected client size, and quick response time requirements. However, this is not necessarily the most efficient solution. There are a few enhancements that could optimize this solution further.

■ Dispatcher can keep track of active service instances and kill inactive ones.

■ User context token-based and dynamically allocated service architectures can be combined to allow for servicing of more clients and optimize use of resources.

■ Dispatcher can start a minimum number of services automatically (to lower startup latency) and increase up to a maximum to prevent resource contention issues.

Table 4.1 summarizes the various architectural alternatives discussed so far.

Table 4.1. Effective Service Architecture Comparison

Architecture	Salient Features	Issue Addressed	Benefits	Challenges
User context token-based	Token identifies client	Privacy	Simple to implement	Timeouts more likely
Client-specific	Defined number of instances automatically started	Privacy, scalability	No token required; No startup latencies	Waste of resources
Dynamically allocated	Instances started as required	Privacy, scalability	No upper boundary	Clients experience startup latencies
Hybrid of all	*Min* predefined instances that grow to a *Max*. Tokens identify clients.	Privacy, scalability	Bounded at both ends; optimal use of resources; no startup latencies for *Min* clients.	Complex

4.5   Where Do You Stand?

With the discussion so far, you have learned a lot about e-Speak as a service deployment platform. Let us remind you of a few key points. You now know how to:

■ Create an e-Speak interface

■ Write an e-Speak service

■ Connect and register your service with the service engine

■ Write an e-Speak client (that also connects to the service engine)

■ Find and invoke methods of a service

- Send data back and forth, using e-Speak's serialization capabilities
- Create a dedicated service instance for each client
- Design e-Speak-based services with simple but effective load balancing and data integrity techniques

At this point, you have enough information to create services that can be accessed by multiple clients. Although this might sound like a relatively trivial skill, there are some fairly interesting problems that can be solved with just the information we've presented up until this point of the book. Let's see what real-life applications can be created with just this knowledge:

- A company-wide application to reserve conference rooms or audio conferencing numbers
- A help desk engineer call routing utility
- A network printer search utility to find the best available printer for your document
- A fileserver application

In subsequent chapters, we build on these concepts to create more advanced services. These complex services use abstractions that are closer to human thinking about service descriptions and quality of service. In an ecosystem designed to serve human beings, such abstractions are necessary from a usability standpoint.

CHAPTER 5

Vocabularies and Contracts

- ◾ Vocabularies
  example working directory:
  \Examples\Ex05HotelVocabulary

- ◾ Contracts
  example working directory:
  \Examples\Ex06AirlineContract

- ◾ Registering in Multiple Contracts and Vocabularies

Chapter 5

VOCABULARIES AND CONTRACTS

In Chapters 3 and 4, we laid the basic foundations to deploy services and create service clients. The concepts used in those chapters helped us in explaining how clients and services establish a communication channel to exchange information. However, both of those chapters were based on predefined or established relationships. Relationships between Scott and the local Porsche distributor are a specific kind of service and client interaction. These relationships form out of an existing business relationship and do not necessarily have a dynamic component.

There is another category of business relationships, as well. In this category, relationships develop when clients are interested in a *class* of service, rather than *a specific service*. There is no explicit affinity between a client and a particular service in such relationships. This would be analogous to our need for plumbers. Most of the time, we do not have a special affinity for a particular plumber (like we do with our personal physician) but we simply want the pipes fixed!

E-Speak facilitates establishing such dynamic relationships through the service registration and quality of service mechanisms. The registration in previous chapters was based on a very simple attribute — Name. Again, that assumes that the client knows the *name* of the service and can locate it that way.

It is important to understand the origin of the attribute Name. Service registration with an e-Speak service engine means providing values for certain attributes. A set of related attributes forms a *vocabulary*. As a result, a vocabulary provides means to *describe* a service. A service described in such a way can be *discovered* by others and used. For more robust service usage, however, a service must also comply by a *contract*. A contract *defines* quality of service for a given service. It also describes means by which a service user can interact with it. In a nutshell, a contract describes *the rules of engagement* for a service. Figure 5.1 depicts the relationship between a service, a client, and related vocabulary and contract.

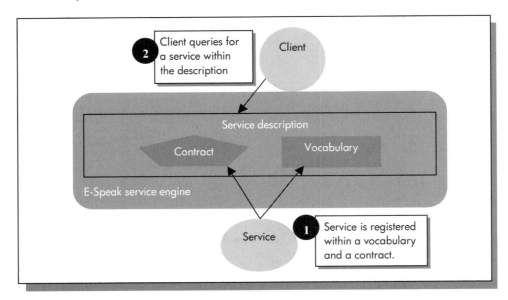

Figure 5.1. Service descriptions.

E-Speak's constructs for vocabularies and contracts are in an evolutionary stage. In this chapter, we look at the programmatic constructs — namely, `ESVocabulary` and `ESContract`.

5.1   Vocabularies

In Chapters 3 and 4, we registered the services with a simple attribute — `Name`. However, such a simple attribute will not always be enough to describe a service adequately with the service engine. A service can be described by many inherent characteristics. Together, these meaningful characteristics allow for a robust description of the service. For example, when talking about a car, it would not be enough to say the car is an *Audi*. You would want to know the *color, the engine power, the number of doors*, whether it has a *sun/moon roof*, and numerous other characteristics.

By the same token, services can be described by important aspects of their offering. For example, in the User Data service, you could use department name, operating system (OS) platform, or even version to describe your service (in addition to `Name`). It is easy to see that there is no dearth of attributes to describe a service with. How many attributes should one use? To answer this, we need *a framework* to describe a service in the best possible way. This framework can provide a way to describe services in a widely adopted *language*. Such a framework is important because it allows clients to create *structured* queries that are more likely to result in an appropriate match between services and clients. For example, when you search on the World Wide Web (WWW) for a particular topic, "Audi+Roseville," you could get back everything from an HP-UX project to a Sacramento State student Web page listing his favorite car and his parents' home address but not necessarily any *Audi car dealerships in Roseville*. However, if you could create a structured search that allowed you to associate values with name-value pairs (attributes) and to execute a search, you might be able to say `car=Audi`, `city=Roseville`, and `typeOfBusiness=Dealer` and receive back a handful of Audi car dealers in Roseville without the student Web pages and projects of Fortune 500 companies (See Table 5.1). Hence, describing a service using attributes is vital for successful implementation of a service-based solution.

5.1.1   Essentials of Vocabulary

The attribute framework must have the following characteristics in order to be effective:

1. Jargon: The framework must take into consideration the users and must encompass attributes that are part of their jargon.

2. Broadness: The description (set of attributes) must be broad enough so that a category of services can be described uniformly, thus allowing clients to

find the appropriate match in a service-agnostic manner.

3. Clarity: The attributes should be as clear as possible so as to avoid ambiguity among the potential users. Otherwise, when searching for a *red Audi*, questions such as *Which red is red?* will pose an obstacle to matching clients and services.

E-Speak provides the *vocabulary* architecture to create an attribute framework to describe services. An e-Speak vocabulary can be thought of as a real-world vocabulary. A vocabulary is a set of words that can be used to discuss a subject — in this case, to describe a service. This type of service description lends itself to forming structured queries to find those services within a certain category. At the very least, a vocabulary must be accepted by two parties — the service provider and service user. When more players accept and use a certain vocabulary, it becomes widely accepted and eventually considered a *standard* way to describe services in that particular category.

A complete e-Speak vocabulary specification consists of property names *and* the *type* of the values they have associated with them; there is also a way to indicate whether an attribute is *required*. A visual representation of a vocabulary is depicted in Table 5.1.

Table 5.1. Visual Representation of a Vocabulary

Attribute Name	Type	Essential
typeOfBusiness	String	No
car	String	Yes
city	String	Yes

A vocabulary is required to *find* a service and, without realizing it, you have, in fact, been using it all along! You used a form of vocabularies — the Base Vocabulary — when you tried to *find* the Hello World service, User Data service, and the Order Status service in previous chapters. These services were registered within the Base Vocabulary. You will see that services are also registered in something called a *contract*, discussed in Section 5.2.

5.1.2   Base Vocabulary

The Base Vocabulary defines a set of attributes that are generic and can be used when a robust vocabulary is not necessary, as in our previous examples. It is preloaded and ready to use when the engine starts up. The attributes that can be used to define simple services under the Base Vocabulary are listed in Table 5.2.

Table 5.2. Attributes of the Base Vocabulary

Attribute Name	Type	Description
Name	String	Name of service
Type	String	Type of service
ResourceSubType	String	Subtype of service
Description	String	Description of the service
Version	String	Version of the service
ESDate	Date	Date associated with the service
ESGroup	String	Group associated with the service
ESTimestamp	Timestamp	Timestamp associated with the service
ESCategory	String	String-list of categories that a service is in

When we registered the Hello World service, we did so with simply one attribute — Name. Although we did not mention anything special about Name, you can now see that it is because of the Base Vocabulary that we could do that.

```
Description.addAttribute("Name", "myGreetingService");
```

The Base Vocabulary allows any resource to be registered; user-defined vocabularies, base contracts, and simply described services are all registered within the Base Vocabulary. In e-Speak, these entities are all resources and are treated similarly. They have to be described and registered within the service engine before they are available.

If we choose to use anything other than the attributes listed in Table 5.2, we need to do some more work to register the service; we would need to create a *user-defined vocabulary*.

5.1.3   User-Defined Vocabularies

The Base Vocabulary is useful but it is very restricting for a service to describe itself because it provides only some rudimentary attributes, such as `Name` and `Version`. To really describe a service effectively, a user-defined vocabulary should be used. This vocabulary allows clients to form structured queries when trying to find an appropriate service.

In our example, a travel agent wants to create a Hotel Information service that will allow hotels to offer their pricing and room availability to potential guests. Roadside Shack, Easy Inn, and SuperGrande Hotel have agreed to deploy this in their respective environments. The travel agent will also create a Hotel Information client that will allow users to search for the appropriate hotel by specifying their search criteria. This is precisely where the concept of vocabularies fits into the picture. The Hotel Information services are registered using the `HotelVocab`. The `HotelVocab` is a user-defined vocabulary that is a set of pertinent attributes used to describe the hotels. The set of attributes that make up the `HotelVocab` is below:

- Name
- City
- Phone
- Email
- AAARating
- HasOnSiteRestaurant
- HasSwimmingPool
- RoomType
- NumberOfRooms
- NearestAirportCode
- URLPrefix

Notice that the `HotelVocab` also contains the `Name` attribute. This attribute does not collide with the `Name` attribute in the Base Vocabulary because user-defined vocabularies do not *inherit* the Base Vocabulary attributes. In general, e-Speak does not have programmatic constructs for inheritance of attributes.

We listed three important criteria for creating a vocabulary (attribute framework). We said that the vocabulary should consider industry jargon, be broad enough, and be clear in order to be effective. If you look at HotelVocab, you will see that it satisfies all three. We chose attributes that were part of the hotel industry jargon — AAARating, for example . We used a broad set of attributes to allow various tiers of hotels to participate. One could argue that a *business-travel* hotel would find the HotelVocab incomplete and would want attributes such as HasFax or HasRoomInternetAccess. However, broadness of the attributes does not imply an all-encompassing attribute set. We need only cover participating services. Finally, the attributes have been named unambiguously.

E-Speak provides several objects to support the creation, registration, and use of vocabularies.

Incorporating Vocabularies

Introducing a user-defined vocabulary requires a few changes to service deployment. First off, the service deployer — Hotel Information service — has to take into account the new vocabulary. Second, the hotel client must also be aware of this same vocabulary in order to find an appropriate service within that vocabulary. For the most part, the service interface and business logic are oblivious to the new vocabulary.

The HotelInformationService will *implement* the HotelVocab. This means that when each Hotel Information service instance is started, it needs to check that the HotelVocab is registered first. The check is required because there is no central service that registered the vocabulary; instead, the services may simply register themselves with the assumption that the vocabulary was already there and register the vocabulary if it was *not* already there. The first bit of code in the HotelInformationService class depicts this:

HotelInformationService.java

```
ESVocabularyFinder myVocabFinder =
   new ESVocabularyFinder(connection);
 . . .
```

```
vocab = myVocabFinder.find(new ESQuery("Name == 'HotelVocab'"));
System.out.println
    ("Found existing HotelVocab instance with following
    attributes:");
```

The class, `ESVocabularyFinder`, is a utility class that e-Speak provides for finding vocabularies registered in the service engine that match a certain criteria. The `find` method is used as you have seen before; it takes the constructed query and performs a search on the service engine for the vocabulary with `Name ==` `HotelVocab`. E-Speak offers the `findAll` and `findNext` methods, as well; these will search for all vocabularies or the next vocabulary, respectively, that matches the search criteria.

Note

The attribute `Name`, in this case, belongs to the *Base Vocabulary*. A user-defined vocabulary, like any other service, is registered in the Base Vocabulary. The Hotel Information service registers its vocabulary in the Base Vocabulary using the Base Vocabulary attribute `Name = HotelVocab`. The attribute `Name`, part of the `HotelVocab`, is used by the Hotel services.

Before a service can describe itself within a specific vocabulary, that vocabulary must be registered with the engine. The Hotel Information service ensures this by registering the vocabulary `HotelVocab` if the search for it fails. The exception `LookupFailedException` thrown by the `find` method is used to detect this. Appendix F contains the exception hierarchy in e-Speak. Any vocabulary can be registered only once. If a service attempts to register an existing vocabulary, the exception `NameCollisionException` is thrown.

Creating a Vocabulary

Creating a vocabulary in e-Speak involves three steps:

1. Creating the description (the set of properties)

2. Establishing the vocabulary element (which contains the description and the connection context)

3. Registering within the service engine

This is very similar to registering a service within the service engine.

The `ESVocabularyDescription` is a container class that keeps all the properties that make up the vocabulary. The services will later use these properties to create attributes to describe themselves. This container class provides methods to include properties of several data types. For example, the Hotel Information service uses several string properties. Hence, it uses the `addStringProperty` method. Appendix D lists all the property methods that are supported by e-Speak.

HotelInformationService.java

```
ESVocabularyDescription esvd =
    new ESVocabularyDescription();
...
esvd.addStringProperty("Name");
esvd.addStringProperty("City");
esvd.addStringProperty("Phone");
esvd.addStringProperty("Email");
esvd.addIntegerProperty("AAARating");
```

All user-defined vocabularies are registered within the Base Vocabulary. Thus, they must specify at least one Base Vocabulary attribute in their description. For `HotelVocab`, the Base Vocabulary attribute `Name` is specified.

HotelInformationService.java

```
esvd.addAttribute("Name", "HotelVocab");
```

The vocabulary description can also be created using an XML file instead of using the `ESVocabularyDescription` object. Once the description (`esvd`) has been completed, the different properties need to be logically bound together into a single entity called the *vocabulary* with the service engine. The `ESVocabularyElement` takes care of this, as seen next. Finally, the vocabulary needs to be registered using the `register` method. Registering the vocabulary returns the *handle* to the vocabulary, which can be used later on to access its properties.

HotelInformationService.java

```
ESVocabularyElement myVocabElement =
    new ESVocabularyElement(connection,esvd);
    // Register the vocabulary
    try
    {
        vocab = myVocabElement.register();
    }
```

You will notice that `vocab` is an instance of the interface `ESVocabulary`. This interface implements the `getProperties` and `getServices` methods, which allow a client to query the vocabulary for properties defined by or services registered within. We can see how this will be useful as we take a look at how the client uses this vocabulary to search for appropriate services.

However, the service is not done with the vocabularies yet. We simply laid the framework (or registered the vocabulary). The specific services have yet to fill in the framework with their *values*. If we take a look at the `main` portion of the `HotelInformationService`, we can see how a service would go about describing themselves using a predefined framework — the vocabulary.

Recall that the service needs to register a description of itself within the service engine. Until now, the description was created using the simple Base Vocabulary. However, in this example, we are going to use the `HotelVocab` that was registered earlier to describe the individual Hotel services. Now that we are ready to register a service, the `HotelVocab` properties turn into attributes to describe the service.

HotelInformationService.java

```
myDescription.addAttribute
```

```
   ("Name", serviceProps.getProperty("Name"));
myDescription.addAttribute
   ("City", serviceProps.getProperty("City"));
myDescription.addAttribute
   ("Phone", serviceProps.getProperty("Phone"));
myDescription.addAttribute
   ("Email", serviceProps.getProperty("Email"));
...
```

The values for these properties are in the hotel's respective INI files.

RoadsideShack.ini

```
Name = Roadside Shack Inc.
City = New York
Phone = 202-555-9999
Email =
AAARating = 1
...
```

Once the advanced service description is created, service registration is as it was in previous chapters. The service needs to be registered and started before it is actually "in business." Also notice that we are using the handle to the service returned by the engine during the registration. In the e-Speak terminology this handle is called an *accessor*. The class ESAccessor provides the accessor to any engine-registered resource. In our example, the accessor is communicated back to the Impl class (the business logic). The method setServiceContext saves this accessor.

HotelImpl.java

```
public void setServiceContext
   (ESAccessor serviceAccessor, ESVocabulary vocab)
   {
myServiceAccessor = serviceAccessor;
myVocab = vocab;
   }
```

Other methods such as getName use this accessor to retrieve information about the registered attributes for a specific instance of that Impl class (i.e., a specific hotel).

HotelImpl.java

```
public String getName() throws  ESInvocationException
{
    return (String)
       (myServiceAccessor.getAttribute
          ("Name", myVocab).getValue());
}
```

Finding a Service with Vocabularies

The three Hotel Information services for Roadside Shack, Easy Inn, and Super-Grande Hotel are registered within the HotelVocab. If you take a look at their respective configuration files, you will see that they do offer a variety of different features. When these hotels deploy their services on the service engine, clients will be able to search for a matching service using the vocabulary.

The Hotel Information client is the user interface to search for an appropriate hotel; it will construct the queries based on the HotelVocab. The ESVocabularyFinder is used to find the vocabulary.

HotelInformationClient.java

```
System.out.print("Name: ");
choice = br.readLine();
if(!choice.equals(""))
{
mySearchQuery.addConstraint("Name == '" + choice + "'");
nonEmptyQuery = true;
}
System.out.print("City : ");
choice = br.readLine();
if(!choice.equals(""))
...
```

Each constraint is added with the name of the property and the input of the user. These constraints get bundled into the `ESQuery` object, which is then used by the `findAll` method to locate all the services that implement the Hotel Information interface, match the user-constructed query, and are on the service engine.

HotelInformationClient.java

```
String interfaceName = HotelInquiryIntf.class.getName();

ESServiceFinder Finder =
    new ESServiceFinder(Connection,interfaceName);
    try
    {
        ESService [] hotelServiceSet =
            Finder.findAll(mySearchQuery);
        . . .
    }
```

All the services that match the user's criteria will be displayed, and further information may be obtained via the interface methods. The `getShortDescription` method provides the user with more information about the hotel.

5.1.4   Service-Defined Exceptions

You can see how this service can incorporate some extensive business logic rather smoothly. The `getPrice` method uses a pricing database to calculate hotel rates and even takes into account any potential discount codes. Take a closer look at the implementation of the `getPrice` method. It throws a `HotelPricingException` if any error is encountered during the price calculation.

If you want your service to throw any user-defined exceptions (nonruntime) they must extend `ESServiceException`, as seen in *HotelPricingException*.

HotelPricingException.java

```
public class HotelPricingException extends ESServiceException
```

```
{
        public String toString()
        {
                return "Error in pricing transaction.
                Check your pricing parameters and try
                your query again";
        }
}
```

5.1.5   In Action

It really does not matter which instance of the Hotel Information service is instantiated first — Roadside Shack, Easy Inn, or SuperGrande Hotel. The Hotel Information service actually checks whether the vocabulary is registered and goes ahead
and registers it if it is not. Let us assume that the Easy Inn service is the first to
deploy its service; by being the first deployed service, it has the responsibility to
register the vocabulary, as seen in Figure 5.2.

The interesting part to note is that the service engine has been started in *in memory* mode, which means that during all registrations of services, vocabularies happen in memory and, hence, are short-lived. In Chapter 10, you will see how these
registrations can be made permanent. Right now, because these are in-memory
registrations, when the registering entity `HotelInformationService` dies, all resources it registered also die with them. So, if the instance for Easy Inn were to
die, the `HotelVocab` would also be lost. The other services would be registered in a
nonexistent vocabulary, rendering it impossible for new clients to begin interaction.

Figures 5.3 and 5.4 display the startup of the Hotel Information service for the
Roadside Shack and SuperGrande Hotel.

Figure 5.5 shows the user interface provided by the Hotel Information client. It can
be run by the command:

```
C:\>java -Despeak_home=d:\e-speak
    Ex05HotelVocabulary.HotelInformationClient
```

We searched for a hotel in any city with a restaurant and swimming pool with at

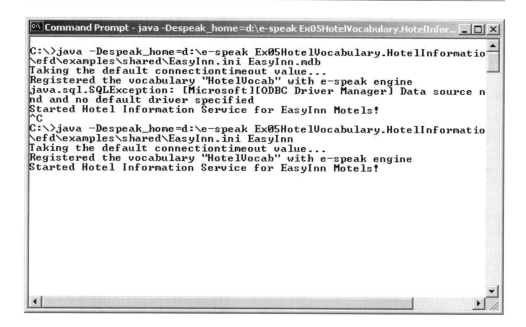

Figure 5.2. Starting Hotel Information service for Easy Inn.

least one room. SuperGrande Hotel was the only one that has a swimming pool and an on-site restaurant and, hence, was the only hotel returned.

It was interesting to see how vocabularies can assist in bringing services and clients together. All three Hotel services shared one implementation of the interface (*HotelImpl*). In a true ecosystem of Hotel services, each service would have the opportunity to develop its own implementations for the *HotelInquiryIntf*. Sharing an implementation for methods such as getPrice would never be acceptable to the hotels as pricing is such a confidential and proprietary company-specific business logic. We have not attached a backend reservation system but that could easily be done (as we did with the pricing database), making this a complete find, price, and reserve hotel ecosystem.

You will see in the next example how an interested party could be responsible for developing and registering the vocabulary and how specific services can manage their own implementations, as long as they abide by an interface (the blueprint for which methods, at least, are required).

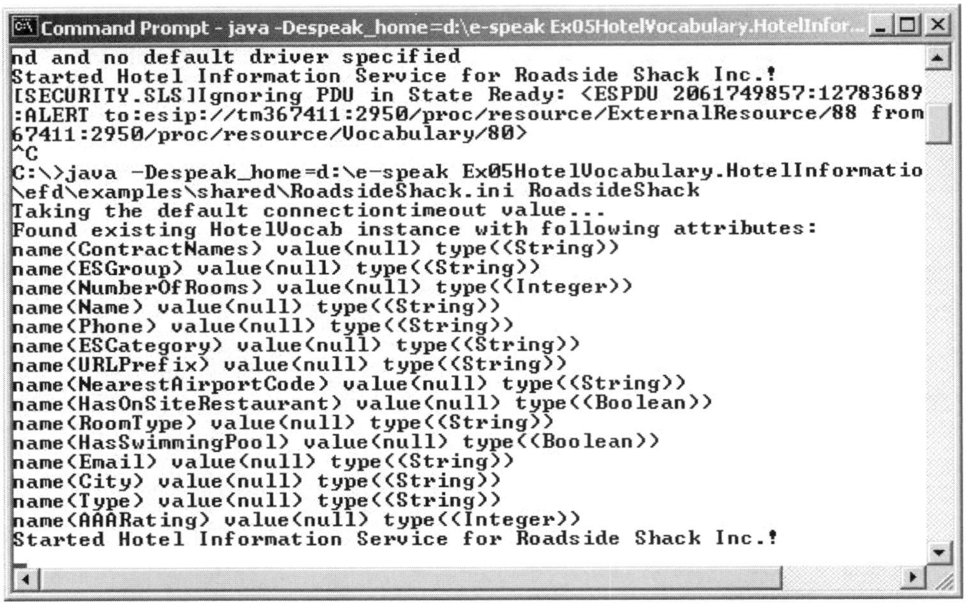

```
 Command Prompt - java -Despeak_home=d:\e-speak Ex05HotelVocabulary.HotelInfor...  _ □ ×
nd and no default driver specified
Started Hotel Information Service for Roadside Shack Inc.!
[SECURITY.SLS]Ignoring PDU in State Ready: <ESPDU 2061749857:12783689
:ALERT to:esip://tm367411:2950/proc/resource/ExternalResource/88 from
67411:2950/proc/resource/Vocabulary/80>
^C
C:\>java -Despeak_home=d:\e-speak Ex05HotelVocabulary.HotelInformatio
\efd\examples\shared\RoadsideShack.ini RoadsideShack
Taking the default connectiontimeout value...
Found existing HotelVocab instance with following attributes:
name(ContractNames) value(null) type((String))
name(ESGroup) value(null) type((String))
name(NumberOfRooms) value(null) type((Integer))
name(Name) value(null) type((String))
name(Phone) value(null) type((String))
name(ESCategory) value(null) type((String))
name(URLPrefix) value(null) type((String))
name(NearestAirportCode) value(null) type((String))
name(HasOnSiteRestaurant) value(null) type((Boolean))
name(RoomType) value(null) type((String))
name(HasSwimmingPool) value(null) type((Boolean))
name(Email) value(null) type((String))
name(City) value(null) type((String))
name(Type) value(null) type((String))
name(AAARating) value(null) type((Integer))
Started Hotel Information Service for Roadside Shack Inc.!
```

Figure 5.3. Starting Hotel Information service for Roadside Shack.

5.2   Contracts

In the previous chapters, you saw how services developed business logic to abide by the service interface. In those cases, the entities creating the service interface and implementation (and even client) were all one and the same. Until now, interfaces have been merely a means to allow the clients to interact with the service. The interfaces defined a set of methods that the service implemented and could then be invoked by the client, once the client received the handle to the service. Also recall that a prior out-of-band interaction had to take place between the service deployer and client, which gave the client the *service stub*. The client already knew what the methods and the invocation sequence were and simply needed to establish a connection to the service (through the address of the service's Inbox). These examples have also assumed that services participating together, as in the Hotel Information example, abided by a single interface (and a shared implementation).

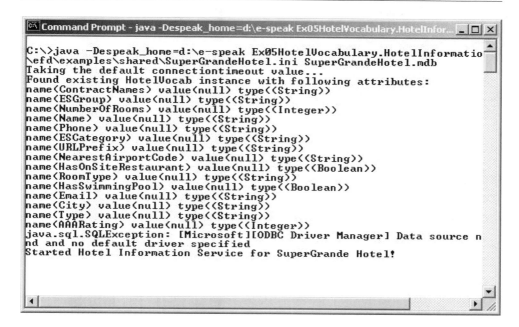

Figure 5.4. Starting Hotel Information service for SuperGrande Hotel.

5.2.1   Real-World Contracts

We need to take a step back from the programmatic construct known as an *interface* and discuss the concepts of rules of engagement, service-level agreements, and licensing to appreciate the power of *contracts* in the services world. As we did with vocabularies, let us take a look at what contracts mean to us colloquially. Contracts are binding agreements between two or more parties that can be (and usually are) legally enforceable. The agreement dictates responsibilities of all the signees and how punitive action can be taken if any party fails to uphold its side. Responsibilities may include anything from expected deliverables to quality of service levels to terms of usage. Contracts can be as simple as a lease for an apartment or as complex as a merger between two Fortune 500 multinationals. However, both set expectations on the involved parties on *what they will do*, what will happen next, *service levels that can be expected*, *escalation routes*, should the need arise, and so on.

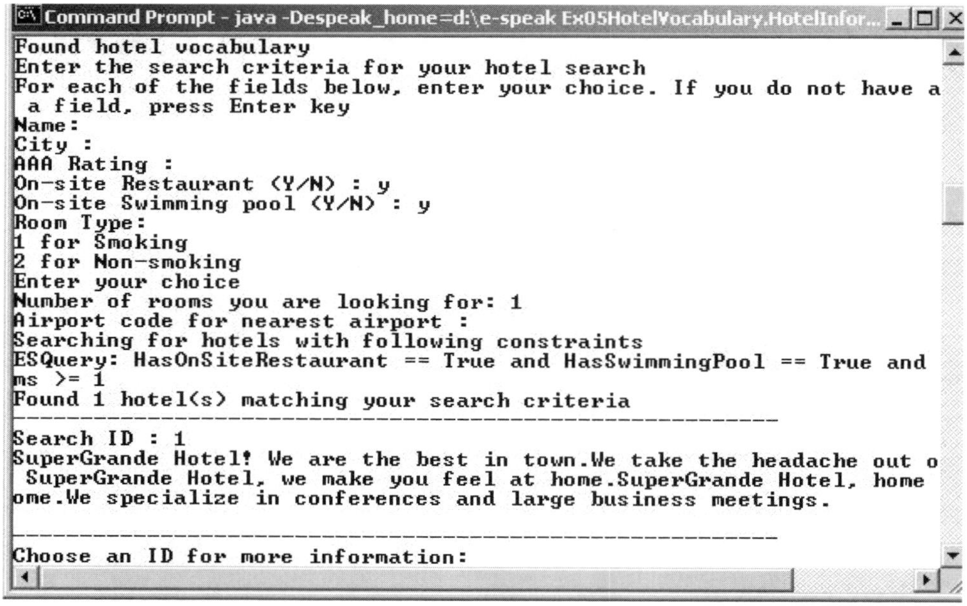

```
Command Prompt - java -Despeak_home=d:\e-speak Ex05HotelVocabulary.HotelInfor...  _ □ ×
Found hotel vocabulary
Enter the search criteria for your hotel search
For each of the fields below, enter your choice. If you do not have a
 a field, press Enter key
Name :
City :
AAA Rating :
On-site Restaurant (Y/N) : y
On-site Swimming pool (Y/N) : y
Room Type:
1 for Smoking
2 for Non-smoking
Enter your choice
Number of rooms you are looking for: 1
Airport code for nearest airport :
Searching for hotels with following constraints
ESQuery: HasOnSiteRestaurant == True and HasSwimmingPool == True and
ms >= 1
Found 1 hotel(s) matching your search criteria
-----------------------------------------------------------------
Search ID : 1
SuperGrande Hotel! We are the best in town.We take the headache out o
 SuperGrande Hotel, we make you feel at home.SuperGrande Hotel, home
ome.We specialize in conferences and large business meetings.

-----------------------------------------------------------------
Choose an ID for more information:
```

Figure 5.5. Query and search results.

E-Speak interfaces also dictate (albeit in a less enforceable manner) what services will do. The interface `HotelInquiryIntf` dictated that a `getPrice` method would provide the client a hotel rate for the specified hotel, month of stay, and kinds and number of rooms, taking into consideration any discount codes. The client expected that this method would be available on the service side because the service registered itself with this interface. By choosing to abide by a certain interface, the service sets the expectation of what *it will do* for the client. This allows the client to interact with the service (and other services in this category) in a predictable manner because the client can anticipate the service to meet certain expectations. Real-world contracts also define quality of service levels and escalation routes. E-Speak provides rudimentary support of these features in the form of `terms of use` and `licenses`. The combined construct, depicted in Figure 5.6, of interfaces, terms of use, and licenses is an e-Speak *contract*. It sets the expectations of how to interact with a service and it could be used to define service-level agreements and terms of use.

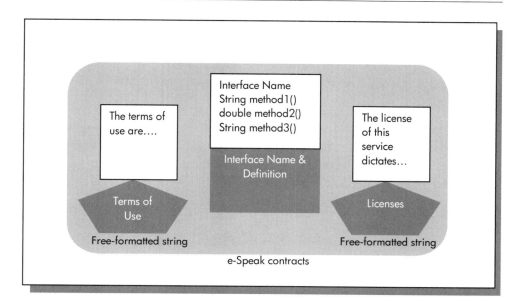

Figure 5.6. Contract construct in e-Speak.

5.2.2   Airline Consortium

In Chapter 1, we introduced the concept of an ecosystem. Ecosystems facilitate the entities participating together — usually under the auspices of a consortium or other governing bodies. Consortiums are made up of interested parties and usually help to provide structure to the interactions of its members and the community in which it exists. In the example, we deploy an Airline consortium made up of several airlines (again, of varying tiers). The consortium provides structure to the interactions of the airlines between each other and especially with their customers. The member airlines have agreed to offer their airline seat information to potential customers via a service. An Airline Information client helps trip planners navigate the framework and search for appropriate airline services to meet their needs. To facilitate this, the participating members were able to define a broad enough vocabulary to encompass all the airlines. However, they could not come to agreement on the interface methods that would be available. The main point of contention was from the *low-frills airlines*. They follow a one-class, first-come-first-served policy, while the rest of the airlines provide three tier classes (economy, business, and

first class). In calculating the ticket price, these airlines needed the class information, and the low-frills did not. Although this could have been handled behind the
scenes with some programmatic assistance (default ticket class, for example), the
business folks from the low-frills airlines did not want to highlight the fact that they
were "classless."

On a separate note, the two groups also differed on quality of service levels that
they would meet. Hence, the consortium compromised, and two contracts resulted.
Faber is a widely accepted contract whereas Weber serves a very narrow vertical
industry that operates domestic-only, no-frills flights. Below are the corresponding
interfaces — FaberFlightIntf and WeberAirlineIntf.

FaberFlightIntf.java and WeberFlightIntf.java

```
public interface FaberFlightIntf extends ESService {
    String getDescription() throws  ESInvocationException;
    double getPrice(String ticketClass, int month,
    String origin, String destination)
    throws  ESInvocationException,
    AirlineConsortiumPricingException;
    String getRestrictions() throws  ESInvocationException;
}

public interface WeberAirlineIntf extends ESService {
    String getAirlineID() throws  ESInvocationException;
    String shortTextDescription() throws  ESInvocationException;
    String longDescription() throws  ESInvocationException;
    double getFares(int month, String origin, String destination)
    throws  ESInvocationException,
    AirlineConsortiumPricingException;
    String termsOfUse() throws  ESInvocationException;
}
```

E-Speak allows the consortium to apply these decisions seamlessly to the Airline
Ecosystem. Figure 5.7 depicts the service layout and shows the interaction patterns of all the players in this ecosystem.

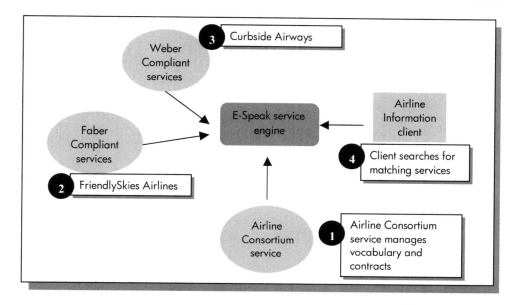

Figure 5.7. Airline ecosystem.

5.2.3   Programming for Ecosystems

As you can see from Figure 5.7, the number of components involved in this distributed system increases as the number of players and the level of complexity increase. The activities to create this ecosystem are similar to those of deploying a service (as in the previous examples). However, now, there is a clear separation of responsibilities and, thereby, some inherent dependencies. Table 5.3 lists these roles and the responsible parties.

In Figure 5.7 and Table 5.3, you can see that the division of responsibilities and number of roles forces the Airline ecosystem deployment to be well planned and thought out. It is important to note here that in a real-world deployment, this would translate into a multisystem deployment; it might even require cross-firewall interactions. We do discuss both multisystem deployment and cross-firewall interactions later.

Table 5.3. Responsibilities in the Airline Ecosystem

Player	Responsibilities	Corresponding Class	Deployment Dependency
Airline Consortium	AirlineSpeak Vocabulary	AirlineConsortium Service	None
Airline Consortium	Weber and Faber Contracts	FaberFlightIntf and WeberAirlineIntf	AirlineSpeak Vocabulary
Weber Members	Deploy Weber-Participating Services	WeberCompliantAirline Service	WeberAirlineIntf
Faber Members	Deploy Faber-Participating Services	FaberCompliantAirline Service	FaberFlightIntf

Registering AirlineSpeak

The Airline consortium is responsible for setting up the appropriate vocabulary for the participating member airlines to register in. This means deploying a service, `AirlineConsortiumService`, that registers the vocabulary `AirlineSpeak` and the two contracts, `FaberFlightIntf` and `WeberAirlineContract`.

You already know what it takes to register the vocabulary. The only difference here is that there is a third party (not any of the service deployers) that is managing this step — separation of responsibilities. Imagine in a real-world deployment. This would be very important to the Airline consortium members because there would be a responsible, accountable, and objective third party handling the foundation. This will ensure a level playing field that facilitates unbiased searches. The class, `AirlineConsortiumService`, creates and registers the `AirlineSpeak` vocabulary for the Airline ecosystem.

Registering Contracts

The Airline Consortium service also registers the contracts (recall that contracts are part of the "description" of a service (Figure 5.1). A contract itself consists of:

▪ Interface name and definition

▪ Terms of use

▪ Conversation scheme

The interface definition is the *Intf.esidl* file. The Airline consortium created two interface files that represent the two groups — Faber (not to be mistaken for the popular Sabre group) and Weber.

The *contract* construct is treated similarly to vocabularies and services. Contracts are registered within the base vocabulary with the `Name` attribute. The `Name` here refers to the base vocabulary attribute for the name of the contract — *Faber Airline Information Contract*, for example.

`ESContractDescription` is a container object that stores the description of a contract, like `ESServiceDescription`. The description, in this case, is the interface (i.e., name and method definitions defined within) and the terms of use.

AirlineConsortiumService.java

```
ESContractDescription FaberContractDescription =
    new ESContractDescription();
FaberContractDescription.addAttribute(ESConstants.SERVICE_NAME,
    "Faber Airline Information Contract");
```

The `setInterfaceName` and `setInterfaceDefinition` methods are provided by the `ESContractDescription` object to bundle the interface name and information into the `ESContractDescription` object — `FaberContractDescription`. You will notice that it stores the *entire* interface contents via the `getBytes` method. Remember that the contract description also includes the *termsOfUse*. The `setTermsOfUse` method is provided to bind the `FaberTermsOfUse` information into the description. Note that the terms of use is simply a text field that can be any free-formatted string variable.

AirlineConsortiumService.java

```
FaberContractDescription.setInterfaceName(FaberContractName);
```

```
FaberContractDescription.setInterfaceDefinition
((new String("Faber Airline Information Contract")).getBytes());
FaberContractDescription.setTermsOfUse(FaberTermsOfUse);
```

At this point, the contract description has been constructed. The contract description, along with the contract context, can be registered in the service engine, using the class ESContractElement.

AirlineConsortiumService.java

```
ESContractElement FaberContractElement = new
ESContractElement(Connection, FaberContractDescription);
try
{
    FaberContractElement.register();
} catch (Exception e) { System.err.println(e); }
```

If a contract with the same Base Vocabulary Name value as a previously existing contract is registered, the register method will throw NameCollisionException exception. The register method also returns a stub to the contract, which can then be used to get information from the contract, such as the interface definition, the name, the terms of use, and so on.

The Faber contract for the *mainstream* participating airlines is now registered. The Airline Consortium service will repeat these same steps to register the Weber contract for the no-frills airlines.

AirlineConsortiumService.java

```
ESContractDescription WeberContractDescription =
    new ESContractDescription();
WeberContractDescription.setInterfaceName(WeberContractName);
WeberContractDescription.addAttribute(ESConstants.SERVICE_NAME,
    "Weber Airline Information Contract");
WeberContractDescription.setInterfaceDefinition((new
    String("Weber Airline Information Contract")).getBytes());
```

```
WeberContractDescription.setTermsOfUse(WeberTermsOfUse);
ESContractElement WeberContractElement = new
ESContractElement(Connection, WeberContractDescription);
try
{
WeberContractElement.register();
} catch (Exception e) { System.err.println(e); }
```

The airline vocabulary and both contracts are now registered with the service engine. You will notice that the Airline Consortium service registers itself with the service engine, as well (including implementing an interface `AirlineConsortiumIntf`). This is mainly for the purpose of keeping the vocabulary and the two contracts alive and registered within the service engine. You will notice that it implements the `getConsortiumName` method, which provides the consortium name, should it be needed.

A Faber-Weber-Compliant Service

Airlines that wish to participate in this Airline ecosystem now need to register their service within the `AirlineSpeak` vocabulary compliant with either the Faber or Weber contracts. We assume that all services complying with a certain contract share one implementation. However, as we mentioned at the end of the Hotel Information example, this is not likely to be a true-to-life deployment scenario. It suffices to say that there are two services and implementations that are customized using configuration files and databases, so that they can be used for multiple airlines. Table 5.4 displays these.

Table 5.4. Contracts, Services, and Implementations

Contract	Service	Implementation
FaberFlightIntf	FaberCompliantAirlineService	FaberCompliantImpl
WeberAirlineIntf	WeberCompliantAirlineService	WeberCompliantImpl

Friendly Skies Airline would like to deploy a Faber-compliant airline service. The `FaberCompliantAirlineService` needs to find the vocabulary, `AirlineSpeak`, and the Faber contract, `Faber Airline Information Contract`. Contracts are found in the same manner as vocabularies. The class, `ESContractFinder`, is a utility class that e-Speak provides for finding contracts registered in the service engine that match a certain criteria. The `find` method is used; it takes the constructed query and performs a search on the service engine for the Faber Airline Information Contract.

FaberCompliantAirlineService.java

```
ESVocabularyFinder myVocabFinder =
    new ESVocabularyFinder(Connection);
String ContractName = "Faber Airline Information Contract";
ESContractFinder myContractFinder =
    new ESContractFinder(Connection);
ESContract myContract = null;
try
{
    vocab = myVocabFinder.find(new
        ESQuery("Name == 'AirlineSpeak'"));
    myContract = myContractFinder.find
        ( new ESQuery("Name == '" + ContractName + "'"));
}
catch (ESInvocationException e)
{
    System.err.println("Error finding AirlineSpeak vocabulary");
    System.exit(1);
}
catch (LookupFailedException e)
{
    System.err.println("Error finding AirlineSpeak vocabulary");
    System.exit(1);
}
```

At this point, you describe the service and register it with the service engine. Ensure that you have set the service context appropriately with the service description and appropriate contract implementation, as shown here.

FaberCompliantAirlineService.java

```
FaberCompliantImpl myServiceImpl =
   new FaberCompliantImpl(args[1],
      serviceProps.getProperty("Description"), myContract);
```

5.2.4   Airline Ecosystem Client

The Airline ecosystem is now fully deployed. The `AirlineInformationClient`
can now use the ecosystem to assist trip planners in their efforts to locate airline
services and find fares. After the client has located the `AirlineSpeak` vocabulary,
it needs to determine which contract within which to search for airlines. This is
important because the airlines associated with either contract cater to very different
market segments, and there may be certain travelers who do not wish to review
matches from the nonpreferred contract. Of course, there may also be travelers for
whom the trip is the most important and, hence, want the ability to review all airlines
in either contract. The client application in an ecosystem needs to understand the
users' needs and provide broad enough search capability.

AirlineInformationClient.java

```
System.out.println("You can narrow the search by
   providing airline service contract preference");
System.out.print("Enter 1 - Faber Contract, 2 - Weber Contract,
   3 - either contract : ");
String contractChoice = null;
try
{
      contractChoice = br.readLine();
} catch (IOException e) { System.err.println(e); }
if(!contractChoice.equals(""))
{
      int intChoice = Integer.parseInt(contractChoice);
      switch (intChoice)
      {
```

```
            case 1: FaberResultSet =
                    findAirlinesWithFaberContract();
                    break;
            case 2: interfaceName =
                    WeberAirlineIntf.class.getName();
                    WeberResultSet =
                    findAirlinesWithWeberContract();
                    break;
            case 3:
            default: System.out.println("Airlines
                implementing either of the contracts
                will be searched");
                FaberResultSet =
                    findAirlinesWithFaberContract();
                WeberResultSet =
                    findAirlinesWithWeberContract();
                break;
        }
    }
```

The `findAirlinesWith*()` methods use the use search criteria, as well as the contract names, and return the set of services (within either a specific contract or both contracts).

The `ESServiceFinder` object still behaves in the same manner. However, in this example, the `mySearchQuery` was built with user input and is based on the custom vocabulary `AirlineSpeak`, and the interface used was defined by the consortium.

AirlineInformationClient.java

```
String interfaceName = WeberAirlineIntf.class.getName();
ESContractFinder myContractFinder =
    new ESContractFinder(Connection);
try
{
        // First search the appropriate contract.
```

```
WeberContract = myContractFinder.find(new ESQuery
   ("Name = 'Weber Airline Information Contract'"));

// Now search services implementing this contract.
ESServiceFinder myServiceFinder =
   new ESServiceFinder(Connection, interfaceName);

// Find all the airlines that match user criteria.
serviceSet = myServiceFinder.findAll(mySearchQuery);
}
```

We now have an Airline ecosystem developed and deployed to help airlines coop-
erate together while still allowing for varying offerings.

5.2.5   In Action

Table 5.3 lists the roles in the Airline ecosystem but also contains the *deployment
dependencies*. Deployment dependencies refer to the components of the ecosystem that must be available for component owners to deploy their portion of the
ecosystem. The Airline Consortium service is the first component that needs to
be available because it registers the vocabulary and the contracts needed by each
airline service.

The Airline Consortium service is started as shown below:

```
C:\>java -Despeak_home=d:\e-speak
   Ex06AirlineContract.AirlineConsortiumService
```

Figure 5.8 shows the successful registration of the vocabularies and contracts.

Two airlines, Friendly Skies Airline and Curbside Airways, wish to comply with the
Faber and Weber contracts, respectively. Since this example is using a shared
implementation for the contracts, the airline services are started via respective *ini*
files that contain the `AirlineSpeak` vocabulary property values for creating the
service description and some additional information. The following is the *ini* file for
Friendly Skies Airline.

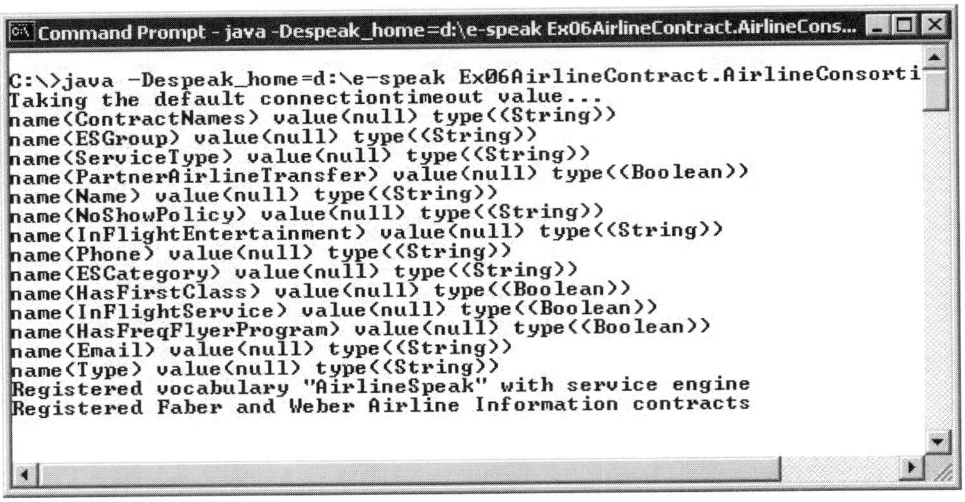

```
Command Prompt - java -Despeak_home=d:\e-speak Ex06AirlineContract.AirlineCons...  [_][□][X]

C:\>java -Despeak_home=d:\e-speak Ex06AirlineContract.AirlineConsorti
Taking the default connectiontimeout value...
name<ContractNames> value<null> type<<String>>
name<ESGroup> value<null> type<<String>>
name<ServiceType> value<null> type<<String>>
name<PartnerAirlineTransfer> value<null> type<<Boolean>>
name<Name> value<null> type<<String>>
name<NoShowPolicy> value<null> type<<String>>
name<InFlightEntertainment> value<null> type<<String>>
name<Phone> value<null> type<<String>>
name<ESCategory> value<null> type<<String>>
name<HasFirstClass> value<null> type<<Boolean>>
name<InFlightService> value<null> type<<Boolean>>
name<HasFreqFlyerProgram> value<null> type<<Boolean>>
name<Email> value<null> type<<String>>
name<Type> value<null> type<<String>>
Registered vocabulary "AirlineSpeak" with service engine
Registered Faber and Weber Airline Information contracts
```

Figure 5.8. Airline Consortium registers AirlineSpeak and Faber/Weber contracts.

FriendlySkiesAirline.ini

```
Name = Friendly Skies Airline

Phone = 123-456-7890

Email = friendly@skies.com

HasFirstClass = TRUE

HasFreqFlyerProgram = TRUE

ServiceType  = DomesticIntl

InFlightEntertainment  = TRUE

PartnerAirlineTransfer = TRUE

NoShowPolicy = NextAvailableFlight

InFlightService = TRUE


Description = Luxury in the skies. Friendly Skies Airline ...
```

Notice that a generic Faber-Compliant Airline service is used with the appropriate configuration (*ini*) file. You start the Friendly Skies Airline service with the following command:

```
C:\>java -Despeak_home=d:\e-speak
    Ex06AirlineContract.FaberCompliantAirlineService
    Shared\FriendlySkiesAirline.ini FriendlySkiesAirlines
```

The `AirlineInformationClient` provides the user interface for trip planners to locate and price various tickets, and is started via the following command:

```
C:\>java -Despeak_home=d:\e-speak
    Ex06AirlineContract.AirlineInformationClient
```

The client starts up the user interface for the ecosystem, and we search for any airline that abides by the Faber contract and has first class. The results are displayed in Figure 5.9.

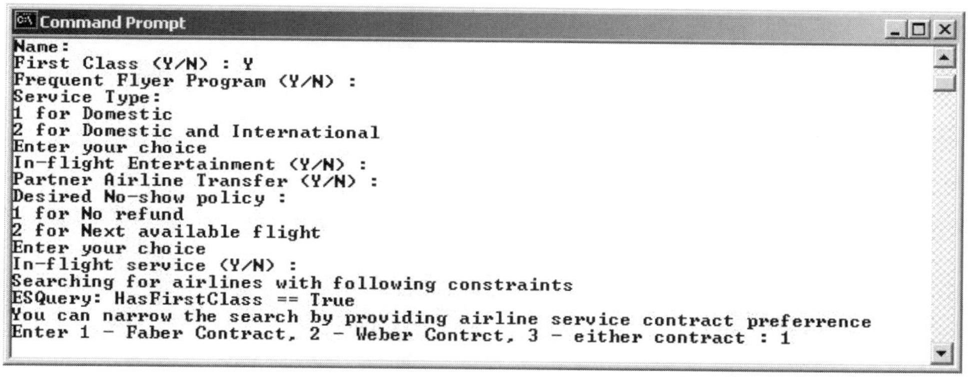

```
Command Prompt                                                    _ □ ×
Name:
First Class (Y/N) : Y
Frequent Flyer Program (Y/N) :
Service Type:
1 for Domestic
2 for Domestic and International
Enter your choice
In-flight Entertainment (Y/N) :
Partner Airline Transfer (Y/N) :
Desired No-show policy :
1 for No refund
2 for Next available flight
Enter your choice
In-flight service (Y/N) :
Searching for airlines with following constraints
ESQuery: HasFirstClass == True
You can narrow the search by providing airline service contract preferrence
Enter 1 - Faber Contract, 2 - Weber Contrct, 3 - either contract : 1
```

Figure 5.9. Airline Information client.

Once the airlines are returned, we can work through the client to obtain fares for a specific airline. At this point, we are interacting with the service and its backend pricing infrastructure. Figure 5.10 depicts this interaction.

The client is versatile enough (albeit rather dull) to facilitate various types of search scenarios. The ecosystem would allow trip planners to find matching airline services for many possible searches, including the following:

▪ The airline with the cheapest tickets for a particular destination

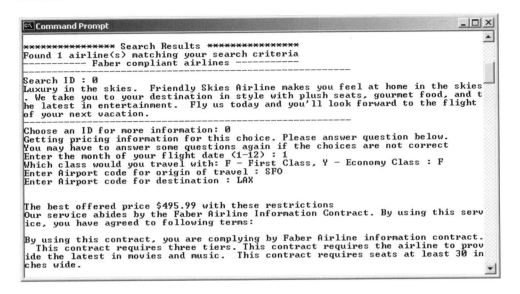

Figure 5.10. Interacting with the Faber service for Friendly Skies Airline.

- The airlines with international destinations, audiovisual entertainment, and refundable tickets

- The airlines with frequent flyer programs and first class

5.2.6   Final Analysis

The concept of contracts is very useful. It can provide structure around the way companies work together. However, contracts are not fully evolved at the programmatic level in e-Speak as well as they are in the real world. The programmatic mechanism publishes the name of the interface that is associated with the contract. It also has "terms of use," but that is a free-formatted string. Semantically, that makes it difficult to structure the "terms of use" definition in a consistent way. For example, in the Airline ecosystem, when the client displayed restrictions and terms of use for the particular airline, it did so using the getTermsOfUse method, which is part of the ESContract object. You could envision taking the "terms of use" to a greater level of sophistication by requiring the terms of use to include specific information formatted in a particular way.

FaberCompliantImpl.java

```
public String getRestrictions() throws  ESInvocationException
{
        return new String("Our service abides by the Faber
        Airline Information Contract. " + "By using this
        service, you have agreed to following terms: \n\n" +
        myContract.getTermsOfUse());
}
```

Therefore, you could create a strong legal contract-like construct, using that string field by providing a structured definition. Figure 5.11 depicts an example of such a construct that could have been used in place of the free-formatted string in the Airline ecosystem. Enforcing this would be left to a separate, higher level entity in an ecosystem (the Airline consortium).

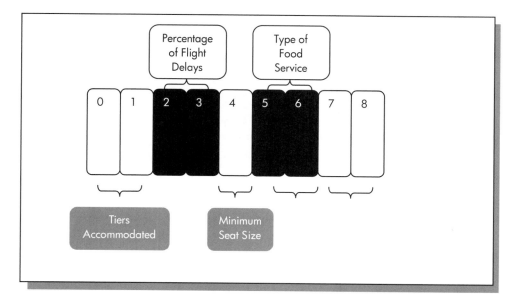

Figure 5.11. Structured terms of use string.

The legal aspects of digital contract formation are not fully figured out yet. In the meantime, however, we can still use these constructs to create a notion of a service level for a service. The license string in a contract element could be used similarly to develop the notion of service licenses. The `getLicense` method of the `ESContractDescription` class provides access to the license associated with a contract.

5.3   Registering in Multiple Contracts and Vocabularies

One might ask whether it is possible for a service to register in more than one vocabulary or abide by multiple contracts. The practical or real-world answer to that is *yes*! It is not uncommon in the real world to see this. You would find the need for using multiple vocabularies when your product or service caters to different audiences. For example, you would use a different set of words (vocabulary) to describe a computer, depending on whether you are talking to a home consumer or a graphic designer.

The need to comply by multiple contracts arises when an organization or product provides different levels and kinds of services for different audiences. For example, a international manufacturing company would need to comply with both ISO 9000 and Six Sigma quality standards to remain competitive. In this case, the company must be able to handle the requirements and expectations of both standards.

The e-Speak infrastructure supports the notion of a service registering in multiple vocabularies or abiding by a set of contracts. There is no specific restriction, as such, about how many or what kind of vocabularies and contracts can be used. To use the example from the previous section, one could imagine a situation where an airline decides to be part of both the `Faber` and `Weber` camps under the `Airline Consortium`. It is also possible that the airline decides to join a different consortium altogether in addition to the `Airline Consortium` — one that perhaps uses a separate set of attributes to describe an airline service. To be compliant with this other consortium at the same time will require the airline to describe its service in multiple vocabularies.

From the programming standpoint, supporting multiple contracts and vocabularies means that the service provider needs to implement all the interfaces corresponding to the contracts it wants to abide by and register the service in all the appropriate vocabularies.

The context for the client as to which vocabulary or contract it is using to interact with the service is *statically bound*. This is because, while developing the business logic, we already know which interface the method being developed is part of. For example, while developing the logic for method `getDescription` we know that it is part of the interface `FaberFlightIntf` and that the logic for method `shortTextDescription`, will be part of `WeberAirlineIntf` interface. Due to this, there is no need for any *dynamic binding* to determine the vocabulary or contract the client is using.

It must be noted, however, that for any methods that are not part of any specific interface, the context must be communicated explicitly. For example, suppose that, when implementing both the `FaberFlightIntf` and `WeberAirlineIntf` interfaces, a common method called `formatText` is used to format the text string as per the requirements of each contract. Both the methods `getDescription` and `shortTextDescription` will invoke this method just before sending the reply back to the client. For the `formatText` method to do proper formatting, the context of the contract must be communicated with it through some parameter. In such cases, an `Enumeration` class object series can be used to denote the context of the contract or the vocabulary.

This chapter demonstrated that deploying ecosystems requires both the cooperation and discussion among industry stakeholders, as well as a comprehensive design (including roles, responsibilities, and governance). As these ecosystems mature and solidify, co-opetition within the industries and more advanced interactions and relationships might be needed. In the next chapter, we discuss how to address trigger-based interactions and service composition.

Advanced Service Interactions

- Events
  example working directory:
  \Examples\Ex07EventHandling

- Service Composition
  example working directory:
  \Examples\Ex08ServiceComposition

- Out-of-Band Data Transfer
  example working directory:
  \Examples\Ex09OutOfBandServiceDelivery

- Service Portals

Chapter 6

ADVANCED SERVICE INTERACTIONS

In the brick and mortar world, related industries often work together providing complementary offerings. A trip to the local video rental store will often result in a deal for soda purchases — rent three videos and receive a free 2-liter bottle of soda or buy groceries at the local grocery store and receive miles on an airline of your choice. Companies, especially those dealing with consumer products, often seek out cooperative marketing opportunities. These provide a win-win situation for the involved parties. This way, the companies receive new customers and increase their chances of repeat business (a much-sought-after asset these days), and consumers receive a deal that may not have been available.

As companies learn how to work together in a co-opetition framework, their interaction patterns may entice vertical and tangential industries to tie up with existing digital ecosystems, such as the Airline ecosystem of Chapter 5. This will allow services to work behind the scenes and provide users with complementary offerings. These related industries can work together to provide complementary solutions and products for users. The key is to foster service interactions that allow for communication and the sharing of data between different services to make the cooperative marketing opportunities a reality.

As more complex service interactions are established, services might find the need to link a set of services together in a specific order. Credit card companies usually first verify a consumer's data, run a credit check, and, finally, issue a credit card.

You can envision the same requirement once a grander ecosystem of smaller related ecosystems works to provide solutions and products to consumers.

To facilitate these complex business relationships, services must be able to interact with each other, share data, and establish linkages. Events allow services to publish triggers (small pieces of data) that can be accessed by other services, then acted upon. The rental of videos is a trigger to notify the sales representative to act and provide the consumer a free bottle of soda.

In this chapter, we see how the Airline ecosystem works with the Hotel services to offer special deals to airline travelers. We also discuss how service composition can be incorporated into the picture and allow for a workflow-like environment where service sequencing is possible.

6.1   Events

We have seen the value of deploying ecosystems in assisting clients and services to foster dynamic relationships in an effective and predictable manner. As the expectations from these ecosystems increase in complexity, relationships that services need to form also need to increase in complexity — at both a business and a programmatic level. Services not only process data from various sources (system information in Chapter 4) but can and will act as trigger or decision points in the workflow. Therefore, services need the ability to trigger subsequent tasks or alter runtime processing.

6.1.1   Real-Life Events and Event Triggers

Events can be thought of as triggers to start off a related set of activities. We use nonprogrammatic events in our daily lives without even realizing it. For example, when you receive a credit card statement, it is a trigger to pay the credit card bill; when you move into a new city, your phone service triggers a whole host of welcome paraphernalia. In the corporate world, events and triggers can be found all along the supply chains — often in business processes and software systems. For example, a decrease in *kanban* levels of a raw material would trigger a purchase order for that material and subsequent restocking.

When services interact with other entities, standard communication or messaging architectures must be constructed.   Foundations such as Common Object Request Broker Architecture (CORBA), RosettaNet, and SAP's Application Link Enabling (ALE) are some of these standards used to format messages in distributed computing environments. Although these provide message formatting standards, for services to *trigger* activity among related services, an event architecture should be used. The event architecture provides the trigger mechanism between services, regardless of the organizational boundaries of the service providers.

Event triggers are important as tools to gauge the condition of a business. They provide pertinent information to decision-making entities (people, processes, systems), based on the occurrence of certain events. A common problem for industries with high fixed costs and low incremental costs, such as airlines or cruises, is that profit margins are reduced (artificially) for trips with low reservations. This is because, in this case, the cost per person becomes very high. Airlines may be able to hedge against this by using event triggers to watch reservation levels *early on* and dynamically provide corrective business action.

To glean the benefits of event triggers, they must be well thought out. Effective event triggers are:

- Communicate occurrence of relevant events
- Provide timely information about the events
- Convey adequate event information

6.1.2   An Event-Based Alliance

We demonstrate the use of event triggers by introducing a business alliance in the Hotel and Airline ecosystems. In this example, we assume that there is an alliance between the Weber-Compliant Airline (Curbside Airways) and the Los Angeles Motel. Such an alliance among complementary services helps to improve existing and obtain new customer loyalty. It also creates opportunities for revenue sharing and ensures optimum occupancy levels, thus preserving business profit margins. Under this alliance, when a trip planner reserves a ticket to Los Angeles on a Weber-Compliant Airline, the Los Angeles Motel is notified. The Los Angeles

Motel can then offer, if it chooses to, a promotional discount to the traveler. For us to understand programmatically how to do this, we first examine e-Speak's event architecture in more detail.

6.1.3   Event Architecture

E-Speak provides a *publish-subscribe* architecture based on its internal messaging for events. In a publish-subscribe architecture, entities publish predefined events through a communication channel to a central authority. The interested parties (in a specific event) must register their interest in subscribing to that event with the central authority. Whenever an event is published, the central authority automatically makes the event available to the subscribers. Subscribers can process the event immediately or in batch mode. The central authority also manages access control and other security for each event.

E-Speak's publish-subscribe event architecture is intuitive in its design. Figure 6.1 depicts a generic view of the architecture. A publisher entity publishes an event along with related information, called a *payload*, to a distributor. A subscriber entity subscribes to an event and designates listeners (to the distributor) for an event. The distributor communicates the occurrence of the event to the listener. The listener acts on behalf of the subscriber and processes the event. The subscriber can designate multiple listeners for different events — each listener processing a certain event.

Figure 6.2 overlays the generic e-Speak event architecture with our example entities and highlights specific roles that services play.

The sequence of interactions in handling an event is as follows:

1. Distributor registers with the engine.

2. Publisher registers its intent to publish an event A.

3. Subscriber registers its intent to subscribe to event A with the Distributor.

4. Subscriber registers a Listener to process event A.

5. Publisher sends the Event to the Distributor, using a `notify` message.

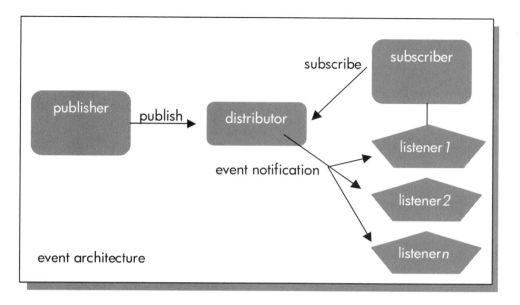

Figure 6.1. Generic publish-subscribe architecture.

6. Distributor notifies the Listener of the event occurrence.

7. The Listener processes event A.

Note

A publisher, a subscriber, a listener, and a distributor can be discrete entities or can be a few number of entities wearing multiple hats. There are no programmatic restrictions regarding this. It depends purely on the desired interaction patterns.

Event

The Weber-Compliant Airline services and Hotel ecosystem alliance revolves around the `WeberCompliantAirlineService.UserQuery` event depicted in Figure 6.3. This event communicates the following pieces of information to the subscribing entity —

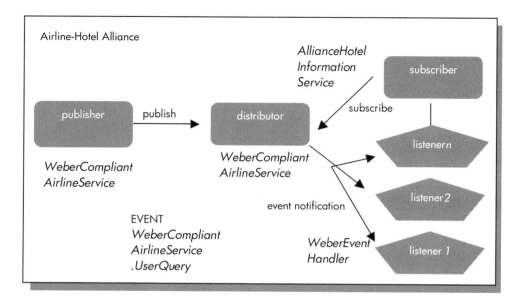

Figure 6.2. Weber-Compliant—Airline Los Angeles Motel alliance.

`AllianceHotelInformationService:`

1. Name of airline

2. The city

3. The travel month

The Weber-Compliant Airline service implementation class, `WeberCompliantImpl`, publishes the event after it processes and calculates the airline fare.

The event is published by instantiating a new event and giving it a predesigned and communicated name. Note that the *name* of the event could be any string text. We have used a Java-style package naming convention as an example. The `Event` class contains the `setPayload` method to associate values to the event data elements included within.

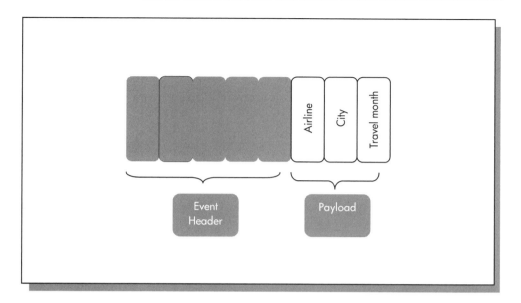

Figure 6.3. Airline–Hotel alliance event.

WeberCompliantImpl.java

```
Event event=new Event("WeberCompliantAirlineService.UserQuery");
event.setPayload(airlineName + "|" + month + "|" + destination);
```

Note

The subscriber registers interest in a specifically named event that has been communicated by the publisher. The publisher must communicate any event name changes to all interested subscribers.

An instantiated event needs to be actively *published* in order for the interested parties to make use of it.

Publisher

The publisher registers *intent* to publish an event with the distributor. It does this by instantiating an object of ESPublisher class. The publisher is instantiated by the Weber-Compliant Airline service, WeberCompliantAirlineService. Events are added via the addEvent method. The method publish registers the myPublisher's intent to publish WeberCompliantAirlineService.UserQuery with the distributor. However, by instantiating the publisher object and adding an event, the event does not get published. The publisher object, myPublisher, is responsible for publishing the created event as and when the *payload* for the event is produced.

WeberCompliantAirlineService.java

```
ESPublisher myPublisher = null;
try
{
        myPublisher = new ESPublisher(Connection);
        myPublisher.addEvent
           ("WeberCompliantAirlineService.UserQuery");
        myPublisher.publish();
        System.out.println("Event publisher for event
           WeberCompliantAirlineService.UserQuery started");
}
```

In the code below, we pass the reference to the publisher, myPublisher, to the service implementation, WeberCompliantImpl.

WeberCompliantAirlineService.java

```
WeberCompliantImpl myServiceImpl = new
   WeberCompliantImpl(args[1],
   serviceProps.getProperty("Name"),
   serviceProps.getProperty("ShortDescription"),
   serviceProps.getProperty("LongDescription"),
   serviceProps.getProperty("AirlineID"), myContract,
     myPublisher);
```

The `WeberCompliantImpl` class, which actually instantiates the event, will use this publisher to publish the event to the distributor via the `sendNotify` or the `sendNotifySync` methods. The events can be published asynchronously or synchronously. When an event is published synchronously via the `sendNotifySync` method, the publishing entity waits for a response from the distributor before publishing the next event.

WeberCompliantImpl.java

```
myPublisher.sendNotify(event);
System.out.println("Notifying participating hotels...");
```

The publisher is not tied with any event in particular; it can publish any number of distinct or similar events.

Distributor

The distributor manages a list of publishers and subscribers, as well as their listeners and the events they are interested in. `WeberCompliantAirlineService` also instantiates the distributor. The distributor receives the published events from the publisher and forwards them to the designated listeners for the specified event. The `ESDistributor` class maintains a list of events. The `addEvent` method adds an event entry into this list.

WeberCompliantAirlineService.java

```
ESDistributor myDistributor = null;
try
{
        myDistributor = new ESDistributor(Connection);
        myDistributor.addEvent
           ("WeberCompliantAirlineService.UserQuery");
        myDistributor.start();
        System.out.println("Event distributor for event
           WeberCompliantAirlineService.UserQuery started");
}
```

Subscriber

The subscriber is the entity that registers interest in an event with the distributor. In our example, the subscriber is the `AllianceHotelInformationService`. The `ESSubscriber` class allows the service to subscribe to events provided by the distributor. It also contains the `addEvent` method to subscribe to events of interest. It also contains a method, `setImplementation`, which designates the listener for the event. The class `WeberEventHandler` is the designated listener. The `subscribe` method registers this *subscription* with the distributor.

AllianceHotelInformationService.java

```
ESSubscriber mySubscriber = new ESSubscriber(Connection);
mySubscriber.addEvent
    ("WeberCompliantAirlineService.UserQuery");
mySubscriber.setImplementation(new
    WeberEventHandler(serviceProps.getProperty("Name")));
mySubscriber.subscribe();
```

Listener

The listener, `WeberEventHandler`, listens and processes the events on behalf of the subscriber, Los Angeles Motel. The distributor pushes the events to the listener as they occur. This allows for immediate processing, although batch mode is also supported. The listener implements `ESListenerIntf`, so both `notifySync` and `notify` from that interface must be implemented. Both these methods process a received event. `notifySync` is a synchronous event handler method that is used when event processing happens to be *critical section* code.

This listener registers a *callback* method, `notify`, with the distributor. When the distributor receives an event, it invokes the callback method, and the listener processes the event. In this case, the processing includes displaying an Applet Window Toolkit (AWT) window with a promotional offer displaying the hotel name and a discount code to use the offer.

WeberEventHandler.java

```
public void notify(Event evt)
{
        int travelMonth;
        String destination, airlineName;

        System.out.println("Received event payload : "
           + evt.getPayload());
        StringTokenizer payloadTok = new
           StringTokenizer((String)evt.getPayload(), "|");
        airlineName = payloadTok.nextToken();
        travelMonth = Integer.parseInt(payloadTok.nextToken());
        destination = payloadTok.nextToken();

        new PromoWindow(handlingEntityName, airlineName,
           travelMonth, destination, discountCode);
}
```

6.1.4   Event Services

You saw in Chapter 2 that almost all resources are services within the e-Speak architecture. In this example, the publisher and subscriber entities have been embedded within the service classes. However, they could have also been converted into services. Treating the event entities as services requires us to *find* those entities, just like other services. One advantage of "service-ifying" them is that we can benefit from e-Speak's security mechanisms, discussed in Chapter 8. Security would allow us to:

- Ensure that a publisher is authenticated to publish a certain event
- Ensure that a subscriber is allowed to subscribe to a certain event
- Ensure that an authenticated listener is handling a certain event

Another advantage of service-ifying the event deployment is our ability to deploy a persistent event model. The distributor, publisher, subscriber, listeners, and event's information are *transient*. It is important to realize that if any of these entities is shutdown and restarted, the publishing and subscribing intent will need to be re-submitted. They, like the service engine, can be made persistent. We discuss this in Chapter 10.

6.1.5 In Action

As always, to run this example, we need to start the service engine. Once the engine has been successfully started, we run the `AirlineConsortiumService`, as explained in Chapter 5.

Now, we start the `WeberCompliantAirlineService` for Curbside Airways, as shown. Remember to start the `WeberCompliantAirlineService` in the working directory for Chapter 6.

```
C:\>java -Despeak_home=d:\e-speak WeberCompliantAirlineService
      ..\Shared\CurbsideAirways.ini CurbsideAirways
```

Figure 6.4 displays the start of this enhanced `WeberCompliantAirlineService`. Notice that the distributor and publisher entities are started and ready for use.

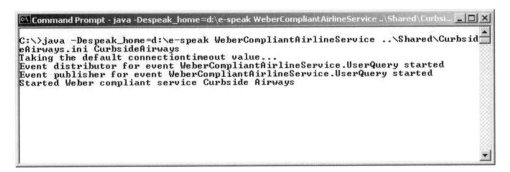

Figure 6.4. Starting the distributor and publisher.

We now start the `AllianceHotelInformationService` (the subscriber):

```
C:\>java -Despeak_home=d:\e-speak
      AllianceHotelInformationService ..\Shared\EasyInn.ini EasyInn
```

Figure 6.5 displays the results of the `AllianceHotelService` starting up, thereby starting the subscriber.

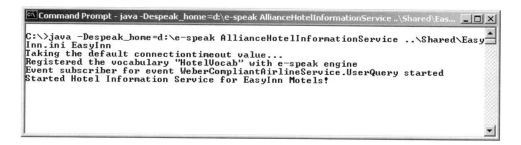

```
C:\>java -Despeak_home=d:\e-speak AllianceHotelInformationService ..\Shared\Easy
Inn.ini EasyInn
Taking the default connectiontimeout value...
Registered the vocabulary "HotelVocab" with e-speak engine
Event subscriber for event WeberCompliantAirlineService.UserQuery started
Started Hotel Information Service for EasyInn Motels!
```

Figure 6.5. Starting the subscriber.

At this point, the hotels and airlines have started up with the event mechanisms in place. The last step is to start the airline client as in Section 5.1. Running the query depicted in Figure 6.6, results in services that match the defined query. In this example, the user is searching for any airline with Economy class within the Weber contract. As before, the trip planner must select an airline service and provide more detailed input to receive a fare quote. We choose January as the month traveling from San Francisco to Los Angeles.

When the user selects to get more information on an airline service, the event triggers are activated, and the Los Angeles Motel discount is displayed in the promotion window, depicted in Figure 6.7.

The promotion window provides the trip planner more information to make use of the discount that the Los Angeles Motel offers. We now start the hotel client from Section 5.2. At this point, we have a choice of either entering generic information to view all hotels in the Los Angeles area or we can specify the specific discount information to view only the Los Angeles Motel. In Figure 6.8, we enter the Los Angeles Motel information and notice that LAX is automatically filled in as the nearest Airport code. This information was inherited from the Airline service query that was completed prior to this step.

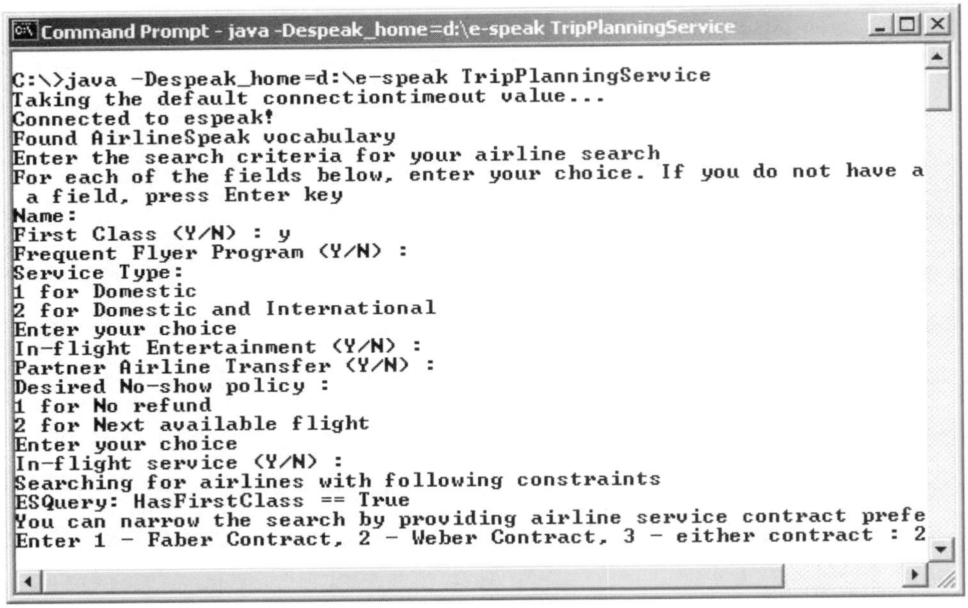

```
Command Prompt - java -Despeak_home=d:\e-speak TripPlanningService    _ □ ×

C:\>java -Despeak_home=d:\e-speak TripPlanningService
Taking the default connectiontimeout value...
Connected to espeak!
Found AirlineSpeak vocabulary
Enter the search criteria for your airline search
For each of the fields below, enter your choice. If you do not have a
 a field, press Enter key
Name:
First Class (Y/N) : y
Frequent Flyer Program (Y/N) :
Service Type:
1 for Domestic
2 for Domestic and International
Enter your choice
In-flight Entertainment (Y/N) :
Partner Airline Transfer (Y/N) :
Desired No-show policy :
1 for No refund
2 for Next available flight
Enter your choice
In-flight service (Y/N) :
Searching for airlines with following constraints
ESQuery: HasFirstClass == True
You can narrow the search by providing airline service contract prefe
Enter 1 - Faber Contract, 2 - Weber Contract, 3 - either contract : 2
```

Figure 6.6. The query.

6.2   Service Composition

In the event section, we saw how two services can communicate with each other
by means of sending simple, free-formatted messages — events. Through these
messages, the Airline service communicated the trip planning query to the Hotel
Information service so that the Hotel service could send the trip planner a promotional offer. From a user's perspective, there were two services that catered to
his or her needs. Certain characteristics of this event-based interaction are worth
noting:

> ▐ The two services were *loosely coupled*. The Airline and Hotel services had
>   no visibility of each other's implementation detail.

> ▐ The level of interaction between the two services in this case was *limited to
>   a certain event* that contained some payload data in proprietary format.

> ▐ The user interacted with the two services *separately*, despite being facilitated

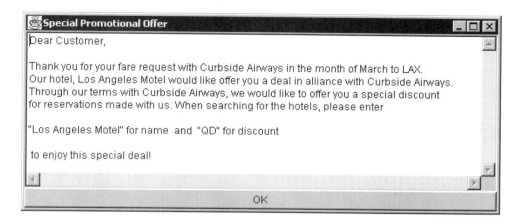

Figure 6.7. The promotion.

by the trip-planning client. The two interaction sessions were independent of each other. This should be expected in a loosely coupled setup such as this.

■ The user made a *conscious* decision to use (or not use) the specific hotel presented by the alliance.

Note

Although we have termed the technology level interaction for events as *loosely coupled*, at the business-level, the two companies (the hotel and the airline) are very closely tied. An alliance such as this would require a fair amount of trust, negotiation, and understanding among the alliance parties to develop, maintain, and promote it.

We call this kind of interaction an example of *service collaboration*. In service collaboration, the interaction pattern among concerned services is characterized as above. There is also another possible form of interaction — *service composition*. In Section 1.2 we discussed the concept of service composition briefly.

Service Composition: *Service composition combines offerings of two or more services to create a new service.*

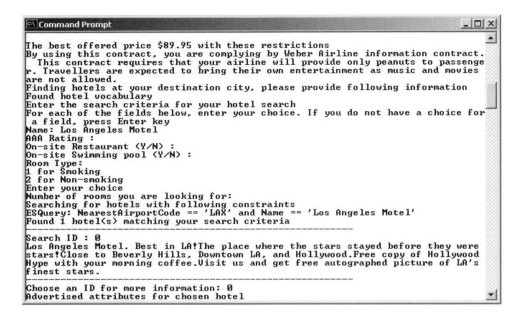

Figure 6.8. The Los Angeles Motel rate through alliance.

Service composition creates a different user experience — one that is inclusive of and different from any constituent service experiences.   The composite service is called a *higher level service* which collects the offerings of *lower level services*. Figure 6.9 shows the relationship between the higher level and lower level services in service composition.

Notice that a lower level service can be a part of several higher level services. In that respect, it is a many-many relationship.

One advantage of service composition is that it makes creation of complex services simpler. A complex service can be thought of as a service that consists of several lower level services. For example, a virtual storefront could be created by assembling together cataloging, order management, payment, and shipping services (each from entities whose core business happens to be providing that particular business service). Each lower level service provides a specialized offering. The lower level order management service would provide only ordering functionality for the virtual storefront (a complex composite service). As you can see, a

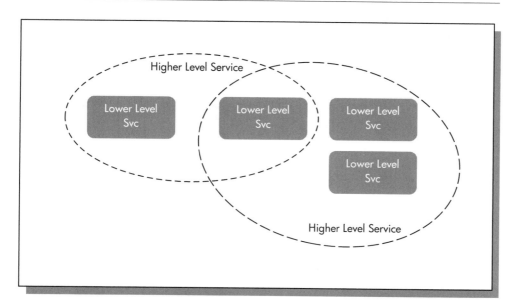

Figure 6.9. Service composition relations.

virtual storefront provider is shielded from the intricacies of supply chain management if a set of reliable supply chain services has been composed into a higher level complex service, thereby allowing the storefront to focus on finding, selling, and advertising high-quality goods.

Using this model of service design, it is possible to create services of any complexity with a good degree of manageability. Conceptually, service composition is analogous to functional decomposition or top-down design approaches used in software engineering.

6.2.1 Service Collaboration versus Service Composition

Service composition is different from service collaboration in several respects. One very important difference is that, while service collaboration helps in the interaction of two services, it keeps the *identity* of the services involved separate. In the previous example, the trip planner was forced to use *different* clients to price the airline and hotel rates. Service composition, on the other hand, *collects* such identities and creates a higher level service with an identity of its own, as will be seen in the example in this section. A few other key distinctions are as follows:

- From a user's standpoint, service composition provides a single interface to *all* the pertinent services. This means that the user will need only *one* session of interaction to get the service.

- Service composition shields the user from knowing about and dealing with any individual lower level service.

- Service composition can create a service with a user experience that could be distinctly different from the experience of the pertinent lower level service.

- Higher level services may not *necessarily* work under heavyweight business alliance agreements with each of the lower level services. Lower level services are designed for simple programmatic composition into a higher level service.

Service collaboration usually involves working together under a pre-established business alliance agreement. For example, the Los Angeles Motel and Curbside Airways partnered to offer promotional discounts for travelers traveling by Curbside Airlines to Los Angeles and staying at the Los Angeles Motel. This would have required several business-level discussions and negotiations by both entities. In service composition, however, the emphasis is not to develop a business alliance and perhaps partake in revenue sharing or customer loyalty schemes. The emphasis is on composing a set of distinct services to fulfill a task or process, as in the virtual storefront example. The virtual storefront would be made up of individual services from a *class* of order management services, a class of purchasing services, so on and so forth.

Composite services need not have any affinity to a specific supply chain service. The composite service would dynamically *find* the appropriate service by using the framework provided by vocabularies and contracts. The composite service searches for services that abided by a certain vocabulary and contract. The term *class* here refers to a category of interest to the creator of higher level service. It is interesting to note that there may or may not be any special business alliance between the composed service and a service instance from that class. In fact, at the business-level, the lower level service provider management may not even be aware of the many higher level services using that particular service.

6.2.2   Composite Travel Service

Composing a higher level service can be analogous to forming a new product team. You need to bring together the right skills, raw material, and team members to make the final product. Some planning, right material, and a set of processes are required to launch the new product. To compose a higher level service that performs a specific task or function, you need to:

- Know the classes of services that are required to carry out the function
- Know the workflow required of these services to perform the task
- Establish connection with appropriate ecosystems that contain the desired classes of services
- Evaluate these ecosystems
- Know the ecosystem framework — vocabularies and contracts established by the ecosystem governing body
- Integrate the appropriate service interfaces and operational processes from the selected lower level services to offer the higher level service.

We have used the Hotel and Airline services developed earlier to create a new composite service to plan a trip. Planning a trip in this case involves pricing an airline ticket and hotel room. Figure 6.10 shows the service tiers in the composed Trip-Planning service.

The `TripPlanningService` class is the composed Airline and Hotel services. If you take a look at the `AirlineSearch` and `HotelSearch` methods, you will notice that they are simply the airline and hotel information clients from previous examples.

TripPlanningService.java

```
AirlineSearch();
System.out.println("Finding hotels at your destination city,
   please provide following information");
HotelSearch();
```

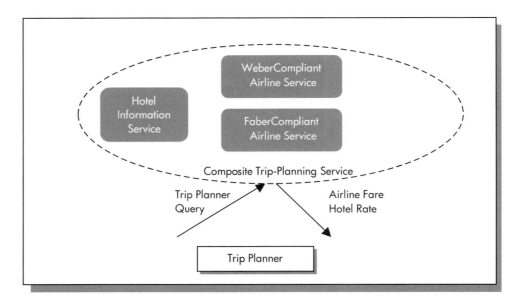

Figure 6.10. Composite Trip-Planning service.

6.2.3   In Action

To run this example, you start the Airline ecosystem and Hotel ecosystem from Chapter 5. Once these have been successfully started, you start the Trip-Planning service from this example, as follows:

```
C:\>java -Despeak_home=d:\e-speak
   TripPlanningService
```

In the Section 6.1, you had to start two clients to price the airline and hotel rates because the trip-planning client was not a composed service. Here, what you are seeing is the composed service, which does present a collected view, rather than an independent view of the lower level services.

6.2.4   Final Analysis

Service composition is a very powerful concept. It pushes distributed computing limits far beyond company boundaries and network firewalls. Because classes of like-minded services are important versus vendor-specific business alliances, we can envision a service world in which services are composed at runtime via the dynamic discovery foundations that e-Speak provides.   From a service user's point of view, a different set of lower level services might be used each time the higher level service is invoked, but that collection of services is *transparent*. Services can publish information about uptime, quality of service, and service levels (as discussed in Chapter 5) and allow higher level services to gather services with more sophistication.

Although powerful, service composition opens up another set of issues that revolves around the fact that the lower level services are not under direct control of the higher level service. The service composer needs to align its service lifecycle with that of all the lower level services. For example, when a lower level service changes behavior, the higher level service needs to incorporate that changed behavior. As the number of lower level services increases, this alignment becomes more challenging.

The Trip-Planning service in this example is not discoverable. It is connected to the service engine to facilitate interaction with ecosystems deployed on the engine. However, if this Trip-Planning service were to be *found* by other service users (human or programmatic), it would need to follow the same set of steps that our e-Speak services do; that is, it would need to abide with a vocabulary and a contract, as well as register and start within the service engine.

6.3   Out-of-Band Data Transfer

In the event section, we looked at how small event data can be communicated to various services or service components using e-Speak's event model. The amount of data we sent with each event was rather small — several bytes in size. In this section, we discuss service architecture to facilitate bulk data transfer.

We have been using the e-Speak engine to do data transfer without realizing it.

All the remote procedure calls (RPCs) between services and their clients are, in fact, a few code messages being sent through the engine. The engine acted as the *conduit* in this case to create an end-to-end channel between two software components connected to it.

In the User Data service in Chapter 4, we first exposed this data transfer mechanism by creating a container class, `StoreSystemData`, and providing some explicit data transfer instructions for that class. In Section 6.1, we showed a data transfer mechanism that required an elaborate setup to move data through the engine. This setup consisted of creating a set of events, payload for the events, and using some additional services to manage the publish-subscribe communication model between collaborating services. There are some fundamental differences between these two data transfer methods.   An event is mainly designed to support loosely coupled interactions, whereas the container class will typically facilitate tightly coupled interactions. The event model is also very efficient in supporting data communication models, such as "publish and subscribe" and push and pull. The container class method is more suitable for request-response interactions. Finally, while the container class streamlines the access and processing of the data it contains via the container class methods, the event mechanism provides free-flowing access to the data. Of course, this also means that such data could be processed inconsistently.

6.3.1 Bulk Data Transfer

The *volume* of data however, poses an orthogonal problem. In either the container class or event-based interactions, there could be a need for voluminous data transfer. However, when the volume of data is large, there is a different set of problems that must be addressed. Like in any message-based system, e-Speak's core messaging infrastructure also *packetizes* the data in a message. In most cases, such as method invocations and simple event payloads, the message is small enough to fit in very few data packets — just one for the simplest interactions.

As the message gets bigger, it must be broken into several data packets, then sent over the underlying TCP/IP communication channel. The number of packets is directly proportional to the size of data and can grow in number for large amounts of data — say several megabytes. When the data packets are sent over the communication channel, they are sent from one node in the network to another until they reach the destination node. Figure 6.11 depicts this in a rather simplified manner.

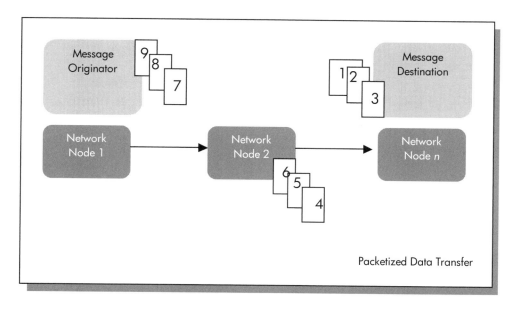

Figure 6.11. Data packet transfer.

When several such data packets are sent from a source machine to a destination machine with other machines in between, there is a chance that they are received in out of order, lost, duplicated, or corrupted, due to some disturbance in the network. As a result, the higher level entities must have mechanisms to recover from these.

In our service architecture, we have always kept the e-Speak engine in the middle of every interaction. When a client searches for a service in an e-Speak engine, it gets back a handle for the discovered service. This handle represents the *mailbox address* of the service in the engine to which the service is assigned during the service registration. In a similar way, the client is also represented by the Uniform Resource Locator (URL) of a mailbox assigned to it. Any interaction between the client and the service happens by means of the messages (a set of data packets) being moved between these mailboxes inside the engine. The service engine acts as the *mediator* between the client and the service during any client-service communication. Thus, any client-to-service interaction consists of two separate interactions — one from the message originator (client or service) to the e-Speak engine and the other from the engine to the message destination (service or client). In both these interactions, there is the possibility of data loss, as we discussed earlier. This makes the probability of data loss double in a mediated interaction (as in the case of e-Speak-mediated interaction), compared with a direct interaction. Note, however, that we are using mediated interaction, due to several other features the engine offers.

In an interaction where the size of the message is small, the effects of data loss, duplication, or corruption can be overcome by several simple checks already present in the TCP/IP stack. As a result, any interaction between a client and a service that involves small messages can be facilitated through the engine without any special mechanism in place. As the volume increases, however, we must address this issue slightly differently, due to the following limitations in the base messaging layer in the e-Speak engine:

- Messages are assumed to be traveling in the best network environment and conditions. If this assumption is false for a network part of or all the time, the messages will be dropped, either during the message originator-to-engine interaction or engine-to-destination interaction.

- Messages are never retransmitted. All messages are assumed to be eventually delivered to the message destination. The originator has no way of knowing whether a message is lost or is corrupted on the way.

- There is no flow control. When large data transfer occurs, there is a possibility that some of the mailboxes involved in the message transfer can reach capacity and may not be able to receive any more data packets until the existing packets are cleared (through consumption of them by the destination entity).

To avoid these problems the solution must be devised with certain characteristics, such as:

- Guaranteed message delivery
- Delivery of messages once and only once (or a certain fixed number of times)

- Ability to detect and recover from corrupted or lost data packets

- Ability to maintain *state* of a message transfer over a long period. This typically means some kind of logging mechanism to log the state

There are several ways in which a solution could be devised for this purpose. Among them are custom packages that are designed on top of the existing e-Speak infrastructure and commercial middleware software, such as Tuxedo or MQ Series. The Reliable Messaging service developed as part of the e-Speak software is distributed as a *contributed* service that addresses this issue. Look in the *contrib* directory in your e-Speak installation for more information.

We, however, recommend a different approach for this. If we step back and list the salient features of e-Speak, we get:

- Ecosystem creation (through roles, vocabulary, and contract description)

- Service registration

- Service discovery

- Mediation (between client-service interaction)

Data transfer is not part of this, and as a requirement, it is an extension of the interaction pattern. The e-Speak mechanism is not designed to facilitate bulk data transfer smoothly; rather, it is designed and optimized to provide the features listed above. There are several products available in the market today that can specialize in providing a reliable messaging infrastructure, and we recommend using those.

6.3.2   Communication Channels

There are no adapters available today between the e-Speak engine and any middleware messaging products. However, assuming that Java Application Programming Interfaces (APIs) are available for those software packages, it should not be difficult to provide that at a higher level. In fact, it would be possible for the communicating entities to use two separate channels to interact with each other.

- In-band communication channel — This is the channel in which the interaction happens through the e-Speak engine. This type of channel is useful during interactions while searching for a suitable service or registering a service with an ecosystem.

■ Out-of-band communication channel — This channel is used during large data transferring needs. The e-Speak engine is oblivious to any interaction happening through this channel between client and service (hence the name *out-of-band channel*). Any software that can provide robust and reliable messaging infrastructure can be used for this purpose.

Figure 6.12 shows the two types of communication channels and their position in the communication architecture *vis-à-vis* the service engine. Using these two channels judiciously, one can take advantage of both of them at the same time. The next example shows this by using the e-Speak infrastructure for the discovery while using a Web server for bulk data transfer. This example also demonstrates how to couple e-Speak with the Web technologies.

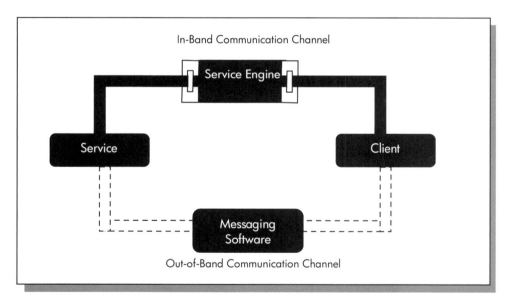

Figure 6.12. Communication channels.

As a business scenario, we use the Hotel Information service developed in the Chapter 5. The only difference in this case is that some additional information is available about the hotel in an audio-visual format. Figure 6.13 depicts the architecture of the new Hotel Information service.

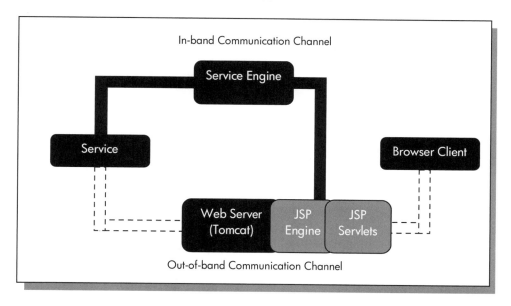

Figure 6.13. Out-of-band hotel information transfer.

In this example, the Hotel Information client is browser-based.   This browser talks to Java Server Pages (JSP) pages deployed on a Web server (Tomcat). The in-band channel (discovering e-Speak-based Hotel services) through the service engine is used to find hotels based on the trip planner's query. All these interactions occur through the in-band channel because the message sizes are relatively small. When more information about a discovered Hotel service is desired — a large audio-visual presentation — the out-of-band channel is used. This channel is formed via the Web server itself.

6.3.3   In Action

To run this example, we need to start the Hotel services from Chapter 5. This will facilitate the in-band channel communications. For the out-of-band channel, we need first to configure and start up the Web server.

Tomcat Configuration

Tomcat configuration requires a few small changes to make e-Speak classes available to the Tomcat infrastructure. These changes are made in the Tomcat installation directory — TOMCAT_HOME.

1. Change the *TOMCAT_HOME\conf\server.xml* configuration file to include a context for our Hypertext Markup Language (HTML) pages. Add the following command to include the context for our HTML pages: /efd.

    server.xml

    ```
    <Context path="/efd" docBase="c:/efd/examples"
       debug="0" reloadable="true"> </Context>
    ```

2. Change the *TOMCAT_HOME\bin\tomcat.bat* to set the ESPEAK_HOME system property in Tomcat's JVM. The changes below should be made for the :startServer and :runServer options in the JVM launch command: start java %TOMCAT_OPTS% ...

    tomcat.bat

    ```
    -Despeak_home=ESPEAK_HOME
    ```

Our Tomcat configuration files are included in the *Shared* directory on the accompanying CD. Once the Tomcat configuration changes have been made, we start the Tomcat server.

```
c:\> tomcat start
```

This will start tomcat in a different window. This window is depicted in Figure 6.14.

Finally, open a browser window and enter the following URL:

```
http://localhost:8080/efd/ex11OutofBandServiceDelivery/
HotelFinder.html
```

Figure 6.14. Starting Tomcat.

This will open a Web page displaying the Hotel Information client, as depicted in Figure 6.15.

Enter any search criteria as previously done and submit the query by clicking on the Search button. The search results are displayed. Figure 6.16 depicts the query results in the browser when the search finds the SuperGrande Hotel.

Click on the link Click here for more ... to get more information about the selected hotel. This link will open an audio-visual presentation that provides information about amenities at the selected hotel. This presentation is delivered to the browser via the *out-of-band* channel between the browser and the Web server, as depicted in Figure 6.13.

The pricing information for the selected hotel can be retrieved by clicking on the Get Price button. This returns the rate for the hotel room, based on query parameters. Figure 6.17 shows this.

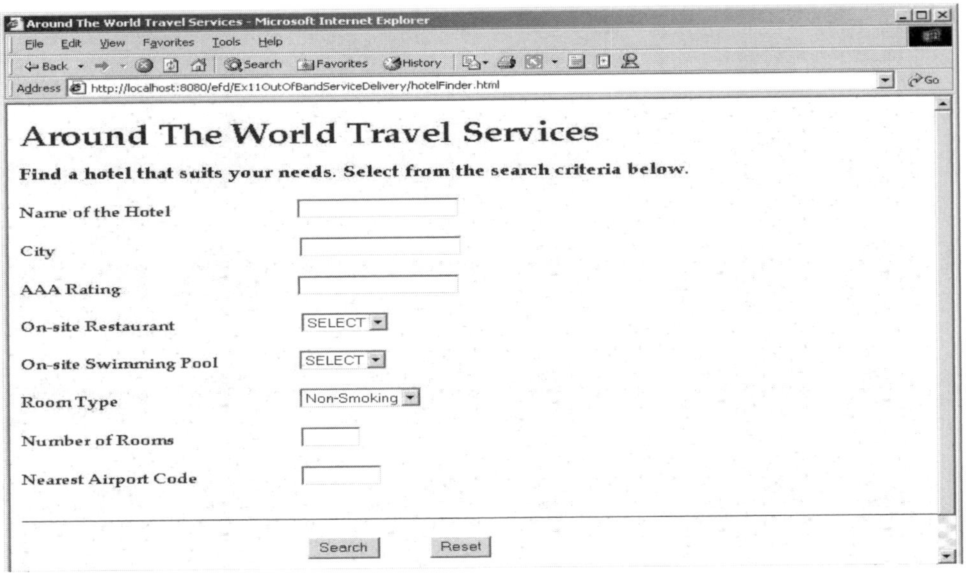

Figure 6.15. Browser-based Hotel Information client.

In this example, we use a multimedia presentation to demonstrate using the out-of-band channel for bulk data transfer. This architecture can be extended to deliver any type of data as a message from the service to the client.

6.4   Service Portals

The advanced service interactions presented can lay the foundation for deploying complex web services on the Web. As we saw in Section 6.2, services can be composed together to create complex, higher level services. In Section 6.3, we showed how standard Web components can interoperate with e-Speak to deploy browser-based interfaces to services. Together, these architectures allow *service aggregators* to collect services of interest and present a Web-based user interface — a service portal. In Chapter 11, we discuss service portals in more detail.

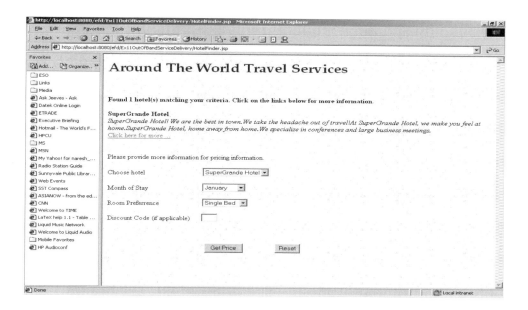

Figure 6.16. Browser-based query results.

Figure 6.17. Hotel rate query results.

Web Service Deployment

PART
Three

IN THIS PART

Multicore Environment

- Multicore Architecture
- The Advertising Service
- Hotel Ecosystem Revisited
  example working directory:
  \Examples\Ex10MultiCore

- Supporting a Multicore Deployment

Chapter 7

MULTICORE ENVIRONMENT

A e-speak-based service solution that is deployed on a single service engine can be good for demonstration purposes, but it would rarely be a solution that is deployed in production. In a real-world deployment, multiple engines will be deployed for a variety of reasons, including:

- Scalability
- Manageability
- Reliability and high availability
- Organizational boundaries

Scalability is important because a single e-Speak engine can become overloaded as the number of services or other resources deployed on it increases. This over-loading can result in a slow response from the services, as experienced by the service users. A set of e-Speak engines that are optimized for load distribution can ensure satisfactory user experience.

Multiple engines also help in managing the deployment of several services. The deployment process of the ecosystem host can create several groups of engines, with each group dedicated to a certain category of services. An example of such categorization is the Travel ecosystem in which the Hotel services are deployed on a separate group from the Airline services, which, in turn, are separate from the travel companies.

To ensure that a service or an engine is available at all times, it is necessary to create a redundancy-based architecture that allows for system downtimes for maintenance purposes.

The organizational boundaries across which an ecosystem is deployed must be preserved. There may be several separate entities participating together in an ecosystem that deploy their own service engines. These may even be behind firewalls; service-client interactions across firewalls is discussed in Chapter 8. In most cases, individual services would be deployed on dedicated engines that were hosted and managed by the entity it served. For example, in the Hotel ecosystem of Chapter 5, each Hotel service could have been deployed on an individual service engine.

For these reasons, an architecture involving interaction among multiple service engines (cores) must be defined. In this chapter, we discuss the multicore deployment environment, with the factors mentioned previously as the driving forces.

Until now, we have been focusing on a single service engine environment in which both the client and service reside. This is perfect for the purpose of examples and even for small-scale e-Speak deployments. For example, an intranet e-Speak deployment might host the service and client application (or JSP (Java Server Pages)-based browser-client) on a single dedicated machine.

In Chapter 1, Figure 1.5 depicts a complete ecosystem. A systems landscaping exercise can help us understand how many different machines and service engines we require to create such an ecosystem. Figure 7.1 depicts a potential deployment scenario wherein the components are deployed on separate service engines.

7.1   Multicore Architecture

Recall that we discussed in Chapter 2 that a service engine is a single logical machine. Thus, multicore deployment means a scenario in which several e-Speak registered resources are deployed on and communicate across several logical machines. To facilitate such communication, the logical machines themselves must be able to communicate with each other. The route from a client on one logical machine to a service hosted on another logical machine can then be established,

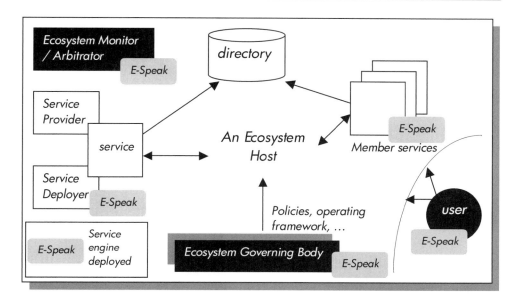

Figure 7.1. Multicore ecosystem deployment.

as depicted in Figure 7.2.

In this setup, the service is deployed on Engine A (Logical Machine A), and the service client is deployed on Engine B (Logical Machine B). The connection between the two engines is established through the Connection Manager resource, as explained in Chapter 2.   As part of this connection, a pair of mailboxes (Inbox and Outbox) is created at each engine for its peer. The client invokes a method from the interface of the service. The service then responds back with the appropriate response. The flow of events in this case is as follows:

1. The client receives the address of the service through the `find` method. In a multicore deployment, e-Speak provides the Advertising service that plays an important role in this step. This service is discussed in detail in the next section.

2. The request from the client is converted into a message, and it is placed in the client's Outbox.

3. The message handler in Engine B picks up this message for delivery. The

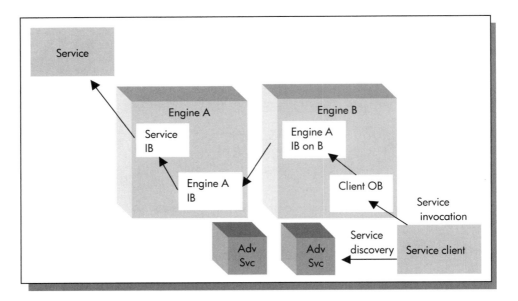

Figure 7.2. Multicore interaction sequence.

envelope of the message denotes that the message is to be delivered to Engine A. Engine B thus delivers the message to the local Inbox it created for Engine A. The message is then delivered to Engine A through the inter-engine connection managed by the Connection Manager.

4. The message handler on Engine A resolves the address on the message envelope to that of the service and delivers the message to the Inbox of the service.

5. The service receives the message, processes the request, and prepares a response message.

6. The response message then travels through the two communicating engines to the client in a similar fashion.

Technically speaking, any logical machine should be able to communicate with any other logical machine. In reality, however, due to manageability and security constraints, a logical machine will talk to a fewer number of peers. Due to this, a *cluster* of logical machines that a logical machine is allowed to talk to must be well organized. E-Speak defines several organization options to establish the communication links between logical machines:

■ An e-Speak group: an e-Speak group is a set of service engines that are closely knit. Typically, this is a set of engines host services that are very close or similar to each other in terms of the functionality they provide. Any search for suitable services initiated on any one of these engines should be extended to other engines in the group, as well.

■ An e-Speak community: an e-Speak community is a set of e-Speak groups that a *client* names in order to specify a meta set of groups that can be searched when a service is desired. Communities represent the client's view of the engine grouping. A client can create a grouping that is different from the grouping on the service side as a result. This provides the flexibility on either end. This policy is commensurate with the local namespace concept discussed in Chapter 2. This lets the clients create their own engine namespaces without knowing or caring about how they are clustered on the service side.

■ A global registry: a global registry is a centralized location that stores metadata of services in a global ecosystem. Registry is analogous to Yellow Pages of businesses, with the exception that it contains *e-services or web services*, not simply business phone numbers. Registries are discussed in detail in Chapter 11.

Figure 7.3 depicts the varying levels of service engines participating together.

The manner in which we deploy groups and communities or even participate in a global registry is accomplished via an intermediary service that stores service registration information. It also makes it easy to search suitable services for clients by adding the ability to extend the search beyond just the local service engine. This intermediary service is called the *Advertising service*. The Advertising service is the mechanism e-Speak provides to allow multiple service engines to exchange and share the service registration information across any number of service engines in the group or community.

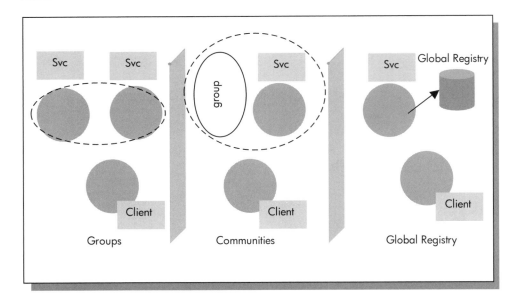

Groups   Communities   Global Registry

Figure 7.3. Levels of multicore interactions.

7.2 The Advertising Service

When services and clients are attached to a single engine, finding a service is a mere task of connecting to the engine and executing a query. However, the scenario changes when services and clients are deployed on separate service engines. There needs to be a resource (or a service) that acts as the intermediary. The Advertising service is an extended e-Speak service that allows services to be located on remote engines. Figure 7.4 depicts a service discovery sequence with the Advertising service. The discovery of a service can happen only if the service has been registered with the service engine *and* advertised by the service engine to an Advertising service, as we depicted in steps 1 and 2 of the figure. Advertising services that are configured to *talk* to each other share resource data, as can be seen in step 3. Finally, clients discover services first in the local service engine, and then in any configured Advertising service groups or communities.

The Advertising service needs to be configured and initiated when the service engine starts so that it can also be started. Advertising service configuration includes

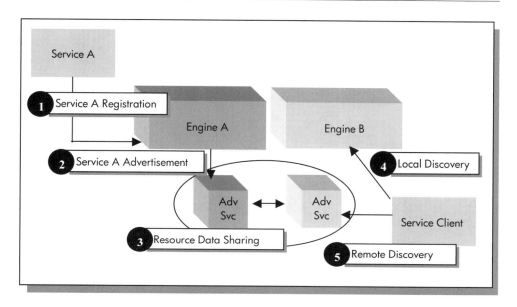

Figure 7.4. Service discovery and the Advertising service.

determining which *group* the Advertising service will participate in. A `find` of a service will occur in all the service engines participating in the group specified. The group allows the Advertising service to put a label on a cluster of services that are related in some way. For example, all the Hotel services could participate in a hotel group and those be "labeled" as such. The group specified by the Advertising service also denotes the group that the associated service engines participate in.

Once the Advertising services and their respective service engines are started, the communication among the different pieces can begin. The Advertising service can be supported by a backend Lightweight Directory Access Protocol (LDAP)-based directory. The LDAP backend directory is recommended for enterprise-wide advertising because it provides a scalable and reliable solution. In Chapter 10, we discuss how the Advertising service and LDAP provide persistent service advertisements. This persistent repository can be used to develop fault-tolerant solutions that allow the Advertising service to fail and restart with the service advertisements intact and available for querying.

The Advertising service can operate in several modes that work at different levels.

Table 7.1. Advertising Service Deployment Scenarios

Deployment Scenario	Runtime Mode	Comments
Internet (worldwide)	Global registry (ESV)	Worldwide applicability and visibility
Intranet (enterprise-wide)	LDAP	Persistent, fault tolerant, highly available
Company LAN (local)	LDAP or SLP	SLP simplifies development and testing
Shared directory	LDAP	Multiple groups can share one LDAP installation

The main difference among these modes is the way the resource information is stored. The Service Location Protocol (SLP) is used to store the directory in memory, while an LDAP-based directory can be used to store this data in an offline mode. The E-services Village (ESV) global registry provides yet another method in which this information can be stored outside an organization and in public domain, if desired. The ESV-based directory is discussed in Chapter 11. We will use the SLP (in-memory mode) in the example that follows. Table 7.1 shows different deployment scenarios for the Advertising service.

To use the Advertising service, when a service registers with the service engine, it must also *advertise* the service to the Advertising service, using the `advertise` method of `ESServiceElement`. The `advertise` method makes the service registration information available to the appropriate peer Advertising services. The Advertising service uses this service metadata available to facilitate queries by clients for desired services that may be on remote engines.

7.3   Hotel Ecosystem Revisited

Remember the Hotel ecosystem from Chapter 5? In that chapter, we deployed all the e-Speak components on a single service engine. However, in a real solution, the Hotel services and the travel client are different companies, with their own identities and networks. We can extend this thought and envision a grander ecosystem in which the individual Airline services and the Airline consortium also deploy their own respective service engines. This would translate into separate service engines for each that are deployed within their own hardware and network infrastructures. Figure 7.5 shows this new Hotel ecosystem deployment.

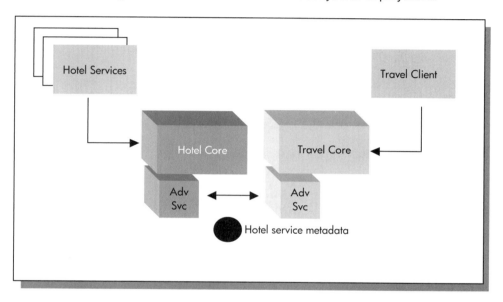

Figure 7.5. Multicore Hotel ecosystem.

In Figure 7.5, notice that we deploy the Hotel services on one service engine and the travel client on another. In a true production deployment, the Hotel services would most likely be deployed on separate service engines commensurate with the organizational boundaries discussed above. We walk through this example to demonstrate how the Advertising service, groups, and communities work together to build this multicore ecosystem. Creating a "multiple logical engines" environment is more of a deployment exercise, rather than a development exercise. The services participating in the ecosystem do not need to undertake any significant programming effort because e-Speak handles all the mediation between different components via the Advertising service and the underlying messaging architecture. The deployment efforts need to focus on planning the partitioning of service engines into groups and configuring the Advertising services for each of the service engines involved to participate in the desired group.

7.3.1 Planning the Hotel Ecosystem

Just as an out-of-band interaction has to happen between a service and a service client (with respect to the service stub required by the service client) to invoke a method on a service, a similar out-of-band interaction must happen between ecosystem players. They need to agree on and be aware of:

1. The appropriate ecosystem vocabularies

2. The host names of different players and their respective roles

3. The relevant group names for Advertising service interactions

In this example, the Hotel services participate in the `HotelGroup` Advertising service group and the Travel service client searches the `HotelGroup` group for the desired services but participates in the `TravelGroup` Advertising service group.

7.3.2 The Advertising Services and Engines in the Hotel Ecosystem

To run the multicore example, the first step is to start the hotel and travel engines.

> **Note**
>
> The machine must be connected to the Internet for the Advertising services to start up correctly.

Although the start commands are the same, note there is a different configuration file for the engines — namely, *TravelCore.ini* and *HotelCore.ini*. This enhanced configuration file carries information about how to start the service engines, as well as the Advertising service.

HotelCore.ini

```
[Tasks]
Start=Core, AdvertisingService

[AdvertisingService]
Class=net.espeak.services.advertise.ypserver.AdvertisingService
Args=-group HotelGroup -mport 1438 -myco codef -esport 12350
    -copath %espeak_home%/config
WaitFor=Core Ready
```

The `Tasks` section denotes the services to be started. We start the engine (core) *and* the Advertising service. The first section configures the service engine start. Notice that the `esport` for each engine, Hotel core and Travel core, are different. This is important in this case because both service engines are on the same hardware machine. Had we actually used two different hardware machines, we could have kept the same `esport`. We are able to start two engines on one hardware environment because of the *logical machine* architecture. However, within an intranet or open Internet, the same procedures described here will work. Service engines communicate in the same manner, as long as regular TCP communication is allowed. In Chapter 8, we discuss the modifications required to facilitate firewall traversal.

TravelCore.ini

```
[Tasks]
Start=Core, AdvertisingService

[AdvertisingService]
Class=net.espeak.services.advertise.ypserver.AdvertisingService
Args=-group TravelGroup -mport 1438 -myco codef -esport 2950
    -copath %espeak_home%/config
WaitFor=Core Ready
```

The second section is the `AdvertisingService` configuration. The arguments provided configure the Advertising service to participate in a *group*, listen on the appropriate group port, and use the service engine on a certain port that it is attached to. Take a look at *TravelCore.ini* and we see that, under the `Tasks` section, we also request that the Advertising service be started. It requires considerably more parameters to start up. The most important ones to note are the `group` and the `Mport`. This is the port on which the Advertising service listens.

We mentioned that the Hotel service engines would participate in the `HotelGroup`. This means that the Advertising service participates in the `HotelGroup` and multicasts resource data on the `mport` specified. In this case, the resource information about the Hotel vocabulary and the Hotel services' metadata are multicast on the `mport`. This will allow any other Advertising services listening on this port to pick up the multicast and make this data available for discovery initiating from the associated local engines.

Note

The Advertising service uses the `Mport` to multicast messages to its peers. These multicasts announce the new Advertising service joining the group. The Advertising services on each engine keep track of their peers that were announced through such multicasts. During search of a service, the Advertising service from where the search is initiated works with its known peers to find appropriate services on corresponding engines. For this mechanism to work, the `Mport` *must* be the same for all the Advertising services that want to work together.

The commands to start the service engine using these modified configuration files are below. Refer to Figures 7.6 and 7.7 to view the started service engines with their respective Advertising services.

```
D:\e-speak\config>..\bin\espeak -i hotelcore.ini
D:\e-speak\config>..\bin\espeak -i travelcore.ini
```

7.3.3   The Hotel Information Service in the Hotel Ecosystem

Although major development changes do not need to be made to services participating in a multicore ecosystem, a small change does need to be made to incorporate the Advertising service functionality. If we examine the Hotel Information

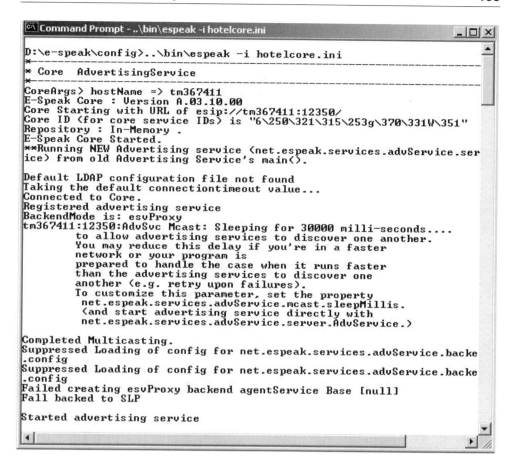

```
Command Prompt - ..\bin\espeak -i hotelcore.ini                    _ □ X

D:\e-speak\config>..\bin\espeak -i hotelcore.ini
*---------------------------------------------------------------
* Core   AdvertisingService
*---------------------------------------------------------------
CoreArgs> hostName => tm367411
E-Speak Core : Version A.03.10.00
Core Starting with URL of esip://tm367411:12350/
Core ID (for core service IDs) is "6\250\321\315\253g\370\331W\351"
Repository : In-Memory .
E-Speak Core Started.
**Running NEW Advertising service (net.espeak.services.advService.ser
ice) from old Advertising Service's main().

Default LDAP configuration file not found
Taking the default connectiontimeout value...
Connected to Core.
Registered advertising service
BackendMode is: esvProxy
tm367411:12350:AdvSvc Mcast: Sleeping for 30000 milli-seconds....
        to allow advertising services to discover one another.
        You may reduce this delay if you're in a faster
        network or your program is
        prepared to handle the case when it runs faster
        than the advertising services to discover one
        another (e.g. retry upon failures).
        To customize this parameter, set the property
        net.espeak.services.advService.mcast.sleepMillis.
        (and start advertising service directly with
        net.espeak.services.advService.server.AdvService.)

Completed Multicasting.
Suppressed Loading of config for net.espeak.services.advService.backe
.config
Suppressed Loading of config for net.espeak.services.advService.backe
.config
Failed creating esvProxy backend agentService Base [null]
Fall backed to SLP

Started advertising service
```

Figure 7.6. Start of Hotel core and Advertising service.

service, we see that there is a slight difference when resources are registered with the engine. The resources (vocabulary and service) must *also* be *advertised*. The `advertise` method publishes the resource metadata to the Advertising service so that it makes it available to other entities. The `advertiseInOtherGroups` method also provided will facilitate advertising the resource information to groups other than the one associated with the local service engine/Advertising service infrastructure.

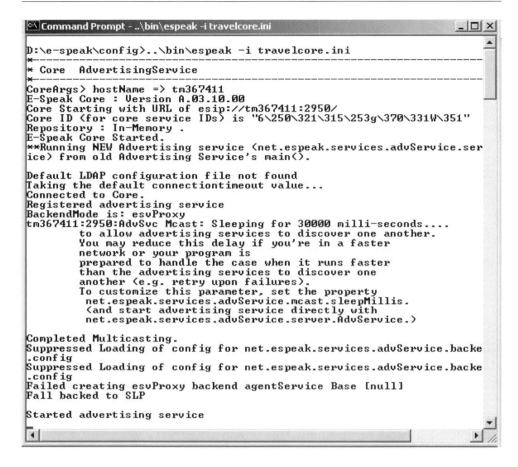

Figure 7.7. Start of Travel core and Advertising service.

HotelInformationService.java

```
try
{
    vocab = myVocabElement.register();
    myVocabElement.advertise();
    ...
    myServiceElement.advertise();
}
```

When the `HotelInformationService` is deployed, the vocabulary and the service will be available via the Advertising service. Our next step is to begin the `HotelInformationService` with its own *service.prop*, both found in the directory for this chapter.

```
C:\java -Despeak_home=d:\e-speak HotelInformationService
   .\Service.prop ..\Shared\EasyInn.ini EasyInn
```

The *service.prop* contains modified configuration information. When the service is deployed and started, we tell it which service engine to connect to. In this case, we are asking it to connect to the service engine on port `12350`, which is the Hotel core. Note that the engine that these Hotel services are deploying on — that is, the Hotel core — is part of the `HotelGroup` group, as is the Advertising service these services get advertised to. Thus, these services are part of the Hotel group, and their metadata will be multicast to all Advertising services *listening* on the `mport` 1438. The results of starting the Hotel Information service are displayed in Figure 7.8.

service.prop

```
hostname = localhost
portnumber = 12350
community = null
```

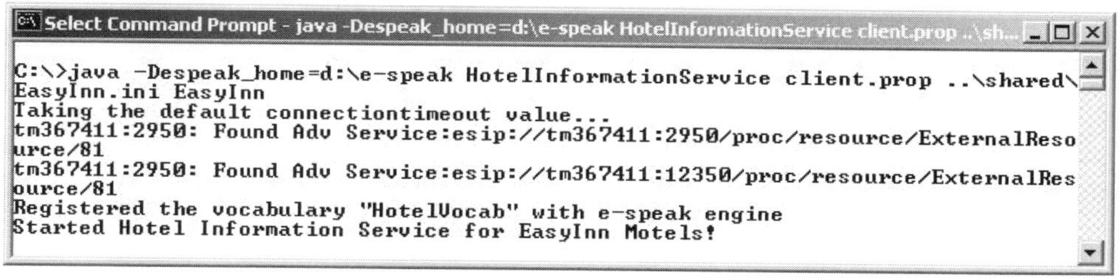
Select Command Prompt - java -Despeak_home=d:\e-speak HotelInformationService client.prop ..\sh...
C:\>java -Despeak_home=d:\e-speak HotelInformationService client.prop ..\shared\
EasyInn.ini EasyInn
Taking the default connectiontimeout value...
tm367411:2950: Found Adv Service:esip://tm367411:2950/proc/resource/ExternalReso
urce/81
tm367411:2950: Found Adv Service:esip://tm367411:12350/proc/resource/ExternalRes
ource/81
Registered the vocabulary "HotelVocab" with e-speak engine
Started Hotel Information Service for EasyInn Motels!

Figure 7.8. Starting the advertised Hotel Information service.

The Client Revisited

As usual, the last step in deploying the ecosystem is for the service user (client) to start. We start the Hotel Information client, also included in the working directory for this chapter. In this case, as well, we start the client with a modified property file. Recall that we need the client to specify which community of groups should be searched when the local engine does not return the desired service. The `community` is denoted in the form of `hostname:service engine port/group`. There can be several comma-separated entries to specify the different groups that can be or should be searched.

client.prop

```
hostname = localhost
portnumber = 2950 # Travelcore service engine
community=localhost:12350/HotelGroup
```

E-Speak provides programmatic ability to change between communities at runtime, using the `ESCommunity` class.

To run the `HotelInformationClient`, run the following command in the working directory for this chapter.

```
C:\>java -Despeak_home=d:\e-speak HotelInformationClient
```

If we launch a query at this Hotel Information service interface, we will notice that there really is no visible difference to the user. However, the services that result from the query are on a *different* service engine. They are deployed on the Hotel core, while the `HotelInformationClient` is deployed, on the Travel core. We can proceed as before, culminating in a hotel rate for the specified destination, dates, and number of nights because the backend processing will also carry on just the same and return the results back to the user.

7.4   Supporting a Multicore Deployment

Current enterprise-level applications involve many components; these components generally have their own lifecycles, deployment issues, and development teams and road maps. However, the unified solution should and does appear to a single whole unit to the end user. The result of this is that, just as complex enterprise application frameworks require a methodical administration plan, so do multicore deployments. Administration and support of a multicore environment involve not only the standard software support practices but also communication, coordination, and negotiation with other parties. This is especially important if a service participates in a mission-critical ecosystem or is an important part of a high-level complex composed service. As the services vision evolves and matures, businesses will rely on business processing or functionality that they might not have any control over, and hence, clear and timely communication will be one of the most important roles of administrators and support engineers of service environments.

Once it is determined that a service needs to be brought down or made unavailable, for reasons such as:

- the hardware it is deployed on needs regularly scheduled maintenance
- the software was diagnosed with a critical problem
- a new version of the service needs to be deployed
- the service has been obsoleted
- the corporate restructuring or other organizational (nontechnical/product) reasons,

E-Speak provides a mechanism to notify Advertising services that the service is unavailable and removes metadata from the online or LDAP repositories. The `unAdvertise` and `unAdvertiseInOtherGroups` methods of `ESServiceElement` remove the entry for the service in the local Advertising service. Once the local Advertising service removes the entry, it will multicast the new, smaller set of resources to its peer Advertising services.

Multiple cores usually involve multiple entities and require communication across network and organizational boundaries. As we cross networks and organizational boundaries, the issue of security and firewall traversal rises to the forefront of the service deployers' concerns. In the next chapter, we discuss how both secured firewall traversal and access control can be deployed in e-Speak solutions.

Security

- Security Levels
- Private Security Environment
  example working directory:
  \Examples\Ex11Security

- Attribute-Based Certificates
- In Action
- Default Security Environment
- Certificate Issuers

Chapter 8

SECURITY

An ecosystem, as described in Chapter 1, consists of several entities, ranging from the ecosystem governing body to the service users. Like a company operating in the real world, a service (which, in fact, represents a company in the ecosystem) also needs to protect its interests in the ecosystem. A service needs to be protected from malicious attacks and other competing services. Security involves securing some combination of the following:

- Access to the service: who has authority to use the service
- Access to different methods of the service: who has what levels of authority on the service methods
- Access to the user data to and from the service: who has access to view and comprehend the data and information flowing to and from the service
- Access to the *user*: who has authorization to communicate with the service user and access user information and data
- Access to the architecture or internal process flows: who has authorization to introspect and extract the business processes that are used by the service

Some part of the service can also be a "trade secret" and must be restricted, even from its legitimate users. The internal pricing structure is a good example of such a trade secret.

Consider the Hotel Information service we created in Chapter 5. This service has a lot of public information, such as the city in which the hotel is located and the contact phone number, and can calculate the rate for a room, based on attributes such as type of the room, the month of stay, and the discount code. It also has some private information, such as the base price for a room and the markup over that. Recall from Chapter 5 that the discount applies only to the markup price. Information such as the base price for a hotel, the markup the hotel charges, and the discount logic are proprietary information to the hotel and must not be shared to the public in general. More importantly, if unauthorized users try to access or change the *private process or information data*, they should be denied access immediately. At the same time, some users do need to have access to that information. Marketing departments, for example, frequently change rates and discounts, based on market trends.

Access control policies play a very important role in this type of scenario. It ensures that, although important, proprietary information is inaccessible to a majority of the users, but a few authenticated and authorized users can get access to it. In this chapter, we look at the security aspect of services. We also demonstrate this security infrastructure by implementing access control for the pricing information. In our example, only the authorized clients (called *pricing administrators*) will be able to view and modify the pricing fields from the pricing table in the hotel database.

E-Speak provides a a very elaborate mechanism for securing the operating environment of a service. In this chapter, we discuss the security architecture provided by e-Speak to secure various aspects of the service.

8.1   Security Levels

The meaning of the word *security* varies a lot in general usage. It is important to discuss the different shades of security to set the proper context. In this book, we use *security* as a resource protection strategy that encompasses several policies. These policies define the behavior of the security architecture at various levels. These policies are, in turn, various *security levels*. Figure 8.1 depicts the different levels of security that can be deployed together to secure various aspects of a service. As we move up in the security stack shown, the result is a more secured environment. Each level, addressing a different aspect of data protection, is discussed next.

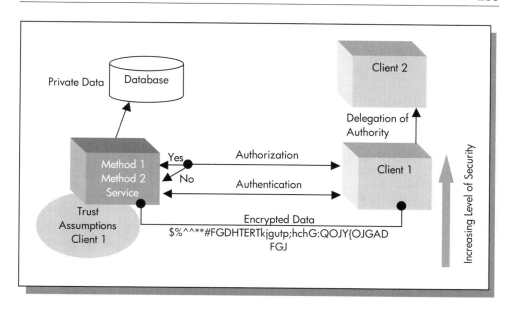

Figure 8.1. Security levels.

8.1.1   Encryption

Encryption is typically associated with codifying data in a *certain* form, so that it is difficult to decipher the data without the proper *decryption* mechanism. Both the encryption — or decryption, in this case — are done using encryption or decryption *keys*. The effectiveness of encryption is directly related to the difficulty in *guessing* or *calculating* the decryption key by a potential intruder. The more difficult it is to guess the key, the more effective the encryption method is. A detailed analysis of encryption techniques is beyond the scope of this book, but there is a variety of encryption mechanisms available.

E-Speak uses a *public key - private key* encryption mechanism. In this technique, a message to a recipient is encrypted using its *public key*. This encrypted message can be decrypted *only* with the *private key* of the recipient. In general, the public key is available to anybody who wishes to send a message to the particular recipient, whereas the private key, as the name suggests, is solely with the recipient. The public key *and* the private key are both required to communicate with a recipient. This is typically called a *key pair*. Figure 8.2 depicts this mechanism.

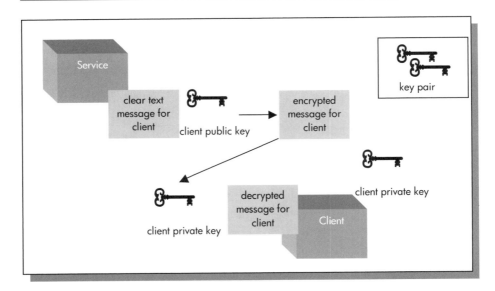

Figure 8.2. Encryption mechanism.

Authentication

Data encryption typically forms the first step in secure communication. It ensures that the *casual* bystander does not overhear *and* comprehend the conversation. There may be solutions in which various components act as conduits for data as it flows to its final destination, thereby *hearing* the conversation, but without the proper decryption keys, it will seem like static or noise. In the computer world, encryption makes it close to impossible for someone to understand the communication by simply *sniffing* the network. Encryption, however, does not inhibit a *rogue* intruder from retrieving the contents of a message in encrypted form. As discussed earlier, once a private key is accessible, anybody can decrypt a message; thus, protecting the network and the keys is very important as well.

The possibility that the private key of a message recipient could be compromised makes it difficult to create a truly secure communication channel. When a response from that recipient is received, we cannot be certain that it really came from the right entity and not from an imposter. This brings the necessity to *authenticate* the communicating entities.

Authentication is a mechanism by which two or more communicating parties in a conversation can ascertain that the other entities involved are truly the same as their identities suggest. Once authentication is complete, the communication can flow smoothly.

E-Speak authentication is done in the form of an electronic document called a *certificate*. A certificate identifies the holder of the certificate. It is this identity that other parties conversing with the certificate holder use to authenticate it. This authentication method involves a *trusted third party* that issues the certificate. The third party, called a *certificate issuer*, must be trusted by all the parties involved in a conversation.

At the beginning of a conversation, the parties wishing to get involved in a conversation present their credentials to each other. These credentials are provided as part of the certificates. If the issuers of the certificates are trusted by all the participants, the certificates are used to authenticate the identities of other participants. The certificate also includes the public key for the certificate holder. The messages to that party can then be encrypted using that public key. Figure 8.3 depicts the interaction and certificate contents.

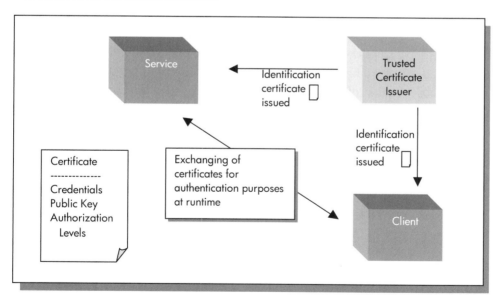

Figure 8.3. Authentication and certificates.

Authorization

An authenticated party can be part of a conversation, but it may not have access or privilege to all information available. For example, typically, users of a service will have certain access privileges when using a service. In fact, there are usually several *levels* among the users — each level with different usage rights. Thus, after a service user is authenticated, it must be authorized to perform a certain operation or to request that a certain task be performed by the service. Usually, a service will create authorization rules based on the *class* or level that the user belongs to, rather than deciding it on an individual basis. Authorization provides an increased level of security by controlling access to privileged information.

Privacy

One of the final levels of security is maintaining the privacy of certain data. Authorization controls the access to the data, even among authenticated parties. Legislated privacy requirements can restrict the usage of data even further. Even though an authorized entity has access to the privileged information, that party might be forbidden to use it without prior knowledge or consent of the primary subject of the data. An example of this is credit-issuing companies. Even though they are authenticated and authorized to have access to the credit cardholder's address, annual income, and preferences, it cannot be shared with anybody without written permission from the cardholder. Moreover, the cardholder can revoke this permission at any time. Privacy of services means that the service can prohibit the end-user from divulging certain data about it (or the data it mediates access to) to other users in the ecosystem.

The four levels of security discussed earlier create a very robust foundation for managing a secure transaction among interested parties. For the purpose of this book and the world of services, these conversations are assumed to be between a service and its users. Recall that a request from a service user (client) to the service flows in the form of messages and the response from the service is also received as a message. An interaction between a service and its client is, thus, a series of messages — messages that form a conversation between the two. Both the client and the service can desire to implement any or all the levels of security measures described earlier. We discuss how e-Speak can help in implementing and enforcing these security measures in this chapter.

A combination of the various security mechanisms discussed earlier provides a progressively more secured environment. However, there are also scenarios in which the security is relaxed a bit. We discuss two such scenarios relevant to this discussion.

Trust Assumptions

In many cases, there is already a built-in trust between two or more parties engaged in a conversation. In such a scenario, the trusting party may be willing to relax the rules of security a bit for a trusted entity. An example of this could be the approval for a travel expense report. If an approving manager trusts the spending judgement of an employee, a travel expense report undergoes a relaxed level of scrutiny. Similarly, a service or a client may relax security around certain shared data or tasks they perform for *specially* trusted entities. Trust assumptions are usually a good way to make an exception to the standard service security policy.

The trust assumption documents are different from the authentication and authorization documents. The authentication documents are generally exchanged among the communicating parties whereas the trust assumption documents are kept locally with the trusting entity, rarely to be shared with anybody. The approval manager almost never divulges his or her trust in the employee to the employee himself!

Delegation of Authority

An entity can take part in a conversation with anybody that trusts the authenticating document (a certificate, in e-Speak world) it provides. The authentication document, thus, is central in starting a conversation. There are situations when an authorized entity is unable to request or perform a certain task, but somebody else it trusts might be willing and able to do so *on behalf of* the authorized entity. Continuing with the approving travel expense example, the approving manager may be planning a vacation and must hand over all the responsibility to some other employee who can do the job and can be trusted. The approving manager can give approval authority to another employee for the duration of the vacation. This is called *delegation of authority*. The ability to delegate creates a powerful mechanism to transfer certain responsibilities to request or perform a task in the web services world.

The e-Speak security infrastructure provides architecture to manage all of the concepts described above. It uses a certificate approach based on the Public Key Infrastructure (PKI) standard. There are two types of certificates available: attribute-based certificates and name-based certificates.

The basis of e-Speak access control is the PKI, sometimes also known as Public Key Cryptography. More specifically, e-Speak implements the Simple Public Key Infrastructure (SPKI). The interested reader is referred to the references at the end of *E-Speak Architecture Guide* for more information on these two security specifications. At the core of the PKI infrastructure are the key-pairs explained above. These keys, the identities, and the authorization tags, bundled together in certificates, form the total security infrastructure for an e-Speak entity.

Every e-Speak entity or e-Speak registered resource is required to have a certificate. This also means that they are associated with a key-pair. The entities are identified by their public key. Entities are authenticated by verifying that they know the corresponding private key. The key-pair for each entity is assumed to be unique. No entity should intentionally share its private key with any other entity in the ecosystem. Doing so violates the assumptions about security. An entity can have many certificates issued by various entities in an ecosystem or even from several ecosystems. Any interaction between the two entities involves exchanging information from certificates issued by each other to encrypt the data, as well as to validate access to any data or functionality. To deploy security, the following could be implemented:

- Create a key-pair for each role that an entity will assume in the ecosystem. Every participating entity must have at least one key-pair.

- Issue an identity authentication for each entity. This certificate identifies the entity and is the basic trust assumption.

- Issue certificates from issuers to the appropriate certificate holders (subjects), specifying access rights.

■ Create a configuration file for each entity that ties together all the security components.

■ Start the entity by specifying the configuration file to deploy entity-specific security components.

It is clear from this description that certificates and key-pairs are important assets for an e-Speak entity to maintain a secure environment — deploy-time and transaction-time. E-Speak's current security environment does not provide protection and management of the key-pairs for an entity. Each entity must provide means to protect these pairs. The e-Speak environment provides a *keystore* to store the key-pairs. This keystore is called *Private Security Environment* (PSE).

8.2   Private Security Environment

A PSE stores key-pairs in an encrypted file on the computer's disk. To open and use the PSE file, a password must be provided. This password is used to encrypt the data (key-pairs) in the file. Access to the PSE file *must* be managed at the operating system (OS) level.

Although it is possible to keep several key-pairs in a PSE file, in reality, only *related* key-pairs must be kept together. For several reasons, it is possible that an entity can have different *roles* when interacting with other entities. Each such role would be associated with the key-pair in the PSE file for that entity. E-Speak supports multiple roles for entities in the ecosystem. While running, the entity can specify the role that it wishes to adorn and use the corresponding key-pairs.

A PSE Manager tool is provided with the e-Speak distribution and can be used to create the key-pairs for any entity. In a production environment, the certificates are typically issued by a trusted third party in the ecosystem. In the Secure Hotel service environment, we have three roles, as described in Table 8.1.

8.2.1   PSE Manager in the Secure Hotel Ecosystem

The Hotel Information service caters to requests from several clients for room rates and other information. It needs to be able to provide this *public* information while

Table 8.1. Roles in the Secure Hotel Service Environment

Entity	Role	Description
Hotel Service	Service	Provide rate information. Needs to protect pricing data.
Hotel Client	Client	Ability to get public information about hotel rates.
Pricing Administrator	Admin	Ability to get and modify pricing fields in the pricing database.

protecting the proprietary pricing logic and related information. The clients must be allowed to get the public rate information and must be denied access for any requests that can expose the internal pricing logic. The pricing administrators, on the other hand, are allowed access to modify the pricing data, using methods provided in the interface of the Hotel Information service. We introduce a new method in the `HotelInquiryIntf` interface to change pricing information.

HotelInquiryIntf.esidl

```
public interface HotelInquiryIntf extends ESService {
...
public void changeRoomRates(String roomType, int startMonth,
   double newBase, double newMarkup)
...
```

As we explained earlier, a separate PSE containing key-pairs for each of the roles needs to be created. Although we keep all the PSE files on the same machine for the purpose of the book, in reality, these PSEs should be kept on individual computers behind the respective organizational firewalls.

Using the PSE Manager tool, a PSE for each of the roles discussed in Table 8.1 can be created as follows:

Start the PSE Manager from the Windows Start menu (Figure 8.4).

The PSE Manager is useful for creating key-pairs for all entities, as well as for granting certificates. With these capabilities, it provides a comprehensive environ-

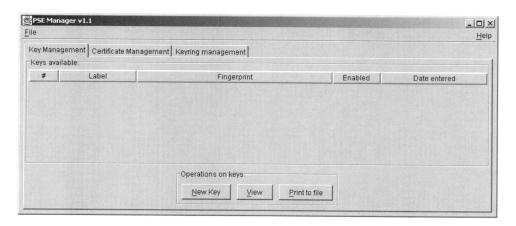

Figure 8.4. PSE Manager.

ment to manage all security instruments needed to deploy security in e-Speak. Click on File → New to create a new PSE environment for an entity. This prompts for a password for that PSE, as shown in Figure 8.5. Recall that each PSE is associated with a password (called *passphrase* in e-Speak security jargon) that is used to encrypt the PSE file.

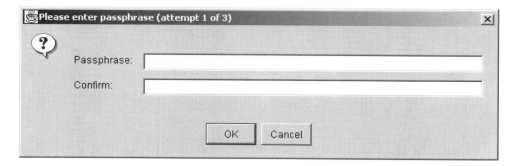

Figure 8.5. Creating a new PSE.

Click on the `New Key` button to create a key within this PSE. This will pop up a dialog box for the *Key Label*. This key label corresponds to a role. Thus, for the role `service` the key label should be mentioned as shown in Figure 8.6. Click the `Ok` button after specifying the key label.

Figure 8.6. Specifying key label for a role.

A new key is generated and appears in the PSE Manager window. The generated key for the role `service` is shown in Figure 8.7.

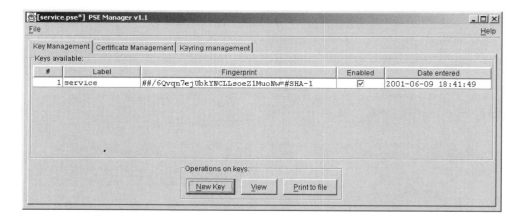

Figure 8.7. Generated key-pair for the role `service`.

Click File → Save to save the generated key-pair. In the example code, this PSE is stored in a file *service.pse*. The PSEs for the other roles associated with the example still need to be created. Specifically, PSEs for the client and the pricing administrator roles would also be created using the PSE Manager. We have provided these PSEs in the files *service.pse, client.pse,* and *admin.pse.* The roles, the corresponding key-pair files, and the associated passwords fot this example are listed in Table 8.2.

Table 8.2. The PSE Files for the Secure Hotel Ecosystem

Role	PSE File	PSE Password
Service	*service.pse*	service123
Client	*client.pse*	client123
Admin	*admin.pse*	admin123

Note

The PSE files and the certificates that are provided with the book are tied to our e-Speak installation. It uses the key-pair from *our* specific e-Speak instance. Since that key-pair is different from the engine key-pair for your installation, the certificates will be rejected by your engine instance.

Note that the PSE contains both the private as well as the public key for a particular role. Once these key-pairs are generated, the entities can authenticate each other and encrypt the data, using the appropriate key, to ensure that only the appropriate entity can retrieve that data. However, the key-pairs are only part of the answer to secure inter-entity communication. The other part is granting access rights by means of certificates.

8.3   Attribute-Based Certificates

As we discussed earlier, certificates are documents that authenticate the identity of an entity. In addition, a certificate can also contain several additional pieces of information. E-Speak provides two types of certificates:

- Attribute-based or authorization certificates
- Name-based certificates

Authorization certificates bind a tag to a public key or a name. Name-based certificates bind a name to a public key or a name. In this example, we discuss and use authorization certificates. Both these certificates consist of some common fields,

such as service identification, issuer, and subject.   Table 8.3 summarizes the
typical certificate fields and their purpose.

Table 8.3. Attribute Certificate Fields

Certificate Field	Purpose
cert	Certificate header
version	Certificate version
cert-display	Display hints for the certificate
issuer	Public key of the certificate issuer
subject	Public key of the certificate holder
deleg	Optional field denoting whether the certificate authorization can be delegated
tag	An expression specifying the access rights
not-before	Earliest date that the certificate is valid
not-after	Latest date that the certificate is valid

8.3.1   Authorization Certificate Structure

Structurally, an authorization certificate is of the form:

```
<cert> = "(" "cert" <version>? <cert-display>?
<issuer> <issuer-info>?
<subject> <subject-info>?
<deleg>?
<tag>
<not-before>
<not-after>
")" ;
```

The first line in the certificate is called the *certificate header*. It starts with a constant field beginning " (cert ". The version field is optional and denotes the version of the certificate. The certificate issuer can set this field for tracking the certificate versions. The `cert-display` field can provide any display-related information that can be used during visual representation of the certificate. The `version` and `cert-display` fields are not used in the current e-Speak implementation. If any certificate contains these fields, they are ignored. However, a utility such as the PSE Manager can use these fields for better certificate management. The `issuer` field denotes the issuer of the certificate. Both the entities engaged in an interaction must trust the issuer of the certificate. The issuer is denoted by its own public key, rather than a name.   The `subject` field denotes the certificate holder. Again, it is denoted using its public key.

The `deleg` field is optional and denotes whether the certificate can be delegated by the subject to some other entity.   The `tag` field is used to specify the access rights for certificate holder. There are two validation fields in a certificate. The `not-before` field depicts the date on which the certificate becomes valid.   The `not-after` field denotes the date after which the certificate is not valid. Together, these two dates determine the validity period of the certificate.

8.3.2   Authorization Tags

Of these fields, the `tag` field is the most instrumental because it grants certain access rights to the certificate holder. The tags are an *expression* that denotes access rights for the certificate holder. These tags can have any valid SPKI string. Note that, although certificates and tags are generated at deploy-time, access rights must be evaluated between any two interacting parties and are, thus, enforced dynamically at runtime. The e-Speak engine uses the `tag` field at runtime to evaluate whether the certificate holder has the access permissions to perform the requested operation and allows or denies that operation accordingly. Authorization tags are used to grant access to a resource. In the Secure Hotel example, the general user requires access to all the methods of the `HotelInquiryIntf` interface except the `changeRoomRates` method. Only the authorized pricing administrators should have the access to that particular method. The authorization tags in the certificates issued to the general users and the pricing administrators reflect these access permissions. The authorization tags are of the form:

```
(tag (net.espeak.method <interface> <method> <serviceId>))
```

The string `net.espeak.method` specifies that the authorization is at the method level. In a similar way, `net.espeak.action` specifies an action-level authorization. The `<interface>` specifies the interface to which the method belongs. The `<method>` specifies the actual method or methods to which the issuer explicitly grants access to the certificate holder. The `<serviceId>` field denotes the ID of the certificate holder. This field is optional. E-Speak provides a default value for this field if it is not specified.

Of the various tag options, we use the `prefix` form tag. In this form, the tag specifies the a prefix string that is used during the validation. In the method-based authorization mechanism, the tag specifies the set of methods with names beginning with the prefix string. In the Secure Hotel example, general users are granted access to all the methods that have the prefix *get*.

The `tag` field for the general user certificate, thus, is as follows:

```
("net.espeak.method" "HotelInquiryIntf" (* prefix "get"))
```

The * can be used as a wildcard. Thus, any of the subfields can use the wildcard to specify the access rights. To grant carte blanche access to a certificate holder, the tag field can be set to:

```
("net.espeak.method" (*) (*) (*))
```

A shorthand representation of this is (*) or (), which can also be used if desired.

Note

The certificate tag is a very versatile field that can be used to specify a rich set of validations. For example, it can be used to grant permissions to files or specify a range on a certain field. The application receiving the certificate can use this field to enforce these validations. The *E-Speak Architecture Guide* provides several examples of tag-based validations.

8.3.3   Granting Access

The PSE Manager used earlier can be used to create certificates — each certificate granting specific access rights from the issuers to the subjects. As we mentioned earlier, e-Speak provides the most restrictive security environment. Thus, each entity involved in an interaction, including the service engine, must grant access to respective parties.

As discussed in the previous section, the service must grant certain access rights to general users, as well as pricing administrators.   Recall that the certificate includes the public keys of both the issuer and the subject. This means that we need access to both these keys, and the two parties must trust the key presented by the other party. In a way, this forms the *trust assumptions* for the entities involved. In the current e-Speak implementation, trust assumptions are in the form of *self-signed certificates*. Self-signed certificates are certificates for which the issuer and the subject are the same. Any entity trusts the other entity that presents a self-issued certificate. In the real world, this is, of course, a rather weak assumption.

Issuing Self-Signed Certificates

To issue a self-signed certificate, only the public key of the entity is required. The steps for issuing a self-signed certificate for the Hotel service follow:

Start the PSE Manager from the Start menu as before. Click on File $\rightarrow$ Open to open the *service.pse* file. This file contains the key-pair for the Hotel service. When asked for the passphrase, provide the passphrase you set before for the PSE. When the PSE file is successfully opened, the PSE Manager window should look similar to the Figure 8.7. Click on the Certificate Management tab and click on the New button. A certificate window appears that shows the fields for the certificate. The issuer key is automatically set to the public key from the PSE. In the Subject section of the window, click on the pull-down menu and choose the PSE option. The location and the key are automatically filled in. Make sure that the issuer and the subject keys match. Refer to Figure 8.8 for more details.

Set the tag section to the string (*). Recall that the wildcard entry provides free access for the service to its own resources. The May Delegate? checkbox indicates whether the subject can delegate this certificate access rights to another

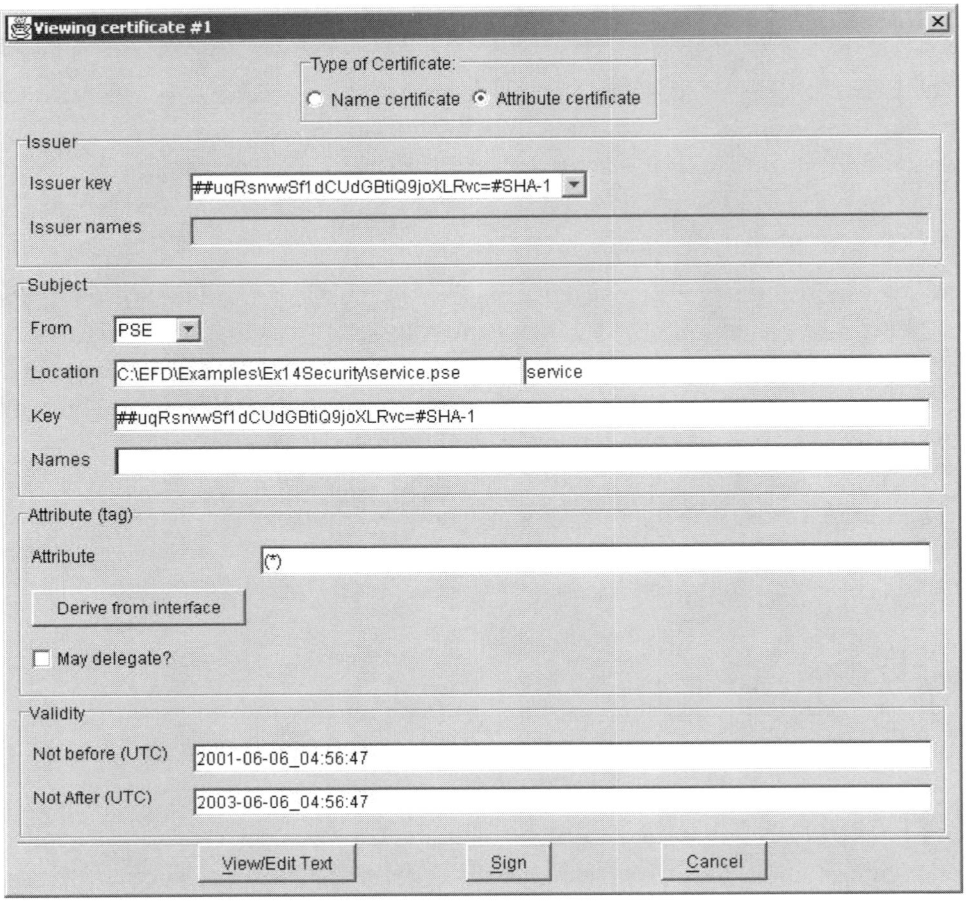

Figure 8.8. Self-signed certificate.

entity. This field is not used in the Secure Hotel example. For a real certificate, on the other hand, this field must be carefully set, based on the trust between the issuer and the subject.

A certificate granting access is usually granted for a specific duration. Usually, this duration is part of the contractual agreement between the issuers and the subject of the certificate. The validity period of the certificate is denoted by the `Not Before` and `Not After` text areas.

Note

The validity period dates have some common checks to ensure that the validity period is correct. The `Not After` date cannot be chronologically before the `Not Before` date. Also, the two dates cannot be the same, although they are set that way by default. This ensures that the certificate is valid at least for one second.

The raw contents of the certificate can be viewed by clicking the `View/Edit Text` button in the Certificate window. The contents for the self-signed certificate for the service are shown in Figure 8.9. The text window showing the contents can be used to modify the contents, thereby changing the certificate.

```
View/edit SPKI certificate text                                                      ×
226\200\032\306\025\240w\'\336\f\371\023x\344\252/\320\207H\313r\007\240t\304\220\037\b\214\221
^\211\274\2543t\331\000\306\"UZE\217\375\232\b\035W\343\r\203\275"))
         (subject (public-key rsa-pkcs1 "\000\021\001\000\001\004\000\331\032.\3506\352\222I\371j
&\bW\210`\036\354!\370\336\020d\340\326:F\316\373]\267\024\201\344y+\030\335\016Q\212\337\230\35
1\255&\275\365\330\206\3419\n\022\210\t\271\216\032\361k\324\273\34053Wi\365/\206\316\2002\253\2
26\200\032\306\025\240w\'\336\f\371\023x\344\252/\320\207H\313r\007\2402t\304\220\037\b\214\221^
\211\274\2543t\331\000\306\"UZE\217\375\232\b\035W\343\r\203\275"))
         (tag (*))
         (not-before 2001-06-06_04:56:47)
         (not-after 2003-06-06_04:56:47)
         )
                    Accept edit              Cancel
```

Figure 8.9. Certificate contents in raw form.

Click on `Accept edit` to close the window. To issue the certificate, click on the `Sign` button. The new certificate will now appear in the PSE Manager window. Choose File → Save to save the certificate. Note that the certificates must be stored in a separate file from the PSE key-pairs. This is because, although the PSE is a *private* keystore and must be kept secure, the certificates are by definition accessed by at least one more entity (the issuer) besides the certificate holder, and access to the certificates is less restrictive than the keystore. It must also be noted that a single entity can have several certificates associated with it — one certificate per interaction per interacting entity. Thus, it makes sense to store all the certificates for an entity in a separate file. For the Secure Hotel service, its certificates are kept in the *servicehotelinformation.certs* file.

Note

It is possible to keep the certificates in several different files. Such an organization would be necessary if the access levels to different certificates for the same entity need to be different. For example, within an entity, certain certificates may be accessible only to the system administrators within that entity, whereas the general users have access only to certain certificates. To enforce such a security policy, it is necessary to keep the certificates in different files. From the e-Speak point of view, this organization of certificates is transparent.

In a similar fashion, all the other entities must issue a self-signed certificate. The files where the certificates for each entity are store are shown in Table 8.4.

Table 8.4. The Certificate Files for the Secure Hotel Ecosystem

Role	Certificate File
Service	*servicehotelinformation.certs*
Client	*clienthotelinformation.certs*
Admin	*adminhotelinformation.certs*

Granting Access to Other Entities

Certificates to the other entities can be issued in a similar manner. In this case, however, a different combination of PSE files is needed. For example, to issue a certificate from the service engine to the Secure Hotel service, we need access to public keys of both the entities. In the PSE Manager, this is achieved using the PSE keystore of the issuer entity and the self-signed certificate of the subject entity. Thus, to issue a free-access certificate from the service engine to the Secure Hotel service, the following steps are required:

Start the PSE Manager. Choose File $\rightarrow$ Open and load the service engine PSE. Note that the service engine PSE is in the file $<installDir>\config\securestore.bin$. The password for this PSE is `default passphrase`. This is the default e-Speak engine PSE passphrase set during installation of any e-Speak engine. This PSE contains three roles — `core`, `service`, and `client`. By default, the engine assumes the role with the tag `client`. We explain the reason behind this shortly. To differentiate between these roles (service and client) and the roles with similar names that we have defined, they are denoted as `Engine-Client` and `Engine-Service`. It must be noted that the actual roles in the engine PSE are still `client` and `service`, respectively.

Click on the `Certificate Management` tab. Choose File → Open and load the file that stores the certificates for the subject (in this case, *servicehotelinformation.certs*). Visually note the public key of the subject. Click on the `New` button. The certificate window appears. Choose the issuer role to be `client`. Note, this is the role for the engine. Click on the drop-down menu for the `Subject` area and choose `Other`. This pops up a drop-down dialog box to choose a key. Choose the key for the subject. Notice that related fields are automatically filled in. The `tag` field should be set to (*) for free access, as explained earlier.

A set of certificates must be issued accordingly between various interacting entities. Table 8.5, Table 8.6, Table 8.7, and Table 8.8 depict the list of certificates and corresponding authorizations for them. All these certificates are set to have validity until 2003. Note that, except for the certificate issued by the Hotel service to its general user role ("client"), all the certificates grant free access to the certificate holder.

Table 8.5. Certificates for Core in File $<installDir>\config\clientcerts.adr$

Issuer	Subject	Attribute Tag
Engine-Client	engine-client	()
Engine-Core	engine-client	()
Engine-Service	engine-client	()

Table 8.6. Certificates for Secure Hotel Service in File *servicehotelinformation.certs*

Issuer	Subject	Attribute Tag
Service	service	(*)
Engine-Client	service	(*)

Finally, when launching each of the entities, the security environment that it uses

Table 8.7. Certificates for Secure Hotel Client in File *clienthotelinformation.certs*

Issuer	Subject	Attribute Tag
client	client	(*)
Engine-Client	client	(*)
service	client	("net.espeak.method" "HotelInquiryIntf" (* prefix "get"))

Table 8.8. Certificates for Secure Hotel Pricing Administrator in File *adminhotelinformation.certs*

Issuer	**Subject**	**Attribute Tag**
admin	admin	(*)
Engine-Client	admin	(*)
service	admin	(*)

must be specified. The security environment is specified in a configuration file and it is then communicated to the JESI library classes instantiated for the specific entity. Because the security environments are different for each entity in this example, we need adequate number of distinct files specifying it. For the Secure Hotel service, for example, its security configuration is in file *service.cfg*.

service.cfg

```
! Set a property prefix.
@prefix=net.espeak.security

! Activate the security
.activate = on

! Name of the PSE file
.pse.storefile = service.pse

! Mode for verifying the passphrase
.pse.mode   = passphrase
```

```
! The passphrase for the PSE
.pse.passphrase = service123

! Role of this application (key label)
.pse.role = service

! Name of the file containing the certificate (without
! the role prefix - service )
.pse.certfile = hotelinformation.certs
```

When launching the service `net.espeak.util.config.file`, the command-line property specifies the configuration file to use. The configurations for the service client and the pricing administrators are in the files *client.cfg* and *admin.cfg*, respectively.

8.4   In Action

To run this example, start the engine in the usual manner. You need to start the Hotel service and the clients differently compared with previous examples. In a separate window, enter the following command from the example working directory to start the service:

```
C:\> java -Dnet.espeak.util.config.file=service.cfg
    HotelInformationService ..\Shared\EasyInn.ini EasyInn
```

Ignore the warning message regarding the loggers. This warning is a result of the configuration file, *service.cfg*, not having any information about the error loggers. This will start the default e-Speak error logger. The JESI libraries automatically take care of the presentation of certificates to appropriate entities (the service engine, in this case).

If the security environment is not deployed properly, the engine will not accept the registration request from the service, and the engine window will show an unauthorized request message, as shown in Figure 8.10.

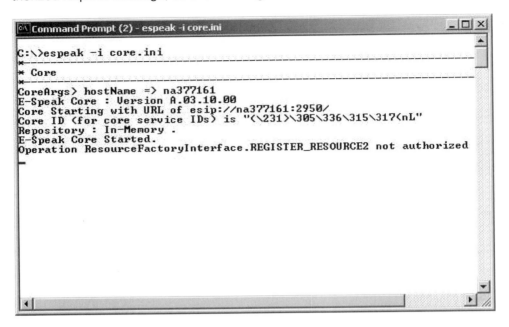

Figure 8.10. Engine message for unauthorized access.

This will also cause the service to terminate. If this happens, check the certificates and the roles of corresponding entities and ensure that the certificates are granted to and from appropriate roles. Recall that the configuration file denotes the role that the entity assumes.

After successful start of the service, start the general user by issuing the following command:

```
C:\> java -Dnet.espeak.util.config.file=client.cfg
    HotelInformationClient
```

The client goes through dialogs similar to previous examples. After a hotel is chosen, the user is given an option to either view the price for a room type or change rates for a room. When the first option is chosen, the client provides the pricing information as in earlier examples. For the second option, remember that the certificate set that the client has does not have permission to access the method to change the rate information for the room. If the client tries to do that, the exception `ESInvocationException` is thrown and the client terminates, as shown in Figure 8.11.

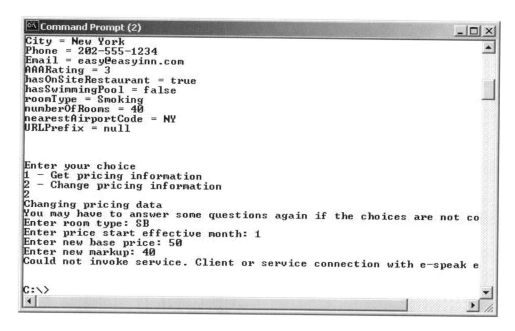

Figure 8.11. Room rate change with unauthorized access.

To invoke this method successfully, the client needs to provide the access rights for the pricing administrator. This can be achieved by:

```
C:\> java -Dnet.espeak.util.config.file=admin.cfg
    HotelInformationClient
```

The client can successfully change the rate information, as depicted in Figure 8.12.

In either case (authorized or unauthorized access), the service window shows the Structured Query Language (SQL) statement to update the database.

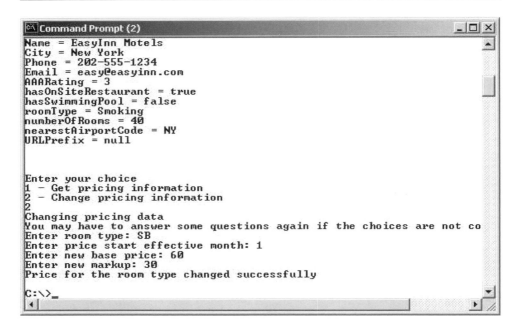

Figure 8.12. Room rate change with authorized access.

8.5   Default Security Environment

Until this example, we had not used the security environment, despite the e-Speak policy of using most restrictive access control. So how did the programs run without any security until now? The answer to that question is the way in which the service and client classes were being run. In the previous examples, we set a property for this when starting the service or the client. For example, the Hotel service was started as:

```
java -Despeak_home=c:\e-speak HotelInformationService
     ..\Shared\EasyInn.ini EasyInn
```

The property `espeak_home` denotes the location of the e-Speak installation. When this property is set, the JESI library components use it to locate the *default security environment*. More specifically, they look for *<installDir>\config\espeak.cfg*, *<installDir>\config\securestore.bin*, and *<installDir>\config\clientcerts.adr*. The necessary security parameters to run any resource through the JESI library are provided in these files. Note that, as discussed earlier, these are the same files that are used to start the engine, as well.

Since all the entities in such a scenario use the same configuration file, keystore, and certificate set, from the security standpoint, they are all identical. Each of the entities (in this case, the engine, a service, and a client) uses the role `client` from the keystore and presents the same set of certificates. Since the role `client` grants free access to itself, all entities started this way can access any resources managed by other entities started in the same manner.

The same argument is also true in the multicore environment. In that scenario, the two engines use the same set of roles, key-pairs, and certificates. In a real-world scenario for a multicore environment, the two engine installations will not share the security components, and each of them must grant each other certificates with specific access rights.

8.6   Certificate Issuers

In the example discussed in this chapter, we used the PSE Manager to create key-pairs and grant certificates to various entities. There was no special entity that was specifically responsible for this. In reality, however, this model is not likely to succeed. Any entity can create any identity using this mechanism and present it when asked for one. This poses a security threat because entities can pose as each other. Such identity thefts will violate the fundamental trust assumption in the security — a certificate represents the *true* identity of an entity.

Fortunately, there is a solution to this problem that already exists. In this solution, the task of granting key-pairs and identity certificates is assumed by an entity called a *certificate authority* (sometimes abbreviated as CA). A certificate authority has the responsibility to verify the identity of an entity before granting key-pairs and identity certificates. In such a scenario, the identity certificates issued by the certificate authority take the place of the self-issued certificates we used in this example. The `Issuer` field in such a certificate is set to the public key of the certificate authority. Naturally, this creates the problem of trusting the certificate authority.

In the real world, several certificate authorities can assume the responsibility of granting certificates. The company VeriSign, Inc. is a good example of certificate authority. When an ecosystem decides to use a certificate-based security mechanism, it must also choose a set of certificate authorities it will trust. Typically, the decision as to which certificate authorities should be trusted is made by the ecosystem governing body. The member services and clients then must get a certificate verifying their identity from one of the *approved* certificate authorities.

Securing services is a very important part of the service lifecycle planning and development phases. Designing for security must be a high priority for the service developer and deployer. However, the software architecture discussed in this chapter is just one aspect of security.

More importantly and sometimes easily forgotten is attention to *revoking privileges*. Ensuring that the authentication databases are updated and fresh is an important part of security, as well, because it assists in determining who has access and to what level. Proper *cancellation* and *termination* procedures must be followed to lock out access for those that have since lost the authorization for a service. For example, a service pricing administrator may move on to a new position but the appropriate certificates may not have been revoked in a timely fashion.

Another important security consideration is securing the physical environment. The services should be deployed on servers that are located in a secured environment or data center where only authorized users have physical access to the service. The network surrounding the service also needs to be secured to ensure that the service does not increase the vulnerability to malicious attacks. The firewall is an effective mechanism for network security.

Firewall Traversal

- Firewalls and E-speak Services

- Accessing a Service Inside a Firewall

- Hotel Ecosystem with Firewalls
  example working directory:
  \Examples\Ex12FirewallTraversal

- In Action

- Security Considerations

- Accessing a Service Outside a Firewall

Chapter 9

FIREWALL TRAVERSAL

In Chapter 7, we demonstrated the use of the Advertising service to link several engines together. Typically, service engines of different entities (or companies) will be protected and separated by firewalls. Firewalls protect local area networks from malicious intrusions and access to internal assets. Internet firewalls allow network administrators to define a centralized gate that tries to keep unauthorized users, such as hackers, crackers, vandals, and spies, out of a protected network; it usually prohibits potentially vulnerable services from entering or leaving the protected network; it provides protection from several types of routing attacks.

Firewalls simply act as access control gates in both directions. Network packets are examined for authenticated origin and destination (IP addresses) and could be rejected if traveling to or from unauthorized IP addresses. However, should an intruder manage to make its way through the firewall, it can cause havoc because the firewall gateway does not have control inside the firewall. E-Speak authentication or user-access level security provides an added layer of security beyond the firewall protection. This is discussed in Chapter 8.

In the previous chapters, we deployed services on single engines without any firewalls. We do realize, however, that firewalls play a very important role in any corporate deployment; thus, firewall traversal is an important feature of the e-Speak technology.

The Hotel ecosystem, made up of Hotel services and a Travel service client, were deployed on multiple cores in Chapter 7; however, there was no firewall protection. In this section, we deploy the Hotel ecosystem with firewalls to protect the Hotel services and the Travel service client. The firewall around the Hotel services can protect the services from malicious attacks on the pricing database or even denial of service attacks.

9.1   Firewalls and E-speak Services

The firewall works well to secure the e-Speak services behind it. The network administrator will configure the firewall to grant access, depending on the entity trying to access the internal assets and services. For example, company policies might grant unrestricted intranet access; these policies can be modified to allow access to an authorized third-party. This third-party entity could be a co-development partner or a vendor with special ties. Figure 9.1 depicts this type of access policy.

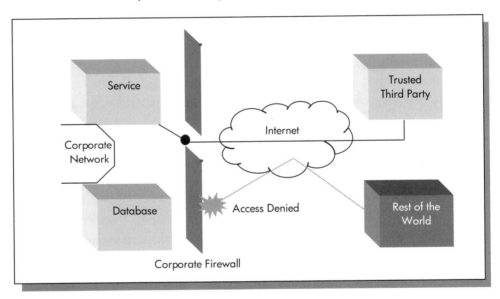

Figure 9.1. Punching firewall holes.

However, companies that do allow access to external entities need to go through a rather heavyweight process of *punching a hole in the firewall*. This can allow companies to access *specific* assets as per an established relationship. The process usually involves business- and technical-level discussions, as well as an intense security evaluation to ensure that the *hole* will not increase the vulnerability to malicious attacks. The process can be very cumbersome (mainly from a business side, rather than the technology side), and hence, the kinds of partners for which this happens would be few and far between. Similarly, when the special nature of the relationship ends, the *hole* that was created needs to be plugged, which again requires some level of tracking and administration.

However, observe our Hotel services in the Hotel ecosystem. The relationship formed between a service user (delivered via the Travel service client) and the service is inherently dynamic in nature. It would be difficult and counterproductive to know ahead of time who all the service users are so that provisions could be made allowing them access to the Hotel services. Recall that we cannot simply move the Hotel services outside the firewall because that would leave some of the backend processing systems vulnerable to attack. There needs to be some way to protect the e-Speak services behind a firewall while still allowing dynamic access by service users served via e-Speak search and match-making functionality.

The two interactions that are interesting to examine are listed here and depicted in Figure 9.2:

- Allowing internal clients to access external services
- Allowing external clients to access internal services

For our example, the latter is more applicable: How do we allow external service users access to the Hotel services located inside firewalls? The issue of allowing internal clients access to external services is discussed at the end of this chapter.

An external service user needs restricted access to a protected service (service within a firewall). The service user needs to be able to review the metadata of a service, as well as invoke methods on a discovered service with associated data. These interactions must occur through the firewalls involved.

9.2   Accessing a Service Inside a Firewall

E-Speak provides two architectures to allow access to a service inside a firewall from a client inside another firewall.   The firewall gateway and the connector

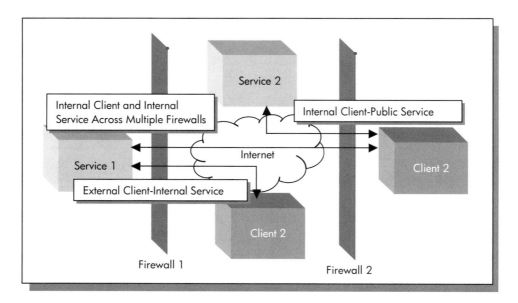

Figure 9.2. Firewall interaction types.

scenario both achieve this goal.

The e-Speak firewall gateway is a *software* gateway. It mediates access to e-Speak services deployed behind a firewall from external clients (either in the public Internet or behind a different firewall). It does so by authenticating and authorizing access from the external clients using Session Layer Security (SLS) certificates.

The second architectural option is the *connector scenario*. The example included in this chapter demonstrates use of the connector scenario.

9.2.1   Connector Scenario

The connector scenario, Figure 9.3, exposes services deployed behind a firewall to service users on the Internet or behind a firewall of another company. The connector scenario uses a set of e-Speak engines to provide *virtual connections* between the service and the client.

A typical connector scenario consists of three engines:

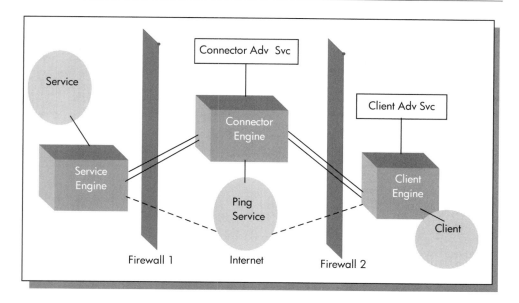

Figure 9.3. Connector scenario.

1. The engine deploying the service inside a firewall

2. The engine deploying the client inside a different firewall

3. The engine managing the virtual connection between the service and the client

This solution is depicted in Figure 9.3. Remember that firewalls are usually finicky about inbound traffic. Outbound traffic is less restricted and is usually facilitated by a Web proxy (for Hypertext Transfer Protocol [HTTP] communication) or a socks server (for Transmission Control Protocol [TCP] communication). The connector scenario relies on the ability to initiate outbound communication from inside the firewall. The connector scenario is designed via:

- Virtual Connections
- Ping Service
- ConnectorFTUtil

9.2.2   Virtual Connections

The client and service engines establish virtual connections with each other through the connector engine. There are two ways to open such virtual connections. One method is by using the `ConnectorFTUtil` libraries provided by e-Speak. This is discussed in detail during the Hotel ecosystem example for this chapter. The second method is by using an explicit Application Programing Interface (API) provided by e-Speak, `openvirtualconnection`.

9.2.3   Ping Service

Once established, the virtual connections must be kept alive.   The connector engine uses the Ping service to ensure a long-lived connection. The periodic pinging provided by the Ping service is required because firewalls are ideal for short-lived communication and drop open connections with periods of inactivity.

9.2.4   `ConnectorFTUtil`

The `ConnectorFTUtil` is a contributed library provided with the e-Speak installation in the *contrib* installation directory. These libraries are used to establish the virtual connection through corporate firewalls between services and their clients. The virtual connection is established when the service provider exports its service metadata from its service engine to the connector engine, then advertises it to the connector advertising service. The client discovers a service in the connector advertising service, as well, and imports it from the connector engine to the client engine. This interaction can be seen in Figure 9.4.

The `ConnectorFTUtil` library provides utility methods to handle the import and export, advertising, and discovery of services behind firewalls. In our example, we show how to use these methods in facilitating the Hotel ecosystem.

Another feature of the connector scenario is its ability to provide some level of fault tolerance. It does protect against some failures in any of the connector components detailed earlier. It provides fault tolerance by proactively catching exceptions at various stages of the service interaction and tries to recover from them. It makes sure that it has a valid `ESConnection`; it makes sure that it has a connection to

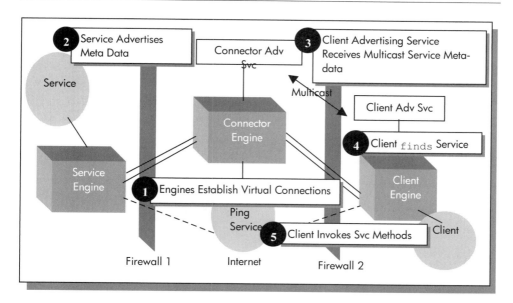

Figure 9.4. Client-service interaction sequence through `ConnectorFTUtil`.

the connector core; it ensures that it can find the connector advertising service. If these activities are consistently successful, it will register the actual service and advertise it in the connector advertising service. Lastly, the Ping service keeps pinging periodically to ensure a live connection. If, during any of these steps, the `ConnectorFTUtil` gets an exception, it goes back and tries to ensure that all the previous steps can be done.

To use these libraries, we must compile the relevant `FTUtil` classes if they are not already compiled. To create these libraries, compile the Java files located in `<installDir>\contrib\faultToleranceUtil`. The class files will be generated in `<installDir>\contrib\lib\faultToleranceUtil`. Remember to add the entry for `<installDir>\contrib\lib` in the `CLASSPATH` system variable so the libraries can be used.

9.3   Hotel Ecosystem with Firewalls

In many of our examples, we have been building on the basic Hotel ecosystem; we added events to facilitate interservice notifications; we deployed it across multiple service engines. In this chapter, we see how protecting the service and the client behind firewalls can be accomplished; specifically, we demonstrate how the `connectorFTUtil` class is used to facilitate firewall traversal. Figure 9.5 depicts the set of service engines and firewalls used by the Hotel ecosystem.

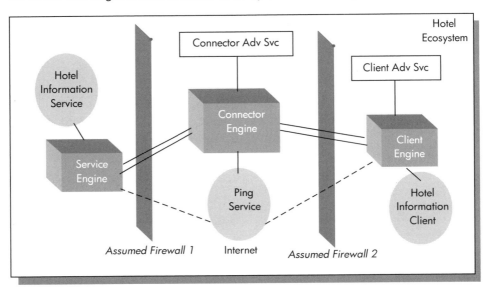

Figure 9.5. Hotel ecosystem and the connector scenario.

9.3.1   Hotel Information Service

In Figure 9.5, we notice that the service advertises the Hotel vocabulary and service with the connector engine located in the DMZ.

In the `HotelInformationService` class, the `connectorGroup` contains the Uniform Resource Locator (URL) of the connector engine. Our example works on a single engine. Hence, it includes `localhost`; however, the likely production scenario would be something similar to `abc.com:2950/HotelGroup`.

HotelInformationService.java

```
private static final String connectorGroup =
    "localhost:2950/HotelGroup";
```

When the Hotel Information service is ready to connect and register the vocabulary, it utilizes the `FTUtil` and `ConnectorFTUtil` classes. It needs to establish connections with both the local service engine and the connector engine. `cftUtil` is the connection object that establishes these connections. `args[0]` is the service property file that denotes the local service engine context.

HotelInformationService.java

```
cftUtil = new ConnectorFTUtil(args[0], connectorGroup);
```

The method `checkAndGetConnectorAds` tries to find the connector advertising service. This establishes a connection to the connector engine, if not already established.

The methods `VocabWrapper` and `createPersistentVocab` create a persistent vocabulary, once the vocabulary object (`esvd`) has been instantiated. It first checks in the local engine whether a vocabulary exists. If it does, it uses that to create a `vocabElement`. If it does not exist, it creates a `vocabElement` from the vocabulary description given, then registers the vocabulary.

HotelInformationService.java

```
try
{
        cftUtil.checkAndGetConnectorAds();
        FTUtil.VocabWrapper myVocabWrapper =
            cftUtil.createPersistentVocab("HotelVocab", esvd);
        myVocab = myVocabWrapper.getVocabulary();
        myVocabElem = myVocabWrapper.getVocabElement();

} catch (Exception ex) { System.out.println(ex); }
```

Once the vocabulary has been registered and created, the next step is to describe the service using this vocabulary and register *it*. The `createPersistentService` method ensures that the service registration is persistent within the connector engine so that, if a failure occurs, it can be recovered from without losing the metadata of the service (or vocabulary).

The `advertiseInConnectorGrp` method is used to advertise the service in the connector advertising service. It is based on the `advertiseInOtherGroups`, from the `ESServiceElement` class.   This method also exports the service and its vocabulary metadata to the connector engine. This exported service and vocabulary is later imported by the client engine, as described previously, so that a virtual connection can be established between the client and the service engines thereby creating a virtual connection that bypasses the firewall and allows for communication across the firewalls between the client and the service.

HotelInformationService.java

```
myServiceElement = cftUtil.createPersistentService
    (myServiceImpl, serviceName, myDescription);
cftUtil.advertiseInConnectorGrp
    (connectorGroup, myServiceElement, myVocabElem, myVocab);
```

The Hotel Information service remains the same thereafter.

9.3.2   Hotel Information Client

Remember that the Hotel Information client also connects from behind its firewall to the connector engine in the DMZ. Hence, the client also defines the connector group to discover services within. Note that it is the same connector group that the service uses. This is important to facilitate the importing of service meta information; there must be a common connector engine between the two entities.

HotelInformationClient.java

```
private static final String connectorGroup
    = "localhost:2950/HotelGroup";
```

As in the Hotel Information service, the `cftUtil` object establishes the connections with the local engine and the connector engines. The Hotel Information client establishes the connection with the connector service engine, using the `verifyAndGetESConnection`. It then checks the connection with the connector advertising service, using the `checkAndGetConnectorAds` method.

HotelInformationClient.java

```
cftUtil = new ConnectorFTUtil(args[0], connectorGroup);
cftUtil.verifyAndGetESConnection();


cftUtil.checkAndGetConnectorAds();
```

Recall that the client needs to find the vocabulary before it can construct a query to facilitate the discovery of a service. The `findVocabInConnectorAds` method finds the vocabulary by looking it up in the connector advertising service. This also imports the vocabulary, once it is found; remember that importing the vocabulary essentially makes it available on the local engine of the client.

HotelInformationClient.java

```
vocab = cftUtil.findVocabInConnectorAds
   (new ESQuery("Name == 'HotelVocab'"));
```

Once the vocabulary is found, the client can construct the search criteria to facilitate service discovery. At this point, everything is the same as before; it is only at the time that we execute the search based on the constructed query that we use the methods provided by the connector library. The `findServiceInConnectorAds` method handles the search and imports the service information to the local engine.

HotelInformationClient.java

```
ESService hotelService = cftUtil.findServiceInConnectorAds
   (interfaceName, mySearchQuery);
```

Table 9.1. Components of the Connector Scenario

Engine	Role	Components Started	Configuration File
Hotel Service Engine	Service Deployer	Local Engine	*service12345.ini*
Connector Engine	Mediator	Connector Engine Advertising Service, Ping Service	*connector.ini* *pingservice.prop*
Hotel Information Client Engine	Client Deployer	Local Engine Advertising Service	*client20000.ini*

Since the virtual connection has been established, the client is able to invoke the service methods as before. As we see in the "In Action" section, the fact that the client is using the service behind a firewall is transparent to the user.

9.4   In Action

We are ready to see the Hotel ecosystem in action; the beauty of the architecture is that we really will not see anything different per se in the runtime environment. There are some deployment issues that needed to be taken care of; however, once the connector scenario libraries are included in the service deployment and service discovery, the firewalls are completely transparent to the end service user — the traveler.

As per Figure 9.5, we see that three service engines need to be started to facilitate the interfirewall communication. Each has its own configuration file that lists what components should be started. Table 9.1 details the components started on each engine and the role played by that engine.

Since running this example, copy the configuration files and the *pingservice.prop* file listed in Table 9.1 from the working directory for this chapter to the e-Speak installation directory — *<installDir>\config*.

To run the example, we start the connector engine first. This is the engine that should be located outside any firewall or in the DMZ of a company.

```
D:\>espeak -i connector.ini
```

A look at the *connector.ini* shows us that it starts more than a simple engine and an advertising service on port 2950. It also starts PingService. The PingService pings the components of the Hotel ecosystem deployment to ensure that the virtual connections are alive and ready to accept communication from either side (to or from the component). Figure 9.6 depicts the start of the connector component.

connector.ini

```
[Tasks]
[Tasks]
Start=ConnectorCore, ConnectorAdvertisingService, PingService

[ConnectorCore]
Class=net.espeak.infra.core.startup.StartESCore
Args=2950

[ConnectorAdvertisingService]
Class=net.espeak.services.advService.server.AdvService
Args=hostname=localhost portnumber=2950
    net.espeak.services.advService.group=HotelGroup
    net.espeak.services.advService.mcast.port=1438
    net.espeak.services.advService.backend.protocol=slp
    net.espeak.services.advService.mcast.sleepMillis=10
WaitFor=ConnectorCore Ready

[PingService]
Class=faultToleranceUtil.PingServer
Args=pingservice.prop HotelGroup
WaitFor=ConnectorAdvertisingService Ready
OnExit=closeall
```

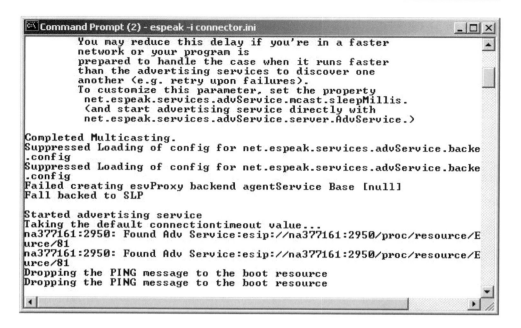

Figure 9.6. Starting the connector components.

The file *pingservice.prop*, used by the Ping service, denotes the port number of the connector engine. This is the engine that the Ping service is deployed on.

pingservice.prop

```
#Port number where connector core is running.
portnumber = 2950
```

We then start the Hotel service engine. This engine hosts the Hotel Information services inside the hotel firewall. The Hotel service engine starts as follows:

```
D:\e-speak\config>espeak -i service12345.ini
```

If we look at *service12345.ini*, we see that it simply starts a service engine on port 12345. It does not start an advertising service (recall that the services *directly* advertise the resources in the connector advertising service).

service12345.ini

```
[Tasks]
Start=ServiceCore

[ServiceCore]
Class=net.espeak.infra.core.startup.StartESCore
Args=12345
```

Figure 9.7 depicts the runtime image of the Hotel service engine. Notice that there are PING messages that appear. To keep the *virtual connection* alive, the Ping service pings the service engine at certain intervals. We see the same PING messages on the client engine because the Ping service will ping it, as well (this is especially important when both the service engine and the client engine are behind firewalls).

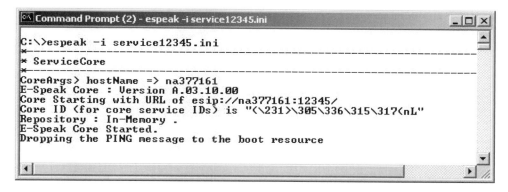

Figure 9.7. Hotel service in the connector scenario.

We now start the client engine that hosts the Hotel Information client. Although there are no *firewalls* on our setup, we can deploy this on systems behind separate firewalls, and the example functions the same, with two changes. First, the host names would need to be *fully qualified* for machines such as the connector engine. Second, the appropriate number of certificates must be issued between the different components so that a secured transaction environment is deployed.

The command to start the client engine follows:

```
D:\e-speak\config>espeak -i client20000.ini
```

Via the file *client20000.ini*, the client engine and the client advertising service are started. This advertising service receives multicasts (discussed in Chapter 7) from the advertising service on the connector engine; thus, the resources that are available on the connector engine will *also* be available on the client engine.

client20000.ini

```
[Tasks]
Start=ClientCore, ClientAdvertisingService

[ClientCore]
Class=net.espeak.infra.core.startup.StartESCore
Args=20000

[ClientAdvertisingService]
Class=net.espeak.services.advService.server.AdvService
Args=hostname=localhost portnumber=20000    \
    net.espeak.services.advService.group=HotelGroup
    net.espeak.services.advService.mcast.port=1438
    net.espeak.services.advService.backend.protocol=slp
    net.espeak.services.advService.mcast.sleepMillis=10
WaitFor=ClientCore Ready
```

At this point, the infrastructure to facilitate the Hotel Information services and client is ready. We simply need to start the enhanced Hotel Information service and client, and the scenario of discovering and invoking methods is as we have seen before.

We start the Hotel Information services by explicitly giving the property file *service.prop*. Recall that the property file instructs which engine to connect to, among other things. We have provided one of the Hotel Information service commands; the remaining Hotel Information services for other entities, such as SuperGrande Hotel, can be started in the same fashion.

```
C:\>java -Despeak_home=d:\e-speak HotelInformationService
    service.prop ..\shared \EasyInn.ini EasyInn
```

Finally, we start the Hotel Information client; we again explicitly provide the client property file.

```
C:\>java -Despeak_home=d:\e-speak HotelInformationClient
    Client.prop
```

In this case, the property file also denotes which community the client should use for discovering services. We execute the discovery in the `HotelGroup`, which is also the group that the connector advertising service is part of, as we saw in the file *connector.ini.*

client.prop

```
hostname = localhost
portnumber = 20000
community = localhost:2950/HotelGroup
```

The rest is a matter of interacting with the interface provided by the Hotel Information client. There really is no difference in the interaction pattern of the service user. Figure 9.8 depicts the successful discovery; it looks like the discovery results of previous attempts. The e-Speak infrastructure provides the firewall architecture, allowing the mechanisms to be transparent to the user.

9.5   Security Considerations

The security implications of this scenario are not as risky as it might appear at first glance. If we look at the components behind the firewall, we see that their risk is constant that is, whatever risk they inherently have by way of being attached to an intranet that ultimately, is attached to the public Internet (Web proxies, mail transports) remains the same.

The third component, the connector engine, is the added risk in this scenario. If the connector machine is compromised in any way, the virtual connection would ultimately drop because, if the connector machine is unreachable, the Ping service would fail, thus *breaking* the whole solution. If somehow a rogue process manages

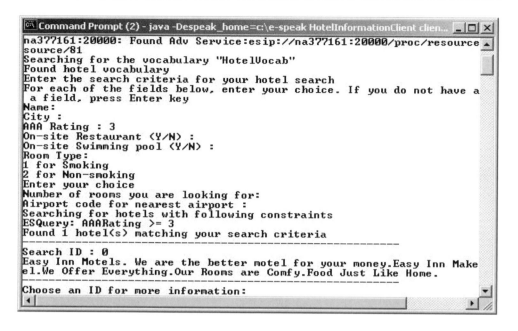

Figure 9.8. Firewall traversal discovery results.

to displace the e-Speak service engine and act as the connector with malicious intent, all it would have visibility to is the encrypted packets flowing through the virtual connection from the service to the client and vice versa. The hacker could listen to that traffic but would *not* be able to comprehend it because it is encrypted, using either the keys of the client or the service. It also would not be able to pose as either because the rogue process would need the keys (located safely inside the client and service firewalls) to do so.

In Chapter 8, we discussed certificate security provided by e-Speak. Prior to the ecosystem setup, the clients and services would have had some certificate-issuing processes, perhaps during a registration process. The clients accessing the service or the service communicating back to the client would need the appropriate engine certificates, which would not be present in the environment of the rogue process. The data flowing through the rogue process would also be protected because of the encryption, which, again, needs public and private keys to decrypt it. Both the certificates and keys are protected behind the respective firewalls, thus limiting damage and risk to the hardware and intra-engine communication levels.

9.6   Accessing a Service Outside a Firewall

Earlier, we mentioned that there are two firewall traversal scenarios possible. In the last few sections, we discussed accessing a service inside a firewall. There is also the outward-facing firewall traversal to facilitate. In this direction, services are located outside a firewall, and the service users are located inside the firewall of a company. Although the connector scenario would work for this, it is not required if the service is located in the public Internet and would be too heavy for such a deployment. However, we did mention that firewalls are concerned, to a lesser extent, with outward traffic. Hence, Web proxies and SOCKS servers are deployed to facilitate the outward HTTP or TCP traffic, respectively. The interaction would be as it is in any multicore scenario except that the SOCKS servers and Web proxies would need to be configured to accept the service-bound outward traffic. The property files and configuration files would need to use fully qualified host names to make this interaction work.

We demonstrated how one firewall traversal deployment could be constructed with the e-Speak architecture. Several industries would have problems in opening any other port other than port 80 (the standard Web proxy port) and, hence, an HTTP-based firewall traversal architecture is preferred; this would mean traffic that flows over HTTP and Hypertext Transfer Procotol over Secure Sockets layer (HTTPS) channels. For example, the banking industry is very strict in its firewall policies and makes it a standard practice to not make any concessions for ports (other than port 80).

The fact that services and clients can interact from behind firewalls brings us one step closer to the service economy discussed in Chapter 1. However, the resource (service and vocabulary) registrations are all transient at this point. With the exception of the connector service registrations, if the engine or advertising service are down (accidentally or purposefully), the registrations need to happen again. Persistence of resource metadata is the next step to a true production service environment. In the next chapter, we discuss various technologies to make persistence possible in the e-Speak infrastructure.

Persistence

- Persistence

- Persistifying Service References
  example working directory:
  \Examples\Ex13Folders

- Persistifying Services
  example working directory:
  \Examples\Ex14Persistence

- Core Repositories

- Persistifying Advertising Services

Chapter 10

PERSISTENCE

The earlier chapters in this part of the book concentrate on the architectural side of deployment. In a nutshell, we discuss how multiple engines can be deployed across firewalls in a secured manner. These chapters focus on how to deploy services and clients for *normal* functioning of the environment. Normal functioning of the environment refers to catering for known states, such as multiple engine deployments, secured transactions, and firewall traversal. In this chapter, we discuss the *operational* aspects of deployment and how to plan for deployment situations when things are *not normal*.

More specifically, we discuss what happens when the service engine or the advertising service do not respond as expected. If solutions are deployed as we described until now, they will *fail* during the downtimes of one or more e-Speak components and will not return easily to a *known* state because significant data loss would occur.

For a resource or a component participating in an ecosystem, the experience should be *continuous*. It should appear to it that the ecosystem is *always on*. Note that this does not imply that the individual resources in the ecosystem should be available at all times; rather, it should *appear* as though a certain resource (or functionality) is always available, despite the individual components providing that functionality not being available at various times. Such an operational quality is called *persistence*. Persistent system designs make the operational downtimes of various components transparent to the users of that system. For example, in our Travel ecosystem, if the engines that the hotel and airline services are deployed on fail, the service deployers would need to reregister themselves with the engine but, more importantly, any client interactions in progress at the time would have to be started again from the first step. This is clearly a quality of service limitation that would be a barrier to use in a true production deployment. Clients cannot be expected to recover from a failure by "restarting" their interaction. In very large workflows, this would be an expensive proposition. Hence, achieving a persistent transactional environment that can recover from some basic failures is important in a web service technology. Couple the technology ability and some hardware-level redundancy, and a fault-recoverable service environment could be deployed.

10.1   Persistence

To achieve persistence, two capabilities are essential. The first is a process or thread management issue that could be handled at the Operating System (OS) level. The transfer of control capability in e-speak-based systems can be achieved using certain off-the-shelf products, such as Hewlett Packard's MC ServiceGuard. The second is an application-level issue. The notion of the *state* of an application or process differs from application to application, and, as a result, must be handled by the application itself. In summary, persistence is both an application-level and an OS-level issue:

- OS-level ability to transfer control from one active component (or an instance) to another

- Application-level ability to transfer the *state* from one component (or instance) to the other

We concentrate on building application-level persistence in this chapter. The current e-Speak implementation manages state information at several different levels:

- Service user (client)-level persistence

- Service-level persistence

- Core-level persistence

Client-level persistence is a client-specific issue; however, one area that the engines can create a standard policy around is "persistifying" the references to services that a client discovers. Such a persistified reference can save a client from the lookup operation. In a situation when the client invokes certain functionality from the found service on a periodic basis, this can ensure that the client reaches the same service during this interaction and provides greater performance because references of desired services can be *cached*.

Service-level persistence refers to design of the service. From the service engine point of view, service-level persistence is a service-specific issue and must be handled by the service deployer. However, because the engine itself is a deployer for some services, such as the advertising service and the event distributor service, it needs to address persistence specifically for those core-managed services. In this chapter, we discuss building persistence in core-managed services, such as the advertising service and other services in the ecosystem.

Core-level persistence addresses the persistence of information that the service engine holds. This includes the state of the core-managed resources, as well as the resource metadata for external resources, such as vocabularies, contracts, and services. If a service engine goes down, another instance of the engine can use this information to reinstate the state of the engine.

Usually, achieving persistence requires storing references to related resources as well as some state information, in an offline storage. The stored information can be used by the new instance of the persistified resource to reinstate the state and associations. E-Speak provides a core-managed resource called *folder* for this purpose.

10.2   Persistifying Service References

The examples discussed in the previous chapters rely on the ability of the service client to discover and use a service dynamically. The dynamic nature of this is at the core of the services-based economy. However, there are situations when it is desirable to be able to reach a specific service.

For example, suppose that a client develops a beneficial relationship with a *specific* service because of quality of service levels, location, or special discount offered by the service. This is a very common scenario in a day-to-day business environment. Just as two or more services can develop an alliance, as explained in Section 6.1, a vendor-customer alliance or partnership is also possible. Such an alliance is built on mutual benefits through the closer links.

As a result of the understanding reached between the client and the service, it is desirable on both sides that the client finds *that* specific service whenever it tries to look for the specific functionality offered by the service. This is somewhat against the dynamic nature of the ecosystem but must be facilitated, due to its practical applicability and necessity.

A reference to a discovered service must also be maintained if the interactions with the service are long-lived (i.e., they take a long time to complete). An example of this is an accounts receivable service. It is usual practice in the business world to make payment against a purchase order in no more than 30 days. This means that the entity receiving the order can make a payment any time during the 30-day period. To reach the same service to make the payment, it is necessary to keep a reference to it.

A client can also share the reference to a service with some other entity in the ecosystem. This is like referring a newly discovered restaurant to our friends. This reference can help friends choose a restaurant without spending a lot of time and energy to find one that suits their taste. Because friends know each others' preferences, they can go ahead without exhaustively researching the restaurant.

In the business world, too, it is common to *refer* services or companies to business partners. In the example situation we discuss in this section, this reference is in the form of preferred hotels for a company. It is common in the corporate world for companies to outsource the travel arrangement services to a third party; this takes the worry out of travel arrangement for the company. The travel service company can make reservations for hotels, cars, and airlines on behalf of its customer. Because the travel service provider serves several customers from different parts of the world, it will in general, have several choices of hotels, car rental agencies, and airlines to choose from. The customer, on the other hand, may have only a handful of preferred entities in each of those industries. Often, preferences for certain providers are based on duration of stay, latest ratings for the hotel or airline companies, and level of the employee who wishes to travel. The travel service provider maintains this list of preferences and may change them from time to time, based on the experience of the travelers.

Consider a scenario in which an employee of BigCo Motor Company is traveling to New York on a business trip and needs to reserve a hotel. BigCo has outsourced the travel arrangement services to a company — American Essential Travel Services (AmEs for short). BigCo also has a list of preferred hotels that the employee must choose from. When a BigCo employee asks AmEs to reserve a room for business travel, AmEs is required to choose a hotel from BigCo's preferred list. Figure 10.1 depicts this scenario.

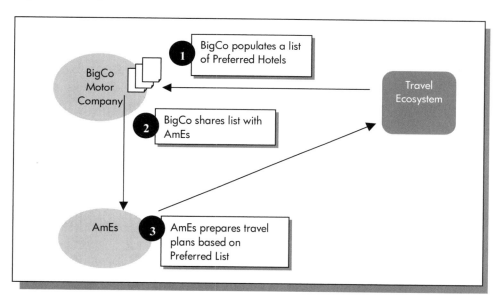

Figure 10.1. The outsourced Travel Service ecosystem.

10.2.1   AmES Travel Reservation Services

A closer look at the problem reveals that the critical component of the relationship between BigCo and AmEs is the up-to-date preferred vendor lists. The process of making reservations and finding economical deals is a speciality of the travel service provider and does not pose a problem. However, it is difficult for AmEs to keep a list of BigCo's preferred list, for two reasons:

1. The preferred list is dynamic in nature. Based on employee feedback and preferences, as well as the company's economic condition, the list of preferred hotels can change frequently. This means that AmEs will need to get periodic updates from BigCo, including the changes in the preferred list.

2. AmEs must serve several other companies and their employees. Even if AmEs and BigCo can refresh the preferred list, the process, when repeated over all AmEs customers, can quickly become a complex operation (although this is largely how things are done today).

Ideally, the responsibility of maintaining the preferred list should be given to the respective AmEs customers. When any employee from a customer company makes a reservation, AmEs can quickly refer to the preferred list of the employee's company and do a room availability and price check for a hotel from that list. BigCo, for example, has the following criteria when selecting a hotel for its preferred list:

▪ The hotel must have an AAA rating of at least three.

▪ There must be an on-site restaurant.

To be able to design and implement this scenario, we need the ability to share the service references between the two companies involved, in this case BigCo and AmEs. When BigCo discovers a hotel based on the criteria above, it stores the reference to the found service in such a way that it is easy to share it with AmEs.

10.2.2 Folders

Folders in e-Speak are an extended service. The Folder service lets the user manage services they discover or create. The interface to a folder is similar to a file system on a computer. Folders also help in creating local namespaces for a service or a service client. Recall that e-Speak does not mandate a globally unique naming scheme. Instead, it requires resource names to be only locally unique. Folders can be used to create a local namespace for the resources of interest. A client can discover a set of services and retain the references to them, using its own naming scheme. The names in its namespace can be completely independent from the names other clients have for the same set of services.

A folder provides a local namespace. Like the file system in an operating system, folders have a hierarchical structure. Just like a file system, each engine has a *root folder*. The root folder contains all the subfolders that are created by the engine clients or by the engine itself. The engine also provides a *home folder* for each engine client (any entity connecting to the engine). The engine client program can then create its folder structure as desired to manage the resources of interest in the ecosystem it participates in. Figure 10.2 depicts the hierarchical structure of folders.

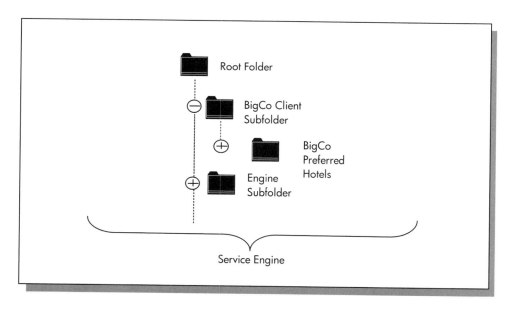

Figure 10.2. E-Speak folder hierarchy.

As can be seen from this figure, BigCo's preferred hotel list is a subfolder of BigCo's default home folder. Further classification of hotels could be provided using a folder hierarchy within the preferred hotel folder. A list of preferred airlines for BigCo can also be created in a similar fashion.

Note

An e-Speak client can create a hierarchical folder structure under its home folder. *Each* folder in the folder hierarchy is a local namespace. Thus, there can be name collisions across multiple folders. This behavior is allowed in the e-Speak local namespace scheme. This is similar to having multiple files with the same name in several directories. In either case, care must be taken while referring to the appropriate resource.

The class `ESFolder` provides the necessary methods to manage the folders for an entity connecting to the engine. In our example, the class `BigCoFolderService` is responsible for managing the folders for BigCo. This class creates, populates, and deletes folders as required. The position of a new folder in the folder hierarchy must be decided before it can be created. This position can be absolute from the client's home folder or relative to the *current* folder.

In this scenario, the flow of events is as follows:

1. BigCo folder service creates the list of preferred hotels, based on BigCo's criteria.

2. AmEs hotel finder uses this folder when a BigCo employee submits a travel request to provide room availability and pricing information.

3. Employee chooses one of the hotels from the list.

4. BigCo updates the preferred hotel list in the folder, based on employee feed-back.

5. AmEs uses the updated list from the folder for the next request from a BigCo employee.

Creating Folders

When an engine client connects to the engine, it is assigned a home folder. To use this home folder programmatically, a method `getHomeFolder()` in the `ESConnection`

class can be used. Alternatively, it is also possible to get the *current* folder immediately after connecting, which has the same effect. The class `ESServiceContext`
used in this example provides the methods to retrieve and set a variety of context
information, such as current folder, community, and category for the entity connecting to the engine.

BigCoFolderService.java

```
ESServiceContext context = Connection.getServiceContext();
ESFolder currentFolder = context.getCurrentFolder();
```

A subfolder under the current folder can then be created. The method from the
class `ESFolder`, `createSubFolder()`, can be used to create subfolders. A folder,
just like a service or a vocabulary, is an engine-registered resource. Thus, we
must provide a description for it before registering (in this case, creating). Because
a folder is considered an extended *service*, `ESServiceDescription` can be used
to describe it. We use the Base Vocabulary in this example to describe the folder.
It is possible to use a separate folder vocabulary if desired. Using these classes,
the folder `BigCoApprovedHotels` is created as follows:

BigCoFolderService.java

```
ESServiceDescription myFolderDescription =
    new ESServiceDescription();
myFolderDescription.addAttribute("Name",
    "BigCoApprovedHotels");
myHotelsFolder = currentFolder.createSubFolder("BigCoHotels",
    myFolderDescription);
```

The search for the hotels satisfying BigCo's criteria can be done independently of
the folder structure. The process for the search is similar to the previously discussed examples. In this case, the search criteria are very specific.

BigCoFolderService.java

```
ESQuery mySearchQuery = null;
...
mySearchQuery = new ESQuery(vocab, "AAARating >= 3");
mySearchQuery.addConstraint("HasOnSiteRestaurant == True");
...
ESService [] hotelServiceSet = Finder.findAll(mySearchQuery);
```

In the example code, the creation of the folder `BigCoApprovedHotels` is conditional upon finding at least one hotel through the search criteria described above. After a successful hotel search, the references to the found services are stored in the folder `BigCoApprovedHotels`. This reference is in the form of an accessor. As explained in Chapter 5, an accessor to an e-Speak registered resource provides a handle to that resource. The accessor can be used to interact with that resource. The `BigCoApprovedHotels` folder stores the accessors for the found services so that the accessors can be used at a later time by any BigCo-approved entity, such as AmEs, using that folder.

The `ESFolder` method `add()` is used to add an entry in a folder. This method requires a *name* for the entry. As we discussed earlier, this name needs to be unique only in its local namespace. For this example, the naming scheme used is the prefix `BigCoHotel` followed by a number. Using this naming scheme, all the found hotels can be added to the folder with unique local names.

BigCoFolderService.java

```
for(int i=0; i<hotelServiceSet.length; i++)
{
    ESAccessor serviceAccessor =
       ((ESAccessorHandle) hotelServiceSet[i]).getAccessor();
    ...
    myHotelsFolder.add(nameBase + i, serviceAccessor);
    ...
}
```

The entries in the `BigCoApprovedHotels` folder can be immediately tested for correctness. The `listNames()` method from the class `ESFolder` can be used for this purpose. This method returns a `String` array containing all the names in a specified folder. Note that this method does not provide the accessors associated with those names. The method `getService()` must be used for that purpose. Using the name from the string array and the interface name, this method returns a stub for that service. This stub can be used to invoke the service methods (from the specified interface). In this example, the interface of interest is `HotelInquiryIntf`.

BigCoFolderService.java

```
for(int i=0; i<hotels.length; i++)
{
    System.out.println(hotels[i]);
    ESBaseService myService =
        myHotelsFolder.getService(hotels[i],
        HotelInquiryIntf.class.getName());
    System.out.println(
        ((HotelInquiryIntf)myService).getShortDescription());
    ...
}
```

The service `BigCoFolderService` creates a list of BigCo-approved hotels in this manner. The AmEs Travel service uses this list when making travel arrangements for any employee from BigCo. To do this, the AmEs Travel service must be able to find and use the `BigCoApprovedHotels` folder.

Using Folders

A folder, an e-Speak registered resource, can be treated as any other resource registered with the service engine. It can be described, registered, advertised, and discovered like a service or vocabulary. Like these resources, a folder must also be discovered first before it can be used. The class `ESFolderFinder` is used for this.

Functionally the `ESFolderFinder` class is equivalent to the `ESServiceFinder` or `ESVocabularyFinder` class. It provides the `find()` and `findAll()` methods to search for one or a set of folders matching a certain criteria specified, using an `ESQuery` object.

Because AmEs serves employees from several companies, it needs to maintain a list of those companies, along with pertinent information about their folders containing the "preferred hotel list" specific to that company. The information that AmEs needs to maintain includes the description attributes used to describe the folders. In this example, the folders are described in the Base Vocabulary using the `Name` attribute. This attribute information has been kept in a *hash*, along with the company's name.

AmEsHotelFinder.java

```
static void prepareHash()
{
    // Prepare the Hash of the company names and
    // corresponding folder names.
    companyFolders = new Hashtable();
    companyFolders.put("BigCo", "BigCoApprovedHotels");
}
```

If the folders were described using some other vocabulary, this hash (or some other suitable data structure) would also contain attributes from that vocabulary that can be used for searching. When a traveler makes a request for hotel information, he or she is asked about the employer. This information is then used to get to the appropriate entry in the hash. Once a valid hash entry is found, the vocabulary attributes from that entry can be used to search for the folder associated with the company.

AmEsHotelFinder.java

```
ESFolderFinder myFolderFinder=new ESFolderFinder(Connection);
try
```

```
{
    companyFolder = myFolderFinder.find(new
        ESQuery("Name == '" + folderName + "'"));
}
catch (LookupFailedException e)
{
    System.out.println("Could not find approved hotel list for "
        + companyName);
    System.exit(1);
}
```

Once a folder is found, AmEs uses the entries in that folder to determine the list of preferred hotels and provide the user with pricing information. The methods `listNames()` and `getService()` are used, as explained earlier, to interact with the folder object and retrieve the accessor associated with the service names. The pricing interaction is the same as that in the `HotelInformationClient` class in earlier examples.

Before we are ready to run the example, there is a configuration change that needs to be done to improve the offline persistence.

10.2.3   E-Speak Account Persistence

The folders provide an excellent way to preserve references to any engine registered resource. As previously discussed, they can be used by not only the creators but also by their business partners. To be effectively used, the folders themselves must be preserved. Note that a folder is an e-Speak resource, and when the engine shuts down or crashes, the folder is destroyed along with it.

E-Speak allows the folders to live longer than their creators. In other words, even if a service or a client that created a folder terminates, it could be maintained within the engine. Such folders are called *persistent folders*. In our example, this means that, even if the `BigCoFolderService` is no longer running, the folder `BigCoApprovedHotels` can be made persistent by the engine and used by `AmEsHotelFinder`. From a system design standpoint, this is a preferred design because it decouples the operations of the two entities that these classes represent. Due to this decoupling, the two services can be down (for maintenance or any other reason) completely independent of each other.

The root folder and the home folder are, by default, persistent folders. Persistence properties are inherited from the parent folder by using `createSubFolder()`. Thus, any folder that is created as a subfolder to the root folder or a home folder is also a persistent folder. E-Speak also provides persistence policies for other resources, such as vocabularies and contracts.

One notable exception to the policy around persistence is that of a *guest* account.

The Guest Account

Each service engine connection is associated with an account with the service engine. The name of the account to be used for a connection can be specified in the property file provided to the `ESConnection` object. When the property file does not specify any account name, a default account called a *guest account* is used. The guest account has account name `guest` and password `guest`.

On one hand, the guest account relieves the developer from managing the account during the early development stages. We have been using the guest account until this point in the book.   The side effect of using the guest account is that no persistent resources can be created. As per the e-Speak persistence policy, all guest account resources are considered *transient*.   When the engine client (i.e., a service or a service user) that connected to the engine using the guest account, disconnects from the engine, all the resources it created are destroyed. This also includes the folders. To create a persistent set of resources, an account other than the guest account must be used.

Using Nonguest Accounts

To use a nonguest account, the account name must be specified in the property file. The engine will persistify the appropriate resources created by the client, even if it disconnects for some reason. All these resources are available to the client next time it connects. The resources will be persistified until they are destroyed by the client or the engine is shutdown. If the engine is run in the persistent mode, the resources can outlive even an engine shutdown. The persistent mode for the engine is discussed in Section 10.4. For every account, the engine creates a dedicated *domain* called a *protection domain*. A protection domain is essentially a collection of resources and policies that are specific to a particular account.

The account name for an entity connecting to the engine can be specified in the `ESConnection` property file, using the `accountname=` tag. Here is the entry for BigCo:

Bigco.prop

```
accountname=bigcouser
```

Note

E-Speak provides a more elaborate account administration mechanism through the Account Manager. Using this mechanism, a secure account can be created that is tied to the key-pair of an entity. The programmatic access to the Account Manager functionality can be used create a comprehensive account management structure.

When a folder is created using an account, it can be tested for persistence using the `isPersistent()` method.

BigCoFolderService.java

```
if(myHotelsFolder.isPersistent())
{
    System.out.println("The folder BigCoHotels is persistent");
}
```

10.2.4   In Action

To run this example, we need to start the Hotel services along with the engine. This will deploy the Hotel ecosystem. To validate how the search criteria works, start all three Hotel services. The service `BigCoFolderService` can be started as follows:

```
c:\> java -Despeak_home=c:\e-speak BigCoFolderService BigCo.prop
```

This service connects to the engine and creates a protection domain and a persistent folder, `BigCoApprovedHotels`. It then searches for the eligible hotels in the Hotel ecosystem and adds references to each eligible hotel in the folder. Figure 10.3 shows this sequence of events.

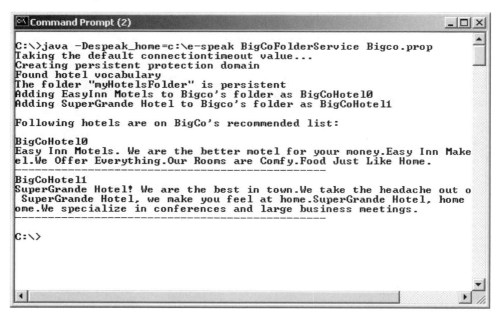

Figure 10.3. The BigCoFolderService program.

Notice that the `BigCoFolderService` program terminates after this. Because the folder `BigCoApprovedHotels` it created is persistent, it should survive the service termination. Now start the `AmEsHotelFinder` service:

```
c:\> java -Despeak_home=c:\e-speak AmEsHotelFinder Client.prop
```

When prompted for the company name, enter "BigCo." The AmEs service will search for the BigCo preferred hotel list folder and display descriptions of those hotels. Figure 10.4 depicts this.

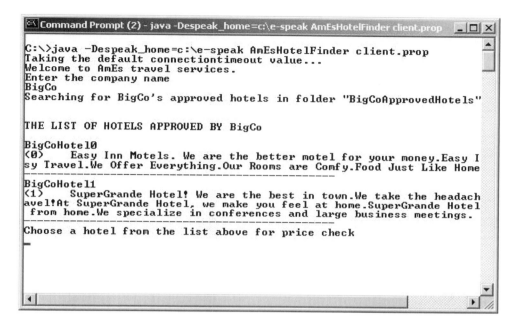

Figure 10.4. The AmEsHotelFinder service.

The AmEs service shows the names for the hotels given by BigCo. This is because of the way the references are stored in the `BigCoApprovedHotels` folder. The user is then prompted to choose from this list. Note that there are more hotels available in the Hotel ecosystem; however, the choice is limited to a few when a BigCo employee makes travel arrangements. The price check is similar to previous examples.

10.3   Persistifying Services

In the last section, we discussed how service references can be stored in folders so that others can use them. In that example, the AmEs service used the hotel references created by BigCo. This provided an elegant way to persistify the references to the found services. But how can the services themselves be persistified?

A persistified service is more desirable than a nonpersistified service. By definition, nonpersistified services lose the data and resources they create when shut down (on purpose or accidentally). This means that if, for some reason, a service crashes while interacting with a client, the client loses the transactional data along with the connection. When the service resumes again and the client tries to complete the transaction, it has to start from the very beginning because the new instance may not have the context for that transaction. A persistent service, on the other hand, can make such crashes and scheduled downtimes transparent to the client.

10.3.1   Crashtime Behaviors of Service and Client

To understand how to provide persistence, we first look at what happens when a service fails during some interaction. The next experiment can give us an idea about the behavior of various entities involved.

Crash Test

Start the engine as usual. From the example working directory, start the Hotel Information service for any hotel and start the Hotel Information client. Provide the parameters to the client so that the Hotel service you started can be found. Go through the client-service interaction until the pricing transaction is reached. Just before the pricing request is sent to the service, kill the Hotel service by pressing the <CTRL> and <C> keys in the window that started it.

The service terminates without much fanfare. Notice that this event has no ramification on the client side yet. The client process does not register the service termination at all, due to the loose coupling between the two. However, when the client tries to interact with the service after this, it will encounter the exception `ESInvocationException`. This can be verified by trying to complete the pricing transaction. Once the pricing data is entered by the user and the client attempts to invoke method `getPrice()`, the exception is thrown.

As can be seen from this experiment, an untimely termination of service (due to a system crash, maintenance, or any other reason) leaves a client in a dangling state. Even if a new instance of the service is started, this does not help the situation.

The client-side exception still persists. Figure 10.5 depicts this more clearly.

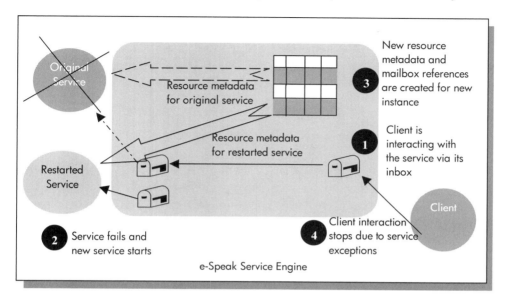

Figure 10.5. Abnormal service termination.

Recall that, as explained in Chapter 4, the client-service interaction in e-Speak translates to messages that are exchanged between the interacting parties. Each interacting party has a mailbox allocated to it by the service engine. When a service goes down, from the service engine perspective, the listener or the recipient to the corresponding mailbox is no longer reachable. Thus, when the client invokes a service method, it results in the exception `ESInvocationException`. This is similar to the postal service scenario; if the address for the recipient is invalid, the mail is returned to the sender.

When a new instance of the service is started and registered with the service engine, it is allocated a *new* mailbox by the engine. The service engine has no way to tell the difference between a new instance being started and a restart of a terminated service. From a client's perspective, the dangling mailbox problem still persists, and any attempt to invoke using the same service reference will continue to result in `ESInvocationException`.

There are two ways to recover from this situation. First, the client would discover the service again and try to start the interaction wherever it was left off. This would require the client to maintain some state information about its own operation and to ensure that it has reached a new instance of the *same* service and not some other service that adheres to the same contract and matches the search criteria. The additional work required on the client side certainly makes this option undesirable; especially in light of a solution that can be implemented on the service side itself.

Recovering from Abnormal Service Terminations

As Figure 10.5 shows, when a new instance of the service is started, it is usually assigned a new mailbox in the service engine. If, however, the new instance can establish itself on the same mailbox that the original service instance was using, it can respond to any requests from clients that were interacting with the original service instance and are unaware of the service termination. From a client's perspective, this is a better solution because this makes the service terminations and restarts transparent to the client. Two issues must be addressed to implement this solution:

- A reference to the original service instance must be available to the new service instance.

- The mailbox associated with the original service instance must be live and assignable to the new service instance.

In this section, we address the first issue. The second issue must be handled at the engine level and is addressed in the next section. The process for preserving a service reference is similar to the one discussed in the previous section. In this case also, a folder with the service reference is created. The main difference in the two scenarios is, of course, that in the previous section, the `BigCoFolderService` preserved the references to all the Hotel services in its ecosystem, whereas in this case, the Hotel service keeps only a reference to itself. The self-reference to the service is maintained at a folder named `serviceFolder`. When a service is started, it first checks whether the folder `serviceFolder` exists. It is created again only if it does not exist in the home folder of the service. This process is similar to the one used in the example introducing folders.

HotelInformationService.java

```
try
{
   myFolder = currentFolder.getSubFolder("serviceFolder");
   . . .
}
catch(InvalidNameException e)
{
   myFolder = currentFolder.createSubFolder("serviceFolder");
   . . .
}
```

In the example code provided, the file *Service.prop* provides the necessary parameters for the `ESConnection` object. This file creates an account, `HotelAccount`, to create a persistent domain for the Hotel service that uses the property file. If multiple Hotel services are started using the same property file, they share the same self-reference folder. In reality, each Hotel service has its own folder and an account associated with it.

To persistify a service, we need at least two e-Speak objects:

1. The service accessor

2. The service handler

The service accessor is discussed earlier. It is essentially a pointer to the resource metadata that is associated with the service. The service accessor is assigned by the service engine during service registration. A service handler object associated with a service is part of the e-Speak messaging infrastructure. It receives service messages and delivers them to the requested service implementation. Whereas an accessor is associated with any engine-registered resource, such as services, vocabularies, contracts, and folders, a service handler is associated only with service-type resources and can be shared among several services.

When a service is registered with the engine, it is assigned a service handler to handle the messages for the service. A service can explicitly specify the handler to be used for the implementation, using the method `setHandler()` of the class `ESServiceElement`. If a handler is not specified, the service engine provides a default handler. Any service handler, including the default service handler, can handle messages for several services at the same time. In our examples so far, we have used the default handler. All the services that are started in these examples are served by the default service handler. The class `ESServiceHandler` provides the necessary abstractions for this.

To replace an earlier instance of a service fully, the new instance must get associated with the accessor and the service handler of that instance. Through this, the resource metadata information in the engine now points to the new service and any messages to the mailbox associated with the old instance are directed toward the new instance. Figure 10.6 shows this.

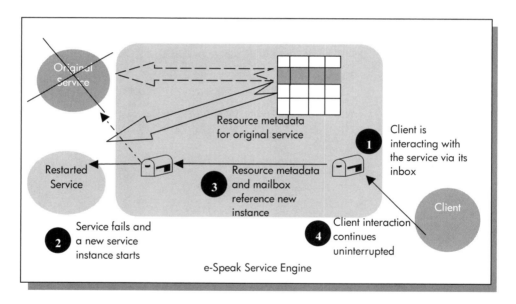

Figure 10.6. Replacing a service instance.

The accessor and the service handler of the original instance must be preserved to be able to assign them later to the new instance. The folder `serviceFolder` is used for this purpose. When an instance of the Hotel service is started, it searches or creates this folder, as discussed earlier. It then searches for the accessor and

service handler to see whether any previous instance was instantiated. The folder
entries are created as unique key-value pairs. The key for the accessor for the
Hotel service is designed to be the `Name` property, which is loaded from the corresponding *.ini* file. The service handler is stored under the key that is the "stringified"
version of the property `Name`, concatenated with the word `Handler`.

HotelInformationService.java

```
String serviceName = serviceProps.getProperty("Name");
String serviceHandler = serviceName + "Handler";
```

An entry in the persistent folder is created only if there is no previous entry under
the two keys. If a previous entry is found, the new instance must associate itself
with the old accessor and the service handler. It also should not register the service
again. This process is essentially restarting the old service instance. The JESI
library provides a separate method, `restart()`, for this purpose. If, on the other
hand, no prior entries for the accessor and the service handler are found, they
must be created and the service must be started. The `start()` method we have
used until now is precisely for this purpose. The logic flow, in short, is as follows:

HotelInformationService.java

```
if(myFolder.containsName(serviceName) &&
   myFolder.containsName(serviceHandler))
{
// A previous instance of the service existed.
// This instance must associate itself with the accessor
// and the service handler of original instance.
}
else
{
// This is the first or fresh instance of the service.
// It needs to create entries for accessor and the service
// handler that subsequent instance can use if required.
}
```

Creating the fresh persistence entries for the accessor and the service handler requires a reference to corresponding objects. The accessor is provided by the engine during the service registration. The service handler reference depends on whether a default or dedicated handler is used. In this example, a dedicated service handler is used. The ESConnection class provides reference to the default handler through the method getDefaultServiceHandler(). A dedicated handler must be explicitly associated with a service element, using the setHandler() method.

HotelInformationService.java

```
ESServiceHandler myServiceHandler =
   new ESServiceHandler(Connection);
...
myServiceElement.setHandler(myServiceHandler);
ESAccessor myServiceAccessor = myServiceElement.register();

try
{
   myFolder.add(serviceName, myServiceAccessor);
   myFolder.add(serviceHandler, myServiceHandler.getAccessor());
   ...
}
catch (NameCollisionException e)
{
   ...
}
```

Associating an instance with the accessor and the handler of a previous instance involves searching for the corresponding references and assigning them to the new instance. To associate the accessor, a service element is created *using* that accessor, whereas the service handler must be explicitly associated.

HotelInformationService.java

```
ESAccessor myAccessor = myFolder.getAccessor(serviceName);
```

```
ESAccessor myServiceHandlerAccessor =
   myFolder.getAccessor(serviceHandler);
ESServiceElement myServiceElement =
   new ESServiceElement(myAccessor);
...
ESServiceHandler myHandler =
   new ESServiceHandler(myServiceHandlerAccessor);
myServiceElement.setHandler(myHandler);
myServiceElement.restart();
}
```

Notice that, in the code segment, the service is not registered or started. If a call to the `register()` method is made, a new entry in the engine is created for the service. Equipped with this setup, a service can now be persistified. When an existing instance of the service terminates abnormally for any reason, a new instance can be started to replace it. If this replacement happens in a short time span, it can be completely transparent to the service client. In this example, all the transactions in the interaction between the service and the client are *independent* from each other. In a real-world application, a reference (e.g., a cookie) may be required to be maintained to preserve the *state* of the interaction. If such a reference is used, the new instance must also load the state of the existing interaction(s) with client(s) to create a completely transparent experience for the client(s).

10.3.2   In Action

The steps for running this example are the same as the ones used in the experiment described at the beginning of this section. Start the engine and start the Hotel service for any hotel using the `HotelInformationService` class from the working directory of this example.

Notice that the folder `serviceFolder` is created because this is the first time the Hotel service is started, as is depicted in Figure 10.7. Start the client as before from the example working directory and provide search parameters such that the Hotel service started is found. Follow the dialog until the pricing request is reached. Kill the service process by pressing <CTRL> and <C> in the service window. Start

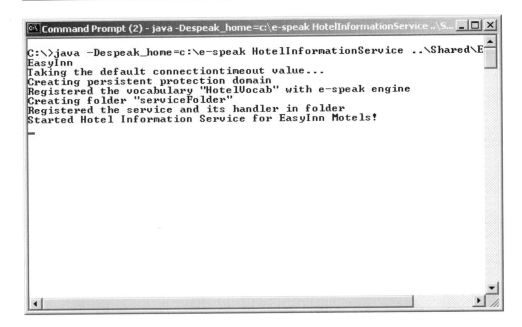

Figure 10.7. Starting a fresh instance of a persistent Hotel service.

the service again to launch a new service instance. This time, the folder entries, along with the `HotelVocab` vocabulary from the original instance, are detected, and the service restarts by associating itself to the original accessor and service handler, as depicted in Figure 10.8. The client will be able to complete the pricing transaction without any problem or error now.

In this discussion, we concentrate on how the service can create a persistent experience for the client. Because a client-service interaction is bidirectional, it is desirable to create a persistent client, as well. A persistent client makes the client-side downtimes transparent to the service. The same mechanism that we discussed so far can be used to persistify a client, as well. Moreover, the service can also maintain a reference to the client, as discussed in the previous section, to ascertain that it can reach the same client during an interaction. The self-reference and cross-reference mechanisms can be employed to create a highly persistified experience on both the client and service sides.

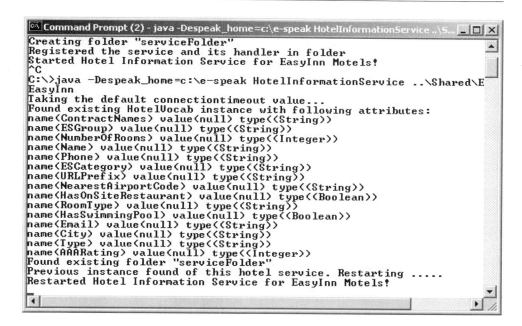

```
Command Prompt (2) - java -Despeak_home=c:\e-speak HotelInformationService ..\S   _ □ ×
Creating folder "serviceFolder"
Registered the service and its handler in folder
Started Hotel Information Service for EasyInn Motels!
^C
C:\>java -Despeak_home=c:\e-speak HotelInformationService ..\Shared\E
EasyInn
Taking the default connectiontimeout value...
Found existing HotelVocab instance with following attributes:
name(ContractNames) value(null) type((String))
name(ESGroup) value(null) type((String))
name(NumberOfRooms) value(null) type((Integer))
name(Name) value(null) type((String))
name(Phone) value(null) type((String))
name(ESCategory) value(null) type((String))
name(URLPrefix) value(null) type((String))
name(NearestAirportCode) value(null) type((String))
name(HasOnSiteRestaurant) value(null) type((Boolean))
name(RoomType) value(null) type((String))
name(HasSwimmingPool) value(null) type((Boolean))
name(Email) value(null) type((String))
name(City) value(null) type((String))
name(Type) value(null) type((String))
name(AAARating) value(null) type((Integer))
Found existing folder "serviceFolder"
Previous instance found of this hotel service. Restarting .....
Restarted Hotel Information Service for EasyInn Motels!
```

Figure 10.8. Starting a fresh instance of a persistent Hotel service.

10.4   Core Repositories

The client- and service-side persistence mechanisms discussed earlier are effective in creating a seamless functionality experience on either side. The solution used in those cases is based on using folders and, thus, is dependent on the availability of the engine.

Recall that a folder is an extended e-Speak service that provides the same set of abstractions for folders as the service, vocabulary, and contract. A folder is, thus, an e-Speak managed resource. If the engine instance that manages a folder goes down, the reference to the folder is lost! This makes the service engine the weakest link in the persistence solution deployed so far.

Fortunately, e-Speak does provide a persistence mechanism for the service engine itself. This persistence mechanism, based on the database technology, provides a very robust offline storage of the resource metadata contained in a service engine. In e-Speak jargon, the resource metadata is stored in a *repository*. To persistify the service engine means persistifying or preserving the repository of that engine.

10.4.1   Repository Types

The e-Speak service engine supports two types of metadata repositories.   The *in-memory repository*, as the name suggests, is a resource repository that is maintained in the memory. This is the default repository that is part of the standard e-Speak installation. Because this repository uses RAM to store the resource metadata, when the engine is shut down or is unavailable for some reason, the repository data is lost. Although useful for development and troubleshooting, the in-memory repository is not useful for production-level deployments.

In the other type of repository, data is maintained in a database. The service engine uses the Java Database Connectivity (JDBC) Application Programing Interfaces (APIs) to interact with the database. Database tables are used to classify and store resource data. Due to JDBC technology, the repository is not tied to a database from any specific database vendor, although Oracle 8.0 or higher is the recommended database.

10.4.2   Setting Up a Database-Based Repository

The file *espeak.cfg* is used to denote the type of repository to be used when starting the engine. The parameters related to the repository are already set to the in-memory repository during e-Speak installation by default. Before changing these parameters, it is necessary to install the database components. Then create a database for use by the engine. For the purpose of this book, we have used Oracle 8i personal edition (version 8.1.6). This version can be downloaded from the Oracle Tech Network (OTN):

```
http://technet.oracle.com/software/products/8i_personal/
software_index.htm
```

Oracle Database Installation

When installing the database, use the "Typical" installation option and note the values for parameters `Global Database Name` and `System Identifier` (SID). We have used the value `OraES` for both these parameters in our examples.

By default, when the Oracle install utility installs the database, it automatically starts the database engine as an NT service. Be aware that this will most likely tax the limits of your system resources. Open the Start Menu, Oracle OraHome81, Database Administration, Database administration for Windows NT. Then click on Oracle Managed Objects, Computers, <Your host>, Databases, <Your database> (OraES, in this case). Right-click on database and choose the Stop Service option. This will stop the service. To change the runtime setting permanently, right-click on the database again and choose Startup/Shutdown Options. Click on the Oracle NT service tab and choose Manual for Oracle NT service Startup Type. Click on the Apply button. Then reboot the machine to have the changes take effect. To verify that the database service is not running, look in the Task Manager process listing for the process `ORACLE.EXE`. The database service must be started before the engine process is started in the JDBC repository mode.

> **Note**
>
> The `HKEY_LOCAL_MACHINE\SOFTWARE\JAVaSoft\Java Runtime Environment\CurrentVersion` registry entry may be changed by the Oracle installation program from 1.2 to 1.1 if you choose to install the Java components. Because these are not used during repository functioning and a value of 1.1 for Java version will hinder other Java applications, including the e-Speak service engine, this registry entry *must* be reset to 1.2.

Once installed, the database settings can be used to set up the e-Speak repository. The repository parameters in the file $<installDir>\config\espeak.cfg$ must be set accordingly. Here are some relevant entries:

espeak.cfg

```
net.espeak.infra.core.repository.Repository_Params.Store_Type=
```

```
         JDBC
   ...
   net.espeak.infra.core.repository.JDBCGlue.driverName=
         oracle.jdbc.driver.OracleDriver
   net.espeak.infra.core.repository.JDBCGlue.connectionString=
       jdbc:oracle:thin:@(DESCRIPTION =(ADDRESS = (PROTOCOL = TCP)
       (HOST = na377161)(PORT = 1521))
       (CONNECT_DATA = (SID = ORAES)))
   net.espeak.infra.core.repository.JDBCGlue.sqlStringSize=255
```

A working version of the configuration file is included in the example working directory under the name *espeak.cfg.persistence*. To use this file, copy it to the directory *<installDir>\config* and rename it to *espeak.cfg*.

10.4.3 Using a Database-Based Repository

To use the database-based repository, the necessary database schema required for the engine must be created. This schema consists of the specific tables that the engine uses to save resource data, as well as the state of the core-managed resources. The engine provides an -r option to build the schema. The same option can also be used to delete the contents of the database and create an empty set of tables.

Note

Notice the dual purpose of the -r option of the engine. If used accidentally on a nonempty database, this option can completely wipe out the persistency information stored in the database. It is a good idea to create a separate file that uses this option and let only the system administrator have permission to access and use that file.

A configuration file, *refresh.ini*, is provided in the example working directory for this. To use it, copy it to the directory *<installDir>\config*. To create the empty schema, start the Oracle database engine, as shown in the Figure 10.9.

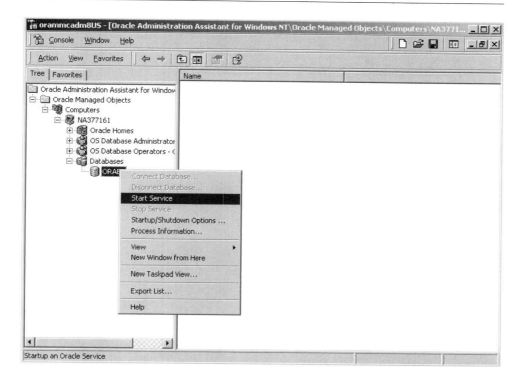

Figure 10.9. Starting the Oracle Database service for the e-Speak repository.

Once you get a message that the database service has started successfully, open a command window and go to the directory $<installDir>\config$ and run the e-Speak utility as follows:

```
c:\> espeak -i refresh.ini
```

A series of messages indicating successful refresh and starting of the engine is displayed:

```
Repository: JDBC-based
JDBC-based Repository is booting ...
E-Speak JDBC-based Repository is clearing the persistent state!
E-Speak Core Started.
```

The repository is now ready to record the resource metadata and state information. We use the basic functionality in the engine to ensure end-to-end persistence.

10.4.4   In Action

To check the persistence of the engine and, thus, the end-to-end component chain, we need to check that the engine retains the folder metadata. As explained earlier, the in-memory repository does not exhibit this behavior. We will concentrate only on the service engine link in the example. A client that implements the self-reference, such as the service in this example, can be used to restart the client program.

Start the database engine, as discussed earlier, and start the engine using the file *core.ini*. The repository schema must be first created, using the -r option discussed previously. After the engine starts successfully, start the Hotel service from the working directory of the example. The command to start the service is unchanged from the previous section in this chapter. After the service starts, its metadata will be stored in the database. This can be viewed using the Oracle DBA Studio tool.

Start the Oracle DBA tool through Start, Oracle, OraHome81, Database Administration, DBA Studio. When prompted, start the tool in standalone mode. Use the default login `system` and password `manager`. The visual representation of the database `ORAES` can be seen. In the DBA Studio window, click on ORAES, Schema, Scott, Tables. This shows all the tables created by the user Scott (the user name provided during the engine startup). Click on various tables to see their structure. One of these tables represents the Hotel service registered. Figure 10.10 shows such a table.

With the specific table highlighted, choose Object, Table Data Editor from the menu. This shows the data in the table. Figure 10.11 shows the entry for EasyInn Motels.

To simulate the service engine shutting down, press <CTRL> and <C> in the engine window. This causes all the engine clients to shut down, as well. In effect, this simulates multiple components in an ecosystem going down. Now start the engine in the same window, using the configuration file *core.ini*. The engine uses

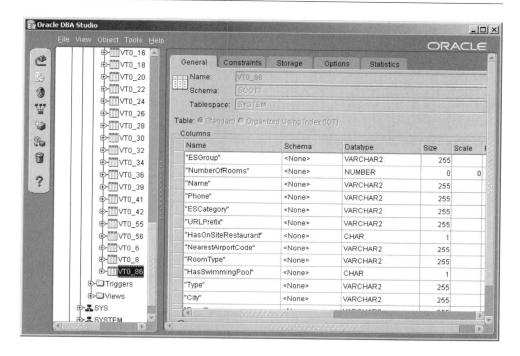

Figure 10.10. Resource metadata table for Hotel service.

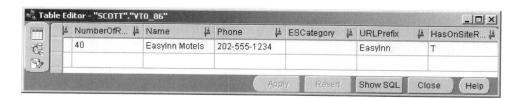

Figure 10.11. Repository table entry for EasyInn Motels.

the persistent database to rebuild the resource metadata, as well as the state of the core-managed resources.

To verify the persistence of engine data, start the service in its window. The service detects the vocabulary and the earlier instance of it, and restarts the Hotel service by binding to the accessor and service handler of the earlier instance.

10.5   Persistifying Advertising Services

In an earlier section, we discussed how to persistify service references on the client side so that it can be used by other instances of the same client or a different client altogether. Ecosystem members, including service clients, depend on the advertising services to discover services that cater to their needs. In a highly populated ecosystem in which different entities frequently seek other entities to partner with, the advertising services play a very important role in the ecosystem infrastructure. As a result, persistifying the advertising service is important.

E-Speak facilitates advertising service persistence through directories based on the Lightweight Directory Access Protocol (LDAP). An LDAP is a standardized directory lookup and population protocol. Essentially, it is a mechanism to organize reference information for any entity, such as a person or a service. Using an LDAP-based directory, an advertising service can keep the reference information for a service on the hard disk. If an LDAP-based advertising service fails, the new instance of the advertising service can use the data in the LDAP repository to rebuild the service information. The interaction is much the same as discussed in Section 10.2 in this case.

An LDAP-based advertising service also improves the scalability of service lookup. Several advertising services belonging to the same group and using the same LDAP directory can be created. In this case, all the advertising services share the same resource metadata. This ensures that, no matter which advertising service is searching for a suitable service, it finds the same references as any other advertising service in that group. Due to this, the service user is free to use the next available advertising service and can be assured that the results are consistent. The advertising service configuration also allows multiple groups to share an LDAP directory. In such a case, each group would be a subdirectory under the main directory.

The interaction with the LDAP directory is completely self-contained in the advertising service itself and is transparent to the user of the service. The configuration file *<installDir>\config\espeak.cfg* provides the default settings for an advertising service. These can be overridden by the *.ini* file used to start the advertising service. The parameter `net.espeak.services.advService.backend.protocol` specifies the protocol to be used. When this parameter is set to `ldap`, the advertising service connects to an LDAP server and keeps the service references in it.

The parameter `net.espeak.services.advService.config` specifies the file that contains the configuration information for the advertising service, including the LDAP directory login information. The configuration file also helps in sharing the configuration information across several advertising service instances. A typical advertising service configuration file would consist of:

```
net.espeak.services.advService.backend.protocol=ldap
net.espeak.services.advService.backend.ldap.host=myLdap.hp.com
net.espeak.services.advService.backend.ldap.port=389
net.espeak.services.advService.backend.ldap.rootDN=myDirMgr
net.espeak.services.advService.backend.ldap.passwd=myPassword
net.espeak.services.advService.backend.ldap.organization=hp.com
net.espeak.services.advService.backend.ldap.proxyHost=myWeb-\
proxy.hp.com
net.espeak.services.advService.backend.ldap.proxyPort=8088
```

Because the advertising service uses standard LDAP APIs, any LDAP directory software can be used. The current e-Speak release is tested with the Netscape Directory Server.

Ensuring persistified components in an ecosystem is the first step toward making services ready for global accessibility. Persistence ensures that quality of service levels are preserved. However, highly persistent ecosystems and services need to be found before they can be used. Online ecosystem directories collect services and make them available to a larger audience. Such directories are the topic of discussion in the next chapter.

Service Registries

- A Registry as a Directory
- E-services Village
- Maturing of the Registry Concept
- The Future of Registries

Chapter 11

SERVICE REGISTRIES

The ecosystem is an underlying theme throughout the service vision. The ecosystem is the playing field for service users, service providers, and consortiums. This playing field allows entities to register their services, discover other services, and follow some consortium or other governing body guidelines. One central component of this ecosystem is the central registry that houses the services and provides the discovery platform. Service providers desiring to make their services available to a general, worldwide audience can do so via global registries such as E-services Village (ESV) — available at `http://www.eservicesvillage.com`. Managed and hosted by Hewlett-Packard (HP), ESV is based on the e-Speak technology. Service users can also use this worldwide registry to incorporate desired functionality into their offering or business processes. Figure 11.1 depicts the interactions that are facilitated by the registry technology.

Until now, we have demonstrated that secured ecosystems consisting of several services (such as those associated with the Travel ecosystem) available on multiple core infrastructures can be developed and deployed. However, simply deploying a service on a network somewhere does not facilitate discovery by truly *blind* service users. A news Web site could have the most up-to-date news from around the globe but if news aficionados cannot happen upon the site, it has not been successful in bringing news to its audience. In the same manner, services deployed for public consumption need a vehicle to make their presence known to those who would be interested. Global online business directories provide that vehicle.

In this chapter, we discuss registries in more detail, using the reference environ-

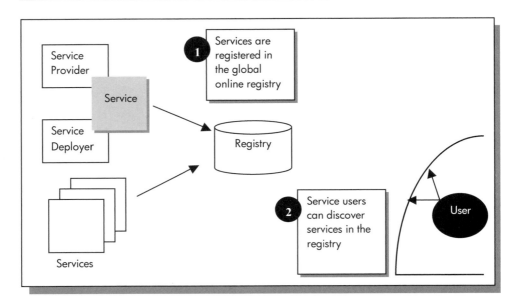

Figure 11.1. Ecosystem interactions facilitated by a registry.

ment provided by `www.eservicesvillage.com`. Although the semantics of discovery and registering services in this discussion are specific to ESV, conceptually, any service registry would provide similar (and more sophisticated) features and tools.

11.1   A Registry as a Directory

A registry is nothing more than a platform for service users and service deployers to discover each other. It is an online directory that provides both browser-based and programmatic access to its service description content. From Chapter 5, we learn that service description is the vocabulary associated with the service and the contract the service abides by. Hence, registries hold the framework information that consortiums and other governing bodies develop so that service providers can register their services in a *predictable* manner. Recall that this predictability allows service users a consistent discovery mechanism.

11.1.1   Business Value of a Directory

We can visualize the business need for a registry or directory by applying it to the Travel ecosystem used throughout this book.

The Travel ecosystem consists of several Airline and Hotel services deployed on several service engines.   Service discovery happens within a specified set of engines (determined by the `advertising group`). Although this works quite well for the defined set of service providers and trip planners, it limits the accessibility of these services to those who *know about* the particular advertising group and other specific deployment details, such as the multicast port, and so on. If these services wanted far-reaching accessibility and visibility, they should make their offerings available in a manner conducive for that.

Figure 11.2 takes our Travel ecosystem and adds the facility for a global online registry such as `http://www.eservicesvillage.com` (discussed in further detail below).

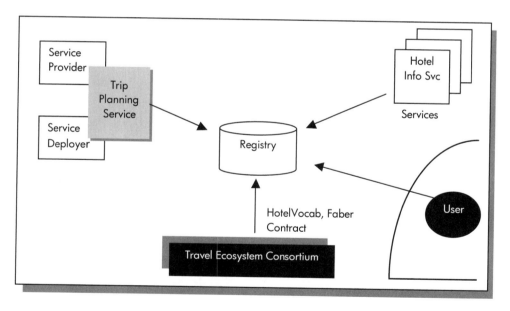

Figure 11.2. Travel ecosystem and a registry.

From this figure, we see that the registry allows service users to browse more information, delve through interaction definitions, and evaluate competing and complementary offerings. The registry further promotes the dynamic discovery of two *unaware* parties, as long as the registry is a well-known entity. It also provides service providers wishing to compose higher level services a catalog of services to choose from during composition.

11.2   E-services Village

The e-Speak technology provides one such registry reference implementation. Available at `http://www.eservicesvillage.com`, it is both browser- and programmatically accessible. The browser representation can be seen in Figure 11.3.

ESV is a developer's edition of a global online public registry for e-Speak services. It provides a home for those designing and defining their solutions and strategies. Programmatically, service deployers that wish to register their services for global visibility and accessibility can register directly to the ESV public registry.

11.2.1   Features of ESV

In Chapter 1, we discuss the roles of various ecosystem members. These roles have very different responsibilities in the ecosystem, and although a specific entity may wear different hats, the role it plays at any point determines the kinds of needs it has. ESV takes into account these various ecosystem roles and provides features catered specifically for various ecosystem members.

ESV provides a rich set of functionality to allow service deployers, service providers, service users, and governing bodies to interact with the registry.

Governing Body or Consortium

The governing body or consortiums usually specify the framework that ecosystems participate within. In Chapter 5, we discuss their role in helping lay out the framework for discovery and interaction via the vocabulary and contracts abstractions. The *market tools* that ESV provides allow these governing bodies (also called *market makers*) to:

Figure 11.3. ESV registry.

☐ Create and manage (including deletion) category and category *hierarchies*

☐ Create and manage (including deletion) vocabularies

☐ Create and manage (including deletion) contracts

☐ Secure the above ecosystem abstractions

ESV is a global registry.   Hence, it could contain several ecosystems. Thus, the *category* or the specific market segment that the ecosystem caters to is important, as well as the vocabulary and contract framework. The category hierarchies are primarily to facilitate browsable searching.

XML is accepted as an important way of HTTP-based communication. ESV allows for creation of vocabularies and contracts, using XML specifications through an upload of an XML document that specifies the vocabulary or contract to be registered.

The market maker tools that provide these features are browser-based wizards that walk the market maker through the process. In Section 11.2.4, we demonstrate these wizards in action.

Service Deployer

The service deployer may be the same as the service provider; however, in the ecosystem, we differentiate between the two. This distinction is helpful because it allows the provider of the business logic to be separated from the entity that manages the service registrations.

Assuming that a service is ready to be deployed and made visible in ESV, ESV provides the service deployer with a set of wizards to facilitate the following:

- Step-by-step wizard for self-registration of services in ecosystem
- Wizard for codeless registration of business processes as web services (including non-e-Speak services)
- Wizard for codeless registration of business processes as web services

Codeless registration of business processes allows for the abstraction of the service to be registered while the actual service itself resides at the service deployer. This could be firewall protected because e-Speak's firewall traversal technology facilitates using firewall-protected services as discussed in Chapter 9. XML and Web-based specification of service descriptions are supported by ESV, again to facilitate XML-centric computing that has become so prominent.

There are also some additional features of ESV that make the service deployer's efforts of maintaining an ESV presence a bit easier. These are listed below.

- Saving auto generated e-Speak wrapper at the client side: When an ESV service is registered, there is e-Speak wrapper code that is generated and saved on the client side that registered the service. This wrapper is used during service management, such as automatic restart.

- Automatic restart of services: When an ESV-registered service fails, it can be easily restarted by using the e-Speak wrapper code generated by the ESV service registration process.

- Signed applet: A wizard-provided signed applet allows for the e-Speak wrapper code to be saved and for the service to be *started* on the client side.

- Access control for services: Access control restricts usage of the services to authorized entities.

To understand the vocabulary and contract specifications to abide by, the service deployer may need to browse the registry or use information provided by the ecosystem it plans to deploy within.   An out-of-band interaction may occur to grant access to the category (which represents an ecosystem or specific market) to the service deployer between the market maker and the service deployer. At this point, ESV access control is `ESVid`-based and, hence, not the most sophisticated architecture. However, it does provide rudimentary access control if required by the market maker. The services are secured in a similar fashion; that is, the access control provided to service deployers allows for `ESVid`-based access control. Thus, service is secured by the `ESVid` associated with the service user. As ESV (or other registry technologies) matures, one of the hurdles these need to surpass is the security surrounding the registration, management, deployment, invocation, and maybe even discovery of registry-based services. We discuss the future of registries in more detail in a later section of this chapter.

Service User and Service Provider

Facilitating discovery of services is the primary purpose of online directories such as ESV. The sophistication provided by the e-Speak technology and the ESV lookup feature set does facilitate discovery. ESV provides a few different kinds of lookup mechanisms:

- Attribute-based lookup of services: This advanced lookup mechanism allows vocabulary-savvy users to look up services in a market or ecosystem based on attributes associated with a specific vocabulary.

▣ Keyword lookup of services: Keywords can be associated with services at the time of service registration. This lookup allows for more generic searches based on a *desired class* of services.

▣ Browsing through service category hierarchies: This is the simplest form of lookup that allows the service user to browse the various categories and locate a desired service.

ESV also provides a *bookmarking* mechanism to identify favorite services that are used often. These are listed in the ESV user's home page in the `Bookmarked Section` of the My E-services Village personalized home page.

In Chapter 6, we discuss composed services or high-level services. Service providers that are composing lower level services together to make the high-level services can use the lookup features provided by ESV to identify the specific lower level services they desire. Hence, this functionality is important for service providers because it also facilitates market and competitive research, assuming that a service is not secured via access control.

11.2.2   Community

As is standard in many portal technologies, ESV provides user management capabilities to register new users and maintain their accounts. Associated with each user is a personalized home page — My E-services Village. This personalized page manages the registration entries made by a particular `ESVid`. For example, a market maker user with registration entries for vocabularies, contracts, and categories would see these entries in the associated My E-services Village home page. The My E-services Village page also provides the delete functionality to remove a registration from the ESV directory and the list of bookmarked services for easy access. A typical My E-services Village home page is depicted in Figure 11.4.

Building community around the ESV users is an important part of the online directory. The community fosters the incubation and experimentation with e-Speak services. Facilitating communication related to services is an important part of ensuring that services are useful and can meet users' needs. Service-provider brand identity can be promoted by associating the branding and logo of the service

Figure 11.4. My E-services Village.

provider with the service registration. This ensures that the service providers can differentiate themselves from other providers of a similar service.

ESV also allows service users to rate the services and provide feedback to the service provider associated with a service. These comments and ratings are also visible to future potential service users. However, the comments and ratings (as in all cases) cannot be wholly relied upon. These are comments from endusers and, with that, contain the frustration and perhaps experience bias that the user has with the service. The law of averages may alleviate some of the extreme responses in either case. For now, service users are likely to rely on their own experiences in determining whether to use a service. In the future, unbiased ratings and reviews may come from experienced service appraisers that review services based on their inherent and consistent quality.

Table 11.1 provides a summary of the roles and the feature set provided for that role.

Table 11.1. E-services Village features for ecosystem members

Role	Feature
Governing body	Define markets
Service deployer	Register services
Service user	Discover services

11.2.3   Technology

ESV is based on the e-Speak technology, so it benefits from the scalability and strong security inherent in e-Speak. It also provides a level of richness that is not yet available in the current competitive technologies, such as the Universal Description, Discovery, and Integration (UDDI) 2.0 specification (discussed in detail in Chapter 14). HP has joined the UDDI effort and, as a Working Group member, has the ability to influence the direction of the UDDI specification. The knowledge and learning gained from the ESV experience will help to converge the two technologies, creating a more standards-based and rich-registry technology.

11.2.4   In Action

The ESV registry is an ideal place for incubating the services that we developed in this text. The Travel ecosystem governing body decided to publish the Travel ecosystem framework in the ESV. This includes the Hotel Information services and the Faber participating Airline services. In this section, we walk through the browser-based wizards to accomplish some of the tasks that various ecosystem members can perform via ESV.

Creating a Market

A market is an e-Speak service category that contains a predefined set of vocabularies and contracts — an ecosystem. Any registered ESV user can create a market. ESV includes a tool called *Define a Market*, which is a group of wizards that allow users to create markets without writing any code. The market-maker wizards are accessible from the My E-services Village page. In Figure 11.4, those wizards are available on the right-hand navigation bar.

Creating a market entails choosing the specific location within the category hierarchy, creating the vocabulary for the specific ecosystem, and finally, creating the associated contract. In this example, we set up the *Travel ecosystem* that we discuss throughout this book. Figure 11.5 depicts the start of the market-maker wizard; the wizard uses a trail map approach to walk the market maker through the process.

Figure 11.5. Creating a market.

The first step is to decide where to place your market in the category hierarchy. Because we are registering a Travel ecosystem, we choose to place it in the Industries root category by clicking on `select`, next to the category of choice. The category selection is based on a Hierarchical Category Menu System, and thus, the market maker and service deployers need to drill down to the appropriate sub-category to locate an appropriate space for the category or service registration. Figure 11.6 depicts this selection and the subsequent step, which names the category (market).

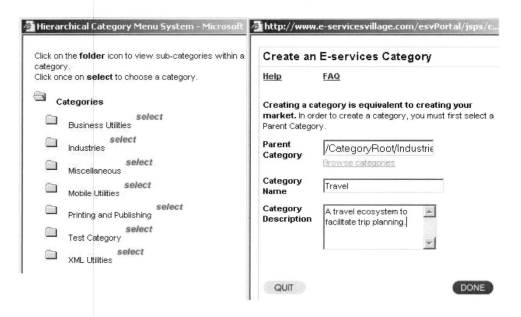

Figure 11.6. Creating the market category.

Once the category has been successfully created, you will be able to see it in your My E-services Village page.

The error handling of the ESV registry is not fully developed, and hence, there may be times when an error is displayed that does not indicate what the true problem is. It may help to ensure that you are not trying to register a category that is already present in the parent subcategory you are working in.

At this point, the market maker needs to register the vocabulary and contracts for the Travel ecosystem. Referring back to Figure 11.5, we see that creating the associated travel vocabulary is the second step of the wizard. As we mentioned before, there are two choices to registering the vocabulary — the wizard-based approach or the XML document-based approach. We use the wizard-based approach in this example. After selecting the `travel` category we created earlier, the market maker names the vocabulary and provides a description for it; this is similar to what we did for creating the category and this is depicted in Figure 11.7.

Figure 11.7. Creating the hotel vocabulary.

After clicking on `Next`, we get the attribute form that allows you to enter the attribute and type information for the vocabulary elements. Recall that the `HotelVocab` consists of:

- Name
- City
- Phone
- Email
- AAARating

- HasOnSiteRestaurant
- HasSwimmingPool
- RoomType
- NumberOfRooms
- NearestAirportCode
- URLPrefix

Entering this information into the form and clicking on `Next` creates the `HotelVocab` in the category `travel`. If it is successfully created, you will see a message stating so; however, the ESV environment may report a false success. Again, as the technology matures and evolves, logging and error handling are expected to improve.

The final (and also optional) step to creating the market is to associate a contract with it. Figure 11.8 depicts a portion of the contract form that appears.

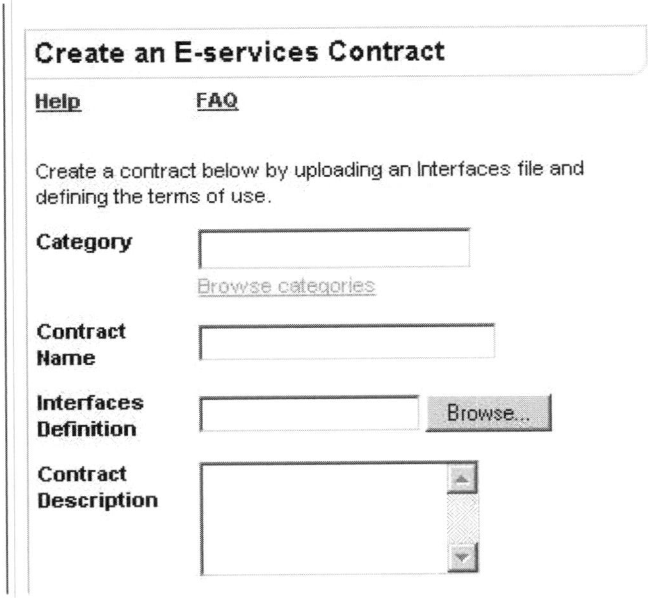

Create an E-services Contract

Help   FAQ

Create a contract below by uploading an Interfaces file and defining the terms of use.

Category

Browse categories

Contract Name

Interfaces Definition   Browse...

Contract Description

Figure 11.8. Creating the airline contract.

The important component of this step is indicating the interface definition for the services that participate in this ecosystem. If we look at the Travel ecosystem we use in this book, we see that the airlines had two competing contracts: Faber and Weber. In this Travel ecosystem, the Faber contracts are supported, so we choose the *FaberFlightIntf.esidl* interface definition. The contract form also includes licenses and terms of use sections that can be used to dictate some more specific service-level agreements and legal constraints. However, it is unlikely that any of the constraints placed in these sections will be legally binding because the legality of such constructs is still unclear. As *Internet law* matures and decisions are made that can take precedence, it will remain ambiguous as to what is and is not enforceable and, of course, to what degree is it punishable.

Registering a Service

At this point, the Travel ecosystem is created and ready to be used by service deployers to deploy the participating Hotel and Airline services. Registering a service within this ecosystem involves completing the eight-step wizard depicted in Figure 11.9.

We are registering a Trip-Planning service in the Travel ecosystem. You could have registered any one of the Hotel or Airline services, as well. As is the case in many of the ESV wizards, the naming form appears as the first step (depicted in Figure 11.10).

The next few steps involve associating the service with the Travel ecosystem framework. We indicate the category: `/Category/Root/Industries/Travel`. We then indicate the vocabulary: `HotelVocab`. Figure 11.11 depicts the vocabulary form. The vocabulary associated with the particular subcategory appears in the pull-down menu, starting with default.

Once the `HotelVocab` is chosen, the wizard will load the attribute form, based on the attributes associated in that specific vocabulary. It looks similar to Figure 11.12.

The next step in registering the service is linking the service class file and indicating where the e-Speak installation is on the system hosting the service. After that, the list of contracts that appear in the specific ecosystem are displayed (again in a drop-down menu), and the appropriate one needs to be chosen, as depicted in

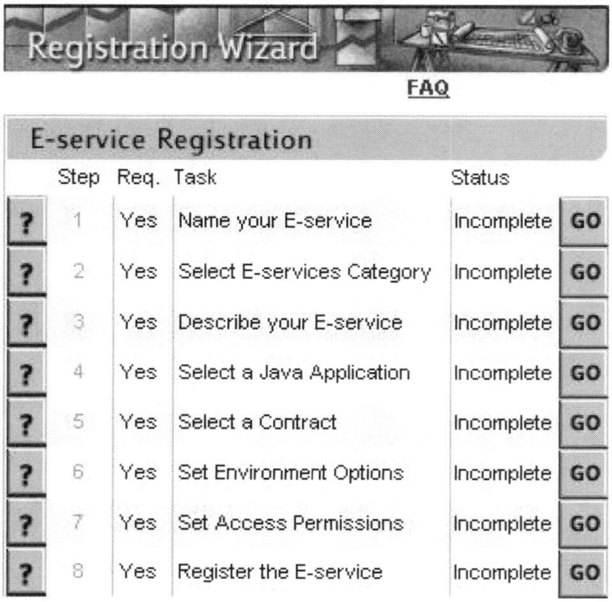

Figure 11.9. Eight-step service registration form.

Figure 11.13.

The next form of the wizard (Step 6) is where several environment options are set. For example, if this service is behind a firewall, you indicate where your Java Virtual Machine (JVM) installation is and a few other parameters. This information is used in a later step to *start* the registered service, so that if users find the service, they can proceed in using it. Step 7 provides access control. Again, the access control is based on the ESVid, so it is not as sophisticated and still requires the service provider to have some level of access control for the traffic that does not come via ESV. In Chapter 8, we discuss how services can be secured using certificates. At this point, we are ready to *register* the service because the wizard has all the information it needs to do so. A signed applet appears, carries out the processing of the class file selected, and registers the service with ESV. A window appears with the logging information that is produced as a result of the applet. Figure 11.14 depicts this information.

Figure 11.10. Step one in service registration.

When this processing completes, the service is up and running and registered in ESV. Figure 11.15 summarizes the steps that were covered in this process.

A registered service can be discovered through the search wizard and workflow, which are similar to the registration wizard and workflow. Using the search wizard, a service within a specific category and vocabulary can be discovered and used.

11.3   Maturing of the Registry Concept

Registries are a very important part of the services vision. However, registry technology available today is still very nascent. There are several industry-level issues that need to be addressed and certain mindshifts that need to happen before the concept of registries (both public and private) moves into the mainstream — in much the same way that Web-searching portals of the likes of Yahoo! and Excite became popular only when Web sites were easily deployed and became accepted

Describe your E-service
Help
FAQ
You must choose an existing vocabulary to describe your E-service. Once you have chosen the vocabulary, you will be asked to populate each of the vocabulary attributes. These attributes form the description of your e-service, and enable clients to find your e-service with simple or sophisticated queries.
Vocabulary
default
QUIT
NEXT

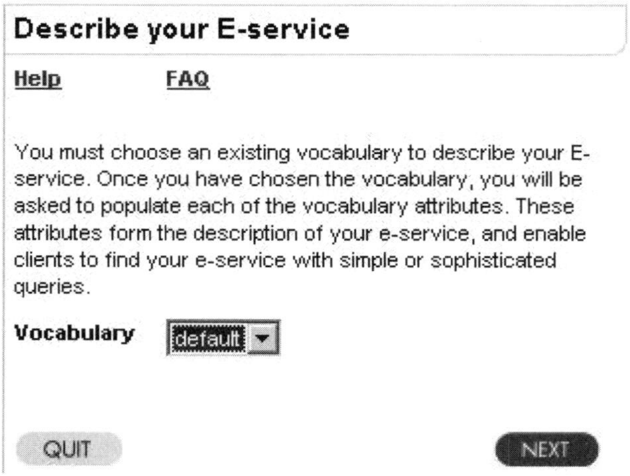

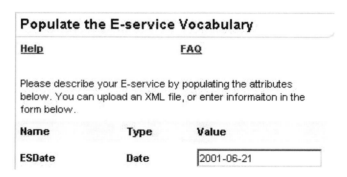

Figure 11.11. Vocabulary step in service registration.

Populate the E-service Vocabulary
Help
FAQ
Please describe your E-service by populating the attributes below. You can upload an XML file, or enter informaiton in the form below.
Name
Type
Value
ESDate
Date
2001-06-21

Figure 11.12. Vocabulary step in service registration.

in people's minds as a mechanism for information gathering.

11.3.1 Business Paradigm Shift

The focus on core competency was the spark of the outsourcing trend that has now become a billion-dollar industry. Companies now outsource everything from trade show planning and participation to major marketing communication and pub-

Figure 11.13. Contract step in service registration.

lic relation efforts. Core competencies of a shoe manufacturer would not normally include photographing the latest basketball star in its shoes; hence, the relationship between a company and the advertising agency is created. The shoe company can spend its valuable time, talent, and money resources on designing the ultimate shoe while the ad agency keeps up with the latest thinking on attracting the attention of the so-fickle teenage population.

Web services and the ability to make the Web work for you could allow companies to go even beyond such large-scale efforts. Web services can be thought of as a unit of specialized functionality. Deploying this specialized functionality in an accessible manner allows other businesses to incorporate the functionality in their business processes. In the Travel ecosystem, the Trip-Planning service was a specialized whole unit for trip planning that could have been composed into a higher level service consisting of trip planning, trip reservation, and trip monitoring. All could be *provided by* different service providers but, to the company using these travel services, it appears to be a seamless whole that allows its employees to con-

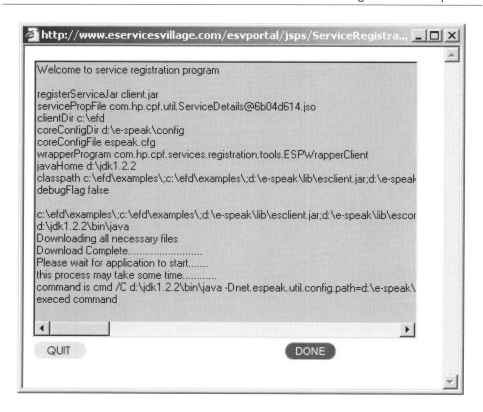

Figure 11.14. Applet step in service registration.

duct business travel without engaging an *in-house* travel department or managing an expensive outsourcing relationship.

This example can be replaced by a supply chain business-to-business scenario in which parts of the supply chain are really specialized units of functionality provided by experts. Imagine a logistics-planning service provided by leaders such as Ryder or Federal Express. This service can be used by a smaller New York City hand carrier's business processes to determine each hand carrier's schedule. This makes the NYC hand carrier's business *dependent* on the availability of the logistics-planning service. This level of engagement implies trust that, at this point, develops as a result of the human interactions between concerned parties. Trust is contracted and enforced legally via legal documents that stand up to courtroom

Figure 11.15. Summary of service registration.

battles.

The business paradigm shift really entails bartering dynamic trust between businesses (the service provider and the service user). Governing bodies and consortiums can play a role in bartering this trust (just as they facilitate interaction between service providers and service users).

Role of Consortium

Consortiums or governing bodies provide an *unbiased* forum for industry participants, users, and other interested parties to discuss obstacles and issues that
affect the success of the industry or space. For a service-centric economy built on
a registry, *bartering trust* is definitely one such obstacle to mitigate.

In Chapter 1, we talked about the roles of the governing body and the ecosystem
arbitrator. These *unbiased* entities (usually made up of competitors and partners)
can work to build the trust in an ecosystem.

Setting up a monitoring system that keeps tabs on the interactions between service providers and service users is extremely important for fostering trust in the
service users — especially those who stake their businesses on services found in
an ecosystem. The Securities Exchange Commission (SEC) monitors (via various
forms, procedures, and laws) companies that are publicly traded. Without the back-
ing of the SEC, many investors would be very wary of investing their hard-earned
money in the stock market.

Despite a strong monitoring system, there may be situations that arise between a
service provider and service user.   With the absence of a crisp legal foundation
in the Internet space, there can be some level of arbitration and dispute resolution
provided by a third-party arbitrator. The arbitrator should be accepted as the dispute resolution entity; therefore, it needs to be a truly independent entity. When a
consumer pays by check and there are insufficient funds in the consumer's bank
account, the dispute between the store and the consumer is usually handled by
a bank or other financial institution, rather than between the two parties. Ecosystems and registries can be facilitated by an arbitrator that is entrusted with the
responsibility of finding fair and amicable resolutions for disputes.

Of course, service appraisal facilities and rating mechanisms can also do a lot
to help foster trust in the ecosystem. The ability to research the performance of
services and to review service levels will increase as the service-centric economy
matures and develops a transactional history.

11.3.2   Security

Security continues to be a major concern as businesses start to consider opening up their assets for public consumption. In Chapter 8, we discuss security provided by the e-Speak platform and its ability to protect the transactional environment between the service user and service deployer. Security with respect to registries is just as concerning. The concerns center around issues such as:

- Securing and restricting the *use* of services
- Securely managing and versioning services
- Securing the transactional data that goes across the wire
- Having fine-grained access control

Security of the interaction patterns that occur via the registry infrastructure is be-ing worked on and developed by various initiatives and standards. However, in the interim, private registries with stricter access control and limited exposure can achieve some of the benefits while reducing the risk.

11.3.3   Private Registries

The concept of a service registry is still new to the computing industry, and as a result, registries are not pervasive or widely accepted. Any existing public reg-istries, including the ESV, have yet to gain the trust of service users and service providers exposing their public workflows or business processes. This can limit the adoption of the service-based business paradigm because the gap between the service users and the service providers cannot be bridged effectively without the registries. The situation is very similar to the Web sites on the Internet. A lot of users use the search engines to discover sites they do not even know exist. In this case, however, the search engine is a registry of Web sites that is trusted by the users.

In such a scenario, a private registry that operates in a secure and controlled envi-ronment is an excellent alternative. A private registry, usually established to serve a private ecosystem, is under tight control by the ecosystem host or governing body. Access to a private registry is granted based on the policies of this host or governing body. Also, typically, the host or the governing body is the beneficiary of such an ecosystem. An example private ecosystem is discussed in Chapter 4. The access control mechanism to a private registry must be more elaborate, compared with the lightweight user-password mechanism employed by ESV. In such a case, the registry would be behind a firewall that this opened to select ecosystem members.

Although the private registries give total control to the host over the environment and services registered in it, it has two inherent disadvantages, compared with a public registry. First, the registry owner (ecosystem host) must provide all the necessary operational infrastructure to operate the registry. The second reason has more to do with the dynamism in service interaction. Because the private registry owner has complete control over the registration, in a way, it already knows about *all* the services that can provide a certain functionality. This limits the dynamic discovery aspect of services. Also, the optimal choice of the service user, in case of a private registry, is limited to the services registered in that registry. It is possible that there would be more optimal choices in the service network that exists beyond the concerned registry. The service user using the private registry would be completely oblivious to the existence of those services. Despite these disadvantages, private registries, managed carefully, can provide the core benefits of a registry.

11.4   The Future of Registries

The future of registries is being discussed and thought about by several members of a growing industry consortium. This consortium, Universal Description, Discovery, and Integration of Business for the Web (UDDI for short), includes several technology and business companies. Their desire is to make web services and their usage and discovery a standard business practice. As part of their efforts, they develop specifications that determine how best to provide registries that will facilitate scenarios like those discussed in this chapter. However, they also work closely with potential endusers to learn how to mitigate issues such as those discussed as part of the tertiary concerns. Chapters 14 and 15 discuss UDDI in more detail.

Applied E-Speak

PART Four

Case Studies

CHAPTER 12

Chapter 12

CASE STUDIES

The examples and discussion in earlier chapters have provided a solid foundation for incorporating particular e-Speak features and functionality into a service and its environment — whether it be security, across-firewall transactions, or registry interactions.

In this chapter, we take these same e-Speak concepts and apply them to two real-life business situations. In the first case study, we delve into the business-to-business world and watch how e-Speak can facilitate a procurement process for a large company. In the second, we see how e-Speak can facilitate location-based mobile services and helps print an important document at the nearest printing store.

We describe these scenarios by walking through the service lifecycle as applicable for deploying an e-Speak service-based solution. Applying e-Speak in such situations is the focus of this chapter, so we take you through developing the vocabularies to use, the type of security to enforce, and the high-level system landscape for the services developed with the help of the examples in this book.

12.1 Procurement

During their product generation processes, manufacturing companies need several types of raw material and parts. Generally, required raw material and parts for manufacturing a certain product are *well known* in a manufacturing process. This includes specifics such as:

- Quantity required per unit
- Quality level
- Substitute material

When a manufacturing run (either forecasted or customer-specific) is planned, the raw material and parts are procured. Companies usually stock up these parts based on product generation requirements, using market forecasts. These parts *must be* available (on hand or readily obtainable) so that the manufacturing processes can flow smoothly. Typically, manufacturers manage relationships with several vendors to supply these. Usually, *just-in-time* manufacturing procedures dictate that when inventory of raw materials or parts goes below a certain level, the procurement procedures determine the inventory requirements for the raw material and parts. A procurement order to restock the inventory to support the manufacturing plan is then placed with an appropriate vendor.

These requests are directed toward the set of suppliers that the company has established relationships with. The suppliers can then respond with their bid (quote) for supplying the desired quantity. A quote usually minimally includes the price for the quantity and the terms related to supplying at that price. An example term that could be associated with a quote could its *expiry date*. Because the market price for many raw materials fluctuates frequently, the expiry date protects the supplier from vast differences between the quoted price and the market price.

Optimizing procurement processes has long been recognized as a valuable tool to provide a competitive advantage to companies. The optimization, in this case, involves several factors. It is not always the *cheapest* supplier that wins orders. The quality, credit rating of the vendor, other references, and recommendations, as well as the company-vendor relationship history, all play a role in the awarding of a contract to a specific vendor. Something as fleeting as the procurement manager's bad *vibe* around a particular vendor might also throw a few vendors off the playing field. Similar criteria come into play when a supplier makes a decision to respond to a manufacturer's need for raw material and parts. For example, even if a supplier has a good relationship with a manufacturer, it may decide not to respond to a particular request because the order is perhaps too small or too large for the supplier to handle. Optimizing the chain of events from the point in time when a inventory need is recognized to the time it is received (i.e., the procurement cycle) is a complex undertaking, mainly because so many *nontechnical* factors affect the final decisions made.

The process by which a buyer and a seller come to an agreement to engage in a trade is called the *RFQ* process. An RFQ (request for quote) is a very commonly used procurement process for obtaining goods, raw material, supplies, labor for contract work, and other services from vendors. This is also called *direct procurement* because, in this case, the customer buys the goods directly from the vendor. It is interesting to note that the RFQ is a generic process that is useful whenever someone has a need for service to be performed or goods to be obtained outside the scope of their entity and needs to locate the appropriately skilled entity to fulfill that need. A state government desiring to widen a major freeway may develop an extensive RFQ to put forth in the civil engineering industry.

12.2   RFQ Basics

The most generic process of direct procurement involves the following steps:

1. The buyer posts a list of required items to appropriate suppliers.

2. The RFQ document includes specification, configurations, and other raw material or parts criteria.

3. The RFQ is reviewed by one or more suppliers.

4. The suppliers then submit a bid or quote in response to the RFQ.

5. The buyer reviews and awards the contract to one or more of the responding suppliers.

6. The goods and money exchange hands.

The RFQ process can be classified into the following categories:

◾ Single-Step RFQ: In this case, the buyer knows exactly what it wants (especially true in the case of tangible products). This is the process defined above. Industries that typically use single-step RFQ are the electrical, mechanical, semiconductor, medical equipment, aviation, metals, and customized parts industries.

■ Two-Step RFQ: In the two-step RFQ process, the buyer asks for a *proposal* based on a generic requirement (consisting of a description of the desired product or service) in the first step. This is generally used when the exact requirements, specifications, and desired result are not easily described. The document distributed by the buyer is called a *Request For Proposal* (RFP). The selected RFPs go into the second step, in which companies negotiate on the requirements and the price associated with those. Industries such as software services and civil construction employ a two-step RFQ process. In general, an RFQ is used for needs that can be described in a very specific manner. An RFP is used either when the products are complex or requirements are not very well understood. In such a case, the first step helps in solidifying the requirements, so that the supplier can quote a price based on these.

■ Multistep RFQ: In this type of procurement, there may be several steps before the actual bidding begins. Government contracts, typically, follow a multistep RFQ. The first rounds are related to supplier selection. For example, a certain contract may require that the supplier company have certain certificates of standardization or it must employ environment- and animal-friendly procedures in its manufacturing. Some companies are selected based on their abilities to satisfy the early step requirements. These chosen companies then can participate in RFQ processes similar to the single-step or two-step RFQ processes.

Another important factor is the process by which the buyer chooses to announce the RFQ. In general, a buyer can announce two types of RFQs:

■ Private RFQ: In this case, the buyer creates the RFQ and sends it to *preselected* suppliers; these suppliers could be a subset of the entire supplier list. These are the only ones eligible to bid on the particular RFQ. The list of suppliers is subjective to the buyer's selection criteria and may vary from time to time. Usually, companies use private RFQs if they have a special trust and confidence in the suppliers' ability to deliver on the RFQ. A private RFQ is easy to administer. However, it limits the participation of the suppliers. The received quote is *best* only among the group of chosen suppliers.

■ Public RFQ: In a public RFQ, in contrast to the private RFQ methods, the buyer creates the RFQ and announces it to the public for bidding. All or any suppliers are free to bid on such an RFQ. The public RFQ ensures that all the interested suppliers get a chance to bid, but it is also difficult to administer.

12.3   RFQ Business Process Flow

In general, an RFQ goes through several stages during its processing cycle. We define below a very general description of the business process associated with RFQ processing. There are several variations in practice that are specific to each industry. Also, in most real-world implementations, there is a uniqueness associated with each company's business flows. Figure 12.1 depicts this process flow.

1. Buyer identifies needs for purchase of direct procurement material and creates the RFQ, which typically includes a list of items, specifications, diagrams and pictures, terms and conditions, quality requirements, and delivery schedule for the material that needs to be purchased.

2. Buyer chooses an RFQ methodology. This determines the steps involved in the RFQ process and the potential set of suppliers who are eligible to respond.

3. After complete review of RFQ data, buyer posts the RFQ.

4. Appropriate suppliers determined by buyer's RFQ methodology get an invitation to participate in the RFQ process.

5. Interested suppliers review the RFQ and decide whether to send a response to the RFQ.

6. Each interested supplier prepares the bid for the RFQ, which typically contains information about prices for the items requested by the buyer, delivery schedule, and supplier's terms and conditions.

7. Supplier, after review, submits the bid to the buyer.

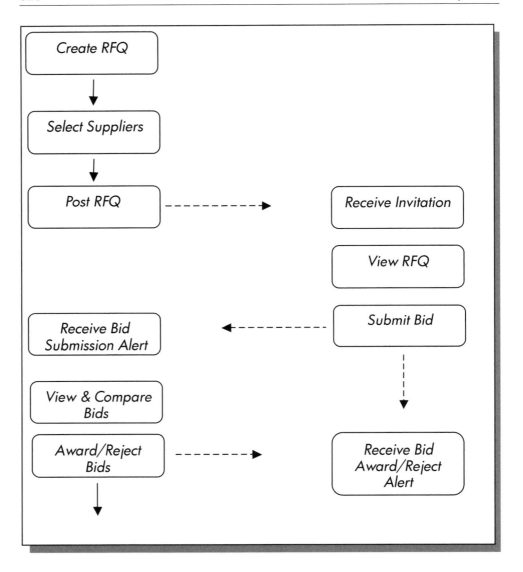

Figure 12.1. General RFQ process flow.

8. After a certain prespecified date, the RFQ is closed.

9. Buyer reviews all the submitted bids.

10. Buyer then rewards the bid to one of the suppliers. The selection of a specific supplier is based not only on quoted price but depends also on other crucial factors, such as quality and availability of material (or some other deciding criteria appropriate to the situation).

11. Buyer will send the appropriate bid award and rejection notification to participating suppliers.

12.4   RFQ Processing for AmCAR, Inc.

In our case study, we consider a car manufacturer, *AmCAR, Inc.* AmCAR is a leader in the car industry and is known for its innovative car designs. AmCAR has manufacturing plants around the world to optimize the cost of manufacturing. These plants manufacture several different car models, based on the local market preferences and demands.

Manufacturing cars requires AmCAR to have several raw materials and parts on hand. Everything from the tires to the sunroof glass, to the metal for doors is procured from various suppliers. AmCAR has been in the car industry for many years and has developed an *extensive* list of suppliers. Its suppliers are categorized by tiers denoting preference levels for each tier. Ideally, all procurement would happen from the top-tier suppliers, but as we noted before, suppliers also have a *choice* to respond to a company's material needs, and hence, managing a host of suppliers (multiple ones for any part in particular) is a very important part of the procurement process.

In most cases, AmCAR floats an RFQ to its list of suppliers. The supplier that submits the most optimal bid is awarded the contract for that particular part list. Recall that the optimal bid is a combination of price, circumstance, and general *confidence* about the situation and the suppliers involved — especially when Am-CAR's top-tier vendors choose not to respond to an RFQ. In some cases, AmCAR decides to award partial contracts to two or more suppliers to complete the desired quantities.

12.4.1   Status Quo

Presently, AmCAR uses a paper-based RFQ processing system. RFQs are generated by hand, based on reports from the inventory systems (what is available) and the manufacturing plan (what is needed). The inventory systems trigger notifications when inventories of raw material, parts, and supplies go below a certain optimum level, and those triggers are reports that are sent to various procurement managers. Each AmCAR procurement manager is responsible for a defined set of material *and* the set of vendors that provides those material. This process is very labor-intensive and cumbersome to work with for both AmCAR and its suppliers. Some of the limitations with the current process are that it:

- is prone to errors because RFQs need to be manually created from the reports; a misplaced decimal could push a raw material beyond the appropriate quality levels.
- can bottleneck easily as responsible procurement managers get involved in other things, go on sick leave, take vacations.
- can be subjective because the procurement managers would add their impulses and situational biases.

Due to the complexity and these limitations, the RFQ process is inefficient and costly. AmCAR has experienced problems — even shut down production lines because of understocked raw material, parts, or other supplies.

12.4.2   Service-Based RFQs

The supply chain business strategy team at AmCAR decided to design a new automated procurement process. This new project, pet-named *Omega-3*, would deploy a fully automated process that would be used for procurement of parts and raw material.

As part of the proposal to the project's sponsor, the team listed the following benefits of Omega-3:

- Reduced procurement cycles

    □ Cost reduction

    □ Effective selection and negotiation with suppliers

In short, a much more efficient process would result. To reduce the risk of breaking the procurement process altogether, the team has chosen to implement Omega-3 in a phased manner. Rather than using it for the pan-AmCAR parts procurement system, the solution will be used during the advanced prototyping phase of a new car model — the *Excelsior*. Every year, AmCAR manufactures a limited number of preview cars with all the new bells and whistles and advanced aerodynamic technologies. These preview models are tested for their marketability and quality and, if approved, brought to market in subsequent years. Because the main *customers* for these cars are car shows across the country, the risk of deploying a new procurement process is reduced greatly.

As part of the new product introduction process, a bill of materials for the *Excelsior* is created. The executive sponsor, although supportive of the project, insisted that *existing suppliers* should be part of the new system. The existing process of floating an RFQ and selecting a quote from one of the responding suppliers will still be used; however, it will be automated by Omega-3.

12.5   AmCAR RFQ System

The Omega-3 system follows the process flow described earlier. AmCAR has decided to use its existing relationships with its tiered suppliers to float the bids through the new system. The Omega-3 efficiency and benefits are experienced through an automation of the manual process described earlier. As the automation is planned to be end-to-end, there will be software components deployed in the environments of both AmCAR and its suppliers. The list of eligible suppliers is determined by AmCAR.

12.5.1   Service Lifecycle: Strategic Planning

AmCAR uses a private RFQ announcement model because any RFQs are expected to be floated only within the tiered suppliers; the Omega-3 solution needs to be able to restrict the visibility of any RFQs, based on certain criteria. In this *strategic planning* phase, the appropriate partners, operating interaction patterns, business models, and frameworks for the service need to be developed.

Partners

AmCAR has solicited a few of its top-tier suppliers to participate in the pilot run of the Omega-3 solution. For now, AmCAR has restricted this pilot phase to the tire manufacturers and will deploy to the other raw material and parts vendors for the Excelsior car in a phased manner. Of the tire suppliers AmCAR has relationships with, the following have signed up for the Omega-3 program: GoodTire, Inc., WoodFire, Inc., and Texon Tire, Inc. The process followed in the discussion can then be repeated with suppliers of other distinct parts or required subsystems.

Interaction Patterns

The Omega-3 system includes an RFQ-generating component that generates the RFQs based on triggers from the inventory systems and manufacturing plan (for products and prototypes). The generated RFQ includes:

- Tire specifications
- Tire quantities
- Delivery dates required
- Cost information
- Credit terms desired

This RFQ is then *sent* electronically to *specific Omega-3 pilot* tire suppliers. Upon *receipt* of the RFQ, the Omega-3 tier suppliers will review it and develop an appropriate response, if desired, in the form of a quote. AmCAR *awards* the specific contract to the supplier that provides the most optimal bid.

Business Models

AmCAR's tire procurement department and the group of three tire vendors form an ecosystem. The appropriate business-level relationships and discussions around this ecosystem must happen at this stage. This ecosystem uses Omega-3 as the platform to transact its business of procuring tires for the *Excelsior* prototype.

Since the RFQs are private in nature — being floated to only very specific vendors — the ecosystem is also *private* in nature. It exists to serve the car manufacturing needs of only AmCAR corporation. The access to this ecosystem is controlled by AmCAR, and AmCAR also makes business and technical policy decisions to operate this ecosystem. It is not unusual for big companies to create such private ecosystems that cater to their needs and the needs of their partners. Note that AmCAR could have also decided to participate in some existing public ecosystem. However, the executive sponsors wanted as much control over their internal and critical procurement processes as possible; hence, deploying a private ecosystem was desired.

Note

There are several advantages to a private ecosystem. For the ecosystem host, which is usually the ultimate beneficiary of the ecosystem as well, a private ecosystem gives a high degree of control over the functioning of the ecosystem. The business and technology policy decisions can be made by the host swiftly and to the extent that they benefit the host itself. A private ecosystem is also a good alternative in absence of a (competent) public ecosystem. In such a case, the private ecosystem, if successful, can be transformed into a public ecosystem. The SABRE system developed by American Airlines is a good example of such a transition.

Framework

Because AmCAR is designing, developing, and implementing the Omega-3 platform to enable the interaction between the ecosystem members and itself, it acts as the *ecosystem host*. It is also the *governing body* for this ecosystem because it makes the policy decisions for this private ecosystem. Recall that the governing body is *responsible* for the operating framework in the ecosystem: the vocabularies, contracts, and other operating procedures.

As the governing body, AmCAR defines the vocabularies and contracts associated with each ecosystem member. These vocabularies and contracts are binding to all the members, and adherence to them is essential for smooth functioning of the ecosystem.

12.5.2 Service Lifecycle: Requirements

The requirements phase of the lifecycle encompasses the discussions with the procurement managers involved, the executive sponsors, and the three Omega-3 tire vendors. Based on these discussions, several criteria or functional requirements were developed to adhere to in designing Omega-3. These requirements can be summarized as follows:

- Support for private RFQ
- Support for targeted RFQ delivery
- Support for anonymous contract announcements
- Support for easily discoverable RFQs
- Support for easily discoverable bids
- Support for real-time notification of new RFQs and bids

With these requirements understood and the partners lined up, it is time for the Omega-3 team actually to design the service and the operating environment of the ecosystem.

12.6 The AmCAR Procurement Ecosystem

Figure 12.2 depicts the AmCAR Parts Procurement ecosystem.

A *Procurement e-Speak service* that belongs to the AmCAR procurement department manages the RFQ process, as described earlier. This service is responsible for creating an RFQ and publishing it to the Omega-3 suppliers via the *AmCAR*

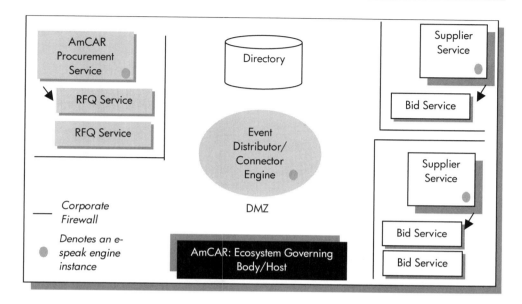

Figure 12.2. AmCAR Parts Procurement ecosystem.

Procurement ecosystem. The suppliers are represented in this ecosystem by the Supplier services and the bids themselves.

The Omega-3 team analyzed the results of the strategic planning phase, and a scan of the competitive landscape and competitive technologies (Chapters 14 and 15) for distributed computing that could facilitate the cross-entity transactions between AmCAR and its suppliers resulted in choosing the e-Speak platform.

The designed architecture and interaction patterns among participants of the AmCAR Procurement ecosystem are shown in Figure 12.3. Notice that any transaction initiating entity needs to operate an instance of the e-Speak service engine. These engine instances communicate with each other to share resource metadata for resources registered with them and manage the event distribution solution. This figure shows only the tire suppliers, but a similar infrastructure will exist for the other suppliers as they begin to come on board with the Omega-3 platform.

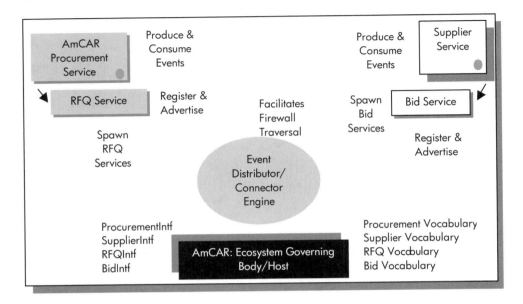

Figure 12.3. Architecture of the AmCAR Procurement ecosystem.

12.6.1 Procurement and Supplier E-Speak Services

With the selection of the e-Speak platform, the services (Procurement and Supplier) need to be described, registered, and discovered in a similar fashion to those discussed in the examples of this book. The AmCAR Procurement service is responsible for floating new RFQs, using information extracted from a system that contains the product information and the bill of materials (BOM). Each RFQ is an engine-registered service, as well, that is described, registered, and advertised in the ecosystem. The Supplier services respond to the RFQ positively by generating a quote or negatively by rejecting the RFQ. Like the RFQs, individual bids are also engine-registered services in the ecosystem. The ecosystem directory is a private registry where the services are registered, so that they are discoverable and could be interacted with. Figure 12.3 shows the Supplier e-services from tire suppliers that participate in the new AmCAR procurement process.

Recall that services follow a defined set of steps to participate in an ecosystem. The services describe themselves, register themselves, and finally, advertise to others. The description is based on a defined vocabulary schema that the governing body develops. In this case, the governing body, AmCAR, has developed the following vocabularies:

- Procurement vocabulary
- Supplier vocabulary
- RFQ vocabulary
- Bid vocabulary

12.6.2   Ecosystem Vocabularies

The Procurement service vocabulary consists of the Base Vocabulary attributes: `Name` and `Version`. Since the names of these services are explicitly known to the participating parties, no other descriptive attributes need to be made available for the discovery of this entity-level service.

The individual RFQs, however, are not known prior to the transaction time. Therefore, the vocabulary associated with RFQs is more elaborate. After discussions with the procurement managers, the following `RFQVocabulary` was developed. The vocabulary is depicted in Table 12.1.

Table 12.1. RFQ Vocabulary

Attribute	Description
RFQ number	Reference number used for RFQ
RFQ description	Description of the RFQ
Start date	Date on which the RFQ is posted onto the RFQ system and is available for bidding
End date	Date after which no bids are accepted: i.e., the RFQ is closed
Category list	The category to which the RFQ belongs; e.g., RFQ belongs to tires category

Table 12.1. RFQ Vocabulary *(continued)*

Contact information	Information on how to contact the buyer
Billing details	Billing address
Shipping details	Shipping address
Payment details	Credit card, escrow, demand drafts, or otherwise
Vendor information	General-purpose information about the buyer. Examples: name, Web site
Note	Free-formatted text for comments from the buyer
Terms and conditions	The different terms and conditions include payment terms, transportation terms, conditions for sale, and other terms
Item	Item for which quote is requested from suppliers
Item code	A unique item code
Item name	Name of the item
Item description	Description of the item
Unit of measurement	The basic unit by which the quantity of the item is measured
Quantity	Quantity of the item
Expected delivery schedule	Expected delivery date for the item
Quality	Quality requirements for the item
Attachments	These might be specs or drawings related to items
Dimensions	Dimensions of the item
Unit of dimension	Unit of measure of the dimension; e.g., cm, meter, feet
Weight	Weight of the item
Unit of weight	Unit in which the weight is specified; e.g., kg, lb, oz

Working with the Omega-3 vendors and the procurement managers, the vocabularies `SupplierVocabulary` and `BidVocabulary` were developed. The former is used

to describe the supplier by publishing details themselves. The `BidVocabulary` publishes the bid information. Tables 12.2 and 12.3 depict these vocabularies.

Table 12.2. Supplier Vocabulary

Attribute	Description
Supplier company	Name of the supplier company
Address	Address of the supplier company
Telephone	Telephone number
Fax	Fax number
Contact information	Information about contact person
Category list	Supplier(s) will be classified into category based on the type of material they sell

12.6.3   Interaction Patterns

In Chapter 5, we discussed the fact that a service *description* consists of the vocabulary attributes, as well as the contract it abides by. The Omega-3 development
team has also worked on interfaces that the various services need to provide to assist those that discover these services. There is a variety of information retrieval
methods that start with the prefix *get* and a few information update methods that
start with the prefix *change*. Table 12.4 depicts a subset of these methods.

12.6.4   Event Architecture

The Procurement service generates a new RFQ when the inventory system sends
it a trigger. Once the RFQ is generated as a service, the Procurement service registers and advertises it out to the AmCAR Procurement ecosystem. The Supplier
services then generate Bid services that registered and advertised in the same
ecosystem.

Part of the Omega-3 system includes an event architecture that notifies the Sup-

Case Studies   Chapter 12

Table 12.3. Bid Vocabulary

Attribute	Description
RFQ number	Associated RFQ number
Bid reference	Reference number used for bid
Bid description	Description of the bid
Contact information	Information about how to contact the supplier
Payment details	Payment mode
Remit to	Remit to address
Vendor information	General purpose information about the supplier. Examples: name, Web site, etc.
Note	Free running text for comments from the supplier
Quote	List of quotes for items specified in RFQ
Item code	A unique code that identifies the item
Item name	Name of the item
Item description	Description of the item
Unit of measurement	The basic unit by which the quantity of the item is measured
Quantity	Quantity of the item
Price	Price of the item
Expiry date	The date after which the quote is not valid
Tentative date of delivery	Date on which supplier can deliver the item

plier services when an RFQ has been registered and advertised and notifies the Procurement service when a Bid service has been registered and advertised in the ecosystem. These events are depicted in Figure 12.4.

In our example, `TireRFQEvent`, published by the Procurement service, will be received *only* by the Supplier services. The Supplier services for the tire suppliers will be *listening* for only the `TireRFQEvent`, as shown in Figure 12.4.

Once the RFQ availability event is received by Supplier services, these services will discover the RFQ and retrieve related information. If interested, the Supplier

Table 12.4. Ecosystem Members, Contracts, and the Interfaces

Service	Contract	Methods
ProcurementService	ProcurementIntf	getRFQsPosted()
SupplierService	SupplierIntf	getSupplierName()
		changeMyContactName()
RFQService	RFQIntf	getQuantity()
		changeEndDate()
BidService	BidIntf	getPrice()
		changeExpiryDate()

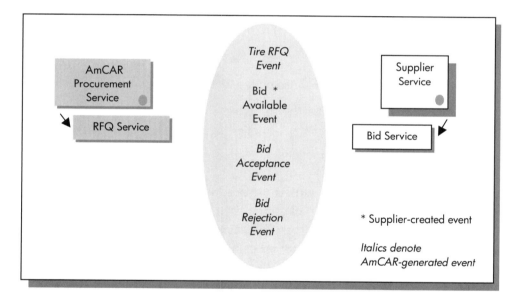

Figure 12.4. Omega-3 RFQ event architecture.

service prepares the bid for the discovered RFQ and advertises it. A second event is generated at this point. This is the `BidAvailableEvent`. The Procurement service *listens* for this event and discovers the advertised bid after it. The various bids are reviewed as they are discovered until the `EndDate` for the open RFQ is reached; at this time, the RFQ is closed, and the system no longer accepts bids.

As the Omega-3 system matures, there might be a systematic way to award the contracts; however, in this pilot phase, the Omega-3 system selects the winning bid. This bid is reviewed by the procurement managers. The Procurement service then generates two more events — a `BidRejection` and a `BidAcceptance`. The terms of the bid and the RFQ are then carried out, resulting in an exchange of money and goods.

12.7   Deployment

Now that the discovery and invocation framework has been considered, the Omega-3 team needs to develop the *deployment* architecture for the AmCAR Procurement ecosystem. The deployment of Omega-3 needs to:

- Be secure
- Operate across multiple firewalls on respective engines
- Provide a persistent architecture
- Facilitate easy event access by all entities
- Support out-of-band interactions

In the following discussion, we expand the security requirement in detail because it is an extremely important part of the deployment. The lack of a strong security policy could cause concern among participants. Hence, any deployment that involves opening up some portion of a business process to partners is going to be scrutinized for security holes. We then touch briefly on each of the remaining deployment criteria in the previous list and highlight the interesting aspects to consider.

12.7.1   Omega-3 Security

Securing the AmCAR Procurement ecosystem is a major part of the Omega-3 deployment. Security involves:

- Securing and protecting the data

- Enforcing authentication
- Configuring authorization levels
- Maintaining data integrity
- Honoring individual network boundaries

Securing and Protecting the Data

The ecosystem needs to ensure that the data was not only secured but also protected from unauthorized access. Encryption of the RFQ and bid information being registered and transferred in the ecosystem is facilitated by the public-private key infrastructure. However, simply encrypting this data is not enough. It should also be protected; imagine a tire vendor being able to view a competitor's bid. This unauthorized access would provide an unfair advantage over others. The Omega-3 tire suppliers that agreed to participate in this ecosystem all insist that the strictest of data privacy be deployed. They did not want to risk the chance of their Bid services being *viewed* by any of the other vendors. AmCAR's management is also sensitive to all this data being transferred over the Internet. It feared other car manufacturers gaining access to information about the well-guarded, new *Excelsior* model. Hence, strict authentication was designed into the Omega-3 system.

Authentication

Authentication ensures that the entity communicating is actually who it says it is. This is facilitated by identity certificates and the certificate authority. The certificate authority in this case is AmCAR as the ecosystem host and monitor. Whenever contact is initiated in this ecosystem, an entity will be required to authenticate itself before proceeding to use the authorization levels it was granted.

Authorization

Once an entity is authenticated in the ecosystem, it still needs authorization rights to interact with the services. Table 12.5 lists the ecosystem members and the contract method authorization rights it grants and to whom.

Table 12.5. Authorization Granted in AmCAR Procurement Ecosystem

Issuer	Subject	Accessible Methods
ProcurementService	SupplierService	get*
ProcurementService	RFQ	get*
RFQ	SupplierService	get*
RFQ	ProcurementService	get* and change*
SupplierService	ProcurementService	get*
SupplierService	Bid	get*
Bid	ProcurementService	get*
Bid	SupplierService	get* and change*

Recall that e-Speak includes the strictest level of security policy. If no certificates are exchanged, absolutely no authorization rights are granted. Access is expressly granted via certificates and authorization tags. Therefore, if a non-Omega-3 supplier tries to access a posted RFQ, it will be denied access because it does not have the appropriate authorization certificates.

Overall Security

General data integrity is preserved via the on-the-wire protocol; in this case, it is the TCP/IP and the ESIP protocols. Thus, using these standard protocols relieves the ecosystem and its participants from dealing with data integrity. However, should a failure in the environment occur, especially mid-transaction, the services need to have fallback mechanisms because the e-Speak infrastructure does not contain reliable messaging by default. The overall solution needs to incorporate a reliable messaging component to provide the fullest data integrity.   The firewalls help protect the ecosystem members' various intranets by honoring individual network boundaries and reducing the risk of exposing a company's business logic to the general public.

12.7.2   Other Deployment Features

Deploying across corporate firewalls on several engines with a persistent architecture is completely possible with the e-Speak technology. Figure 12.5 depicts the set of systems that make up the AmCAR Procurement ecosystem and denotes the locations of various e-Speak engines, as well as corporate firewalls.

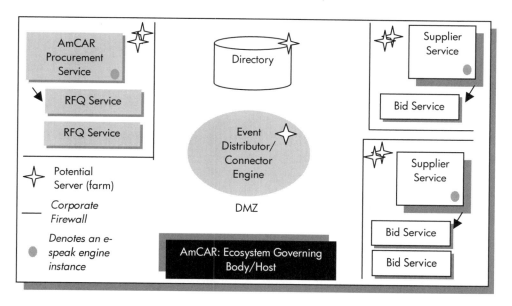

Figure 12.5. AmCAR Procurement ecosystem systemscape.

The appropriate advertising groups and communities need to be formed and deployed (via the advertising services configurations) to facilitate discovery and invocation across the set of engines making up the ecosystem. Figure 12.5 depicts a potential advertising service grouping and the set of advertising services deployed.

Recall that at least one e-Speak engine must be located in the DMZ to facilitate firewall traversal as per the *connector scenario* discussed in Chapter 9.

As far as possible, the registration and advertisement information, as well as the services, must be persistent. These could be made persistent by using a persistent repository and non-guest accounts for service registration and advertising.

Often, an RFQ or a bid will be accompanied by supplementary information. The tire procurement team has a set of very detailed tire specification documents that *can be* made available should the supplier need them. These are not part of the RFQ themselves because they are very large documents. An out-of-band interaction environment is deployed with a Web server to serve the documents to the Bid or Supplier services. The details of this type of deployment are available in Chapter 6.

12.8   Location-Based Mobile Services

While in the software industry Web services are making waves, in the hardware world, mobile devices seem to be in fashion. Literally millions of these smart devices have been sold worldwide. There are several different types of such devices available today, including pagers, cell phones, and Personal Digital Assistants (PDAs). Several other new *information appliances* are being designed and will be available on the market soon. There are two noticeable trends in the mobile industry today: integrated devices that have dual (or multiple) functionality and *services* on top of the device. Both of these dimensions are enhancing the usability of these devices and making them more indispensable. The integration trend has resulted in devices such as Sony Clié (integrates an MP3 player with a PDA) and HP Jornada (integrates a cell phone with a PDA).

The value-added services, on the other hand, use an existing device and build a functionality stack on top. Services such as corporate email and mobile information systems for the sales force of a company are examples of such services. These *mobile services* are where e-service and Web service technologies are a result of the intersection between the mobile space, e-services, and web services. One important class of mobile services is *location-based services*.

Location-based services, as the name suggests, provide location-savvy functionality. As the user's location changes, service invocation results in a different outcome. Some examples of location-based services are: finding the nearest point of interest, dating services, and on-the-spot product promotions. In this section, we discuss a special case of point-of-interest, location-based services.

12.8.1   Mobile Printing Scenario

Consider Ron Danforth, a salesman with a CoolSoft, Inc. — a company that makes accounting and financial software products for small and medium-size businesses. As part of his responsibilities, Ron is required to travel all over North America — his sales region — to talk to business owners and explore sales opportunities.

Being in the software industry, it is imperative for Ron to stay abreast with the latest happenings in the software industry, as well as in the financial services world — his clientele. In addition, he also needs access to customer-specific documents required during customer visits. These include product data sheets, customer information, such as buying history, and details of any contracts with the customers. Before mobile devices became popular, Ron used to take his laptop computer everywhere so that he would be able to connect to the Internet from his hotels and get the information he wanted. These days, however, Ron prefers to take his handheld device, *Corona*, on shorter trips. Corona is a top-of-the-line mobile device that has a PDA integrated with a cell phone. The PDA part of the device is also equipped with a wireless communication subsystem. Using the wireless subsystem, the device can connect to the Internet through a wireless Internet Service Provider (ISP). Corona can store contact information, limited customer data, and limited product information. Corona can satisfy most of Ron's information needs; however, it does not provide access to everything because of its limitations.

First, storage space limits the amount of data it can carry. Second, the current wireless protocols supported on it provide a very low bandwidth. This prevents downloading large documents through the communication link. Finally, because it is a handheld device, it has a very small *form factor* (screen size). This limits the amount of information that can be displayed on its screen. To optimize available storage space on the device, Ron takes only the company private data he needs on the device. He uses the Internet connection, albeit slow, to download any public information. These limitations make it difficult for Ron to have the information he needs; especially on important sales visits. According to him, it would be great to have a summary of the information (for example, news headlines) on the device, then get elaborate information on a specific item (for example, the article associated with a news headline) in print format when desired.

There are two problems that prevent Ron from making this scenario a reality. Due to bandwidth limitations, it is difficult to download detailed information. Even if he manages to download the information, he does not always have access to a printer. A mobile printing solution can help Ron stay informed, even if he is on the road. To understand the solution, it is useful to know more about the world of mobile devices.

12.8.2   Mobile Technologies

Although wireless communication technologies have been around for several years, they did not intersect with computing technologies. This is because wireless technologies were primarily focused on voice communication. Devices such as walkie-talkies and cell phones are examples of early versions of the devices that used wireless technologies. Recently, however, a number of more intelligent devices utilize wireless technologies for different purposes. These include handheld and pocket computers that extend the PDA functionality on the device, pagers, and Wireless Access Protocol (WAP)-enabled cell phones. This new breed of devices is much more intelligent, compared with earlier devices. They usually include a processor and an Operating System (OS) kernel that bring them closer to a computer. In fact, Microsoft-enabled devices are called handheld and pocket PCs!

The feature of the mobile devices are defined by three dimensions — platform, protocols, and services. The platform provides the core of hardware and software functionality. The protocols are part of the communication subsystem that help the device connect to the rest of the digital world, and the services enhance the value of the device by adding more features. Figure 12.6 depicts the mobile space. The connectivity options available on a device play a crucial role in the effectiveness of any service offered on it.

Mobile Communication Protocols

To connect to the public network, a handheld device needs to communicate with a gateway that is connected to the Internet. The connection protocols vary from device to device. For cell phones, the WAP has been available for some time.
  For PDA-type devices, protocols such as CDPD (Cellular Digital Packet Data) and GPRS (General Packet Radio Services) are gaining popularity. Both of these

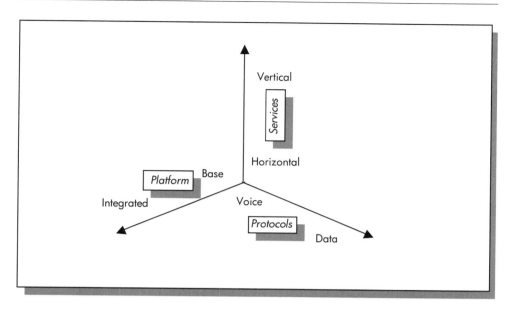

Figure 12.6. Dimensions of mobile device features.

technologies fall under the *Wireless Wide Area Network (WAN)* technology class. These protocols provide *public* network connectivity through a wireless service provider. Another class of wireless access protocols is also emerging, called *Wireless Local Area Network (LAN)* protocols. The protocol 802.11b is a good example of such a protocol. Wireless LAN protocols, as the name suggests, provide access to a local area network. A wireless LAN infrastructure is typically deployed within a corporate network boundary. Wireless LANs are characterized by bandwidth that is much higher, compared with wireless WAN bandwidth. However, a wireless WAN is more pervasive, compared with a wireless LAN. The wireless LAN technologies offer connectivity for a device within a close proximity from the LAN access point. Compared with that, wireless WAN connectivity is possible virtually anywhere.

A *hot spot* is a location from where high-bandwidth connectivity (typically through wireless or wire-line LAN technology) is available. Examples of hot spots are corporate offices, airports, and coffee shops. Usually, these locations are equipped with high-speed Internet connectivity. A device that is connected to the network from a hot spot can transact more effectively, due to the availability of high band-

width. Whenever possible, a user would prefer to have device connectivity established from a hot spot. However, when it is not possible to do so, the wireless WAN
technology is another option. Together, the wireless LAN and WAN technology can
provide close to an "always connected" experience from a mobile device. The mobile ecosystem that facilitates mobile printing on demand consists of such devices
and a backend connectivity infrastructure.

Many Web sites are mobile-device savvy and can filter the content before it is sent
to such a device. This filtering is called *repurposing*. A repurposed site appears,
potentially, much different from the original Web site. Several features (for example,
graphics and navigation icons) not supported on the device are omitted for a better
user experience. Repurposing can also limit the amount of information sent to
the device, and thus, only a subset of the information, that which is deemed vital,
may be sent to the mobile device. Repurposing is a very effective and bandwidth-
friendly way to get the gist of the information to a mobile user.

12.8.3   Mobile Printing Ecosystem

A solution to Ron's problem requires alliances between various entities, such as
print service providers and location-savvy components in the mobile marketplace.
It would be easy to think of this new set of interactions in terms of an *ecosystem*
that serves a specific need — namely, mobile printing. The *Mobile Printing ecosystem* can bring necessary services together and define the interaction among them
to facilitate mobile printing needs similar to Ron's. Figure 12.7 depicts one such
ecosystem.

The user of the ecosystem services in this case is a mobile professional who would
like to stay connected with the Internet while on the road and would like to get as
much information as he or she needs by circumventing the limits of the mobile
device used. The service user uses the mobile device to connect to the Internet
through one of the connectivity options described earlier and gets to the desired
information. The general activity of *web surfing* is not necessarily visible to the
ecosystem in this case. Presumably, the Web sites providing the information of
interest to the user are repurposed for the device. When a user is interested in
receiving detailed information, the interaction with the mobile printing ecosystem
begins.

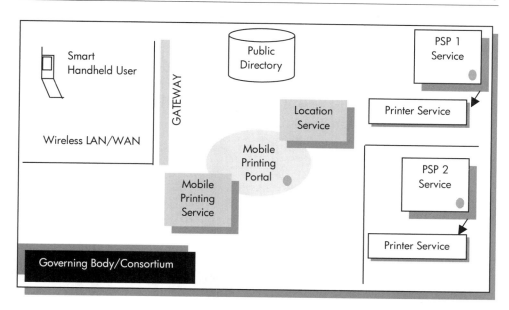

Figure 12.7. The Mobile Printing ecosystem.

At the center of the mobile printing ecosystem is the ecosystem host. The ecosystem host brings together the mobile device users and the print service providers. From that aspect, its role is similar to the procurement ecosystem host, discussed earlier in this chapter. A request from a service user typically includes the Uniform Resource Locator (URL) of the information that needs to be printed and the *location* of the user. The request also specifies certain print-quality instructions, such as color or black-and-white copies or two-sided and photo-quality printing.

Several methods and technologies to specify locations are available in the market today. A location service that effectively determines the exact location of the service user is an important part of the mobile printing ecosystem. Once the location of the service user is determined, a suitable Print Service Provider (PSP) must be located that can fulfill the user's print request. This search, based on the e-Speak service discovery mechanism, can take into account several predefined and user-specified parameters to find a printing provider. To enable this discovery, each PSP must register a service representing itself (or each of its stores, if it is a chain) with the ecosystem and describe its capabilities. The vocabularies required in the ecosystem can be defined by an independent consortium or the ecosystem governing body. Using the service descriptions and the location of the user, the Mobile Printing service can locate the most optimal PSP that can fulfill the user's request. Once a suitable PSP (or PSPs) is found, the service notifies the user about the PSP locations and other attributes, such as price and rating associated with that PSP. The user then decides whether to respond to any offer and communicates his or her decision to the Mobile Printing service. The service then submits the request to the appropriate PSP.

Once a PSP receives a print request, along with an associated URL, it prints the document for the user. Within its setup, the PSP uses an e-Speak service engine for load balancing purposes. When a print request is submitted to a printer farm, an e-Speak engine determines the best way to schedule the print job. Using the print-quality instructions from the service user, as well as the printer description registered with the engine, the best printer to print documents from a user request is determined. From this list, the printer that has the appropriate load is chosen to print the document. Note that it is also possible to change the priority in the print queue to move a print job in that queue, if required. When printing is completed, the PSP can notify the user so the user can pick up the document at a designated time.

The interaction sequence in the Mobile Printing ecosystem is as follows:

1. The Mobile Printing ecosystem host creates the necessary platform for its functioning.

2. The ecosystem host invites appropriate entities to populate the ecosystem. These entities include the governing body, foundation and extended services, and potential service users.

3. The PSPs that wish to participate in the ecosystem register their print capabilities with the ecosystem.

4. The user submits a mobile printing request to the Mobile Printing service. The request includes the user's location, the URL of the document(s) to be printed, and print-quality and pickup instructions.

5. The location service determines the list of potential PSPs that can fulfill the user request.

6. Using the user parameters, the Mobile Printing service selects the best PSP that can fulfill the user request.

7. The Mobile Printing service communicates the list of PSPs and pertinent data for the user's consideration.

8. The user determines whether he or she wishes to submit the print request to one of the PSPs.

9. The user submits electronic payment (digital wallet-based or credit card) to the PSP.

10. The PSP receives the print request and determines the best printer from its printer farm to queue the print job.

11. Once the document is printed, the PSP notifies the user that the document is complete and provides directions from the current location or a specified location to the PSP.

12. The user retrieves the document from the PSP at the designated time.

12.9   Summary

The e-Speak technology and its architecture provide a robust infrastructure that can be used to develop business-class services, such as the Procurement service; and mobile services, such as Mobile Printing service, discussed in this chapter.

12.9.1   The Mobile Printing and Procurement Ecosystems

It is useful to note the differences between the two ecosystems presented in this chapter. The two ecosystems catered to two different market segments. The Procurement ecosystem functions in the Business-to-Business (B2B) area and is a private ecosystem that serves the purpose of a specific company. The Mobile Printing ecosystem, on the other hand, caters to the Business-to-Consumer (B2C) marketplace. It is a public ecosystem that is open to the general consumers and services in the public domain. It is not designed to serve any particular entity in particular. The Procurement ecosystem is a very tightly bound ecosystem. All the ecosystem members are aware of other entities in the ecosystem, and the role of each ecosystem member is known ahead of time. The Mobile Printing ecosystem, in contrast, is a loosely coupled ecosystem where the ecosystem members are not necessarily well known in advance.

It is worth noting that these ecosystems are not completely different from each other. They still use the ecosystem concepts described earlier. Both the ecosystems can be treated as a functional unit and can participate in a higher level ecosystem. This composition of ecosystems is a useful concept to bring several ecosystems together, similar to service composition that brings several services together.

12.9.2   XML-Based Ecosystems

The interactions and transactions in the case studies were based on the Network Object Model (NOM), discussed in Chapter 2. In the next chapter, Chapter 13, we discuss both e-services and web services. Web services, as you see in that chapter, relies on the Document Exchange Model (DEM), with XML over HTTP as the primary transport mechanism.

These ecosystems can be deployed based on the DEM paradigm. The interaction patterns that are invocation based would be replaced with specially formatted XML documents. For example, the RFQ service would be an XML document representing the RFQ. It would be sent to the selected suppliers who, upon receiving, would have some XML processing components that will take the XML-RFQ and develop an appropriate XML-Bid to submit in response.

In the same way that the vocabulary and contract information needed to be shared and agreed to by various parties in the ecosystem, the XML documents need to be formatted in an agreed-upon format. The tags used to describe the RFQ and the bids must be well known so that the processing components on either side of the interaction can work with the received document. The main difference is the transport mechanism — whether it is object-based or document-based. More about these types of technologies can be found in Chapters 14–16. In the next section, we discuss the role of services in the mobile computing environment.

E-services and Web Services

Chapter 13

E-SERVICES AND WEB SERVICES

In Chapter 1, we briefly touch on the differences between the two industry terms, e-service and web service. Although Hewlett-Packard's (HP's) e-service vision incubated the industry thought around Internet-based services, the term *web services* has (like most children do) gone off to have a slightly different meaning. The difference between these two terms and related concepts is mainly caused by the technologies supporting the different service visions. E-services are supported by e-Speak, and web services are supported by more standards-based and interoperable technologies. There is also a difference in prioritization between the two. Whereas the e-Speak technology provides a more comprehensive solution, web services technologies (discussed in Chapter 15) rally behind interoperability, and hence, in trying to saddle agreement among standards bodies, is somewhat behind in reaching the completeness of e-services and e-Speak.

From an industry perspective, it would be desirable to converge the two visions. This convergence would bring forth a solution that has the completeness of e-services *and* the standards-body adoption and interoperability of web services. We try to emphasize the similarity between the two visions and expedite the convergence between the two. Both facets — completeness and interoperability — are crucial to wide adoption of service-based computing thereby resulting in a very personable and rich experience for the users of the Internet. Some of the convergence between the two can already be observed as e-Speak embraces the Simple

Object Access Protocol (SOAP) messaging standard and as e-Speak technologies are submitted to standards bodies for wider adoption. HP is also consciously using the term *web service* to describe its newer technology offerings (discussed further in Chapter 16.

Because e-Speak is an e-services reference implementation, it implements most of the features that can be found in competing web services solutions. While both technologies have provisions for issues in service-based economies, there are differences in what is used to *answer* them. Prominent among them are:

- Service Invocation
- Security Provisions
- Low-Level Interoperability Infrastructure
- High-Level Interoperability Infrastructure
- Service Description
- Service Registries and Service Discovery
- Security
- Orchestration of Public Business Processes
- Integration with Behind-the-Firewall Workflows

In the next few sections, we draw out some of the differences highlighting advantages of either, wherever possible. The goal in this comparison is not so much to prove which technology or vision is better than the other, but more to point out differences that must be resolved to arrive at the comprehensive strategy that is inclusive of *both*. For each of these, the discussion first summarizes the e-Speak A.03.11 feature, followed by the general approach used by different flavors of web service implementations.

13.1   Service Invocation

E-Speak services are primarily Internet- and intranet-accessible distributed components, called *resources*, that can be invoked in a secure manner from any *e-Speak* registered client. The focus of this book has been on how to develop, deploy, and invoke e-Speak-based e-services. The key point to note is that e-Speak is required on either side of the interaction in order to provide the secured channel and robust discovery mechanisms. It is precisely in this arena, service invocation, where e-services and web services differ significantly.

13.1.1   Web Service Approach

Currently, the term *web services* is generally accepted to signify services that can be invoked over any TCP/IP network. Usually, a client invokes a web service by using the Hypertext Transfer Protocol (HTTP) POST protocol to send an XML request to a web service. The web service then receives the request, processes the XML, creates an XML response, then sends the XML response back to the client in the HTTP response. Processing of an incoming XML document, here, can mean a large spectrum of activities such as transforming it into another language or invoking a number of potentially behind-the-firewall processes.

To provide the channel that allows clients to access web services, most web services infrastructure vendors use *off-the-shelf* web servers with special *web services plug-ins* that can map received XML documents to backend servlets or objects, or another XML-savvy entity.

Although web services are typically invoked using the HTTP protocols (or HTTPS protocols, when security is required), they can also be invoked by clients emailing XML requests to web services. It is also possible for clients to send XML requests into web services via message queues or even by using the File Transfer Protocol (FTP). In fact, any technology that can be used to transfer an XML request from a client to a web service (and from the web service back to the client) can be used as the underlying transport mechanism for web services. This interaction pattern can be seen in Figure 13.1.   The primary mode of interaction for web services is based on the Document Exchange Model (DEM).

As discussed in Chapter 2, DEM is primarily suitable for asynchronous interactions that are *long-lived*.   The long-lived interactions are the interactions that take significantly longer time to complete, compared with the interaction between tightly coupled distributed objects. Table 2.1 compares the two interaction models. Web services use DEM as the primary interaction method.

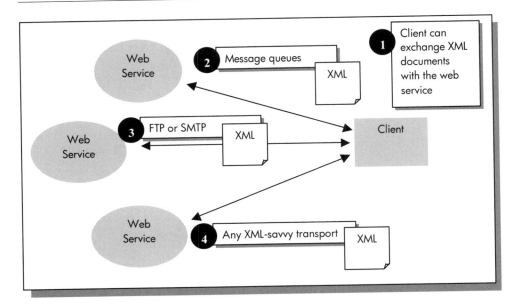

Figure 13.1. Invoking web services.

The current e-Speak engine is primarily based on the Network Object Model (NOM); it also supports the DEM, to some extent. The implemented DEM features use XML as the foundational technology. Throughout this book, however, we have used NOM-based examples because e-Speak's NOM model is much more developed and complete. The important e-Speak contribution is the *same* set of abstractions provided for both the interaction mechanisms. Thus, at a conceptual level, the e-Speak interaction mechanism subsumes the web services model. However, due to support for standard protocols and related tools in web services, the Document Exchange Model is easier to deploy for the web services.

13.2   Security Provisions

E-Speak is first and foremost a platform that provides very secure and reliable business-to-business (B2B) integration solutions that include end-to-end security. As such, it provides an innovative, trust-based security that goes above and beyond the level of authorization available through off-the-shelf security solutions constructed using Secured Sockets Layer (SSL) and X.509 certificates in addition to the HTTPS protocol. Although the aforementioned security standards are a part of the implementation of e-Speak's unique security, e-Speak's SLS protocol provides fine-grained security at a level not found elsewhere within the industry's current web services offerings. Only with a security technology as rich as SLS can businesses form truly secure virtual private service networks using the public Internet. This security mechanism is discussed in Chapter 8.

13.2.1   Web Services and Security

All the major web services platforms being developed and marketed today rely on Internet standards for transporting and securing communications. This means that they leverage technologies such as SSL, HTTPS, X.509 certificates, and Secure Multipurpose Internet Mail Extensions (S-MIME). This is a very reasonable design decision to make because all the popular Internet infrastructures already support such security standards. Using standards-based security provides an evolutionary migration path into the world of web services computing, rather than introducing an entirely new and nonstandard security model.

So how does e-service security based on e-Speak compare with that available with today's web services solutions? Many of the current solutions provide, at the most, very lightweight, large-grained solutions that leverage HTTPS protocol provided by the web servers upon which the services are built. If only large-grained security access is needed (that means that one can decide who can access their *entire* web server but not who can access individual business documents or parts of business documents), then there is less of an advantage in using e-Speak's SLS. However, if a fine-grained access control is needed over vital business documents, then a good choice for trust-based security is to use the SLS protocol.

For complex business interactions that involve several parties, a fine-grained security model, such as the one provided by SLS, must be adopted. For this, the SLS-based security model or something with similar abilities must be adopted by standards bodies.

13.3   Low-Level Interoperability Infrastructure

The low-level interoperability infrastructure refers to the protocols and standards that are used during messaging and communication. When two or more systems interact with each other, the protocol for the communication channel and the structure of the messages sent over that channel must be defined and agreed on by all the parties. This level is considered *lower* because it does not attach any semantic meaning to the messages or to the sequence of the messages. That is the responsibility of some *higher* level interoperability standard.

The development of e-Speak started prior to the introduction of web services standards such as SOAP and Web Services Description Language (WSDL). Therefore, the architects who designed e-Speak needed to devise their own enveloping and document transport technologies. The work in this area is in the form of e-Speak's messaging architecture, as discussed throughout this book.

E-Speak defined a messaging architecture that was very similar to today's SOAP specification. Each message contained an envelope that itself contained a header and a body. Routing and transport information was stored in the header; business documents were stored within the body. The underlying technology used to transport these messages is MIME-based, and the assumption was that most implementations would use HTTP or HTTPS protocols to exchange business documents. In the recent releases of e-Speak service engine and the Service Framework Specification (SFS), e-Speak's service modeling specification, support for SOAP-based messages has been included.

13.3.1   Web Services Trends

SOAP is an enveloping technology that allows XML business documents to be transmitted using standard Internet protocols. SOAP is becoming the de facto standard transport mechanism for web services infrastructures. Prior to the advent of SOAP, web services solutions provided their own proprietary schemes for exchanging business documents with trading partners, as is the case with e-Speak. Most used XML to represent the business documents, but none shared the same techniques for enveloping those documents or transmitting them across the Internet. The industry as a whole seems to be converging to the SOAP specification for most web services messaging, so that the infrastructures of various vendors can interoperate.

13.4   High-Level Interoperability Infrastructure

A high-level interoperability infrastructure is just as important as the low-level infrastructure that is used to transport business documents. It is a set of agreed-upon standards for nearly everything that the lower level standard does not address. Coupled with the lower level interoperability standards, the higher level standards provide a complete interaction specification between interacting entities. Typical high-level interoperability standards include:

- Format of business documents
- Specification of the business processes
- Document security and security policies
- Guarantee of document delivery
- Quality of service metrics, such as response time

E-Speak's SFS describes a business interoperability framework that rides on top of its messaging technology. The idea is that businesses conducting e-commerce would use this messaging standard and the business level interaction protocols to exchange business documents. The business documents themselves and the semantics for the exchanges of documents would be specified by rules outlined by the SFS. The SFS assumes that business documents exchanged by services are represented as XML and that XML Schema is used as the metadata describing those documents. However, it is not currently widely adopted by the web services industry.   SFS goes as far as describing the semantics for the following types of two-way interactions (or *conversations*, in the SFS jargon):

- Clients querying the e-services for the XML descriptions of their public interfaces
- E-services advertising themselves throughout an e-Speak service network
- Clients finding e-services throughout an e-Speak service network

◻ Business initiation dialog between a service and its clients

◻ Contract negotiation

◻ Representation of conversation semantics that an e-service supports

13.4.1   Web Services High-Level Interoperability Infrastructure

The three most relevant specifications that address similar issues in the web services world are those proposed by RosettaNet, ebXML, and Microsoft's BizTalk 2.0 framework. These are discussed in greater detail in Chapter 15. Note that the service framework is only one part of the e-Speak stack. Thus, it is possible to adopt a more standard service framework into other e-Speak components in the future. At the time of writing this book, no standard in particular seems to be dominating the market.

13.5   Service Description

Service description is one of the most important concepts that e-Speak brought to the industry. Service description is at the core of the service-centric computing and the dynamic interaction. E-Speak provides the following types of service description attributes:

◻ Formats of exchanged business documents: In e-Speak, text attributes, and under the DEM model, the XML DTD and XML Schema languages are used to describe business documents. The SFS also describes some standard formats for documents that provide "horizontal" services, such as querying an e-service for its public interface.

◻ Service signatures: E-Speak offers an e-services infrastructure to provide a mechanism for querying the public interfaces of services and representing those public interfaces as XML files. This is called *service introspection*. Although not very rich today, service introspection can, in principle, provide very elaborate information about a service. This service metadata can be used to make a decision about whether to engage with a service.

▪ Business process definitions: Originally, e-Speak was designed for single message-in, message-out service invocations. The service engine used in this book is currently based on this architecture. With that execution model, all that would be required to describe a service is which business objects or documents it accepts and which business objects or documents it responds with. After a few e-Speak implementations, it was clear that e-services would be multiple-step "conversations." To describe the semantics of such services, the e-Speak development team proposed the Web Services Conversation Language (WSCL).

▪ Bindings (addresses) for accessing services: Since its inception, e-Speak was designed for distributed computing. As such, one of the most important components of e-Speak was its federated registry of services — much like the Common Object Request Broker Architecture (CORBA) Trader Service. As e-Speak matured into an Internet-accessible e-services infrastructure, HP deployed the E-services Village (ESV). Any e-Speak service that is deployed onto the e-Speak core advertises its Uniform Resource Locator (URL) into the ESV. Clients that want to access the service then retrieve its address by looking it up in the ESV. All binding information for e-Speak services is stored in the ESV.

13.5.1   Web Services and Service Description

Web services also recognize the importance of describing themselves such that they can be found and used by service users. Web services provide similar description features sets.

▪ Formats of exchanged business documents: Since XML has become the standard language used to represent business documents exchanged with web services, the XML DTD and XML Schema languages are used to describe business documents.   Many industry-specific business documents are also being standardized by organizations such as RosettaNet, ebXML, and BizTalk.org.

▪ Signatures of web services: Web services are invocable chunks of software that are triggered by sending them XML business documents. For each web service, there is a *signature* that is defined by the shape and content of the input documents that can be sent to it and the output business documents that it will respond with. Currently, the WSDL is the de facto standard for describing this information. However, ebXML proposes an alternative language called a Trading Partner Profile (TPP). Clients of web services may want to obtain these signature definitions. Often, web service providers will place these signature definitions on Web servers or register them with a public registry, such as the one provided by Universal Definition Description Integration (UDDI) group.

▪ Business process definitions: The concept of business process definitions for web services is much less standardized, compared with the *signature* concept. This is because there is still debate within the industry about whether there is really a requirement for multistep web services and, if so, how to describe the semantics of those web services. There have been many alternative suggestions for languages to use for these descriptions. Some of them are XAML, Microsoft's XLANG (pronounced *slang*), IBM's Web Services Flow Language (WSFL), HP's WSCL, ebXML's BPSS, and BEA's XOCP. The competing standards are discussed in detail in the subsequent chapters.

▪ Bindings (addresses) for accessing web services: Bindings are the technical details for accessing web services. These details include what enveloping technology to use for transporting the messages, such as SOAP or ebXML's Message Specification. In addition, bindings typically include the address (usually a URL) to access the web service. Binding information can be placed within WSDL files. However, because addresses of web services may change more often than their signatures, it often makes sense to store binding information independently of the type of information stored within a WSDL file. Therefore, all web services registry technologies allow you to place binding information directly into the registry and associate it with a web service.

13.6 Service Registries

As mentioned in Chapter 11, e-Speak's ESV is the Internet-accessible registry used to advertise and discover e-Speak-based services. Each service that advertises itself into ESV can associate its address with a rich *ontology* that fully describes its features and properties. Ontologies can be thought of as the categories of services — each category with a specific set of associated vocabularies and contracts. When clients query ESV for services, they can leverage the ontology infrastructure to create rich queries, enabling them to acquire access to exactly the services they desire, as seen through the examples discussed in this book.

13.6.1   Web Services and Service Registries

Web services are distributed components of processing that are accessible across a local network or even across the World Wide Web (WWW). Because clients will often access services whose addresses (URLs) they do not know ahead of time, there needs to be a mechanism whereby web service providers can *advertise* the existence and addresses of their web services and whereby clients can *look up* services by company name, service name, signature, or other property. In a sense, what is required to do distributed web service-based computing is the equivalent of a phone book's "white pages" and "yellow pages."   This is the service that is provided by UDDI and ebXML's Registry.

13.7   Orchestration of Public Business Processes

Orchestration is the management of the orderly exchange of documents that occurs between businesses conducting a transaction over the Internet. Orchestration can be thought of as the infrastructure for executing the "public business process" that binds together trading partners.

Usually, when two or more trading partners decide to collaborate with each other, they get exposed to internal (private, behind-the-firewall) workflows in each other's organizations. These private workflows are very proprietary to the company to which they belong. It is generally desirable to not expose the other partner to these processes for two reasons:

> An internal workflow that is exposed to the world can compromise the business conduct confidentiality of a company. In some cases, the trading partner can use the knowledge to its advantage.

■ On the other hand, for trading partners, this means that any time the internal process changes, it may need to amend its behavior while responding to it. Becoming aware of and adapting the internal nuances of one partner company may be feasible, but it is certainly difficult to do it for several business partners.

Orchestration addresses these issues by exposing only the public processes of a company to potential trading partners. The private workflows, as the name suggests, are kept internal only to the company they belong to. Due to this separation between public and private workflows and processes, there must be a layer in the architecture that does integration of public and private processes. Figure 13.2 depicts this scenario.

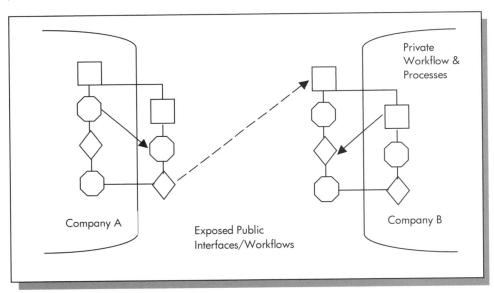

Figure 13.2. Separation of public and private workflows.

The orchestration in e-Speak is called *conversations*. Currently, e-Speak 3.11 does not contain an *orchestration* component that can execute public business processes. However, HP is currently conducting research into this area. WSCL is a step toward implementation of conversations. Future versions of e-Speak are expected to support conversations or some standard orchestration mechanism.

Most, but not all, web services solutions provide a component that performs business process orchestration. In the web services world, there are many products that provide orchestration of public business processes.   Within the .NET and BizTalk 2.0 product suite, the BizTalk Orchestration Server provides this service out of the box. IBM's solution is to provide public declarations of orchestration, using WSFL. It allows the MQ Integrator product to manage public business processes. BEA Systems' Collaborate provides orchestration services. Many of the other vendors are developing similar components as part of their web services offerings.

13.8   Integration with Behind-the-Firewall Workflows

Just as important as the public "interfaces" and public business processes that web services provide are the behind-the-firewall business workflows that perform most of the actual business logic. The need for integration between the two workflows is discussed in the previous section. Ideally, a workflow manager should be used to perform this integration.

The e-Speak engine and the SFS provide a sound foundation for deployment of e-services. However, e-Speak 3.11 does not provide any workflow engine to execute business operations behind a firewall. Instead, e-Speak is useful as the Internet access point through which clients can access web services. Behind the firewall, however, HP expects that workflows will be executed using a workflow engine, such as HP's own Process Manager. In future versions of e-Speak, a smooth integration with Process Manager can be expected.

Many workflow engine vendors, such as NetFish, which was recently purchased by IONA, provide graphical tools for defining business workflows and runtime engines for executing them. These workflows run behind the firewalls of enterprises. Web services is the technology that allows clients to access these workflows over the Internet.

Here is a list of some of the predominant web services vendors and the products they offer for conducting behind-the-firewall workflows:

■ Microsoft's BizTalk Messaging Server, in conjunction with COM+ and

Exchange Server

- IBM's MQ Integrator
- BEA Systems' Process Integrator
- Vitria's BusinessWare Automator
- IONA's Enterprise Integrator
- Bowstreet's WebEngine and Bowstreet Models
- NeuVis' NeuArchitect Integration Server, Logic Server, and Messaging Server

13.9   Summary

Table 13.1 summarizes some of the differences between the two industry terms and their underlying technologies. These are not highlighted as points of differentiation but mainly to draw out the likely convergence points and the trends in the industry as the efforts come together and evolve.

Table 13.1. Comparison of E-services and Web Services

Feature	E-services	Web Service	Comments
Service invocation	Primarily network object-based	Document exchange-based	—
Security provisions	Fine-grained (method level) possible	Large-grained control possible	Web services security is evolving
Service description	Vocabularies, Contracts	XML Schema, Several process definition languages	No specific emerging standard
Service registries and discovery	ESV	UDDI	ESV is evolving into a UDDI public registry

Table 13.1. Comparison *(continued)*

Low-level interoperability infrastructure	Provided for by SFS	Provided for by SOAP	SOAP is strongly supported; likely to be industry standard
High-level interoperability infrastructure	SFS	Several	No clear standard emerging yet
Orchestration of public business processes	None provided	Several in the market	—
Integration with private workflows	Loose integration with HP Process Manager	Several available	—

It seems that Internet and intranet services, whether they are e-services or web services, need to address the full spectrum of issues that arise in the services lifecycle. Technologies, tools, and knowledge need to be developed to support the development, deployment, and runtime environments of services in a secured and reliable fashion. The full set of technologies available (discussed in further detail in Chapters 14 and 15) can be woven together to create such an ecosystem.

Comparable Technologies

- E-Speak Engine
- Registry Technologies
- Service Framework

Chapter 14

COMPARABLE
TECHNOLOGIES

In this chapter, we discuss the most predominant comparable technologies that compete with the primary components of e-Speak. Since each technology addresses its own set of concerns, there is not a perfect overlap between e-Speak components and their counterparts in the industry. However, similar functionality and features are available in various technologies. In Chapter 2, we describe the three main components of the e-Speak offering:

1. E-Speak service engine

2. Service registry

3. Service framework

In the following discussion, we look at each e-Speak component and discuss technologies that play a similar role; a quilt of these technologies could realize the service-centric vision, although it would be difficult to design, manage, and maintain.

14.1   E-Speak Engine

The e-Speak engine provides an infrastructure for doing object- and message-based distributed computing within a company's intranet, as well as between enterprises over the Internet. Recall from Chapter 2 that the e-Speak engine provides a logical machine, a resource paradigm, and interaction mechanisms. Many of these services are available in different forms in other distributed computing middleware products. This section briefly discusses other distributed computing middleware technologies with features similar to those of the e-Speak engine.

14.1.1 CORBA

Common Object Request Broker Architecture (CORBA) was designed by an international organization of over 800 member companies called the *Object Management Group, Inc.(OMG)*. Teknekron, Expersoft, and Digital Equipment Corp. (DEC) were some of the earliest implementers of the standard. The earliest Object Request Brokers (ORBs) were based on the C and C++ languages.

An ORB is a middleware technology that hides client-side and server-side application code from any of the low-level networking Application Programming Interfaces (APIs) that are required for writing distributed applications. ORBs — at least today's ORBs — are used strictly for object-oriented application development.

Although the architectures of the earliest CORBA ORBs were based on the CORBA 1.0 specification, they were not interoperable. This meant that a client using one vendor's client-side ORB libraries could not communicate with a different vendor's server-side ORB. This posed quite a problem for companies that wanted to adopt the CORBA standards but that were concerned about being locked in to one vendor's implementation of the CORBA standard. The CORBA specification evolved to include the Interoperable Object Reference (IOR), the General Inter Orb Protocol (GIOP), and the Internet Inter Orb Protocol (IIOP). These standards helped pave the way for interoperability between the ORBs of different vendors.

As Java gained in popularity, CORBA ORB vendors began to implement Java-compatible and Java-based CORBA ORBs. Today, most commercial CORBA ORBs are Java-based. Currently, the most popular commercial CORBA ORBs are produced by: IONA, BEA Systems, IBM, Borland, and Sun. In addition to commercial ORBs, there are numerous freely available open-source CORBA ORBs written for Java and C++.

The CORBA standard reintroduced into the programming community some object-

oriented concepts that it already knew but had forgotten. Possibly the most important concept (one that has made its way into Java, RMI, JINI, Microsoft's COM+,
and Web services) is that of an interface definition. Each CORBA object is an
Internet-accessible object that has a set of public methods that clients can invoke.
These methods comprise its public interface. In CORBA, you define the interface
of an object using a C-like language called *Interface Definition Language* (IDL).
The IDL forms the contract between clients and the CORBA objects they call.

All CORBA ORBs today provide tools to allow you to generate client-side proxies
and server-side skeletons from IDL files. The client-side proxies are the objects
that a client application calls in order to communicate with remote CORBA objects.
When client application code invokes a method of a proxy, that proxy performs
the low-level networking API calls required to communicate with a remote CORBA
object — but the client application developer is never exposed to this networking
code. Each client-side proxy has the same public interface as the remote CORBA
object it represents. This enables the client-side application code to invoke the
proxy object as though it were the actual remote CORBA object. What this means
is that you can write a client application that communicates with distributed software running somewhere else on a network, but you never have to write any of the
low-level networking API calls in order to create your application.

The server-side skeletons that are also generated from IDL files serve the same
purpose (for the CORBA server object) as do the client-side proxies. Namely, the
skeletons contain the low-level networking API calls that can receive remote invocations from clients, then invoke the appropriate methods on the CORBA server
objects they represent. A programmer writing a CORBA server object never needs
to see any of the lower level networking API calls. Instead, the programmer simply constructs an object — using Java or C++ — and the CORBA ORB connects
the skeleton to the object that the programmer has written. This object that the
programmer writes contains largely the business logic.

Once the programmer has coded the server-side CORBA object(s), he or she creates a main function that does three things:

1. Initializes the CORBA ORB

2. Registers relevant object(s) with the ORB

3. Goes into a "loop forever and accept method invocations" state

Many CORBA ORBs actually allow you to associate a name with CORBA objects you register with the ORB. That same name can then be used by client applications to "look up" the CORBA object. Usually, the client-side application code queries the CORBA ORB to "find" the CORBA server object. The client-side ORB will then return the client application code an instance of a client-side proxy through which the client communicates with the server.

One of the primary design goals for CORBA was to come up with a technology that allowed clients written in one language to communicate with CORBA server objects potentially written in a different language. To make this work, the OMG created the GIOP and IIOP protocols. These protocols are very simple message formats that can be used to find objects, invoke methods on objects, and delete objects. These message formats contain only data types that can be translated into External Data Representation (XDR) format. This means that C++ objects, Java objects, and any other language-specific formats cannot be represented using GIOP and IIOP. What this means is that, once a CORBA message is on the wire, you cannot determine what language was used to create the client or CORBA server. But the limit that this introduces is that you cannot pass objects over the network "by value" because they cannot be streamed into GIOP or IIOP messages.

There are other distributed object middleware technologies in market, but CORBA is the most widely used technology today, due to the length of time that it has been available and the number of developers familiar with its programming model. Many of today's CORBA ORBs allow you to access remote objects over the Internet; however, it is primarily a technology for accessing objects within your own enterprise.

14.1.2 DCOM and COM+

In the 1993 timeframe, Microsoft released its Distributed Component Object Model (DCOM). This technology was originally called *Network OLE* after Microsoft's Object Linking and Embedding (OLE) technology.   In its functionality, DCOM is an ORB much like CORBA's ORB. Like CORBA, DCOM has interface definition languages (IDL and Object Description Language [ODL]), client-side proxies, and server-side stubs. It also has code generators that can generate proxies and stubs from IDL and ODL files. Its underlying messaging protocol, however, is based on DCE-RPC rather than the OMG's GIOP.

Whereas CORBA is very object-oriented in nature, Microsoft's DCOM is much more like standard RPC technology. In CORBA, each server-side object has a unique identity — its IOR. When a client application retrieves a reference to a CORBA object, the client is communicating with a specific object instance — one that no other client is communicating with. And if a client calls one method of a CORBA object that stores some data in that object, the client can later call another method on that same CORBA object and retrieve back some or all of that data. The reason this works is that each CORBA object has a "state" and "identity" — it really is an object with its own data segment. In DCOM, however, objects do not have a state or identity.

A client using DCOM to communicate with a remote object can never be sure what data is stored in that object. In fact, if a client obtains a remote object from the DCOM ORB and stores data into that object, then later attempts to retrieve the same object, it cannot. This is because DCOM objects do not have identity and state — they are not really objects. Instead, DCOM objects are more like a collection of services (each method on a DCOM object is a service) that you can call. None of these services share state with each other, even though they are all bundled together within the same DCOM object.

Although it is slightly less of a distributed object technology than CORBA, DCOM is still a very useful technology. One of the most useful aspects of DCOM is that it can be used to interconnect objects written in any Microsoft-supported language, including Visual Basic, C++, C, and Java. Because of its ease of use, programmers have used DCOM to solve a number of business and application integration problems. But as DCOM-based solutions grew in complexity, it soon became evident that a federation of autonomous distributed objects written in Java, C++, and Visual Basic would be very difficult to deploy and to administer. And there was very little in the way of actual distributed transaction support in the DCOM ORB and in Microsoft products.

In 1996, Microsoft announced the Microsoft Transaction Server (MTS). This was an innovative technology that was possibly the motivation for Sun's Enterprise Java

Bean (EJB) specification. MTS introduced the concept of a server that contained deployed and running DCOM objects. It provided deployment, transaction control, security, lifecycle management, and all the services that a truly robust distributed computing infrastructure demands. Once MTS was released, Microsoft advised all future DCOM developers to build their solutions so that their DCOM objects run within the control of MTS servers, rather than simply on their own, without the added services that MTS provides.

Microsoft soon realized that a robust distributed object computing infrastructure was essential for any enterprise-class operating system. Therefore, starting with Windows 98 and Windows 2000, Microsoft has made DCOM and MTS technologies part of its Operating Systems (OSs) rather than add-on services. The DCOM-MTS infrastructure that is integrated into Microsoft's newest OSs is now called *COM+* rather than *DCOM* or *DCOMMTS*.

COM+ is basically a combination of DCOM, MTS, and MSMQ (Microsoft Message Queue) technologies. Along with its new name, COM+ offers this entire suite of features for developing distributed applications:

▢ Self-Describing Components: All objects have deployment-time attributes, such as security constraints, transactional behavior, etc. This is an outgrowth of the DCOM component descriptors found in MTS.

▢ Queueing: Now you can invoke COM+ objects asynchronously by sending them messages, rather than by directly invoking their methods.

▢ Events: This includes typical event features, such as notification and the publish-and-subscribe mechanism. Equipped with that, COM+ objects can look like normal objects with remote methods, but they send messages along a message queue, rather than making synchronous method calls on a remote object.

▢ Transactions: COM+ provides a few new transactional APIs above and beyond what were previously provided as part of the MTS infrastructure.

▢ Security: Access control can be specified at three levels: globally at the application level, at the component level, and at the method level. The security mechanism takes advantage of Microsoft's Active Directory technology and can include use of Kerberos (in addition to Public Key Infrastructure [PKI] and NT LAN Manager [NTLM] security).

◻ Load Balancing : You can use COM+ to specify a "router" machine that will dispatch object creation calls to the least-utilized of a farm of COM+ servers.

Although some third-party vendors have created gateways that allow clients to invoke COM+ objects from across the Internet, COM+ is predominantly a technology for accessing objects within an enterprise.

14.1.3   RMI and JINI

Java, which was released in the 1995–1996 timeframe, was designed from the start as a network-aware language. Therefore, it came with a built-in package of network objects (`java.net.*`), such as Socket, ServerSocket, and Uniform Resource Locator (URL). These were low-level APIs that closely resembled the socket APIs available on most versions of the UNIX operating system, as well as on various flavors of Microsoft Windows.

In addition to the `java.net.*` package of objects, Java also provides a package that implements an all-Java ORB known as *Remote Method Invocation* (RMI). The RMI classes are an enhancement to Java that basically ensures that every J2SE- or J2EE-based Java Virtual Machine comes with an embedded Java ORB.

The RMI ORB is very similar to its predecessor, the CORBA ORB. Just like you would with a CORBA ORB, you can use IDLs to generate RMI client-side proxies and server-side stubs or you can generate them directly from Java code, using the Java *interface* mechanism as the well-known contract that defines how clients communicate with servers. Also, just like CORBA's Naming Service (its registry of running CORBA server objects), RMI also has a naming service. And if you look at the "main" code of a server-side application that contains one or more RMI objects, it — like a CORBA server-side "main" — initializes the ORB, registers its object(s), and awaits remote method invocations from clients.

Although RMI and CORBA are similar in architecture, there are many differences between them, as well. The most prominent feature of RMI that is lacking in CORBA is the ability to pass objects over the wire from a client to a server or from a server to a client. This is possible because, unlike CORBA, RMI was not designed to work with clients written in any language talking to servers written in any language. Instead, RMI was designed for Java clients to talk to Java servers.

With this design goal in mind, the wire-level protocol Java Remote Message Protocol (JRMP) was designed to allow for Java objects to be streamed across the network, then "reconstituted" on the other end.   CORBA's GIOP and IIOP do not allow you to pass objects across a network like this.

Being able to pass Java objects around may or may not be a useful feature. Possibly, the major advantage to such a design is not that you really need to pass objects across a network to build applications, but that it allows programmers to make the same assumptions when they call either local methods or methods implemented by remote RMI objects.

CORBA may not be able to handle passing objects across the network by value (actually, the new CORBA 3.0 specification provides techniques for doing this), but it does provide a number of benefits that are not present in RMI based on the JRMP protocol. The CORBA specification has always attempted to take into account the requirements of industrial-strength distributed applications. These requirements include: passing security contexts between objects (so that object A can call object B, object B can call object C, and object C still accesses the security credentials of the client that called A), handling distributed transaction processing, and providing an "interceptor" architecture — allowing third-party security and transaction solutions to be plugged into the ORB. The only distributed object infrastructures that provide security and transaction processing and pluggable security solutions is CORBA. RMI over JRMP lacks this level of sophistication.

Because of its ease of use, many programmers have created distributed computing solutions based on RMI — even though it lacks the levels of security and distributed transaction support available with CORBA ORBs. Because of its overwhelming success, Sun has decided to solve some of the shortcomings that still make developers choose to use a CORBA ORB, rather than RMI. The most recent solution to this lack of functionality in the RMI ORB is for Java to support a hybrid RMI/CORBA technology known as *RMI over IIOP*. This technology provides the ease of use and object-passing features of RMI with the security and distributed transaction processing capabilities available with CORBA ORBs.

In the spring of 1999, Sun announced a network programming model that is based on RMI but that includes a richer set of infrastructure and services for distributed, peer-to-peer computing. This technology was called *JINI*. The basic extensions to

RMI provided by JINI are a set of IP multicast-based protocols known as the *Join* and *Discovery* protocols, the concept of a Lookup Service (a rich registry of advertised RMI objects), and the concept of downloadable client-side proxy objects.

The main idea behind JINI is that service providers are RMI objects that can be communicated with through client-side proxies. These client-side proxies implement Java interfaces known by clients. When servers want to be accessible by clients, they advertise themselves by using the JINI Join protocol to register themselves with any nearby running Lookup Services. During the Join process, servers upload the client-side proxies that clients will require to communicate with them. When clients want to find services, they use the Discovery protocol — requesting remote services by name, properties, etc. The Discovery protocol is sent by the client to any nearby Lookup Services. When a Lookup Service answers the client's request, it provides the client with a client-side proxy for all available services that match the client's search criteria. Once the client has access to a proxy to a service, it makes local method calls to that proxy in order to communicate with the remote service provider. Of course, all this distributed computing magic is implemented above RMI.

RMI is a technology that allows you to access objects only within your own enterprise — it does not work across firewalls. And JINI, because it builds on RMI, is also not well suited for accessing objects from across the Internet.

14.1.4   EJB and J2EE

After Java 1.0 had been released and the developer community started to experiment with this new language, it soon discovered that Java was more suitable as a server-side language than as a language for developing applets that download into Internet browsers. The first server-side applications were based on distributed objects, using the Networking (`java.net.*`) package or the RMI (`java.rmi.*`) packages. Due to its ease of use, RMI quickly became the favored technique for creating complex distributed applications in Java.

Problems began to occur, however, with these newly created distributed computing applications. A single distributed Java application often consisted of many objects running within many Java Virtual Machines running on many different hardware hosts. Just like the early DCOM and CORBA applications that suffered from being too difficult to deploy and administer easily, these RMI applications soon became too costly to deploy. Sun needed to solve this problem by coming up with an environment that could be used to deploy and administer RMI objects more easily. That environment is what eventually became the EJB specification.

The EJB 1.0 specification, released in 1997, described an architecture of *servers*, *containers*, and *enterprise beans*. The concepts seemed strange; Sun was asking programmers to create their distributed object applications by distributing those objects to only a single machine (an EJB server). Yet these concepts did seem familiar. In fact, most of the architectural components of the EJB specification could be found in the MTS that was released by Microsoft in 1996. Some of the features that can be found in the EJB specification are: deployment descriptors (including security and transaction attributes), database access APIs, transaction coordination, and object lifecycle management.

As developers became more accustomed to the constraints imposed by the EJB servers, they soon saw the advantages they received by using them. And development managers and business managers who were held accountable for the success of Java deployments embraced the control and predictability they gained from EJB-based application development.

In an effort to do a more complete job of addressing the needs of enterprise-class software development using Java, Sun announced the Java 2 Enterprise Edition specification. This specification was a set of blueprints for the creating of Java Web servers, EJB servers, and the server-side APIs needed to create Internet-accessible enterprise applications. Today, all of the remaining EJB vendors that are successful follow the J2EE specification as closely as they can. Sun's EJB specification and the J2EE have brought a new level of predictability and quality to the world of distributed object-oriented computing.

The first implementations of the EJB 1.0 specification were based on RMI. That prohibited clients from accessing EJBs remotely across the Internet. Of course, if you coupled an EJB server with a Java Web server as its "presentation technology," clients were able to access EJBs across the Internet by going through servlets running within the Java Web server. The servlets could, in turn, access the EJBs on behalf of the clients. With the some of the recently developed RMI-over-IIOP

EJB servers, it will now be possible to access EJBs directly across the network without the need to go through a Java Web server intermediary.

14.2   Registry Technologies

One of the most important components of any distributed computing solution is a registry that can be used by components and services to *advertise* themselves and by clients to *discover* existing components and services they can access. All distributed object middleware solutions have some form of registry that serves this purpose. And, as the computer industry is beginning to realize, any viable web service solution will need a similar component in order to be of any utility.   E-Speak's E-services Village (ESV) (discussed in Chapter 11) is one of the Internet's first Internet-accessible registries for storing and looking up web services. The sections below discuss other distributed computing registry technologies that serve a similar — but often much more limited — purpose.

14.2.1   CORBA Naming Service

CORBA specified a number of CORBA services that are pervasive throughout an ORB network. One of those services is the CORBA Naming Service. This service is actually a network-visible registry with a hierarchical data model that looks just like a file system. What you would think of as a directory in a file system is called a *Naming Context* in the CORBA Naming Service. Each Naming Context can contain other Naming Contexts, as well as named references to running CORBA objects.

CORBA objects make themselves "visible" to CORBA clients by placing named references to themselves within the CORBA Naming Service (or the CORBA Trader Service, discussed next). Clients then can obtain the remote references to running CORBA objects by asking the CORBA Naming Service for the objects by name. The CORBA Naming Service can store only references to CORBA objects. It cannot be used to store references to other sorts of distributed objects, such as COM+ objects or RMI objects.

14.2.2 CORBA Trader Service

The CORBA Trader Service was proposed by the OMG long after the release of the initial CORBA 1.0 specification. This service, unlike the Naming Service, allows CORBA objects to advertise themselves with a set of associated properties, rather than by a hierarchical "path" name. When clients search for CORBA objects using the Trader Service, clients must specify the IDL interface name they are looking for (such as `BankAccount`) and may optionally specify a set of properties as well, such as `BankLocation=SantaCruz AND StreetName=Pacific`. The Trader Service, like the Naming Service, can be used to advertise and look up only CORBA objects. The CORBA Trader Service has clearly influenced the architecture of many other registry technologies, including the JINI Lookup Service, e-Speak's ESV, Universal Description, Discovery, and Integration (UDDI), and ebXML's Registry.

14.2.3 Windows Registry and Windows Active Directory

Microsoft's DCOM and COM+ have been quite a success — as is evident by the number of solutions based on these technologies and the fact that they are now embedded in all Microsoft operating systems (OSs). But interestingly, Microsoft has never provided an easy-to-use network-accessible registry for advertising and finding DCOM/COM+ objects. In fact, until the release of Active Directory, the only registry that was provided for storing location information for DCOM objects was the local Windows Registry. This meant that if you had a number of client machines that wanted to have access to DCOM objects running on a server, each and every one of their Windows Registries would have to be configured with the location and interface information for the DCOM objects.

With the release of Active Directory, it can be used as a registry to store references to COM+ objects. Although this is a very simple technology with no more power than the CORBA Naming Service, it does provide for a manageable solution for advertising and discovering COM+ objects.

14.2.4   RMI Naming Service

The RMI Naming Service is simply an RMI-specific implementation of a registry that works just like the CORBA Naming Service. The only real difference is that you can store only RMI objects in the RMI Naming Service.

14.2.5   JINI Lookup Service

The JINI Lookup Service is like an RMI-specific implementation of the CORBA Trader Service. It is very similar to the CORBA Trader Service in that RMI objects are advertised into the JINI Lookup Service — and their advertisements have associated with them the Java interface of the object providing the service, as well as optional properties further defining the service being offered.

A major difference between the JINI Lookup Service and the CORBA Trader Service is that the JINI service uses IP multicasts and a special Join protocol and Discovery protocol for advertisement and lookup of services. Also, the client-side proxies for accessing services can be stored along with service advertisements published to the JINI Lookup Service. Of course, the same thing could not be done with the CORBA Trader Service because CORBA does not allow for streaming of objects over the network.

14.2.6   UDDI

The UDDI specification is quickly becoming the de facto standard registry for publishing and finding web services on the Internet. The reason for its sudden success may be due to the fact that a number of companies have signed on to the standard and are contributing reference implementations, as well as Software Developer Kits (SDKs) for accessing UDDI registries from Microsoft, UNIX, and Linux applications written in a number of languages. The companies contributing to UDDI have formed an organization — UDDI.org — to prevent the appearance of bias toward any one vendor and to help make UDDI become an industry standard. Companies can play different roles within the organization, from merely observing the current standards to becoming active contributors and all the way up to being a UDDI operator. At the time of writing this book, there are four companies signed up to be UDDI operators: Microsoft, HP, IBM, and SAP.

UDDI operators are those companies responsible for ensuring that their UDDI registries are always available over the Internet and that they exchange all their service registries with the other UDDI operators in a timely fashion. The actual technical specifications for what is required of UDDI operators are spelled out in the UDDI technical specifications.

So what exactly is a UDDI registry? It has a very rigid and simple schema — like that of a Lightweight Directory Access Protocol (LDAP) directory. There are only four different object types stored within a UDDI registry:

1. Business Entity

2. Business Service

3. Binding Template

4. Technology Model

Hanging off the root of the UDDI registry are "Business Entity" nodes. Any business that wants to advertise itself using a UDDI registry must log onto the operator with which it has an account, then create a *Business Entity* node representing its business.

A business could simply stop entering data after adding its Business Entity node into the UDDI registry. But usually, businesses register themselves within the UDDI registry because they want to advertise web services that they provide. To do so, a business will add one or more *Business Service* nodes underneath its Business Entity node. To use a file system analogy, the Business Entity node for a business is the folder of all web services that the business provides. A business will create a Business Service node (within the Business Entity "folder") for each web service it wants to advertise.

Each Business Service node contains the name of the service, its description, and possibly some properties that help classify it. But a Business Service node does not specify what URL a client would use to access that service. In fact, one can think of the Business Service node as a folder that contains the zero or more URLs that can be used to access that web service. The URLs get added underneath a

Business Service node by the business that is publishing its web service. Some-times, when an administrator at a business deploys a web service, he or she will use a UDDI browser to select the Business Entity node, then the correct Business Service node. Then the administrator will create a *Binding Template* node, which contains the URL for accessing the running web service. In a more automated configuration, a web service could use a UDDI API to add the appropriate Binding Template representing its URL. The web service could, likewise, programmatically remove that entry when it is shut down.

The final type of data object that can be stored within a UDDI registry is called a *TModel* (short for Technology Model). This is sort of a *catch all* for storing many types of things, including categories (like the categories on a portal such as Ya-hoo!); global identifiers that can be used to specify characteristics of Business Entity, Business Service, and Binding Template nodes; and "public interface" de-scriptions. The most interesting use of TModels is as a way to describe the public interface of a web service.

When a web service is published into the UDDI registry, the URL that clients would use to access it can be specified by creating a Binding Template. But this is only an address for accessing the service — it says nothing about the types of XML documents that the service will accept or the types it will send back. Nor does it specify the choreography or business process(es) implemented by the service. These are all public interface details that must be associated with the URL in order to specify the service fully. Fortunately, there is a way to specify such things — with one or more TModels. Each TModel can contain a descriptive string, as well as a URL to a descriptive web page or document.

Currently, it is suggested that web services describe their public interfaces with an XML vocabulary, such as IBM's Web Services Description Language (WSDL). This language allows you to fully specify the shapes of the XML messages that a web service will accept and those it will generate.   Currently, Microsoft, IBM, HP, BEA, ebXML, and others are working on a number of specifications for XML vocabularies that describe not the shapes of the messages that a web service can process but the higher level orchestration or "conversation" that clients can carry on with the service. Some of the potential XML vocabularies to use for this purpose are: Microsoft's XLANG, HP's Web Services Conversation Language (WSCL), IBM's Web Services Flow Language (WSFL), BEA's eXtensible Open

Collaboration Protocol (XOCP), or the Trading Partner Agreement (TPA)/ Trading Partner Profile (TPP)/ Collaboration Protocol Agreement (CPA)/ Collaboration Protocol Profile (CPP)/ Business Process Specification Schema (BPSS) languages proposed by ebXML. Regardless of which standards emerge for this purpose, these are the types of documents that should be specified in TModels and associated with BindingTemplate nodes in order to specify their public interfaces.

Finally, it should be mentioned that the technology that allows clients to communicate with UDDI registries is synchronous Simple Object Access Protocol (SOAP). Clients (usually through an object-based API that shields the client software from the underlying Simple Object Access Protocol (SOAP) and XML) use a set of UDDI-specific messages to register and look up: Businesses, Services, Bindings, and TModels. On the wire, these communications with the UDDI registry are simply UDDI-specific XML messages packaged within the Body element of SOAP messages. A client uses Hyper Text Transfer Protocol (HTTP) or HTTPS to POST a request to the UDDI registry, the registry acts on that request in real-time, and finally, the registry returns its response in the HTTP/S reply to the POST.

14.2.7   ebXML Registry Services Specification

ebXML's Registry Service Specification is currently a specification but not yet an implementation. In that sense, it differs from UDDI and from HP's ESV — both of which are implementations of specifications. Although it has not yet been implemented, the ideas behind the ebXML Registry go far beyond what is offered by either UDDI or HP's ESV. These other two registries solve the simple problem of providing the ability to store and retrieve pointers to services by specifying attributes — in the form of name/value pairs — of the services stored. Granted, UDDI provides slightly more than that in the way of its information model, and ESV has a richer "ontology"-based scheme for specifying the properties of services. But overall, their technologies provide repositories of pointers to services.

ebXML's Registry is very rich. It does provide mechanisms for storing pointers to ebXML-compliant services. And it also allows association of properties with those pointers and retrieval of pointers to services by specifying properties of those services. But ebXML's registry goes further. Its registry pays equal — if not more — attention to the many forms of metadata that describe web services. In fact, to store a pointer to a web service within the ebXML registry, you first must have stored the following:

- Metadata descriptions of any of the messages that can be exchanged with that web service.

- A metadata description of the business process that is implemented by that web service.

- The service provider's CPP, which describes the service provider's role in offering its service, as well as the technical details for how to access that service. When a CPP is stored within the ebXML Registry, it is possible to associate a number of properties with it in order to *classify* it. This provides a mechanism whereby clients looking for a specific class of CPPs can query for and find the CPPs that meet their requirements.

When clients want to access web services whose pointers are stored within the ebXML Registry, they begin by searching for those web services whose CPPs promise to deliver the service they desire. Then clients use the CPP information to establish a connection with the web service provider. Dynamically, the client and the service provider form a CPA which describes all the steps — and technical endpoints — that comprise the complete business transaction they will carry out.

The ebXML registry has a much richer set of *lifecycle management APIs* than those provided by either UDDI or ESV. And, unlike these other registries, ebXML's Registry provides an extensible information model through the concept of *slots*. Slots are extra pockets of data that can be inserted into registry entries in order to store more information. Clients of the ebXML Registry use the `Add Slot` and `Remove Slot` APIs to perform schema modification and to add/remove data stored in slots.

Another feature that is unique to the ebXML Registry is rich support for categories and subcategories and sub-subcategories, etc. Categories are extremely useful properties to associate with web services — they allow clients to "drill into" and "drill up from" areas of interest so that they can easily retrieve the service(s) they are interested in.

Finally, the querying and result-filtering features provided by the ebXML Registry are far richer than those provided by the UDDI or ESV registries. Of course, this is necessary because there are so many different attributes that can be associated with ebXML services, such as categories, slots, business documents, business processes, and CPPs. Queries and result filters can be specified by using the ebXML data structures described in the ebXML Registry Information Model document. The ebXML Registry Services Specification also states that compliant registries can offer an interface whereby clients can query the registry using Structured Query Language (SQL) syntax.

Just like with the UDDI and ESV registries, the ebXML Registry offers its services through XML messages that are exchanged between clients and the registry. In the case of ebXML, those messages are compliant with the ebXML Message Service Specification. It is expected that clients will use object-oriented APIs to access the ebXML registry so that they are not exposed to the low-level XML messages and ebXML message envelopes that will be exchanged between clients and the registry. Currently, there is a Java Specification Request — JSR 93 — which species a Java API that will allow Java programs to communicate with both UDDI and ebXML registries in a consistent manner.

14.3   Service Framework

E-Speak's Service Framework Specification (SFS) was initially released in the spring of 2000. It provided an XML-based specification for describing business models, publishing services into registries, querying for services in registries, enveloping business documents (much like today's SOAP standard), e-Speak service interface definitions, and security. Overall, this specification was fairly complete and introduced some valuable concepts; the Internet-accessible business service registry was one such concept, though it would not make its way into web services standards for another year.

The SFS is a horizontal standard — defining an infrastructure upon which to construct a network of intercommunicating services. Other emerging specifications provide a more vertically focused (i.e., industry-specific) stack of technologies that could provide an infrastructure for business-to-business communications over the Internet. In this section, we briefly introduce the emerging standards in the area of Web services: ebXML, RosettaNet, and Microsoft's BizTalk Framework.

14.3.1   ebXML

ebXML is one of the premier standards bodies influencing the direction of web services standards. Although its early work centered around standards for business documents themselves, it soon branched out to create specifications for how to construct an e-business infrastructure.

From the `www.ebxml.org` web site, ebXML's mission is to provide an open XML-based infrastructure enabling the global use of electronic business information in an interoperable, secure, and consistent manner by all parties. ebXML is a set of specifications that together enable a modular electronic business framework. The vision of ebXML is to enable a global electronic marketplace where enterprises of any size and in any geographical location can meet and conduct business with each other through the exchange of XML-based messages. ebXML is a joint initiative of the United Nations (UN/CEFACT) and OASIS, developed with global participation for global usage.

UN/CEFACT (`www.unece.org/cefact`) is the United Nations body whose mandate covers worldwide policy and technical development in the area of trade facilitation and electronic business. Headquartered in Geneva, it has developed and promoted many tools for the facilitation of global business processes including UN/EDIFACT, the international Electronic Data Interchange (EDI) standard. Its current work includes such topics as Simpl-EDI and Object-Oriented EDI, and it strongly supports the development and implementation of open interoperable, global standards and specifications for electronic business.

OASIS (`//www.oasis-open.org`) is the international, not-for-profit consortium that advances electronic business by promoting open, collaborative development of interoperability specifications. OASIS operates XML.org, a noncommercial portal that delivers information on the use of XML in industry. The XML.org Registry provides an open community clearinghouse for distributing and locating XML application schemas, vocabularies, and related documents. OASIS serves as the home for industry groups and organizations interested in developing XML specifications. ebXML has created a number of very rich standards and documentation for those standards. The following is a list of the ebXML standards that are geared toward defining a web services infrastructure:

ebXML Requirements Specification

This document outlines the high-level business and technical requirements motivating the ebXML organization's efforts. It discusses the following topics:

- ebXML vision and scope
- Assumptions about the business requirements for trading partners carrying on e-business over the Internet
- Globalization issues
- The need for registries and repositories
- Technical requirements for interoperability
- Security requirements; legal requirements
- Technical architecture and core components of an implementation of the standard
- Requirements for message transport, routing, and packaging

ebXML Technical Architecture Specification

This document is a description of the overall architecture of a web services infrastructure based on ebXML standards. The Architectural Specification covers the following topics:

- ebXML design objectives
- ebXML system overview
- Recommended modeling methodology
- ebXML infrastructure
- Rules for compliance with the ebXML standards
- Security
- Use cases

Message Service Specification

This specification describes the technical details of a secure, reliable message transport technology for conducting e-business. It contains sections describing the following concepts:

- The ebXML message structure
- The behavior of the Message Service Handler that sends and receives ebXML messages
- A message packaging (enveloping) specification; SOAP extensions required by ebXML (these are similar to the SOAP extensions required by the BizTalk 2.0 Framework)
- The Message Service Handler services; Reliable messaging; Error handling; Security

Collaboration Protocol Profile and Agreement Specification

The ebXML specifications provide very precise technical details about how to represent the business agreements between trading partners, as well as the technical connection points provided by each trading partner to provide web services. TPPs provide the *public interface* of messages that a single trading partner can exchange with other trading partners. TPAs are documents that describe the high-level business flows that occur between trading partners. A CPP describes the implementation details of a TPP. A CPA describes the technical implementation details of a TPA. The Collaboration Protocol Profile and Agreement Specification describes the details of the CPP and the CPA documents.

ebXML Business Process Specification Schema

The BPSS is a language for describing the orchestration of message exchanges between trading partners. This document describes in detail the syntax of the BPSS language. It includes sections describing the following features of BPSS:

- An overview of the language

- How BPSS is used in the ebXML architecture

- How to specify two-party and multiparty collaborations

- How to model core business transaction semantics

- Specifying legally binding contracts using BPSS

- Nonrepudiation, authorization, and document security

- Messaging reliability

- How to reference CPPs and CPAs from within BPSS documents

- Runtime transaction semantics represented by BPSS

- Representing roles within BPSS

- Guaranteed delivery

ebXML Registry Services Specification

This document describes the architecture and features of the ebXML Registry Service. This is a blueprint for a registry service. The registry architecture specified by this document goes far beyond what is provided by in the UDDI standards. ebXML calls for a much more *active* registry than what UDDI specifies — one that understands service lifecycle operations, provides for rich descriptions of services, and responds to SQL queries.

ebXML Registry Security Proposal

This document specifies a security model to be adopted by ebXML-compliant registries.

ebXML Registry Information Model

This document describes the information model used to represent web service entries within ebXML registries. It is similar to the UDDI's XML Structure Reference.

ebXML and UDDI Registries

This document describes how to store references to ebXML repositories as TModels within a UDDI registry. The idea presented here is that you can store a web service reference within an ebXML Registry, then store a pointer to that reference in a UDDI registry. That way, web services clients can always find web services by querying a UDDI registry — even if those web services are ultimately ebXML-compliant services whose references are stored in an ebXML Registry.

14.3.2   RosettaNet

RosettaNet is a nonprofit organization of over 400 high-technology companies specializing in the areas of information technology, electronic components, and semiconductor manufacturing. The goal behind RosettaNet is to promote a set of standards for conducting e-business transactions between high-technology companies. This is the only standards body mentioned within this chapter whose focus is on a single "vertical" sector of the economy.

RosettaNet defines three primary components that together enable the implementation of a standards-based web services infrastructure for conducting electronic business. These components are:

1. RosettaNet Dictionaries

2. RosettaNet Implementation Framework (RNIF)

3. RosettaNet Partner Interface Processes (PIPs)

RosettaNet Dictionaries are the standard XML business documents (and elements contained within them) that can be used to provide for a consistent language for conducting business between companies. Only with such a set of standard business documents could a truly open infrastructure of businesses intercommunicate dynamically.

The RNIF is a very detailed specification for the messaging formats, and wire protocols that RosettaNet proposes become the standard for conducting e-business over the Internet. The specification includes:

▢ Information exchange between trading partners using XML

▢ Transport

▢ Routing and packaging

▢ Security

▢ Signals

▢ Trading partner agreements

Whereas RosettaNet Dictionaries provide the business documents that are exchanged between businesses, the RNIF specifies the technology infrastructure that must be in place to connect those businesses electronically.

Possibly the most noteworthy component of the RosettaNet specifications is the concept of a PIP. A PIP is an agreed-upon set of document exchanges that comprise business-to-business transactions. RosettaNet defines a number of useful PIPs that trading partners can use today to conduct business over the Internet. Web services products that are RosettaNet-compliant provide implementations of some or all of these PIPs. A PIP contains four primary types of information:

1. A definition of the business process

2. A narrative describing the business impact of adopting the PIP

3. References to which RosettaNet Dictionary elements will be exchanged

4. An implementation specification that details the exact technology that will be used by a trading partner to execute the PIP

Interestingly, although RosettaNet has done a good job of describing what belongs in a PIP, it does not currently prescribe an XML vocabulary (such as ebXML's BPSS, IBM's WSFL, HP's WSCL, or Microsoft's XLANG) for containing the metadata description of a PIP.

14.3.3 Microsoft's BizTalk 2.0 Framework

Microsoft's BizTalk 2.0 Framework is an e-business infrastructure specification that builds on the technologies provided by the SOAP 1.1 standard. Although it is not the result of a consortium of businesses or a nonprofit organization, the BizTalk 2.0 Framework specification does build upon many Internet standards from the W3C. In fact, Microsoft has made a concerted effort to develop this framework within the context of industry-accepted standards.

In a sense, Microsoft's BizTalk 2.0 Framework is more similar to HP's SFS than it is to ebXML or RosettaNet. The BizTalk 2.0 Framework, like HP's SFS, does not focus on many of the higher level concepts such as TPAs, PIPs, and "orchestration." Also, both Microsoft and HP have developed their specifications without much involvement from outside organizations — whereas both ebXML and RosettaNet are standards that were created by organizations, rather than individual companies.

The BizTalk 2.0 Framework is by far the simplest of the e-business specifications being discussed in these sections. In fact, it simply specifies the SOAP extensions that would be required to provide sufficient levels of:

- Security
- Nonrepudiation
- Auditing
- Guaranteed delivery
- Versioning
- Management

The BizTalk 2.0 Framework does not even specify a technology for advertising or discovering web services. Later revisions to the document may refer to the UDDI specification for these aspects of a web services infrastructure.

In the next chapter, we look at the competitive landscape for e-services and web services, and discuss the platforms and software available from major software vendors.

Competitive Landscape

- Recognized Leaders
- Strong Industry Participants
- Honorable Mentions
- Summary

Chapter 15

COMPETITIVE LANDSCAPE

The services-based economy is truly recognized by industry leaders and thinkers as the next wave in the high-tech world or the *Next Chapter of the Internet*. Keeping in mind that, several software companies, including a few software giants, have invested in this space and developed technologies that aim to promote service-centric computing. Figure 15.1 depicts an assessment of these efforts by Gartner, Inc. in June 2001 based on the vendors' vision and their ability to execute that vision.[1] In this chapter, we briefly discuss some of the most prominent web services initiatives and technologies available in the market as of spring 2001.

15.1 Recognized Leaders

Microsoft, IBM, and Hewlett-Packard (HP), are recognized as leading the effort for both furthering the web services economy and providing technologies to support it. In this chapter, we primarily focus on the technologies provided by the leaders.

15.1.1 Microsoft

Microsoft's DOT NET (or .NET) is the first web service technology mentioned in this chapter because Microsoft — along with IBM, HP, and possibly Bowstreet — has taken a leadership role in defining what web services means and how to make them a reality. The DOT NET strategy is a significant change in the way software

---

[1] Gartner Magic Quadrant, D. Plummer, June 2001.

401

applications are constructed and deployed.

Microsoft's DOT NET announcement was quickly followed by several white papers describing the web services components, such as SOAP (Simple Object Access Protocol), the BizTalk 2.0 Framework, and UDDI (Universal Description, Discovery, and Integration). Microsoft also released software developer kits (SDKs) for DOT NET, UDDI, and BizTalk 2.0. This generated a lot of interest among the developer community as these components and related white papers explained Microsoft's vision for web services by providing developers with sample infrastructure components that would allow them to test-drive web services and DOT NET concepts.

The early foundations for Microsoft's DOT NET are SOAP (which began its life as XML-RPC) and the CLR (Common Language Runtime). CLR is Microsoft's new Operating System (OS) infrastructure that allows software applications and components written in different languages to intercommunicate. It is like a virtual machine that can execute Visual Basic, Java, C#, C++, and other languages. At an architectural level, the CLR resembles Sun's JVM (Java Virtual Machine). It provides garbage collection, namespaces, metadata, etc. But unlike Sun's JVM, the Microsoft CLR integrates smoothly into the overall operational infrastructure that Microsoft provides, including: IIS, COM+, ASP+, and DOT NET web services.

Although Microsoft's CLR work may end up being extremely useful for advocates of multilanguage development and Java-like languages, the web services portion of DOT NET does not really require much of the CLR infrastructure on the server side. And clients of DOT NET web services can be written in any language — Microsoft CLR-compatible or not. In fact, a developer can easily connect a Perl client running on a Linux operating system to a web service provider written using DOT NET software. And *this* is what web services are all about. This flexibility has also assisted Microsoft in its ability to gain developer mindshare and strong support of the DOT NET platform.

DOT NET clients communicate with services by exchanging XML documents — usually via HTTP/S POST messages. Recall in Chapter 13, we denoted this XML-centric framework as one of the key differences right now between e-services and web services. XML documents that are exchanged contain no trace of what language was used to generate them. So, for example, Java web services clients can easily communicate with COM+ web services written in C#. The languages used to write the clients and servers just do not matter.

> **Note**
>
> At the core of the web services vision lies the interoperability and the desire for platform/language independence. The important thing is that the client and the server can exchange XML documents with each other — and that both the client and server can interpret any "enveloping" that is used to wrap and transport those documents.

Developing clients and servers that can parse and create XML documents is rather simplistic at this point. The open source community provides a number of XML parsers and generators based on the Document Exchange Model (DEM) and Simple API for XML (SAX) standards. These parsers and generators exist for all the languages used to develop Internet-based applications today. Microsoft continues to provide up-to-date DOM- and SAX-based libraries that can be used from any Microsoft-supported language (such as C#, C++, Visual Basic, and JavaScript).

The tricky part of getting clients and servers to be able to communicate by exchanging XML documents is for there to be a universally agreed-upon "enveloping" technology used to *wrap* the XML business documents that are exchanged. Earlier, the most likely candidate for transporting XML data between clients and servers was the XML-RPC standard — proposed by DevelopMentor. This was a standard that allowed clients to invoke methods synchronously on servers by sending the servers XML documents containing the name of the method to invoke and the parameters to pass into the method. Once a server received an XML-RPC message, it would invoke the requested method, then return the results of that method invocation (the return value — if any — from the method call) as an XML document. The XML-RPC request was sent by the client to the server in an HTTP POST, and the HTTP response to that post contained the XML-RPC response.

On the inside, XML-RPC defined an XML vocabulary representing an "envelope" that contained a "body." Within that body was the XML payload that a client was sending to the server (and that the server returned to the client). The rules were that the transport-specific information should be contained in the HTTP POST message and the envelope part of the XML-RPC message, and the body of the XML-

RPC message would contain the *business document*. Because XML-RPC was originally about making method calls, the business document transported within the body was actually an XML representation of either a method invocation (if you were a client sending the XML to the server) or an XML representation of the results of a method call (if you were a server returning a result to a client).

XML-RPC was a good starting point, but it was designed primarily for synchronous calls. This is not a very scalable solution when there are very many clients concurrently invoking services provided by a single server. A better solution would be an enveloping technology that allowed for synchronous or asynchronous communication of XML documents. On top of that, it would allow the XML business documents exchanged to be either XML representations of method invocations or full-blown business documents — such as *purchase orders*, *invoices*, and *receipts*. DevelopMentor worked with Microsoft to extend the definition of XML-RPC to include these new features. This work later was renamed *SOAP*. The SOAP specification has been submitted to the W3C (World Wide Web Consortium) for standardization.

Early SOAP toolkits provided client-side code and a *listener* Active Server Page (ASP) that assisted in creating web services and invoked them from any Microsoft-supported language. At that time, because a standard for describing the "public interfaces" of web services was not developed, this toolkit used Microsoft-proprietary Service Definition Language (SDL). This language was used both to generate the client-side proxy for calling a web service and for configuring the server-side listener so that the listener knew the action to be performed when it received a web service call.

The DOT NET Framework SDK was available soon after the SOAP toolkit. This SDK was much richer than the early SOAP toolkit. It provided a plug-in for Internet Information Server (IIS) that allowed IIS to *understand* when it was hosting a servlet containing a web service. And the SDK provided a simpler-to-use client-side Application Programming Interface (API) for invoking web services from Visual Basic or C#. In fact, this SDK provided a C# compiler and early release components of the CLR. With this new SDK, all a developer had to know to create a web service were the extra ASP labels required to *tag* or denote the code as a web service. Here is an example from the DOT NET documentation of a very simple web service written in Visual Basic using the DOT NET SDK:

```
<%@ WebService Language="VB" Class="TimeService"%>
Imports System
Imports System.Web.Services


' Declare a new class for our new service. It must inherit
' from the system-provided base class WebService


Public Class TimeService : Inherits WebService


' Place our functions in the class. Mark them as WebMethods


Public Function <WebMethod()> GetTime (ShowSeconds as Boolean)
    As String


' Perform the business logic of our function Find current time,
' format as requested, and
' return the string


        Dim dt as DateTime


If (ShowSeconds = TRUE) Then
  GetTime = dt.Now.ToLongTimeString
Else
GetTime = dt.Now.ToShortTimeString
End If


    End Function


End Class
```

As can be seen in the example above, all the developer has to do to create a web service using the DOT NET SDK is create an ASP (giving it an `asmx` extension), provide the `WebService` label in its header, and add the `<WebMethod()>` tag to the start of the method to expose as a web service.

Below is a Visual Basic client that can invoke the service. The code (again) is very

simple; it hides the SOAP and XML parts of the web service invocation from the
programmer:

```
Imports System.Xml.Serialization
Imports System.Web.Services.Protocols
Imports System.Web.Services
Imports System

Public Class  TimeService
Inherits System.Web.Services.Protocols.SoapClientProtocol

Public Sub New()
 MyBase.New
 Me.Url = "http://191.1.1.3/AspxTimeDemo/TimeService.asmx"
End Sub

Public Function <System.Web.Services.Protocols.
   SoapMethodAttribute("http://tempuri.org/GetTime")>
   GetTime(ByVal
     <System.Xml.Serialization.XmlElementAttribute(
       "ShowSeconds", IsNullable:=false)>
     showSeconds As Boolean) As Integer
       Dim results() As Object = Me.Invoke("GetTime",
 New Object() {showSeconds})
   Return CType(results(0),Integer)
End Function

Public Function BeginGetTime(ByVal showSeconds As Boolean,
   ByVal callback As System.AsyncCallback,
                  ByVal asyncState As Object)
   As System.IAsyncResult
     Return Me.BeginInvoke("GetTime", New Object()
       {showSeconds},
       callback, asyncState)
```

```
End Function

Public Function EndGetTime(ByVal asyncResult
                          As System.IAsyncResult)
   As Integer
      Dim results() As Object = Me.EndInvoke(asyncResult)
      Return CType(results(0),Integer)
End Function

End Class

Public Module foo

Public Sub Main ()
Console.WriteLine ( "Creating proxy..." )
Dim Proxy As New TimeService ()
Dim strResult As String
strResult = Proxy.GetTime ( True )
Console.WriteLine ( "Result: " and strResult )
End Sub

End Module
```

At around the same time that Microsoft released its DOT NET SDK, it also released its UDDI SDK. The UDDI SDK provided client-side libraries for registering and looking up services whose metadata is stored in a UDDI registry. The first version of this SDK was fairly poorly documented, but the sample browser that came with it did work and could be used to query Microsoft's UDDI registry, as well as IBM's and anyone else's as long as it was UDDI 1.0 compliant.

As of this writing, Microsoft, IBM, and others have zeroed in on Web Services Definition Language (WSDL) as the XML vocabulary for describing the *public interfaces* of services. And the web services industry is adopting UDDI as the de facto standard for advertising and looking up web services. However, at the same time that technology companies are doing a good job of attempting to define and implement the infrastructure for web services, there are standards organizations, such as RosettaNet and ebXML, that are defining higher-level concepts that will be necessary in order for truly rich business-to-business (B2B) communications to work using web services. And the more time that these standards organizations spend defining how businesses will intercommunicate, the more they are reaching *down the technology stack* and defining the standards for implementing their specifications.

So what this all means is that the web services work being done by Microsoft, IBM, HP, and the W3C is beginning to collide with standards being proposed by RosettaNet and ebXML. This collision of standards will likely help the entire industry to mature the direction of web services. However, in the short term, what this means is that the standards are still in a great deal of flux.

Microsoft is building its DOT NET story from the ground up, slowly releasing the low-level technologies that implement parts of the overall strategy. This strategy provides credibility and makes it easy for developers to experiment with their web services technologies. Other vendors, such as HP, have released *complete solutions* — such as e-Speak. These solutions come less frequently than the small components that Microsoft and IBM release, but when they are released, they allow application developers and software integrators to create more *complete* web services solutions.

Microsoft BizTalk 2.0 Framework

The goal for the BizTalk 2.0 Framework Specification is to provide an *interoperability* framework that allows servers to conduct business securely over the Internet. It basically adds the extra layers above SOAP that are required to provide an interoperability framework.

Microsoft's BizTalk 2.0 Framework is the *business infrastructure* that rides on top of its lower level web services infrastructure based on SOAP. BizTalk 2.0 evolved from an earlier version of BizTalk (1.0). BizTalk 2.0 takes into account web services and makes sense in the context of web services and Microsoft's DOT NET initiative.

The BizTalk 1.0 Framework was announced prior to web services (and thus DOT NET). It was basically a message routing and transformation technology that would allow businesses to *front-end* the backend transactions with a unified presentation layer. Clients could submit business documents to a BizTalk 1.0 server using Microsoft Message Queue (MSMQ) or IIS or Simple Mail Transport Protocol (SMTP). The server would then translate the message — if necessary — into the format that the backend service provider could understand. Then the BizTalk 1.0 server would send the message along to the Inbox (a real SMTP Inbox, a Uniform Resource Locator [URL], a message queue, etc.) of the service provider. So basically, BizTalk 1.0 was all about routing messages and transforming them.

The BizTalk 2.0 Framework is at least two additional things — a specification (that can theoretically be implemented in any language on any OS) and an implementation. The implementation is Microsoft's BizTalk 2000 Server. The BizTalk 2.0 Framework Specification is straightforward and sensible. It builds on the simple method invocation roots of SOAP and extends SOAP — by introducing new sub elements of the SOAP `Header` element — to provide a robust, reliable transport mechanism for conducting business over the Internet.

SOAP does not define any way to associate documents together into a *conversation* or *sequence* of related documents. SOAP does not specify how to guarantee that messages are delivered or that they are not *stale* (i.e., not too old). A robust transport and enveloping technology must take into consideration these issues and more. This is where the BizTalk 2.0 Framework comes in. The framework defines properties for business documents that are transported using SOAP. A BizTalk document is a SOAP 1.1 message in which the body of the message contains the business documents, and the header contains BizTalk-specific header entries for enhanced message-handling semantics. The following concepts apply to BizTalk documents and are specific definitions from the BizTalk 2.0 Specification:

- Lifetime: The time period during which a document is meaningful. A document must not be sent, accepted, processed, or acknowledged beyond its lifetime.

- Identity: A universally unique token used to identify a document.

- Acceptance: The act of being accepted for delivery by a receiver. A received document is accepted if it is recognized as being intended for an endpoint served by the receiver, including documents that are copies or duplicates of previously received documents (based on the identity). Acceptance does not mean that all header entries and the body have been inspected and their contents verified for any specific purpose.

☐ Idempotence: The ability of a document to be transmitted and accepted more than once with the same effect as being transmitted and accepted once.

☐ Receipts: BizTalk Framework includes end-to-end protocols that prescribe certain receipts to be sent by the receiver to ensure delivery semantics in some cases. These receipts are first-class BizTalk documents with a pre-scribed syntax. There are two receipt kinds defined in this specification:

  ☐ Delivery: A receipt to acknowledge that the receiver accepted a given document for delivery.

  ☐ Commitment: A receipt to acknowledge that, in addition to being accepted, a given document has been inspected at the destination endpoint, all header entries marked `mustUnderstand="1"` have been understood, the correctness of their contents (as well as the contents of the body) have been verified, and there is a commitment to process the document.

In addition to specifying the headers required to guarantee a level of reliability and traceability, the BizTalk 2.0 Framework also discusses security techniques and the overall responsibilities for a BizTalk 2.0-compliant server. The most fundamental elements of a BizTalk 2.0 server are:

☐ Interoperability: BizTalk servers need to be able to intercommunicate with each other using a well-known transport and enveloping technology (SOAP). They also need to use standard Internet messaging technologies to transport SOAP messages. These include: HTTP/S, SMTP, and File Transfer Protocol (FTP), to name a few. The business documents that are exchanged need to be understandable by all intercommunicating nodes. Therefore, XML Schema and Data Type Definitions (DTDs) are used to provide metadata describing the content and meaning of XML business documents exchanged between BizTalk servers.

☐ Service Description: BizTalk servers must provide metadata that describes service access points and their public interfaces. Microsoft's first vocabulary for doing this was called *Service Control Language* (SCL). This later evolved into SDL. The industry as a whole is now converging on using WSDL.

■ Service Discovery: In 1999, the year that web services made their debut, there were a number of possible technologies that could have been used for service discovery. At that time, X.500 directories and the Lightweight Directory Access Protocol (LDAP) were strong candidates. They provide a very simple technology for storing strings in a directory and for accessing those strings. Often, these *directory* technologies were used to store public phone book entries, public *keys* for Internet security, and other strings that might be useful across large distances but that could be administered within a federation of directory servers. These technologies came *out of the box* with a well- known and rigid schema. However, they would allow you to extend their schemas for your needs.   At about this time, IBM proposed ADS (Advertisement and Discovery of Service) and Microsoft proposed DISCO (Discovery of Web Services).

IBM and Microsoft could not agree on which directory or lookup technology made more sense, and there were other players getting into the web services game, so they agreed to work with Ariba on a different, less proprietary standard for discovery and lookup of services.   To develop this standard, the companies formed the Universal Description, Discovery, and Integration Organization (www.uddi.org). Together, they created the UDDI 1.0 specification. This specification describes a very simple XML-based API that UDDI registries must support. These XML messages are communicated between clients of the registry and the UDDI registry using synchronous SOAP messaging. The UDDI API allows web services providers to register entries describing their companies, services provided by companies, URLs for obtaining services, and public interfaces describing services. The UDDI API also allows clients of web services to discover those services.

In its beta form, the BizTalk 2000 Server did not communicate using SOAP. Instead, clients could communicate with it using HTTP POSTs of non-SOAP messages or they could use Microsoft's MSMQ. But the BizTalk 2000 Server does introduce some concepts that are missing from the BizTalk 2.0 Framework Specification. These seem to be essential for real-world B2B communications to be enabled over a web services infrastructure. One of these concepts is that of a business process. Currently, the BizTalk word for business processes is *XLANG schedules*.

XLANG Schedules

An XLANG schedule is a set of steps — just like a workflow — that are invocations of objects, sends of messages, and receives of messages. All of the steps together form a business process. In its current implementation, BizTalk Server comes with a version of Visio that allows you to draw these business processes. The processes are then described using an XML vocabulary invented by Microsoft and called *XLANG*. An XLANG document describes a business process, and a running instance of one of these business processes is called an *XLANG schedule*.

Along the lines of the business process is the concept of *orchestration*. Basically, orchestration is the runtime component of an architecture that executes XLANG schedules. It is the part of the infrastructure that remembers where you are in a business process with a business partner. And it knows what steps of that process you have already completed. Orchestration enables execution of long-lived business processes.

Microsoft is proposing XLANG as the preferred XML vocabulary to use to describe public business processes. However, in its current form, XLANG does not do a very clean job of differentiating between the public steps of a business process and the private ones (recall from Figure 13.2 that it simply combines them all together, just like most workflow engines do today).   HP has submitted to the W3C an XML vocabulary called *Web Services Conversation Language* (WSCL) for describing public business processes.   IBM has also announced a similar XML vocabulary called *Web Services Flow Language* (WSFL). Regardless of which vendor's proposals influence the standards for describing business processes, the concept of a conversation or orchestration of messages flowing between business partners over the Internet is one of the primary contributions that the BizTalk 2000 Server has brought to the nascent web services industry.

15.1.2 IBM

IBM is one of the industry leaders in the move to define and standardize web services. It has been in this role since just about the time that Microsoft announced SOAP and IBM decided to support the SOAP specification.

IBM's involvement seemed to be driven by its push in the early 1998 timeframe to support the open source movement and the Linux OS. Around this time, IBM started to invest heavily in open source and published its AlphaWorks Web site (`//www.alphaworks.ibm.com`). This site allowed anyone to download technology previews of XML parsers, XML transforms, security components, and eventually, web services technologies. In addition to maintaining the AlphaWorks web site, IBM also became active in the Apache Project — contributing many of its XML technologies to that effort. IBM's path to web service support and contribution is similar to Microsoft's — both these companies have published several white papers and released web service SDK components. However, it is not reinventing itself around the concept as Microsoft seems to be doing. Instead, IBM appears to be more of a large research and development organization that has been advancing the state of the art of web services.

IBM envisions its product offering being folded into the WebSphere line of products. IBM's Web server and application server technologies, therefore, will evolve into a tightly integrated yet *open* web services infrastructure. It appears that whatever form WebSphere takes in the future, it will, as much as possible, be based on open web services standards.

As mentioned above, the AlphaWorks Web site (and its content) has done a great service to help move the developer community toward the concepts of web services. IBM led the introduction of WSDL as the de facto standard XML vocabulary for describing public interfaces of web services. IBM has also been one of the primary forces behind establishing the UDDI organization. It is one of the initial three UDDI operators — those responsible for providing a highly available infrastructure of UDDI registries. (Microsoft and HP are the other two initial UDDI operators.)

IBM's contribution to UDDI may be its most visible contribution to the area of web services. But it has been involved in other areas as well. One of these areas is that of interenterprise transactions (transactions across the Internet). The XAML (Transaction Authority Markup Language) XML vocabulary is a language being defined to describe these web services transactions. Currently, Bowstreet, HP, IBM, Oracle, and Sun Microsystems are leading this initiative.

Another XML vocabulary being championed by IBM is WSFL. This language competes with Microsoft's XLANG and HP's WSCL. WSFL is a language that can describe the steps that comprise a web service. The language also can be used to describe composed services: These are web services that have a public interface (the service they provide) that is implemented by calls to a number of different services (behind the scenes). This is similar to the concept of composed services discussed in Chapter 6. Clients of a composed service know about only its public interface — even though it is implemented by making calls to other web services. WSFL fits into the area of web services known as *orchestration, choreography*, or *conversations*.

It appears that WSFL may be useful behind the firewall, as well as in front of it. In front of the firewall, WSFL can describe the public interfaces of web services. Behind the firewall, however, WSFL may be useful for describing workflows. IBM has a very successful workflow product called *MQ Series*, as well as a message routing and transformation product called *MQ Series Integrator*. WSFL may well be the *glue* that allows these behind-the-firewall technologies to be reachable across the Internet as web services. If this is the case, IBM's WebSphere, combined with WSFL and MQ Series Integrator, is in direct competition with Microsoft's BizTalk 2000 Server and XLANG.

Although WebSphere and MQ Series Integrator are shipping products, IBM's web services technologies are primarily still a work in progress. The best way to understand the current state of its web services work is to log onto the AlphaWorks web site and download the current version of the Web Services Toolkit (WSTK). In the current version (as of June 2001), there are a number of components, including a UDDI registry, a UDDI browser, an Axis server (web services dispatcher that runs above a web server), an embedded version of WebSphere, many tools, and many helpful white papers.

In the current incarnation, IBM's WSTK makes it very simple to create, deploy, and invoke web services. For a deployment platform, you use your favorite open source Java Web Server (i.e., Jakarta/Tomcat), or you can use WebSphere. Then you install the Axis server into your Java Web Server. The Axis server intercepts calls to web services and invokes them on your behalf. In a sense, the Axis server does the same thing that Microsoft's IIS plug-in does with the latest DOT NET SDK. Basically, both of these components are the interceptors that are invoked by the web server when it does not know what to do with the request. These components are able to determine that the request is an invocation of a web service, and they invoke the appropriate web service.

With the WSTK, you write web services in Java and deploy them to files that end in `.jws`. Here is an example *Stock Quote* service that comes with the WSTK:

```
public class StockQuoteService {
  public float getQuote (String symbol) throws Exception {
    // get a real (delayed by 20min) stockquote from
    // http://www.xmltoday.com/examples/stockquote/.
    // The IP addr
    // below came from the host that the above form posts to ..

    if ( symbol.equals("XXX") ) return( (float) 55.25 );

    URL url = new URL( "http://www.xmltoday.com/examples/" +
        "stockquote/getxmlquote.vep?s="+symbol );

    DocumentBuilderFactory dbf =
        DocumentBuilderFactory.newInstance();
    DocumentBuilder db  = dbf.newDocumentBuilder();

    Document doc  = db.parse( url.toExternalForm() );
    Element  elem = doc.getDocumentElement();
    NodeList list =
        elem.getElementsByTagName( "stock_quote" );

    if ( list != null && list.getLength() != 0 ) {
      elem = (Element) list.item(0);
      list = elem.getElementsByTagName( "price" );
      elem = (Element) list.item(0);
      String quoteStr = elem.getAttribute("value");
      try {
        return Float.valueOf(quoteStr).floatValue();
      } catch (NumberFormatException e1) {
        // maybe its an int?
        try {
```

```
            return
        Integer.valueOf(quoteStr).intValue() * 1.0F;
            } catch (NumberFormatException e2) {
            return -1.0F;
            }
        }
    }
    return( 0 );
  }
}
```

As is the case with e-services based on e-Speak, web services need to be de-ployed before they are accessible and usable. To deploy it, you create a *deploy.xml* file and place that file in a subdirectory of the web service's application. Here is what the *deploy.xml* file looks like for the *Stock Quote* service:

```
<deploy>
 <handler name="authen"
 class="org.apache.axis.handlers.SimpleAuthenticationHandler"/>
 <handler name="author"
  class="org.apache.axis.handlers.SimpleAuthorizationHandler"/>
  <chain    name="checks"  flow="authen,author"/>
  <chain    name="rpc"     flow="checks,RPCDispatcher"/>

  <service name="urn:xmltoday-delayed-quotes" pivot="rpc">
    <option name="className"
        value="samples.stock.StockQuoteService" />
    <option name="methodName" value="getQuote" />
  </service>
  <service name="urn:cominfo" pivot="rpc" >
    <option name="className"
        value="samples.stock.ComInfoService" />
    <option name="methodName" value="getInfo" />
  </service>
```

```
</deploy>
```

The client-side code that invokes this service is very simple. Just like with Microsoft's DOT NET SDK, the client code uses a generated *proxy* to invoke the service. As you can see, neither the client Java code nor the server-side Java code contain any native XML — even though the client and server communicate over the Internet using XML. Here is the client:

```java
import java.net.*;
import org.apache.soap.*;

public class GetQuoteClient
{
  public static void main(String[] argv)
      throws MalformedURLException, SOAPException
  {
    if (argv.length != 1)
    {
      System.err.println("Usage:\n" +
         "java " + GetQuoteClient.class.getName() + " symbol");
      System.exit(1);
    }

    GetQuoteProxy testProxy = new GetQuoteProxy();

    System.out.println("Result: "+testProxy.getQuote(argv[0]));
  }
}
```

The IBM WSTK makes it very simple to implement, deploy, and call web services. The UDDI4J Java API that comes with the toolkit allows developers to create applications easily that can register and find web services by using UDDI registries. Although many of the web services technology downloads that IBM has released are works in progress, it provides a very rich suite of components that could even today be used by early adopters to develop solutions that build upon web services. As IBM integrates these technologies into its core product lines, it will be very well positioned to make a significant impact on the world of web services.

15.2 Strong Industry Participants

Aside from HP, IBM, and Microsoft, there are several other companies that offer products in the web services arena. Not all of these, however, have the same level of product completeness or maturity as the industry leaders. These vendors have a strong offering in a related area, and thus, they could, in theory, pose strong competition for the leaders in the industry. In the next discussion, some of these companies and their product offerings are described.

15.2.1 BEA Systems WebLogic Collaborate

BEA Systems is known for delivering an industrial-strength implementation of Sun's J2EE (Java 2 Enterprise Edition) standard. A few years ago, BEA Systems started to dominate the Enterprise Java Bean (EJB) market with its acquisition of We-bLogic. In addition to its EJB server, BEA Systems also sells *Tuxedo*. Tuxedo is one of the most mature Transaction Processing Monitors (TP Monitors) on the market. BEA Systems has a rich arsenal of middleware technologies that can be used to develop intranet-based as well as across-the-Internet solutions.

Because of its strong middleware story, BEA has become the de facto standard for J2EE servers within many Fortune 1000 companies. However, because more and more companies are trying out J2EE servers and finding that they are a useful tool for developing distributed applications, there are more companies getting into the market of developing and selling J2EE servers. IBM's WebSphere and Sun's iPlanet are two major competitors to BEA's WebLogic. HP's Total-e-Server also competes in this market. In addition to all these commercial — and often expensive — products, there are a few open source J2EE servers coming onto the market.

BEA has realized that, as the market matures and J2EE becomes the standard architecture for application servers, J2EE servers are becoming a *commodity*. To-day, BEA has developed a strategy to develop a higher level middleware stack that relies on commodity J2EE servers and adds value that is not yet available in its competitors' offerings. BEA's strategy generally follows the same architecture as is being pursued by Microsoft and IBM. Namely, BEA is providing a workflow engine product and an Internet-based web services infrastructure that allows enterprises to carry on XML conversations with one another.

Active, a company acquired by BEA, also developed a business process modeling tool. BEA combined the high-level modeling aspects of that tool with its own Tuxedo infrastructure — and other infrastructure components — and created a workflow product called *BEA WebLogic Process Integrator*. Basically, what BEA has done is create an industrial-strength workflow engine that can be used within an enterprise to create applications via an easy-to-use GUI. This is a very useful infrastructure for doing Enterprise Application Integration (EAI), but it does not solve the problem of connecting businesses across the Internet. Realizing that it needed a B2B integration solution, BEA developed its web services product, named *BEA WebLogic Collaborate*.

BEA WebLogic Collaborate

BEA WebLogic Collaborate, the industry's first production web services infrastructure, is based on modern concepts — such as using XML to transact business and providing an infrastructure that supports public conversations between businesses, along with behind-the-firewall private workflows.

BEA has been active within the same web services standards committees as IBM and Microsoft. However, it has not played such a public role in bringing forward standards that it has developed itself. It seems as though BEA is more interested in *tracking* the standards and ensuring that its products adhere to those standards. As of spring 2001, BEA WebLogic Collaborate is based on these standards (among others): XML, SSL, HTTP/S, and RosettaNet. It is hoped that support for SOAP and UDDI are soon to arrive.

Possibly because it was first to market with a web services product or possibly because it wants to provide features above and beyond the standards, BEA has made some implementation decisions that are slightly divergent from today's vision of a UDDI-based universe of web services.   Most notably, the BEA WebLogic

Collaborate product introduces the concepts of *C-Hubs* and *C-Spaces*.

C-Hubs and C-Spaces

A C-Hub is a dynamic marketplace that can be used for trading partners to find one another, to retrieve metadata describing the public interfaces of web services, and to carry on audited and secure business transactions. It is a web services market-maker software. This differs from the UDDI model for advertising and discovering web services. UDDI is simply a directory that can be used by web services to advertise themselves and by clients to find web services. Once a client finds a service, the UDDI registry is no longer needed. In contrast, BEA's C-Hub plays an integral role in the entire conversation that is carried on between clients and the web services with which they transact business.

C-Spaces is the other new concept that BEA's WebLogic Collaborate introduces to the area of web services. The following excerpt from BEA's WebLogic Collaborate documentation provides a high-level definition of a C-Space in its own words:

> A C-space is a virtual place where predefined trading partners can con-duct and coordinate conversations with each other. A C-space has a specific business purpose and logically represents an electronic mar-ketplace or common trading environment. It provides the administra-tion capability, conversation coordination, and underlying messaging services that are used to create a dynamic business-to-business inte-gration environment.

Although C-Hubs and C-Spaces are somewhat proprietary concepts, they rely on many of the standard web services concepts and technologies. And, fortunately, BEA has actually implemented in its product the concept of a conversation that oc-curs between trading partners. (This is something that is missing from Microsoft's DOT NET and that has only been suggested by IBM's web services Flow Lan-guage work.) At the time that BEA released Collaborate, there was no standard XML vocabulary for describing the syntax and semantics of conversations between trading partners. So BEA defined its own XML language, called *eXtensible Open Collaboration Protocol* (XOCP). According to the product documentation:

XOCP refines the business process that governs the exchange of business information between trading partners. The business protocol specifies how to process the messages and how to route them to the appropriate recipients. A business protocol may also specify characteristics of messages related to persistence and reliability.

XOCP competes with Microsoft's XLANG, IBM's WSFL, and HP's WSCL. They are all languages for describing the business process flows that occur between trading partners over the Internet. BEA has attempted to convince the industry to adopt XOCP as a standard, but to date, it has not caught on. If another standard — such as WSFL or WSCL — becomes the standard, BEA's products and those businesses that have started creating solutions based on BEA WebLogic Collaborate will have to endure some modifications to be standards-compliant.

Overall, BEA's WebLogic Collaborate and Process Integrator products are a strong team of technologies that can help businesses begin to offer and use web services today. As these products mature, they will likely adhere to emerging web services standards, such as SOAP and UDDI. And in the future, it may be possible that BEA's suite of web services technologies will be interoperable with other standards-based solutions from Microsoft, IBM, HP, and others.

15.2.2   JSR-109

The way that new Java APIs are introduced into Sun's Java standards is through the Java Community Process (JCP). Each new set of APIs is introduced through JSRs (Java Specification Requests). Each JSR targets a specific area of technology, such as parsing XML documents, making remote method invocations using XML, web services, and so on. *JSR-109* is the web services JSR being led by IBM. It is entitled *Implementing Enterprise Web Services* and defines the programming model and runtime architecture for implementing web services in Java. This is a very important JSR, as is reflected by the members of its Expert group: Art Technology Group, Inc., BEA Systems, Cisco Systems, Cygent, Inc., DevelopMentor, HP, interKeel, IONA, iPlanet, Motorola, Oracle, Rational Software, Silverstream Software, Sun Micrososystems, Sybase, WebGain, and WebMethods Corporation.

The JSR-109 specification brings together a number of previously defined JSRs into a coherent whole that can be used to address the needs of developers, deployers, and clients of web services. Among the other JSRs that are leveraged by this one are:

- JSR-67 (Java APIs for XML Messaging) — also known as *JAXM*. This is a set of APIs that allows applications to send and receive XML messages. The first reference implementation of JAXM implemented ebXML enveloping for transmitting XML messages. Future implementations will adopt the SOAP standard.

- JSR-93 (Java APIs for XML Registry) — also known as *JAXR*. These APIs provide the same type of access to registries as do JNDI (Java Naming and Directory Interface). Where JAXR differs from JNDI, however, is that it provides a technique for accessing XML-based repositories, such as UDDI and ebXML's Registry Services.

- JSR-101 (Java APIs for XML-Based RPC) — also known as *JAX-RPC*. These APIs are used to make simple synchronous method invocations over the Internet via XML documents. You can think of this as a Java API that would allow you to make XML-RPC/SOAP method invocations.

There are other, lower level Java APIs for XML that are also leveraged by this specification. *JAXP* is one of them. It defines the Java API for parsing XML documents. This API implements the DOM and SAX standards. Java APIs for XML Binding (JAXB) is another API used by this specification. It is the JAVA APIs for Binding. Although not yet completed, the finished JAXB specification will provide a technique for creating a Java facade for XML documents. In other words, you will be able to read and write XML documents by accessing them as though they were normal Java objects.

In addition to aggregating all these useful APIs, JSR-109 also discusses the relationships between the current J2EE architecture and an architecture for web services. There are a number of vendors, such as IBM and HP-Bluestone, that have invested much of their efforts into implementing Sun's J2EE standards. These companies would like to see the industry's web services standards take a decidedly evolutionary step extending from Sun's J2EE. That way, their product lines can easily evolve toward the new web services standards. Those vendors that agree that Sun's JCP should determine the future for web services are heavily invested in trying to make the JSR process succeed.

However, the JCP and JSRs are not the only standards bodies working on the issues of web services. For instance, the W3C is the premier repository for all Internet-related standards. The UDDI organization is also playing a very influential role in determining the shape of web services repositories. RosettaNet has done a very effective job of working together with a number of real-world users of web services and has defined a number of Partner Interaction Processes (PIPs) they can use today to transact business over the Internet. And the ebXML organization is playing an ever more important role defining horizontal web services standards for enabling the implementation of Trading Partner Agreements (TPAs), RosettaNet PIPs, and other forms of web services.

Sun and those companies actively participating in the JCP are interested in seeing a web services architecture based on Java APIs and architecturally similar to today's J2EE. However, other companies, such as Microsoft, BEA, and Bowstreet, already have working web services architectures that are not based solely on the J2EE standards. Whether there can ever be an API-level standard for web services is debatable. It may end up being that only the wire-protocol, enveloping techniques, and registry access techniques will be able to be based on standards. And the independent implementations of those standards may be done using a variety of languages and architectures.

15.2.3 Sun's Open Net Environment (ONE)

Recently, Sun Microsystems announced its web services strategy named *The Sun Open Net Environment* (Sun ONE). Interestingly, it was much later to the game than were HP, IBM, Microsoft, and BEA Systems. And the Sun ONE vision appears to be much more of a marketing response to the web services concepts. In fact, many of the Sun ONE white papers released to date from Sun are really more of a statement of which Java APIs to use when building web services running within a J2EE environment.

Sun ONE initiative, at the time of writing this book, did not include any technology previews that could be downloaded and no new server-side software to install and test drive. In fact, what Sun has done best is publicly to give its support for emerging web services standards, then attempt to explain how you can implement those standards using current and emerging Java APIs.

According to the early Sun ONE documentation, Sun supports the following XML standards and protocols: XP (SOAP), UDDI, ebXML, WSDL, and S2ML. It suggests that the following Java APIs will be the foundation upon which J2EE web services can be built: J2EE, JSP and Servlets, JDBC, JAXP, JAXB, JAXR, JAXM, JAXRPC, J2ME, and Mobile Information Device Protocol (MIDP).

Sun ONE has defined an open software architecture to support interoperable web services. The Sun ONE software architecture attempts to address issues such as privacy, security, and identity. It defines practices and conventions to support specific situations, such as client device type and user location. And it supports systems that can span multiple networks, including the traditional Web, the wireless Web, and the home network. The architecture's main goal is seamless interoperability. The Sun ONE architecture is based on a recommended set of open and pervasive standards, technologies, and protocols. Sun plans to collaborate with other companies to foster the development of these new standards through appropriate standards bodies and industry initiatives, such as W3C, OASIS, IETF, UDDI, ebXML, and the JCP program. In particular, Sun will work with others to foster the development of new standards to support shared context.

At its essence, the Sun ONE software architecture is based on XML, Java technology, and LDAP. Sun's technical philosophy is to use common, pervasive technologies and to use what is available as a standard. The Sun ONE documentation introduces a few concepts that describe some of the defining characteristics of web services:

- Smart Delivery: In Sun ONE, this is the name given to that portion of an architecture dedicated to the rendering portion of a service's presentation. The rendering part is how the service shows itself in a browser, in a Wireless Access Protocol (WAP)-enabled phone, or through a voice interface. It is the device-specific part of the web service's user interface. Several technologies can be used to render the user interfaces of web services.

- Service Container: The Sun ONE documentation discusses the high-level architectural benefits of implementing web services as services that run within the infrastructure of a *container*. The documents briefly discuss the features and benefits of J2EE containers. Sun's vision is that web services of tomorrow will be implemented the way the Internet applications are implemented today — as servlets running within J2EE containers.

▢ Smart Management: In the area of management of distributed software, Simple Network Management Protocol (SNMP) has been the most widely accepted standard. Although it has worked wonders in terms of helping infrastructure administrators keep tabs on enormous numbers of hosts deployed throughout the enterprise, SNMP has never provided the fine-level granularity some have wanted in order to administer individual distributed software components. In this domain, Sun has introduced an innovation that appears to be substantial and potentially revolutionary. This standard is actually both a definition for the XML data that travels over the wire (from management agents to management consoles) and a Java API that can be used to instrument software components, as well as to access the management data provided by those components. This new standard is called *Java Management Extensions* (JMX). Within the context of Sun ONE, Sun is suggesting that this will revolutionize the management of web services. In fact, JMX will be equally useful for management of distributed components that are not web services.

▢ Smart Process: This concept is Sun's placeholder for the concepts in web services known as *orchestration*, *choreography*, and *conversations*. Sun recognizes the importance of this aspect of web services but has not provided tools or APIs to help developers actually implement it. In fact, the most it does is to recognize that ebXML is working on the issue and that XAML might be a suitable XML vocabulary for representing orchestration. Unlike IBM, Microsoft, and BEA, Sun has not provided any infrastructure components that can actually provide orchestration.

▢ Smart Policy: In discussing this concept, Sun's documentation begins to explore the very interesting concepts of *context-aware* web services — services that can alter their behavior based on who the client is. Soon, however, its explanation of *Smart Policy* becomes the place where it discusses the fact that a web services infrastructure should provide authentication, authorization, and encryption. The technologies Sun endorses in this realm are: XML,

Kerberos, PKI, Security Services Markup Language (S2ML), and AuthXML.

Some of the Sun ONE documentation does a fair job of explaining how the various web services standards are used with each other in the development and deployment of web services. So to build web services strictly using Java and J2EE, the Sun ONE documentation is a good starting point.

JXTA

At around the same time that Sun announced its Sun ONE vision, it also announced a potentially relevant technology called *JXTA* (an acronym for Juxtapose). JXTA is a peer-to-peer technology that leverages Internet protocols and XML. However, unlike many of the early web services technology previews, which provided only a synchronous, client-server computing model, the JXTA provides an infrastructure in which all communicating nodes are of equal stature. They are all peers. What this means is that any peer can initiate a conversation with another peer. No node is in only a client role or a server role. This is important because it allows you to use an asynchronous computing model. An asynchronous computing model makes it much more straightforward to implement workflows that are shared across a network. If the JXTA concepts catch on and become an indispensable component of web services, Sun may leapfrog some of the early innovators in this space and again take a leadership position similar to what it has done with the Java language.

15.2.4   webMethods

WebMethods was one of the early products that provided an infrastructure for doing B2B integration using the Internet. However, it started its life enabling EAI between various Enterprise Resource Planning (ERP), Customer Relationship Management (CRM), financial, and other applications within enterprises. As webMethods grew in popularity, the company developed a larger and larger arsenal of adapters to backend systems. It has many backend adapters that came prepackaged with the software.

Within the world of web services, possibly webMethod's largest claim to fame is that it was the first product to implement RosettaNet PIPs. In addition, webMethods supports a number of other business integration standards, including Open Buying on the Internet (OBI) transactions, Electronic Data Interchange (EDI) documents, Common Business Library (CBL) documents, Commerce XML (cXML) documents, and other XML messages.

The products that comprise the webMethods B2Bi Solution suite were implemented prior to the advent of many of the current web services standards, such as: SOAP, UDDI, WSDL, etc.   But these products make use of these prevalent Internet standards that were available when they were released: SSL, X.509 certificates, SMTP (for management alerts), XML, XML DTDs, LDAP, and HTTPS.

For early adopters, the webMethods suite of products is a great way to enter the universe of web services. However, because the standards continue to mature, unless the webMethods product line can evolve with the standards, it could end up finding itself behind. Hopefully, with the addition of a workflow component and a stronger adherence to today's web services standards, the webMethods B2B product line will continue to win customers and help integrators create web services-based solutions.

15.2.5   Vitria

Vitria, like webMethods, was one of the first companies to release a line of products addressing the B2B integration domain. Although not initially labeled a web services infrastructure, Vitria's suite of BusinessWare products is exactly that. In fact, Vitria's solutions are some of the most complete in terms of addressing business process modeling and execution, messaging, transformation of data, back-end adapters, security, and Internet standards.

The BusinessWare line of products has its roots in EAI. Although it is very rich in EAI components, it has yet to implement fully the latest web services standards such as SOAP, UDDI, and WSDL. However, Vitria does already implement RosettaNet PIPs as well as use XML, SSL, and HTTPS, so it does support its share of today's web services standards. In addition to using XML over HTTP to communicate with other enterprises over the Internet, Vitria can also be used to communicate with the very large installed base of *legacy* EDI applications — by virtue of its

BusinessWare EDI Module.

Vitria's BusinessWare line of products is composed of the following major components:

- BusinessWare Modeler: This is a UML-based modeling tool that allows "business developers" to describe business processes visually. Each process is
comprised of a set of interdependent processing steps. Each step represents an invocation of backend logic. Business processes are the glue that
ties these steps together. The tool allows developers to associate business
rules with processing steps and transitions between steps. Once a business
process has been described using the tool, it can be stored into the BusinessWare Repository, where it can later be executed by the BusinessWare
Automator.

- BusinessWare Transformer: The Transformer has a visual and a runtime
component. The visual component allows developers to map source document structures graphically into transformed destination document structures. Field by field, a developer can specify transformations to apply to a
message in order to translate it into a different format. This technology is crucial, given the number of different business document formats currently used
in electronic business transactions. This technology allows Vitria to integrate
services and applications that speak completely different languages, including BizTalk, ebXML, RosettaNet, and EDI. The runtime component of the
Transformer executes transformations at the appropriate times within business processes.

- BusinessWare Server: This is the core server upon which the primary architectural components of the Vitria solution execute. The five components that
execute within this server are: BusinessWare Automator, BusinessWare Analyzer, BusinessWare Communicator, BusinessWare Connector, and BusinessWare Transformer. The BusinessWare Server provides a common set of
services that are leveraged by all components that execute within it. These
services include: Security (authentication, authorization, and data encryption), Transaction Management, Persistence (the state of in-progress business processes is maintained), and Repository (which stores metadata, such
as business process models).

■ BusinessWare Automator: This is the Vitria component that executes business processes that have been modeled using the BusinessWare Modeler and stored in the BusinessWare Repository. This component executes the *glue* code that performs most of the EAI portion of a service. However, when it needs to communicate with other businesses over the Internet, it can do so by using the BusinessWare Communicator.

■ BusinessWare Analyzer: This component helps business users view their enterprise transactions. In a sense, it is part of an enterprise's ERP system — providing a view into business processes running throughout the enterprise. Using this component, users can view business metrics, identify processing bottlenecks, and understand process usage patterns. In fact, this component can even provide a real-time "feedback loop" that can send statistics into the BusinessWare Automator in order to modify how it is executing business processes.

■ BusinessWare Communicator: This is the messaging component of the Vitria solution. (Architecturally, it is very similar to BizTalk 2000's Messaging Server.) This component allows business processes — which are executed by the Automator — to intercommunicate with other business processes and applications through various techniques, including: IBM's MQ Series, Microsoft's MSMQ, EDI, and XML over HTTP/S.

■ BusinessWare Connectors: These Connectors are Vitria's adaptors to backend systems, as well as to outside-the-firewall, XML-based services. Vitria, like webMethods, provides a rich set of already implemented Connectors to a number of popular backend systems, such as SAP. The BusinessWare Connector architecture is extensible, and Vitria provides a toolkit that allows developers to implement new Connectors easily for connecting with their applications.

■ BusinessWare Administrator: Vitria's BusinessWare line of products implements a virtual network of integration middleware. There can be a single machine running Vitria software or an entire federation of Vitria machines working in concert. The BusinessWare Administrator is a graphical management and monitoring component that allows system administrators locally or remotely to administer BusinessWare servers.

■ BusinessWare Repository: Business process models that are created with the Modeler tool are stored within this repository. From within the repository, they can be executed by the BusinessWare Automator.

☐ BusinessWare EDI Module: This component is the front-end business presentation component that allows business partners that communicate using EDI to integrate into a company's business processes. In a sense, the EDI Module can be thought of as a Connector that allows EDI transactions to plug into the Vitria infrastructure.

☐ Vitria Business Network (VBN): Vitria's Business Network was designed and announced prior to the advent of UDDI. It was designed as a marketplace that allows businesses automatically to find other businesses, form supply chains with them, and execute business transactions. This is a more heavyweight form of business registry than UDDI; however, it is able to provide levels of security and monitoring that far surpass what is provided by UDDI and even approach what is provided by EDI's value-added networks.

☐ BusinessWare for RosettaNet Framework and BusinessWare for RosettaNet PIPs: These components run on top of the BusinessWare platform. They implement RNIF (RosettaNet Implementation Framework) and RosettaNet PIPs. The RosettaNet specifications call for specific message formats, qualities of service, security, and auditing. The RosettaNet components of the Vitria product line implement these standards. BusinessWare for RosettaNet PIPs is an infrastructure and a set of preconfigured RosettaNet PIPs that execute within the BusinessWare for RosettaNet Framework.

Note that Vitria's products are very similar architecturally to Microsoft's BizTalk 2000 and IBM's web services with MQ Integrator. In fact, all these products implement business process modeling, business process execution, data transformations, messaging, and security. The Microsoft and IBM products rely on more up-to-date web services standards, including: SOAP, WSDL, and UDDI. Vitria, being a slightly earlier-to-market product, does not yet support some of the latest web services standards. And Vitria, unlike Microsoft or IBM, implements its own marketplace (the BusinessWare Server) for advertising services, finding services, and conducting secure business transactions.

Vitria is not currently very active in introducing new web services standards. But because it is already a robust and proven B2B infrastructure, Vitria could benefit quite a lot by simply drafting behind the current web services standards and incorporating them into its products as quickly as possible.

15.2.6   IONA's iPortal XMLBus

IONA is arguably the industry's leading Common Object Request Broker Architecture (CORBA) Object Request Broker (ORB) vendor. For years, IONA's Orbix CORBA ORB has competed with the likes of Visigenic, BEA Systems, IBM, Expersoft, and others. Yet as its competition evolved into other markets, IONA remained strongly committed to maintaining and extending its ORB as the CORBA standard progressed. Today, its ORB implements the CORBA 2.4 specification and parts of the 3.0 specification — such as the Portable Object Adapter (POA).

As IONA's CORBA products have matured, they have expanded into the area of EAI, as well as B2B integration over the Internet. Although relatively new to the web services game, IONA's wide array of integration and middleware technologies combined with its latest web services product — iPortal XMLBus — places it within competition with the likes of BEA, Microsoft, and IBM.

IONA's web services product has evolved out of its EAI and middleware assets. Its EAI product — called *Enterprise Integrator* — has grown out of its early work creating CORBA adapters to the most widely used backend systems and packaged applications. It, like Vitria's BusinessWare Automator, executes business processes and integrates disparate infrastructures and applications. A few of the enterprise packages that can be integrated using Enterprise Integrator are: SAP, PeopleSoft, and Siebel. In addition to its runtime component, the Enterprise Integrator comes with visual tools that allow developers to construct business processes and connect various systems easily throughout an enterprise. It also contains a hub (like a registry) that can be used securely to store and find business processes as well as to execute them.

The first B2B integration product released by IONA was its B2B Integrator. This product includes a number of components: messaging services, data transformation services, security, and auditing. Because B2B Integrator was released earlier than most of today's web services standards were in place, it implements only a subset of them. Some of the standards that are supported by B2B Integrator are:

EDI (ANSI X12, EDIFACT, EDIINT), XML, RosettaNet, ebXML, xCBL, SSL, and LDAP. You can think of this product much like a message router that can transform documents and speak many of the different dialects used in B2B integration.

The most recently announced integration product to come from IONA is its flagship web services solution, iPortal XMLBus. iPortal XMLBus is an XML-based development toolkit and a collection of related technologies for building and exposing web services. iPortal XMLBus enables companies to allow B2B transactions and application integration across the Internet, using their existing Internet infrastructure. Using industry standard directory technology, XMLBus also enables IT developers quickly to browse for, implement, and access web services interfaces to their companies' e-business applications.

XMLBus is a truly standards-based web services product. It goes beyond the initial offering of B2B Integrator — implementing WSDL and SOAP and using UDDI registries for advertisement and discovery of web services. Just like Microsoft's and IBM's web services SDKs, IONA's XMLBus provides a toolkit that allows developers quickly to generate the server-side code required to expose their components as web services. It is interesting to note that IONA's product may be the first to allow developers to create web services from components implemented in any of the three major middleware technologies: COM, EJBs, and CORBA.

15.2.7   Bowstreet Business Web Factory

Bowstreet was one of the first software companies to understand the web services vision. It is active in a number of standards initiatives, including XAML and UDDI. In fact, Bowstreet created a Java-based UDDI registry (called *JUDDI*) and contributed it to the open source community.

Bowstreet's technology has not always been an implementation of the web services vision. It began as a registry of HTML components that could be *wired together*, using its Business Web Factory software to create new Web portals and e-commerce sites. As the concept of ASPs and e-business marketplaces began to gain traction in the software industry, Bowstreet repositioned its products accordingly. It generated a number of white papers discussing the concept of a Business Web of intercommunicating services. Its products were a natural fit for implementing software based on this new paradigm.

Because it was already in the market of selling products designed to help software developers create and deploy services over the Internet, Bowstreet simply repositioned itself again — this time with the web services technology wave. Fortunately, Bowstreet did not just draft behind the emerging web services standards. Instead, it played an active role in helping move the industry forward toward the web services vision. Early on, it contributed by developing XML-based access to LDAP directories, then becoming involved in the XAML effort. Soon, it also became actively involved in the design and development of the UDDI standard.

Although Bowstreet was one of the first companies to take advantage of the web services trend, its products have not really been as readily usable as those offered by Microsoft, IBM, IONA, and others. Even though Bowstreet has been championing the concept of services over the web for long time, its products continue to reflect Bowstreet-specific concepts, such as Business Webs, Builders, and Models. In other words, Bowstreet uses its own terminology to describe the components of its web services offering. And there is little mention of current web services standards, such as SOAP, WSDL, and even UDDI.

Here is an overview of the high-level components of the Bowstreet Business Web product line:

- Builders: These are components that execute logic in order to carry out business functions, as well as to generate content. You can think of each Builder as a step of a complete business workflow. In Bowstreet terminology, a Model (business workflow) executes a set of related Builders in a sequence defined by the business process modeler. Some Builders are useful for constructing user interfaces, such as Web pages to be displayed in browsers. Other Builders carry out data transformations or access databases.

- Models: Models are business processes. They are designed by business developers, using Bowstreet's business process modeling tool. A Model is a process that executes a series of Builders. Builders can be thought of as the low-level "building blocks" upon which Models are constructed. Once a Model is built, it is stored in the Bowstreet Business Web Factory. Then, at runtime, the Model is executed within the Bowstreet WebEngine. Models primarily carry out the steps that were specified by the programmer of the Models. However, the Bowstreet WebEngine can react to user profiles and other context information — causing it to modify the behavior of Models, based on the context in which they are running.

- Bowstreet Business Web: This is the term used by Bowstreet to represent a business's offering of web services. Although it isn't very well articulated by Bowstreet, this concept will eventually take full advantage of the UDDI standards as they emerge.

- Bowstreet WebEngine: This is the runtime component that resides within the firewalls of service providers. This is where Models and Builders are stored, once they have been designed by business developers. This is also the execution environment in which Models and Builders run to provide services for clients.

Behind these proprietary terms and concepts is a compelling offering that offers many of the same architectural services as do the other major web services products available today. Developers working with the Bowstreet product use high-level graphical tools to construct Models (business processes). These Models are represented as XML documents, thereby providing metadata describing the business processes. When Models are executed, they are aware of the context in which they are running. In fact, they can modify their behavior, based on who is requesting the services and what that client's profile indicates. This concept of configurable Models is very similar to the Sun ONE Smart Policy concept. Clients execute services hosted by the Business Web Factory runtime by posting requests as documents sent via HTTP. Once invoked, these services are then instantiated and executed by the runtime engine — called *Bowstreet WebEngine*.

Overall, Bowstreet provides a very easy-to-use infrastructure for programming and deploying web services. However, it provides little in terms of backend adapters, transaction processing, and workflow management. Bowstreet's product line is best suited as a front-end business presentation technology — acting as the first point of contact for clients of web services. In the future, Bowstreet may acquire or build a more robust EAI technology in order to help it better compete with the likes of Vitria, WebMethods, IONA, and BEA. In the meantime, however, it might be best used at the edge of a company's network — where the enterprise connects with the Internet.

15.3   Honorable Mentions

As of the writing of this book, the number of web services products being brought to market is growing rapidly. Therefore, it is impossible to do justice to all the current and emerging products that support web services. The preceding sections were an attempt to describe the current industry leaders in the area of web services. The following discussion describes briefly many of the web services products just now being brought to the market. Because these are brand-new products, information on them is just emerging; therefore, we only briefly touch on the major attributes of each product.

15.3.1   Borland's Delphi 6

Borland is a company that has been producing award-winning software development environments for nearly the last 20 years. As languages and programming concepts have come into vogue, Borland has always been there with relevant and useful products. In the 1997–1998 timeframe, Borland branched out into the area of enterprise computing with its purchase of Visigenic — a CORBA ORB vendor.

Since becoming an enterprise computing company, Borland has invested heavily in cross-platform technologies, such as Java. And it now produces IDEs for UNIX, Linux, and the Windows platform. Its JBuilder Java IDE has become a favorite of many Java developers. And its traditional "Delphi" environment continues to be popular.

Borland recently announced its entry into the world of web services with the release of its Delphi 6 product line. This IDE allows developers quickly and easily to produce web services by using a graphical interface. This IDE is called *BizSnap*. WebSnap, another component of the Delphi product, is a component-based Web application development framework — much like the open source *struts* project. And the final component of Delphi 6 is DataSnap, which is an adapter technology allowing you to construct web services from CORBA, DCOM, and Java objects, as well as from calls to databases such as: Oracle, Microsoft's SQL Server, IBM DB2, and Sybase.

15.3.2 WebGain's Application Composer and Business Designer

Within the last year, WebGain purchased the Visual Cafe Java IDE from Symantec. It then went on to acquire a number of technologies that would allow it to compete in the arena of full software development lifecycle solutions. Its primary competitor in this arena is Rational's latest software development tools. Although its primary focus is on providing a repository-based environment that unifies and streamlines the software development process, some of the tools WebGain has recently released to the market enable developers to construct web services quickly.

Application Composer is WebGain's Rapid Application Assembly product. It is a graphical IDE that allows developers to create executable capsules — its name for executable components, such as J2EE servlets and EJBs. Instead of doing any Java coding by hand, a developer using Application Composer points-and-clicks, wiring together already-programmed Web pages, Java objects, EJBs, and other components. The Application Composer then stores an XML description of one of these assemblies of objects into a capsule definition file. The IDE even allows you to execute and debug one of these capsules, then launch a browser to connect to its user interface and test it out. Application Composer can create a number of different types of capsules, including Java objects, EJBs, J2EE servlets, and, soon, WSDL-based web services.

WebGain realizes that real B2B solutions require the ability to execute business transactions over the Internet. Often, these transactions are complex and consist of multiple steps. WebGain's new product — Business Designer — makes it simple for business developers to design business processes graphically that are then translated into an assembly of executable components. Business Designer is intended to provide both a repository of business requirements and a mapping down to the implementation of those requirements as an executable business process.

15.3.3 NeuVis's NeuArchitect

Initially, the NeuArchitect product from NeuVis appears to be very similar to Web-Gain's Application Composer. But upon closer inspection, one realizes that NeuArchitect provides a richer infrastructure than does Application Composer. Application Composer is basically a code-generation technology, whereas NeuArchitect is that and a great deal more.

NeuArchitect provides three components that developers use to construct and deploy complex e-business solutions very quickly. The NeuVis Modeling System is a UML-compliant graphical environment that allows developers to draw business processes that will be executable across the Internet. Business process models designed using the NeuVis Modeling System are stored as XML descriptors. They can then be instantiated into actual code by the second component of NeuArchitect, the NeuVis Construction System.

The NeuVis Construction System can be thought of as a code-generation environment. Developers use the NeuVis Modeling System to graphically lay out entire applications — from the user interface to the middle tier, and back to the database. But the user of the Modeling System works only with abstract concepts, such as a table, without working with the implementation details of any specific product. When developers then instantiate a runnable example of the application he or she has constructed visually, he or she uses the NeuVis Construction System. This component asks the user to enter any product-specific runtime and deployment information, then generates software that can be deployed and executed within a specific product. The Construction System supports all of today's application server standards, such as Sun's J2EE and SQL.

Once an application has been generated by the NeuVis Construction System, it is deployed to the NeuVis RunTime System. This component consists of the following subcomponents: NeuArchitect Logic Server, NeuArchitect Messaging Server, NeuArchitect Integration Server, and NeuArchitect Session Server. Together these subcomponents of the NeuVis RunTime System work as an EAI infrastructure, allowing you to develop complex applications that span the enterprise.

Although NeuVis's initial focus has been to create a product line that allows developers to create browser-based e-business applications quickly, it has recently extended its offering so that it can be used to generate WSDL-based web services easily.

15.4 Summary

As can be seen from the discussion in this chapter, several vendors have offerings in the web services space. Some of these offerings are the outgrowth of existing product lines. In some cases, especially for leaders such as Microsoft and IBM, completely different architectures and software components have been developed.

There are several new standards that are emerging around web services and so it is difficult for vendors to choose a particular standard to abide by. In the long run, there is likely to be a convergence among various standards and technologies. This will give rise to a more cohesive web services foundational platform and strategy for the industry as a whole. However, there is still plenty of opportunity for differentiating on top of this platform, especially in areas such as service management, monitoring, and private registries. HP, a web services platform vendor itself, is also experiencing this maturing of the industry. It has developed a two-pronged strategy: It is an active member of the major web services standards initiatives, and it is developing its own differentiating software offering.

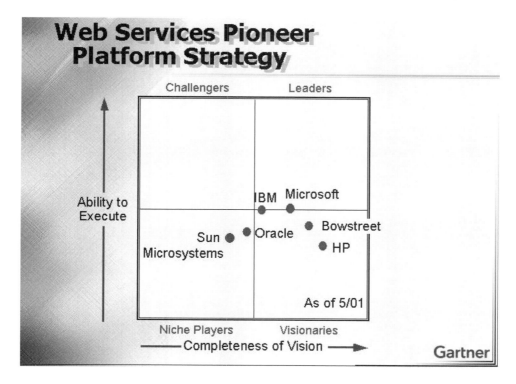

Figure 15.1. Gartner Magic Quadrant. The Magic Quadrant is copyrighted June 2001 by Gartner, Inc. and is reused with permission. Gartner's permission to print its Magic Quadrant should not be deemed to be an endorsement of any company or product depicted in the quadrant. The Magic Quadrant is Gartner's opinion and is an analytical representation of a marketplace at and for a specific time period. It measures vendors against Gartner-defined criteria for a marketplace. The positioning of vendors within a Magic Quadrant is based on the complex interplay of many factors. Well-informed vendor selection decisions should rely on more than a Magic Quadrant. Gartner research is intended to be one of many information sources and the reader should not rely solely on the Magic Quadrant for decision-making. Gartner expressly disclaims all warranties, express or implied of fitness of this research for a particular purpose.

Future of E-services and Web Services at HP

Chapter 16

FUTURE OF E-SERVICES AND WEB SERVICES AT HP

Hewlett Packard (HP) is a pioneer in Internet- and intranet-based services. HP began work on e-Speak, one of the first products focused on e-services and web services, in HP labs in the spring of 1995. The visionary approach to *Chapter Two of the Internet* forced HP to answer some of the interesting questions of a service-based economy on its own. HP subsequently released a few versions of e-Speak, culminating in the supported version: e-Speak A.3.11.

The e-Speak platform has functionality that enables discovery and interaction between partners. These are the same capabilities that the industry is now focused on, through efforts such as Simple Object Access Protocol (SOAP), Universal Description, Discovery, and Integration (UDDI), and Web Services Description Language (WSDL). With the convergence of industry support around these emerging standards, HP is working to integrate these standards into its own e-Speak web services platform, thereby bridging the gap between e-services and web services described in Chapter 13. HP is also a major and active contributor to these and other emerging standards in the area of web services and sharing the knowledge learned as part of the early e-Speak releases. By playing this active role, HP hopes to shape the future of service computing.

In this chapter, we discuss the direction of the current e-Speak A.3.11 platform. This discussion is forward-looking and hence, there might be a slight disconnection between the discussion and the evolutionary product web services offering that is available in late fall of 2001.

16.1   E-Speak Technology

Although the e-Speak technology provided the interaction engine in a service economy, it is morphing greatly from a large, contained instance to a set of components that together serve as the runtime environment for e-services and web services. E-Speak was an early market-defining product for web services. Since its introduction, a number of standards have emerged, standards that deal with such things as:

- The underlying communication protocols (SOAP)

- The service interaction languages (WSDL, Web Services Flow Language [WSFL])

- The registry that stores these standards-based web services (UDDI)

Additionally, there is an emerging development platform with Java 2 Enterprise Edition (J2EE). HP is transitioning to this new standards-based environment as part of the natural evolution of e-Speak.

This means that much of the functionality of the e-Speak engine will be morphed into the J2EE-based application server with web services components. Again, one of the main reasons HP is moving in this direction is to gain the benefits of a large developer community (J2EE) and to have a common platform where all the pieces plug and play together with other vendor offerings.

16.1.1   Internet Operating Environment

The web services offering, along with the HP Bluestone Application Server (HPAS) make up the *Internet Operating Environment* (IOE). The IOE is a new platform for software developers and systems integrators or independent software vendors that are no longer writing applications for an Operating System (OS) but for software *platforms*, such as Java or Microsoft, and, more specifically, to the Internet-enabled platforms. For example, writing an e-Speak service provided *logical machine abstractions* that obviated the need to concentrate at the OS level. New software applications based on the IOE will be web services-enabled, standards-based, and will interoperate with other similar web service platforms.

Removing the OS from the software development picture by relying on standards such as J2EE allows HP to get closer to the elusive goal of a *write-once-run-anywhere* environment. Applications or web services should be able to run on Windows, Linux, and HP-UX. "OS-agnostic" web services support the interoperability goal of the web services movement.

Note

Support of standards, the J2EE environment, and interoperability with web services platforms of other vendors are the defining characteristics of the newer versions of e-Speak, with a stack of value-added components and integration with other HP software, such as OpenView and Process Manager.

16.1.2   Adopting Web Services

E-Speak brought to the industry the concept of e-services. Because the industry seems to be converging on a common understanding and more important acceptance of the *web services* term, HP has also welcomed this term into its software offerings. Its new standards-based platform will be entitled *HP Web Services*. A strategic move by HP, this adoption of the term demonstrates a strong support of standards, interoperability between different vendors and technologies (discussed in Chapters 14 and 15), and a willingness to work with other web service offering vendors to expand the larger web service industry.

16.1.3   Web Services Platform

The HP Web services platform is being designed to be a high-performance web services infrastructure platform that enables companies to create and deploy J2EE- *and* .NET-compliant web services. The platform will evolve to provide the necessary plug-and-play features to enable interoperability, collaboration, and transaction across a host of business processes in the business-to-business (B2B) arena. With that focus, the new platform is expected to provide support ranging from full RosettaNet Implementation Framework (RNIF) compliance to Biztalk and ebXML business process exchanges.

Moving the web services platform into an interoperable state removes the proprietary nature of the e-Speak A.3.11 technology; the proprietary nature meant that companies could not rely on *all* of their partners to implement the same solution.

The HP Web services platform is expected to include:

- Tools for creation/deployment of web services

- A Graphical User Interface tool for browsing web services registered in global business registries

- Tools for mapping existing backend business logic to those of partners

- Quality of service monitoring to guarantee service delivery

- Process Manager integration for management of the internal workflows

- B2B infrastructure components (private workflows)

Support for service interaction protocols such as conversations and workflow are likely to emerge in the next phase (WSCL, WSFL). It will also include a prefabricated pipeline to configure desired business process flows graphically should greater control and flexibility than the standard out-of-the-box flow be desired.

16.2   Registry

In Chapter 11, we discussed HP's registry offering, E-services Village (ESV). ESV is being migrated (as is the rest of the technology) to a standards-based directory. In Chapter 14, UDDI was introduced as a new registry platform to facilitate web service registration and discovery. HP announced in mid-2001 that it would be one of four UDDI Public registry operators.

16.2.1   UDDI

The UDDI initiative announced by Ariba, IBM, and Microsoft defines specifications for and operation of a registry for web services. Loosely coupled web services promise to provide easy development and integration of extended and virtual enterprises. The web services directory promises to provide the environment to deploy these services via central registration, discovery, and integration. All UDDI registry entries are classified by either:

- White pages: general registry company data
- Yellow pages: describing and locating businesses
- Green pages: enabling organizations to describe any web service and how to interact with it

16.2.2   Private Registry Option

HP also has plans to release a UDDI-compliant Private registry for companies and organizations that want greater control over their registry environment — perhaps to facilitate a *private ecosystem*, as described in Chapter 4. This is likely to be a solution also for the service deployers that wish to expose their services publicly but need to deploy them within a controlled set of service users. For instance, an ecosystem governing body or deployer will develop services it considers core competencies and will partner with service providers for additional services to complete a solution. This ecosystem host will then need to aggregate, to control the access of, and to manage the usage of web services in its particular environment. Most ecosystem hosts will want to keep their developed services private and will, thus, need registries deployed behind their firewalls. They will also want the flexibility of implementing various security models, deploying infrastructure services that ease and/or differentiate their services offerings, and instituting business models specific to their industry/business. Finally, the solution for these inherent requirements would need to interoperate seamlessly with other registries, both public and private. It is likely to provide interoperability between its Public node and privately deployed registries based on the HP Private registry offering.

HP is again in a strong position with respect to registry offerings. HP has customers already using private registries and, thus, has unique insight into customer experience and requirements. HP is considered a pioneer in web services and private registry development via its proof-of-concept implementation, ESV. The registry offerings are based on HP's experience in deploying and hosting both private and public registries, thus meeting high quality of service requirements, as well as providing cutting-edge functionality.

16.3   Focus on Standards

Standards are critical to the rapid adoption of web services. Standards reduce the overall cost of the solution and ensure greater levels of interoperability, especially in the B2B arena. Standards remove the obstacle of determining *how* business partners can talk to each other. For example, in the case study presented in Chapter 4, e-Speak was required in all entities of the AmCAR Procurement ecosystem. However, there might be reasons why this is not cost-effective for smaller vendors. A standards-based approach that allows interoperability with *existing* technologies based on web servers and Hypertext Transfer Protocol (HTTP) can ensure that web services reach even the smallest business entity having nothing more than a web server on a computer in the back room. The goal of this standards approach is to ensure that the benefit of creating each additional connection point radically exceeds the cost of creating that additional connection.

Currently, W3C (World Wide Web Consortium) is playing an active role in creating web services business protocol standards, a major shift from its conventional engagement in technical protocols such as HTTP. The current market trend seems to be around creating standards and protocols for service description, registration, and discovery, and focusing on converting J2EE/Java components and .NET components as web services via global business registries. The e-Speak initiative within HP is likely to follow that trend for the foreseeable future.

The web services initiatives's solid emphasis on standards-based technologies has been a debatable issue. Although on one hand, adherence to standards is imperative for wide acceptance of a product, a pure standards-based product is not likely to succeed in the market because it will not have any differentiating characteristics. For the same reason, other companies in the web services industry, such as IBM and Microsoft, are also trying to achieve their differentiated stack.

HP is involved (at various levels) in the following standards:

- Java APIs for XML Processing
- Java APIs for XML Binding
- Java APIs for XML Messaging
- Java APIs for XML-based RPC
- Java APIs for XML Registries

At the same time, HP is building differentiation into its web service and registry product offering.

16.4   Summary

From the outset, HP recognized that the e-service or web service phenomenon was a disruption in computing. Given the lack of established foundations for such an interaction environment, the e-Speak technology was a strong and comprehensive software offering to support the dynamic discovery and invocation that characterized this chasm. As e-Speak evolves into HP's Web services platform, there are likely to be more shifts and adjustments in the industry that will require HP and other vendors of web services to be flexible and quick to adapt. E-Speak is a key element of HP's software strategy — the NetAction suite.   This next generation of e-Speak will leverage HP's investment in the HPAS and will adopt key industry standards such as SOAP, UDDI, and XML digital signatures. HP's visionary role in this space will allow it to offer a unique technology stack for web services and e-services. For the latest information on HP's plans for e-Speak, e-services, and web services, please continue to visit the following web presences:

- `http://www.hp.com/go/webservices`
- `http://www.e-speak.hp.com`
- `http://www.uddi.hp.com`
- `http://www.insidewebservices.com`

Appendixes

PART
Five

IN THIS PART

Appendix A

INSTALLING AND CONFIGURING E-SPEAK

The e-Speak installation package is available for three different platforms:

- Windows NT and Windows 2000
- HP-UX
- Linux

The examples in this book are based on Windows 2000. The e-Speak package for installation is based on InstallShield.

When you run the InstallShield setup program, you are prompted for the directory path of your Java Developers Kit (JDK). Locate your JDK (JDK version 1.2.2 or higher) now and have that information ready. The recommended configuration for the Windows-based e-Speak installation program is:

- 256 MB RAM
- Windows NT 4.0/SP 4 or later
- JDK 1.2.2.

The installation program uses 128 MB during the installation process.

A.1   Installing e-Speak

Insert the CD-ROM in the CD drive. Locate the proper directory to install from. In the case of Windows-based systems, the e-Speak install package is located in the directory $<Drive\ Name>\backslash winnt$. The file $espeak\_A$-03-11-$00.exe$ is the e-Speak install program for Windows. This program is also included in the CD associated with this book. Click on the program to start installation. This will start the e-Speak installation wizard, as shown in Figure A.1.

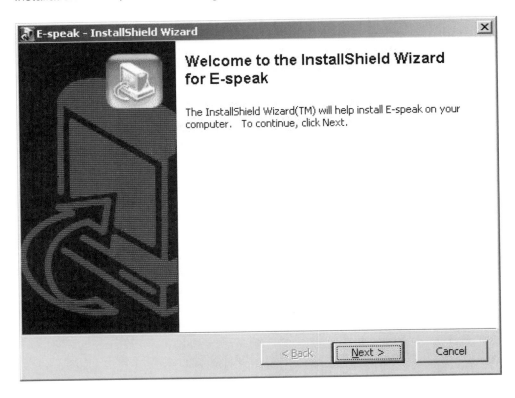

Figure A.1. E-Speak installation wizard.

Click on the Next button to start the install process. This will copy necessary files to the target drive in preparation for installation. Follow the prompts to provide user name and company and related information. When prompted for the Java Runtime Environment (JRE) path, verify and provide where the Java installation is located.

E-Speak requires JDK 1.2.2. The default path for JRE is `C:\jdk1.2.2`. Providing the correct JRE path is vital for successful installation.

The e-Speak installation directory is recommended to be different from the default for running the programs from this book. The default installation directory is *C:\Program Files\e-speak*. The space character in the path can make it difficult to integrate e-Speak with Tomcat and other Web-related tools. We recommend the installation directory to be *C:\e-speak*. Click on the `Browse` button to change the installation directory, as shown in Figure A.2.

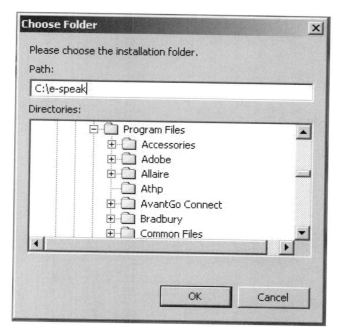

Figure A.2. Changing the e-Speak installation directory.

Verify all the parameters for installation before starting it. The screen just before the installation summarizes the user choices. Figure A.3 shows this screen. If any choices are incorrect, go back and fix them.

Once all files are copied, the installation program will create a default security environment for the installation. This installs the necessary Public Key Infrastructure (PKI) certificates for different security roles. Successful installation of the security

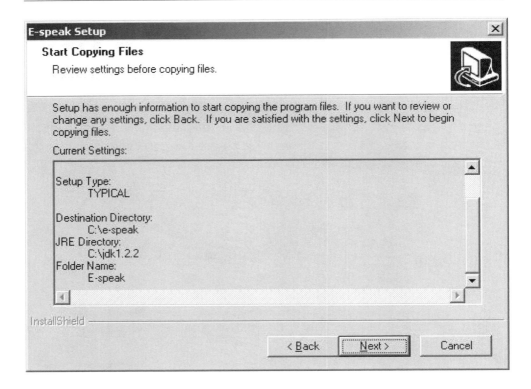

Figure A.3. Verifying the e-Speak installation parameters.

environment is essential for proper functioning of the e-Speak engine. The JRE path specified earlier is used during this stage. The program that creates the security environment is started in a separate command window. This window is closed after the program completes. Note that this step takes several minutes to complete. The installation wizard shows the progress as it goes through the steps to create and configure the default security environment. The command window also provides more details.

This completes the e-Speak installation. After the installation is complete, read the file *readme.txt* that has information specific to the current version, as well as minimum platform requirements. You will need to restart the computer after the installation for the configuration to take effect. After the restart, to verify that the installation is successful, start the PSE Manager program from the Start menu, located at Start → Programs → e-Speak → e-Speak PSE Manager. If this program starts properly, e-Speak is properly installed.

A.2   Uninstalling e-Speak

To uninstall e-Speak:

1. Select Start → Programs → e-Speak.

2. From this menu, select Uninstall e-Speak to uninstall the e-Speak application.

3. Restart the machine.

4. Once the machine has restarted, verify that the e-Speak reference has been removed from Programs in the Start menu.

5. Verify that the $\backslash Program\ Files \backslash e\text{-}speak$ folder is empty.

6. Verify that e-Speak cannot be started.

7. Verify that EspeakProcessManager is no longer in the Services dialog.

8. Verify that none of the processes exist in the Task Manager (you may have Java programs other than e-Speak running):
   java.exe
   espeak.exe
   ESPM.exe

Appendix B

SETTING UP DSN

A database in any system can be accessed using the driver provided for it by the vendor. This typically constitutes a vendor-specific solution to data access. Open Database Connectivity (ODBC) is a data access standard that aims at standardizing the data access mechanisms so that a programmer can write the applications without knowing the nuances of how the driver and the database from a vendor behaves. ODBC provides standard Application Programming Interfaces (APIs) and response guidelines for a database. An ODBC Data Source Name (DSN) contains metadata about a particular database. It contains information specific to the connection and location of the database, as well as the driver that manages the database. Java provides a package, Java Database Connectivity (JDBC), based on the ODBC standard. JDBC provides Java APIs based on ODBC. It uses a mechanism called *JDBC-ODBC* bridge.

The Windows operating system (OS) provides a wizard to create a DSN entry based on the ODBC standard. We have used this wizard to create DSN names for the databases used in the example. Follow the steps below to create a user DSN.

B.1   Datasources

Go to Start → Settings → Control Panel and click on Data Sources (ODBC), as shown in Figure B.1. Under the User DSN tab, select the Add option to add a new DSN.

Now select the database driver for which you want to set up a data source. For ex-

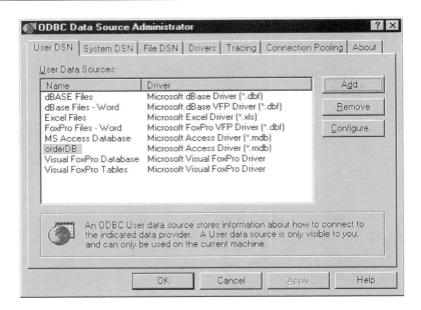

Figure B.1. ODBC Start panel.

ample, you will select Driver for Microsoft Access ($*.mdb$) for the Access database. Click on Finish to complete the task (Figure B.2).

Now you will be prompted for information related to your database. Enter a DSN of your choice (to which you can refer in your programs to connect to the database). This is depicted in Figure B.3.

Click on Select to select the database file located on your system (and $*.mdb$ file, in this case). Locate your database file and click OK. Your DSN is ready for use. This DSN entry can be used for any application that supports ODBC.[1]

---

[1]DSN entries for different databases from vendors such as Oracle or Sybase can be created in a similar fashion, using their corresponding drivers.

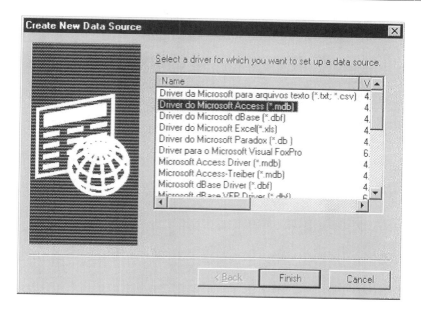

Figure B.2. Choosing the ODBC driver.

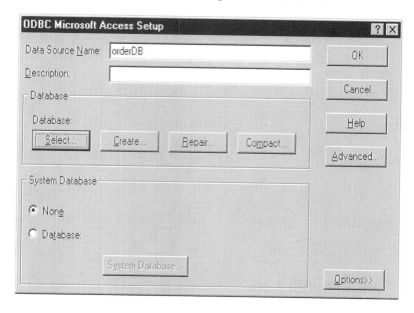

Figure B.3. Attributing a DSN to a database.

Appendix C

DATABASES AND DATABASE WRAPPER UTILITY

This book uses several examples that use a database in the business logic. This database access is provided through the Java Database-Open Database Connectivity (JDBC-ODBC) bridge. The Data Source Name (DSN) entries required for this are explained in Appendix B. The database access logic required in all these examples is similar and is packaged separately in the `DatabaseWrapper` class. This class is in the *Shared* directory.

The constructor for this class requires three parameters — the DSN name, as registered with the operating system, user name, and password. Both the user name and the password for all the databases in the book are set to `null`.

DatabaseWrapper.java

```java
public DatabaseWrapper(String database, String usrName,
                                        String password)
{
    dbName = database;
    dbUserName = usrName;
    dbPassword = password;
}
```

The method `connectToDb()` has the logic to connect to the database. The method `executeQuery()` is a general-purpose method that interacts with the database to perform a database operation. The database operation to be performed must be specified to this method, using a Structured Query Language (SQL) statement. The result of the SQL execution is returned as a `ResultSet` object. The `ResultSet` object contains a table that contains the query results. The individual table rows can be retrieved using the `next()` method from the `ResultSet` class.

Several examples in the book use a database in the business logic. The database schemas for these databases are given below for easy reference.

C.1   Order Database

The order database used in Chapter 4 consists of two tables. The table `users` contains the user information, and the table `orders` contains the orders associated with the customers in the `users` table. The schema for `users` is shown in Table C.1, followed by a sample entry in Table C.2.

Table C.1. Schema for Table `users`

Field Name	Type	Description
`custId`	Text	Primary key
`userName`	Text	User name
`password`	Text	Password
`outputFormat`	Text	Desired output format. T — Text, X — XML
`custName`	Text	Customer name as it would appear in the order status report

Table C.2. Sample Entry for Table `users`

`custID`	`userName`	`password`	`outputFormat`	`custName`
1	scott	scottymn	T	Scott Baumann

The `orders` table schema is as shown in Table C.3. Note that the field `custId` in this table is a foreign key that relates each entry in the table `orders` to an entry in the table `users`. The sample entry for the `orders` table is shown in Table C.4.

Table C.3. Schema for Table `orders`

Field Name	Type	Description
ordNumber	Text	Primary key
custId	Text	Foreign key
ordState	Text	Order state
ordDate	Date-Time	Order date
ordTotal	Number	Order total

Table C.4. Sample Entry for Table `orders`

ordNumber	custID	ordState	ordDate	ordTotal
26FI-34590	2	processing	9/9/2000	100

C.2   Hotel Pricing Database

All the hotels use the same database structure, though in real life, that is not likely to be the case. Each hotel pricing database consists of two tables: `RoomMaster` and `DiscountMaster`. Table C.5 shows the schema for the table `RoomMaster`, and Table C.6 shows a sample entry.

The schema for the table `DiscountMaster` is in Table C.7.

Table C.8 contains a sample entry for the `DiscountMaster` table.

C.3   Airline Pricing Database

The airline pricing database is similar to the hotel database. The pricing logic is used in either case; however, the fields are somewhat different. For the airline database, the table `PriceMaster` has the necessary prices for a certain class,

Table C.5. Schema for Table `RoomMaster`

Field Name	Type	Description
ID	AutoNumber	Record key
RoomType	Text	Type of room. Three possible values. SB — Single Bed, DB — Double Bed, SU — Suite
BasePrice	Number	The minimum price hotel must charge
MaxMarkup	Number	Maximum markup over the base price
EffStartMonth	Number	Month when the rate takes effect
EffEndMonth	Number	Month after which rate is not valid

Table C.6. Sample Entry for Table `RoomMaster`

ID	RoomType	BasePrice	MaxMarkup	EffStartMonth	EffEndMonth
1	SB	60	30	1	7

origin, and destination, and the effective dates for each entry. The schema for this table is in Table C.9.

Table C.10 contains a sample entry for the `PriceMaster` table.

Table C.7. Schema for Table `DiscountMaster`

Field Name	Type	Description
ID	AutoNumber	Record key
DiscountCode	Text	Unique discount code
DiscountPercent	Number	The percentage discount applicable for the `DiscountCode`

Table C.8. Sample Entry for Table `DiscountMaster`

ID	DiscountCode	DiscountPercent
2	10	10

Table C.9. Schema for Table `PriceMaster`

Field Name	Type	Description
ID	AutoNumber	Record key
Class	Text	Ticket class
EffStartMonth	Number	Month when the rate takes effect
EffEndMonth	Number	Month after which rate is not valid
Origin	Text	Travel origin
Destination	Text	Travel destination
Price	Number	Price for a given month range

Table C.10. Sample Entry for Table `PriceMaster`

ID	Class	EffStartMonth	EffEndMonth	Origin	Destination	Price
1	F	1	6	SFO	LAX	495.99

Appendix D

PROPERTY METHODS FOR VOCABULARY ATTRIBUTES

The JESI library provides several methods to add vocabulary attributes — one per data type supported. The complete list of methods is as follows.

D.1   Adding Numeric Attributes

void addBigDecimalProperty(java.lang.String propName) — Adds a property of type BigDecimal with the specified name to the ESVocabulary.

void addDoubleProperty(java.lang.String propName) — Adds a property of type Double with the specified name to the ESVocabulary.

void addFloatProperty(java.lang.String propName) — Adds a property of type Float with the specified name to the ESVocabulary.

void addIntegerProperty(java.lang.String propName) — Adds a property of type Integer with the specified name to the ESVocabulary.

void addLongProperty(java.lang.String propName) — Adds a property of type Long with the specified name to the ESVocabulary.

void addShortProperty(java.lang.String propName) — Adds a property of type Short with the specified name to the ESVocabulary.

D.2   Adding Nonnumeric Attributes

`void addBooleanProperty(java.lang.String propName)` — Adds a property of type `Boolean` with the specified name to the `ESVocabulary`.

`void addByteArrayProperty(java.lang.String propName)` — Adds a property of type `ByteArray` with the specified name to the `ESVocabulary`.

`void addByteProperty(java.lang.String propName)` — Adds a property of type `Byte` with the specified name to the `ESVocabulary` .

`void addCharProperty(java.lang.String propName)` — Adds a property of type `Char` with the specified name to the `ESVocabulary`.

`void addDateProperty(java.lang.String propName)` — Adds a property of type `java.sql.Date` with the specified name to the `ESVocabulary`.

`void addProperty(ESProperty prop)` — Adds a property passed to the method as an argument to the vocabulary's properties.

`void addStringProperty(java.lang.String propName)` — Adds a property of type `String` with the specified name to the `ESVocabulary`.

`void addTimeProperty(java.lang.String propName)` — Adds a property of type `java.sql.Time` with the specified name to the `ESVocabulary`.

`void addTimeStampProperty(java.lang.String propName)` — Adds a property of type `java.sql.TimeStamp` with the specified name to the `ESVocabulary`.

Appendix E

ESCONNECTION **CONFIG FILE ENTRIES**

The ESConnection class object is used to denote the connection parameters that a client uses when connecting to the e-Speak engine. A property file is used to specify these parameters. The defaults for various parameters are listed in Table E.1.

Table E.1. Connection Properties and Defaults

Property	Description	Default Value
accountname	Account name	guestconnection
username	User name	guest
password	Password	null
protocol	Connection protocol	esip
hostname	Host where engine is running	localhost
portnumber	Port the engine is running on	2950
connectiontimeout	Connection timeout value (sec)	100
community	Community the client is interested in	null
eventcontrol	Event parameter	0
coreurl	URL of the engine	esip:localhost:2950

E.1   Using ESConnection **Properties**

The connection parameters in the file appear in the format

```
ParameterName = ParameterValue
```

with one parameter per line. The character # at the beginning of a line can be used to insert a comment. The comment must appear on a line of its own.

If any of them is not specified, a default value is assumed for that parameter.

Appendix F

E-SPEAK EXCEPTION HIERARCHY

E-Speak defines two classes of exceptions to inform clients when an error occurs in the system:

- Runtime exceptions
- Recoverable exceptions

F.1   Runtime Exceptions

Runtime exceptions are thrown when a programming error occurs. These exceptions end the currently running program.

F.1.1   `ESRuntimeException`

The `ESRuntimeException` classes include:

`CorePanicException`
The engine cannot process the request. Although the engine attempts to notify all clients of its inability to continue operating, it also replies with this exception for as long as possible. The engine can continue to accept new messages if the problem is limited to a single message.

`ServicePanicException`

A service cannot process the request. This exception can cause the service to exit, or it can simply mean that a *specific* request caused an unrecoverable internal error; in this case, the service will *continue* to accept new requests.

`RepositoryFullException`

The request attempted to add additional information to the engine's repository when the repository was full. The client can recover from this exception if it can delete one or more resources from the repository. This is a runtime exception because the client has no guaranteed means of recovery. Even if the client can free repository space, some other application may use the space instead.

`OutofOrderRequestException`

The system state is inconsistent with the request.

`ConnectionFailedException`

A resource attempting to connect to the engine failed to establish a connection via the connection manager.

`InvalidParameterException`

Any other programming errors occur. This exception has three subclasses:

- `NullParameterException` is thrown when a null parameter was supplied but not allowed. This error is often caused by passing an uninitialized object.
- `InvalidValueException` is thrown when a parameter is outside the allowable range.
- `InvalidTypeException` is thrown when the specified name is bound to the wrong type.

F.2 Recoverable Exceptions

Recoverable exceptions occur due to a problem with the system state. For example, when a client sends a message to request access to a resource, the message may be undeliverable because the handlers Inbox is full. Recovering from this exception can be as simple as resending the message. The base exception is `ESException`. This exception includes three major subclasses:

- ESLibException

- ESInvocationException

- ESServiceException

F.2.1   ESLibException

This is the base class for client library exceptions. The `CoreNotFoundException` class is a subclass of this class that indicates that an engine could not be found to connect to. To correct this exception, either change the specification of the engine or ensure that the engine is running.

F.2.2   ESInvocationException

This is the base class for all of the exceptions that the engine or a resource handler can throw back to a client during request processing. Exceptions thrown by most handlers are included here to reduce the number of explicit classes of exceptions. This exception has multiple subclasses.

`NamingException`
Regardless of the cause, this exception or any of its subclasses is thrown only for the primary resource name given in the message header.

`NameNotFoundException`
The name resolution process failed to find a given name. The client can recover by changing the `ESName`.

`EmptyMappingException`
A mapping object is associated with the name but has no usable accessors. This condition occurs when the accessor has no elements, the elements refer to unregistered resources, or the resources did not pass the visibility tests. The client can recover by changing the `ESName`.

`UnresolvedBindingException`
All the accessors of the mapping object are search requests. The client can recover by requesting a lookup, using one of the search requests.

`MultipleResolvedBindingException`

The mapping object has more than one explicit binding.

`StaleEntryException`

This exception occurs when the resource no longer exists. The engine removes any unused handles from the mapping object before returning the exception. A retry does not result in this exception unless another referenced resource has been unregistered.

`PermissionDeniedException`

This exception occurs when the client is not authorized to access the resource. The client can recover by retrying with a different set of certificates. One subclass, `SessionRequiredException`, is thrown when a client attempts to send a message to a service with security enabled without first setting up a session. A secure session is necessary for access control checks. This exception is normally handled by the client library and is transparent to the application programmer. The client recovers from this exception by exchanging Session Layer Security (SLS) messages with the service to establish a session.

`QuotaExhaustedException`

This exception occurs when the client attempts to define more resources than the quota assigned to it. The client can delete other resources and re-attempt the request.

`MethodNotImplementedException`

This exception occurs when the client attempts to invoke a method that is not implemented. This is typically used to "stub-out" routines when a service is under development.

`RecoverableCoreException`

This exception occurs when there is a problem while processing the request. The exception includes two subclasses.

`RequestNotDeliveredException`

The engine never started processing the message. This exception can be thrown by the client library if it implements timeouts or by the engine if the corresponding queue is full. It may be possible to recover from this exception by resending the message.

`PartialStateUpdateException`

The engine cannot finish processing the message. You may need to discover what state was changed before attempting recovery (for example, by examining the state of the metadata).

`TimedOutException`

This exception occurs when a message being written to or received from a channel has not successfully completed within the caller-defined time period.

`UndeliverableRequestException`

This exception occurs when the message cannot be delivered to the resource handler. When security is enabled, this exception does not occur in the current implementation. The security subsystem ignores these messages, and the client must wait for a `TimeOutException`. This exception contains two subclasses.

`RecoverableDeliveryException`

Temporary conditions cause a message to fail to be delivered, such as a full mailbox. The client can recover by resending the message.

`UnrecoverableDeliveryException`

A message cannot be delivered due to a more complex condition. The client can recover by selecting a binding that points to a different resource handler.

F.2.3   `ESServiceException`

`ESServiceException` is the base class for all service-defined exceptions.

`ESNameFrameException`

This is the main class of all name frame exceptions. The arrangement allows the client to catch this exception and handle all the name-frame-related exceptions in one catch block.

`NameCollisionException`

The name specified in an add, copy, or similar operation is already defined in the name frame.

`LookupFailedException`

No resources are found that match a search recipe.

`InvalidNameException`
A string designating a name is not found in the name frame.

`ESRemoteException`
This exception occurs if the Remote Resource Manager operation failed for any reason.

F.3 User-Defined Exceptions

User-defined exceptions are supported. If a user-defined exception (nonruntime) is desired, developers must extend `ESServiceException`. This is similar to extending exceptions in Java.

GLOSSARY

A

Accessor. See *Service Accessor*.

Active Directory. Microsoft's trademarked directory service, an integral part of the Windows 2000 architecture. Active Directory is a centralized and standardized system that automates network management of user data, security, and distributed resources, and enables interoperation with other directories.

Advertising Service. A service for looking up resources not registered in the local repository. It returns zero or more connection objects.

ALE. Application Link Enabling. A concept available in R/3 (Release 3.0+) and supports the development of applications across different SAP systems. It incorporates the exchange of business information across these systems while ensuring consistency and integrity of the data. This functionality is achieved with the use of IDocs (information documents), as opposed to the use of a centralized database. It is also used as SAP's interfacing middleware technology. Tools are provided to bundle business data into IDocs, which are then sent to or received from external, non-SAP systems.

Arbitration Policy. A specification within the search request accessor for naming that provides the logic to resolve multiple matches found for a name search.

ASP. Active Server Page. Microsoft's technology for scripted Web pages that can display dynamic content requested by a Web browser.

Asynchronous Interactions. Not synchronized; that is, not occurring at predetermined or regular intervals. The term *asynchronous interactions* refers to interactions between the service and the client in which data can be transmitted intermittently, rather than in a steady stream. See also *Synchronous Interaction*.

Attribute Framework. See *Vocabulary*.

Attributes. A key-value pair that is used to describe the characteristics of a service.

Authentication. A mechanism by which two or more communicating parties in a conversation can ascertain that the other entities involved are truly the same as their identities suggest.

Authorization. Provides an increased level of security by controlling access to privileged information.

Authorization Tags. Used to grant access to a resource. See also *Tag*.

AuthXML. A specification for authentication and authorization information in XML.

B

B2B. Business-to-Business. An electronic, shared infrastructure that provides businesses a platform to interact in real time with buyers, partners, distribution channels, and suppliers. Also can be called a *business-to-business exchange*.

Base Vocabulary. A vocabulary provided with the engine at runtime.

BizTalk. An open framework for B2B (or business-to-business exchange), which is being implemented across all major platforms and most major B2B products from other companies. In addition to being a leading B2B platform, BizTalk is also a new and impressive improvement over previous programming models and presents cost savings when used in internal IT projects.

BPSS. Business Process Specification Schema. The ebXML BPSS provides a standard framework for business process specification.

Builder. An entity identified by a remote resource handler that is used to construct the internal state of a resource imported by value.

Business Logic. Functionality provided by the service — usually focused on a specific task such as a pricing service or a sales tax service. This is the logic that is exposed by the service deployment.

C

C-Hubs. A dynamic marketplace that can be used for trading partners to find one another, to retrieve metadata describing the public interfaces of web services, and to carry on audited and secure business transactions.

C-Spaces. A virtual place where predefined trading partners can conduct and coordinate conversations with each other.

Cancellation and Termination Procedures. The process of revoking access to systems and networks when a party no longer meets the access criteria.

Certificate. A data structure assigning a tag or name to a subject. Certificates are signed using cryptographic techniques so that they cannot be tampered with.

Certificate Issuer. A trusted third party that validates and issues certificates to an entity. See also *Issuer*.

CGI. Common Gateway Interface. Early Web technology developed to launch server-side functionality based on user responses.

Choreography. A web service concept that addresses business process integration between business partners.

Client. Any active entity (e.g., a process, thread, service provider) that uses the e-Speak infrastructure to process a request for a resource.

Client Context. Contextual routing information for a particular client of the service that is valid across messages.

Client Library. The interface specification that defines the interface for e-Speak programmers and system developers that will build e-Speak-enabled applications.

Client-Side Proxy. When a Lookup Service answers the client's request, it provides the client with a client-side proxy for all available services that match the client's search criteria so that the client can make local method calls to that proxy to communicate with the remote service provider.

CLR. Common Language Runtime. Microsoft's new operating system infrastructure that allows software applications and components written in different languages to intercommunicate. It resembles Sun's JVM (Java Virtual Machine).

COM. Component Object Model. It enables programmers to develop objects that can be accessed by any COM-compliant application.

Composition. See *Service Composition*.

Connection Manager. A component of a logical machine that does the initial connection with another logical machine.

Connector Scenario. The connector scenario uses a set of e-Speak engines to provide virtual connections between the service and the client as it exposes services deployed behind a firewall to service users on the Internet or behind a firewall of another company.

Consortium. A group of entities that assemble together in support of a common cause or undertaking. For example, the WAP Forum is a 200-member consortium formed to guide WAP's future. In an ecosystem, consortiums or governing bodies usually define the framework in which ecosystem members will transact.

Contract. A resource denoting an agreement between the client and the resource handler for use of a particular resource. The agreement includes a provision for the client to use an Application Programming Interface (API) known to the resource handler when making the request for the resource. See Also *Resource Contract*.

Conversation. E-Speak's early work proposal for business process integration among (potential) business partners.

Co-opetition. Business environment in which different entities are competing and cooperating at the same time with each other.

CORBA. Common Object Request Broker Architecture. An architecture and specification for creating, distributing, and managing distributed program objects in a network. It allows programs at different locations and developed by different vendors to communicate in a network through an "interface broker."

CORBA Naming Service. A standard service for CORBA applications, defined in the Object Management Group's (OMG's) CORBA services specification that allows you to associate abstract names with CORBA objects and allows clients to find those objects by looking up the corresponding names.

CORBA Trader Service. A CORBA service that allows CORBA objects to advertise themselves with a set of associated properties. Conceptually, this is similar to an e-Speak advertising service.

Core. See *Service Engine*.

Core Event Distributor. A core-managed resource whose purpose is to collect information on e-Speak events and make such information available to management tools within the infrastructures.

Core-Managed Resource. A resource with an internal state managed by the core.

CPP. Collaboration Protocol Profile. Describes a service provider's role in offering its service, as well as the technical details for how to access that service. A CPP stored within the ebXML Registry provides a mechanism whereby clients looking for a specific class of CPPs can query for and find the CPPs that meet their requirements.

D

Database-Based Repository. See *Repository*.

DCOM. Distributed Component Object Model. An extension of COM to support objects distributed across a network.

Decryption. The process of decoding data that has been encrypted into a secret format. Decryption requires a secret key or password.

Delegation of Authority. The process of transferring certain responsibilities to request or perform a task.

DEM. Document Exchange Model. Interentity interaction mechanism that uses exchange of structured documents for communication.

Description. A formal approach to express capabilities of a service using an attribute set that is based on standard specifications.

Distributor Service. A service that forwards published events to subscribers.

DMZ. Demilitarized Zone. The public part of the Internet.

DOM. Document Object Model. A platform- and language-neutral interface that will allow programs and scripts to access and update the content, structure, and style of documents dynamically.

E

EAI. Enterprise Application Integration. A business computing term for the plans, methods, and tools aimed at modernizing, consolidating, and coordinating the computer applications in an enterprise.

ebXML. Electronic Business eXtended Markup Language. A project to use the eXtensible Markup Language (XML) to standardize the secure exchange of business data. Among other purposes, ebXML would encompass and perhaps replace a familiar standard called Electronic Data Interchange (EDI). ebXML is designed to enable a global electronic marketplace in which enterprises of any size, and in any location, could safely and securely transact business through the exchange of XML-based messages.

Ecosystem. A collection of related services. This collection, as a whole, provides a set of services in a specific domain.

Ecosystem Arbitrator. The mediator to resolve various issues/disputes (non-compliance with guidelines, unsatisfactory quality of service, breach of contract or fraud) between the ecosystem members.

Ecosystem Host. Host that facilitates the general functioning of an ecosystem and is responsible for providing the necessary infrastructure for an ecosystem to function.

Ecosystem Member Services. The ecosystem member entities are the very reason why an ecosystem exists. The ecosystem member services form the second tier of the ecosystem — the member class services. The entities in this category use the ecosystem infrastructure to function.

Ecosystem Monitor. An entity that monitors the interactions between ecosystem members and ensures that the members of the ecosystem are following the interactions guidelines set by the ecosystem host and the governing body.

EJB. Enterprise Java Beans. A Java-based specification for creating component-based transaction services. See also *MTS*.

Encryption. The translation of data into a secret code.

Engine. See *Service Engine*.

Engine Client. Any entity connected to the engine. An engine client could be *either* a service or a client.

ERP. Enterprise Resource Planning. An industry term that encompasses a wider set of activities (facilitated through ERP software and applications) that a business employs for its efficient functioning. These activities include product planning, purchasing, inventory management, and order processing.

E-services. A service that abides by a specific framework to offer its services. The framework provides the means to describe and discover the service, audit its service offering, and integrate the service with other services to offer higher level services.

ESIDL. E-Speak Interface Definition Language. Similar in concept to the Java-RMI IDL. See also *IDL*.

E-Speak. An open-source technology suite provided by Hewlett-Packard Company that enables dynamic business interactions.

E-Speak Community. A set of e-Speak groups that a client names in order to specify a metaset of groups that can be searched when a service is desired.

E-Speak Group. A set of service engines that are closely knit. Typically, these engines host services that are very close or similar to each other in terms of the functionality they provide.

E-Speak SDK. E-Speak Software Development Kit. A set of Java interfaces that provides a framework for developing and deploying XML-based services that conform to the Service Framework Specification.

ESSerialization. E-Speak's serialization mechanism, which is similar to Java serialization, except that it is faster and will work across different languages and platforms because it does not depend on the Java architecture. See also *Serialization*.

ESV. E-services Village is a developer's edition of a global online public registry for services, based on the e-Speak technology.

Event. A generated message (akin to a trigger) that results in the recipient invoking a registered callback.

Event Distributor. A core-managed resource whose purpose is to collect information on e-Speak events and make such information available to management tools within the infrastructures.

Event Filter. A subscription specification expressed as a set of attributes in a particular vocabulary that must match those in the event state in order for a client to receive notification on publication of an event.

Event Listeners. Engine-registered clients that are designated as receivers of an event message. An event distributor forwards any event to the event listener for processing that event.

Event Payload. Information associated with an event. Usually, payload is sent along with the event message.

Event State. A reference within an event to its expressed set of attributes in a particular vocabulary. These attributes must match the event filter in order for the subscriber to receive notification of the event.

Event Subscriber. An e-Speak registered client that expresses its interest in the happening of a certain event type.

Event Trigger. A component that initiates a sequence of actions.

Explicit Binding. An accessor that contains a repository handle.

F

Folder. An extended e-Speak service that lets the users manage services they discover or create.

FTP. File Transfer Protocol.

G

GIOP. General Inter Orb Protocol. A transport-independent communication protocol for ORB interoperability.

Governing Body. A service ecosystem entity that sets the policies in the ecosystem. These policies provide the framework for transactions in the ecosystem.

Guest Account. The default account assigned a client when connecting to an e-Speak engine. All resources registered through the guest account are treated as *transient* by the engine.

H

Higher Level Services. Higher level services are a composition of several lower level services. See also *Lower Level Services*.

HTTP. Hypertext Transfer Protocol. A protocol for exchanging files (text, graphic images, sound, video, and other multimedia files) on the World Wide Web.

HTTPS. Secure Hypertext Transfer Protocol. A protocol that encrypts and decrypts user page requests, as well as the pages that are returned by the Web server.

I

IDL. Interface Definition Language. A generic term for a language that allows a program or object written in one language to communicate with another program written in an unknown language. Examples of IDL are: ESIDL, Java-RMI IDL, and CORBA IDL. See also *ESIDL*.

IETF. Internet Engineering Task Force. The body that defines standard Internet operating protocol, such as TCP/IP.

IIOP. Internet Inter Orb Protocol. An object-oriented programming protocol that makes it possible for distributed programs written in different programming languages to communicate over the Internet.

Import Name Frame. A container that holds a name for each imported resource.

In-Band Communication. An interaction between two entities that happens through an e-Speak engine.

Inbox. A core-managed resource used to hold request messages from the engine to an engine client.

In-Memory Repository. A resource repository that is maintained in the memory. This is the default repository that is part of the standard e-Speak installation.

Intelligent Matchmaking. Discovery of a service — choosing, either deliberately or accidentally, a specific service from a class of services, using a specific description.

Introspection. At the language level, introspection is a mechanism used to query functional aspects of an object. Introspection provides information about methods and properties of an object. In the services world, introspection allows an entity to get more information about functional aspects of a service, such as vocabularies and contracts supported, quality of service, and specific interface methods.

IOR. Interoperable Object Reference. Applications in possession of a reference to an object that can invoke calls on that object. Access to CORBA objects by using IORs is achieved transparently to the application by means of the General Inter-ORB Protocol.

Issuer. An entity issuing a certificate. The issuer is denoted in a certificate by its public key. See also *Certificate Issuer*.

J

J2EE. Java 2 Platform Enterprise Edition. A platform-independent, Java-centric environment from Sun for developing, building, and deploying Web-based enterprise applications online.

J2ME. Java 2 Platform Micro Edition. A technology that allows programmers to use the Java programming language and related tools to develop programs for mobile wireless information devices, such as cellular phones and Personal Digital Assistants (PDAs).

J2SE. Java 2 Platform, Standard Edition. A solution for rapidly developing and deploying mission-critical enterprise applications.

JAXB. Java APIs for XML Binding. Provides an API and tools that automate the mapping between XML documents and Java objects.

JAXM. Java APIs for XML Messaging. Enables applications to send and receive document-oriented XML messages, using a pure Java API.

JAXP. Java APIs for XML Processing. Enables applications to parse and transform XML documents using a pure Java API that is independent of a particular XML processor implementation.

JAXR. Java APIs for XML Registries. Provides access to standard XML registries.

JAX-RPC. Java APIs for XML-based RPC. This API provides a transport-independent API for standard XML-based RPC protocols.

JCP. Java Community Process. An open organization of international Java developers and licensees whose charter is to develop and revise Java technology specifications, reference implementations, and technology compatibility kits.

JDBC. Java Database Connectivity. An API that lets you access virtually any tabular data source from the Java programming language.

JDBC-ODBC Bridge. Allows Java programs to use JDBC with many existing ODBC drivers.

JINI. A network technology that provides an infrastructure for delivering services in a network and for creating spontaneous interaction between programs that use these services, regardless of their hardware/software implementation.

Join and Discovery Protocols. Entities that wish to start participating in a distributed system of JINI technology-enabled services and/or devices, known as a DJINN, must first obtain references to one or more JINI lookup services. The protocols that govern the acquisition of these references are known as the discovery protocols. Once these references have been obtained, a number of steps must be taken for entities to start communicating usefully with services in a DJINN; these steps are described by the join protocol.

JRMP. Java Remote Message Protocol. A defined set of message formats that allow data to be passed across a network from one computer to another.

JSR-109. Java Specification Request-109 defines the programming model and runtime architecture for implementing web services in Java.

jUDDI. (Pronounced "Judy".) An open-source Java-based implementation of a UDDI registry and a toolkit for developers to build access to UDDI registries within their own applications. See also *UDDI*.

K

Kerberos. A network authentication protocol. It is designed to provide strong authentication for client-server applications by using secret-key cryptography.

L

LDAP. Lightweight Directory Access Protocol. A software protocol for enabling anyone to locate organizations, individuals, and other resources, such as files and devices in a network, whether on the public Internet or on a corporate intranet.

Load Balancing. Distribution of tasks or workload across multiple resources, so as to get optimum usage from available resources. Load balancing is important in a multiprocessing system.

Logical Machine. An engine and the associated repository.

Lookup Request. Resources with attributes matching the lookup request will be bound to a name in the name space of a client.

Lookup Service. The component that finds resources that match attribute-value pairs in the resource description of registered in the repository.

Lower Level Services. Services that are atomic functional units.

M

Mailbox. A core-managed resource assigned to a connected engine client to send messages to or receive messages from. It can be either an Outbox or an Inbox.

Mapping Object. An object binding an `ESname` to resources or a search recipe.

Member Class Services. The services in an ecosystem that use the standards and rules set by the regulatory class services to offer a certain service that is within the domain of the ecosystem.

Member/Service Directories. See *Registry*.

Message. Data packets used for interprocess communication on a network.

Metadata. Data that is not part of the resource's implementation but is used to describe and protect the resource.

MIDP. Mobile Information Device Profile. Provides a standard runtime environment that allows new applications and services to be dynamically deployed on the end-user devices. **Mport**. Multicast port used by the advertising service to multicast resource metadata.

MQ Integrator. IBM's application integration product based on message brokering technology.

MSMQ. Microsoft Message Queueing. Technology that enables applications running at different times to communicate across heterogeneous networks and systems that may be temporarily offline.

MTS. Microsoft Transaction Service. A service that allows creation of component-based and transaction-oriented applications. See also *EJB*.

N

Name Frame. A core-managed resource that associates a string with a mapping object.

Name Search Policy. A name conflict-resolution tool used by the core to find the appropriate strings when looking up names in a name frame.

.NET. Microsoft's initiative around the web services paradigm. Its goal is to provide a technology stack that is interoperable and make the functional interfaces of the devices and the applications more web services-oriented.

NOM. Network Object Model. Interentity interaction model based on objects communicating with each other through some RPC mechanism.

NTLM. Windows NT LAN Manager. The default protocol for network authentication in the Windows NT 4.0 operating system.

O

ODL. Object Description Language. A Microsoft-proposed IDL.

OLE. Object Linking and Embedding. A compound document standard developed by Microsoft Corporation. It enables you to create objects with one application, then link or embed them in a second application.

ORB. Object Request Broker. A component in CORBA architecture that mediates the interaction between distributed objects.

Orchestration. Microsoft term for creating and managing business processes that span multiple applications, platforms, and web services.

Outbox. The location where the client places a message to request access to a resource.

Out-of-Band Communication. An interaction between two entities that happens without the knowledge or participation of the e-Speak engine.

P

Passphrase. The e-Speak security jargon for *password* in the PSE.

Peer-to-Peer Architecture. A nonhierarchical application design style in which no particular component is in complete control of the overall functioning. The components in this architecture, self-contained, and self-managed, are *peers* of each other.

Persistence. The ability of an entity to retain its state and data in an offline mode.

Persistent Folder. An e-Speak engine-registered folder resource that stays operational even after the service that creates it terminates. See also *Folder*.

Persistent Repository. A database-based repository that stores resource metadata and state of e-Speak core-managed resources. A e-Speak engine can use the data from this repository to reinstate the state of the engine. They are helpful for fault tolerance.

Persistified Service. By definition, does not lose the data and resources it creates when shut down (on purpose or accidentally). A persistent service makes such crashes and scheduled downtimes transparent to its clients.

PKI. Public Key Infrastructure. A set of services and protocols that support the use of public and private key-pairs by applications for security.

Principal. The entity holding the private key corresponding to a given public key.

Private Key. Secret key required for decryption of data. See also *Public Key*.

Private Registry. Service registry that caters to a business entity or entities. These entities have greater control over service registration and discovery.

Protection Domain. The environment associated with a particular Outbox from which resources can be accessed.

PSE. Private Security Environment. A cryptographically secure store for private keys.

Public Key. Nonsecret data that is associated with a given private key by cryptographic techniques. See also *Private Key*.

Publish. A request sent to the distributor service to publish events.

Q

Quality of Service. Defines consistency and predictability metrics for a service.

R

Registry. A directory of e-services and web services, including service description and information on service invocation.

Regulatory Class Services. Services that ensure interoperability among the members of the ecosystem and enforce standards and regulations required for that purpose.

Reliable Messaging Service. A *contributed* e-Speak service for guaranteed message delivery.

Remote Resource Manager. An e-Speak engine component responsible for importing and exporting resources from a remote service engine.

Repository. A passive entity in the core that stores resource metadata and the internal state of core-managed resources.

Repository Entry. The metadata of a resource, as stored in the repository and made available to the engine.

Repository Handle. An index into the repository associated with the metadata of a resource.

Repository View. A resource that can be used to limit the search for particular resources in a large resource repository, much as a database view restricts a search within a database.

Resource. A uniform description of active entities, such as a service, or passive entities, such as hardware devices.

Resource Contract. A resource denoting an agreement between the client and the resource handler for use of a particular resource. The agreement includes a provision for the client to use an API known to the resource handler when making the request for the resource.

Resource Description. The data specified for the attribute field of the metadata, as represented by the client to the core. See also *Resource Specification*.

Resource Factory. An entity that can build the internal state of a resource requested by a client.

Resource Handler. A client responsible for responding to requests for access to one or more resources.

Resource-Specific Data. A metadata field of a resource. Carries information about the resource. Can be public or private to the resource handler.

Resource Specification. Consists of all metadata fields, except the attributes field for a resource in the engine.

RMI. Remote Method Invocation. A Java mechanism for interprocess communication. See also *RPC*.

Root Folder. Top-level folder within an e-Speak engine instance. See also *Folders*.

Root Name Frame. Top-level name frame within an e-Speak engine instance. See also *Name Frame*.

RosettaNet. A consortium of more than 400 worldwide companies. It is a self-funded, nonprofit organization dedicated to creating, implementing, and promoting open e-business standards. These standards form a common e-business language, aligning processes between trading partners on a global basis.

RPC. Remote Procedure Call. A protocol that one program can use to invoke a method from another program deployed on a remote computer on the network without having to understand network details. See also *RMI*.

S

S2ML. Security Services Markup Language. A standard that provides an XML specification for the sharing of security services between companies engaged in B2B and business-to-customer business transactions.

SAX. Simple API for XML. A standard interface for event-based XML parsing.

SDL. Service Definition Language. Microsoft's specification for service description.

Self-Signed Certificates. Certificates for which the issuer and the subject are same.

Serialization. Allows distributed systems to send data through different computer architectures. See also *ESSerialization*.

Service. An active program or a software component, in a given environment, that provides and manages access to a resource that is essential for other entities in the environment to function.

Service Accessor. Handle to the service returned by the engine during registration.

Service Aggregators. An ecosystem entity that composes a set of related services and creates a higher level service.

Service-Centric Economy. An economy where business interentity interaction happens through a network of services.

Service Composition. Combines offerings of two or more services to create a new service.

Service Deployers. These entities can advertise or register their services in such a registry for discovery by service users.

Service Description. A formal and publicized way to characterize features and functionality of a service offering.

Service Discovery. A process of finding a service, based on a description.

Service Engine. The active entity of a logical machine that mediates access to resources registered in the local repository.

Service Framework. A specification that provides guidelines for service design, creation, and deployment.

ServiceID. Service Identity. A field in the metadata that identifies a service.

Service Lifecycle. A sequence of stages that a service will undergo in its life — from strategic planning to obsolescence.

Service Obsolescence. A service lifecycle stage in which a service is obsoleted.

Service Registry. See *Registry*.

SFS. Service Framework Specification. E-Speak's specification for service modeling. See also *Service Framework*.

SGML. Standard Generalized Markup Language. SGML is a standard for the definition of device-independent, system-independent methods of representing texts in electronic form. See also *XML*.

SLS. Session Layer Security. The low-level message protocol used by all e-Speak cores and clients for remote communication.

SMIME. Secure Multipurpose Internet Mail Extensions. A secure and encrypted email protocol.

SMTP. Simple Mail Transfer Protocol. A TCP/IP-based protocol used for sending and receiving email.

SOAP. Simple Object Access Protocol. A lightweight protocol for exchange of information in a decentralized, distributed environment. It is an XML-based protocol that consists of three parts: an envelope that defines a framework for describing what is in a message and how to process it, a set of encoding rules for expressing instances of application-defined data types, and a convention for representing RPCs and responses.

SPKI. Simple Public Key Infrastructure. A specific variant of PKI developed within the IETF and used by e-Speak. See also *PKI*.

State. Data that a resource needs to implement its abstraction.

Stub. A client-side or server-side representation of a remote object. A stub contains the necessary logic for communicating with the remote object. It hides the complexity of network communication and *remoteness* of the object.

Subject. The entity to which the access right or name has been issued. In a certificate, the subject is denoted by its public key.

Synchronous Interaction. A blocking interaction in which the transacting entities are blocked in their transaction sequence until the current interaction is complete.

T

Tag. The field in a certificate expressing an access right.

Terms of Use. Specific service-level agreements and legal constraints.

TLS. Transport Layer Security. Security infrastructure that ensures safety of the data while it is on the wire.

TPP. Trading Partner Profile. ebXML specification that provides the *public interface* that a single trading partner can exchange with other trading partners to interact with it.

Transient Resource. A resource that is removed from an e-Speak engine when the service that created it is terminated.

Trust Assumptions. Specify which certificates will be honored and the acceptable set of tags in each case. Both clients and services may have trust assumptions. Trust assumptions do not appear in any of the e-Speak protocols (core-to-core or client-to-core APIs).

U

UDDI. Universal Description, Discovery, and Integration. The UDDI Project is an open industry initiative enabling businesses to discover each other and to define how they interact over the Internet and share information in a global registry architecture.

URL. Uniform Resource Locator. An address that identifies a document or resource on the World Wide Web.

V

Vocabulary. A resource that contains the set of attributes and value types for describing resources.

VPN. Virtual Private Network. A group of two or more computer systems, typically connected to a private network (a network built and maintained by an organization solely for its own use) with limited public network access that communicates *securely* over a public network.

W

W3C. World Wide Web Consortium. The consortium was created in October 1994 to lead the World Wide Web to its full potential by developing common protocols that promote its evolution and ensure its interoperability.

Web Services. Self-contained applications based on peer-to-peer architecture that can be described, published, located, and invoked over a network, generally the Internet. They interact with and/or invoke each other, fulfilling specific tasks and requests, and carry out specific parts of complex transactions or workflows.

Workflow. The sequence of activities performed in a business that produces a result of observable value to an individual node (entity) of the sequence.

WSCL. Web Services Conversation Language. Provides for the definition of abstract interfaces of web services. It specifies the business-level conversations or public processes supported by a web service.

WSDL. Web Services Description Language. A standard proposed by Microsoft for service description. WSDL is an XML format for describing Internet or intranet services as a set of endpoints operating on messages containing either document-oriented or procedure-oriented information.

WSFL. Web Services Flow Language. An XML language for the description of web services compositions proposed by IBM.

WSTK. Web Services Toolkit. IBM's toolkit for development of web services.

X

X.509. A standard that defines what information can go into a certificate and describes how to write it down (the data format).

XAML. Transaction Authority Markup Language. A vendor-neutral standard that enables the coordination and processing of online transactions.

XDR. eXternal Data Representation. A standard for the description and encoding of data. XDR uses a language to describe data formats, but the language is used only for describing data and is not a programming language. Protocols such as RPC and the Network File System (NFS) use XDR to describe their data formats.

XLANG. A complete language that uses XML as the written format for for describing any business process.

XML. eXtended Markup Language. A platform-independent information exchange format. XML is a special case of SGML. See also *SGML*.

XML DTD. XML Document Type Definition. Specifies formatting rules for XML (or SGML) documents.

XML-RPC. A specification and set of implementations that allow software running on disparate operating systems running in different environments to make procedure calls over the Internet.

XML Schema. Specification for information structure in XML documents.

INDEX

access control, 46, 50, 204, 210, 228,
    316, 476
    fine-grained, 315, 359
Active Directory, 378, 384
ADS, *see* Advertisement and Discov-
    ery of Service
Advertisement and Discovery of Ser-
    vice, 411
advertising service, 58, 185, 187–190,
    192–195, 199, 238, 241, 251,
    288, 289, 343
    group, 188, 189, 192–194, 295
ALE, 149
ASP, 20, 404
asychronous interaction, *see* asynchronous
    communication
asynchronous communication, 5, 54,
    357, 404
attribute, 50, 74, 77, 109, 111–114,
    116, 203, 299, 337
authXML, 425

B2B, *see* business-to-business
B2C, *see* business-to-consumer
BizTalk, 61, 362, 367, 393, 396, 397,
    408–411, 446

business-to-business, 1, 3, 55, 358,
    390, 396, 407, 445, 448
business-to-consumer, 3, 351
business logic, 32, 43, 69, 72, 75, 98,
    298, 342, 446

C-Hub, 419, 420
C-Space, 419, 420
call-by-reference, 58
call-by-value, 58
CDPD, *see* Cellular Digital Packet Data
Cellular Digital Packet Data, 346
certificate
    autorization tag, 215–219, 222,
    223, 342
    cancellation and termination pro-
    cedures, 230
    self-signed, 219, 221, 222
    structure, 216
    subject, 215–217, 219, 223
certificate holder, 207, 210, 216–218,
    221
certificate issuer, 207, 216, 229
CGI, 19, 20
client-server architecture, 17
CLR, *see* Common Language Run-

fulfill your needs

invent

Want to know about new products, services and solutions from Hewlett-Packard Company — as soon as they're invented?

Need information about new HP services to help you implement new or existing products?

Looking for HP's newest solution to a specific challenge in your business?

HP Computer News features the latest from HP!

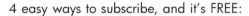

4 easy ways to subscribe, and it's FREE:

*   **fax** complete and fax the form below to (651) 430-3388, or

*   **online** sign up online at www.hp.com/go/compnews, or

*   **email** complete the information below and send to hporders@earthlink.net, or

*   **mail** complete and mail the form below to:

Twin Cities Fulfillment Center
Hewlett-Packard Company
P.O. Box 408
Stillwater, MN 55082

reply now to receive the first year FREE!

name	title
company	dept./mail stop
address	
city	state	zip
email	signature	date

please indicate your industry below:

- [ ] accounting
- [ ] education
- [ ] financial services
- [ ] government
- [ ] healthcare/medical
- [ ] legal
- [ ] manufacturing
- [ ] publishing/printing
- [ ] online services
- [ ] real estate
- [ ] retail/wholesale distrib
- [ ] technical
- [ ] telecommunications
- [ ] transport and travel
- [ ] utilities
- [ ] other: _____

integrated **hp education training** **it just works**

HP's world-class education and training offers hands on education solutions including:

- Linux
- HP-UX System and Network Administration
- Advanced HP-UX System Administration
- IT Service Management using advanced Internet technologies
- Microsoft Windows NT/2000
- Internet/Intranet
- MPE/iX
- Database Administration
- Software Development

HP's new IT Professional Certification program provides rigorous technical qualification for specific IT job roles including HP-UX System Administration, Network Management, Unix/NT Servers and Applications Management, and IT Service Management.

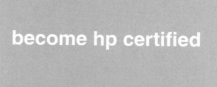

become hp certified

http://education.hp.com

LICENSE AGREEMENT AND LIMITED WARRANTY

READ THE FOLLOWING TERMS AND CONDITIONS CAREFULLY BEFORE OPENING THIS CD PACKAGE. THIS LEGAL DOCUMENT IS AN AGREEMENT BETWEEN YOU AND PRENTICE-HALL, INC. (THE "COMPANY"). BY OPENING THIS SEALED CD PACKAGE, YOU ARE AGREEING TO BE BOUND BY THESE TERMS AND CONDITIONS. IF YOU DO NOT AGREE WITH THESE TERMS AND CONDITIONS, DO NOT OPEN THE CD PACKAGE. PROMPTLY RETURN THE UNOPENED CD PACKAGE AND ALL ACCOMPANYING ITEMS TO THE PLACE YOU OBTAINED THEM FOR A FULL REFUND OF ANY SUMS YOU HAVE PAID.

1. **GRANT OF LICENSE:** In consideration of your purchase of this book, and your agreement to abide by the terms and conditions of this Agreement, the Company grants to you a nonexclusive right to use and display the copy of the enclosed software program (hereinafter the "SOFTWARE") on a single computer (i.e., with a single CPU) at a single location so long as you comply with the terms of this Agreement. The Company reserves all rights not expressly granted to you under this Agreement.

2. **OWNERSHIP OF SOFTWARE:** You own only the magnetic or physical media (the enclosed CD) on which the SOFTWARE is recorded or fixed, but the Company and the software developers retain all the rights, title, and ownership to the SOFTWARE recorded on the original CD copy(ies) and all subsequent copies of the SOFTWARE, regardless of the form or media on which the original or other copies may exist. This license is not a sale of the original SOFTWARE or any copy to you.

3. **COPY RESTRICTIONS:** This SOFTWARE and the accompanying printed materials and user manual (the "Documentation") are the subject of copyright. You may not copy the Documentation or the SOFTWARE, except that you may make a single copy of the SOFTWARE for backup or archival purposes only. You may be held legally responsible for any copying or copyright infringement which is caused or encouraged by your failure to abide by the terms of this restriction.

4. **USE RESTRICTIONS:** You may not network the SOFTWARE or otherwise use it on more than one computer or computer terminal at the same time. You may physically transfer the SOFTWARE from one computer to another provided that the SOFTWARE is used on only one computer at a time. You may not distribute copies of the SOFTWARE or Documentation to others. You may not reverse engineer, disassemble, decompile, modify, adapt, translate, or create derivative works based on the SOFTWARE or the Documentation without the prior written consent of the Company.

5. **TRANSFER RESTRICTIONS:** The enclosed SOFTWARE is licensed only to you and may not be transferred to any one else without the prior written consent of the Company. Any unauthorized transfer of the SOFTWARE shall result in the immediate termination of this Agreement.

6. **TERMINATION:** This license is effective until terminated. This license will terminate automatically without notice from the Company and become null and void if you fail to comply with any provisions or limitations of this license. Upon termination, you shall destroy the Documentation and all copies of the SOFTWARE. All provisions of this Agreement as to warranties, limitation of liability, remedies or damages, and our ownership rights shall survive termination.

7. **MISCELLANEOUS:** This Agreement shall be construed in accordance with the laws of the United States of America and the State of New York and shall benefit the Company, its affiliates, and assignees.

8. **LIMITED WARRANTY AND DISCLAIMER OF WARRANTY:** The Company warrants that the SOFTWARE, when properly used in accordance with the Documentation, will operate in substantial conformity with the description of the SOFTWARE set forth in the Documentation. The Company does not warrant that the SOFTWARE will meet your requirements or that the operation of the SOFTWARE will be uninterrupted or error-free. The Company warrants that the media on which the SOFTWARE is delivered shall be free from defects in materials and workmanship under normal use for a period of thirty (30) days from the date of your purchase. Your only remedy and the

Company's only obligation under these limited warranties is, at the Company's option, return of the warranted item for a refund of any amounts paid by you or replacement of the item. Any replacement of SOFTWARE or media under the warranties shall not extend the original warranty period. The limited warranty set forth above shall not apply to any SOFTWARE which the Company determines in good faith has been subject to misuse, neglect, improper installation, repair, alteration, or damage by you. EXCEPT FOR THE EXPRESSED WARRANTIES SET FORTH ABOVE, THE COMPANY DISCLAIMS ALL WARRANTIES, EXPRESS OR IMPLIED, INCLUDING WITHOUT LIMITATION, THE IMPLIED WARRANTIES OF MERCHANTABILITY AND FITNESS FOR A PARTICULAR PURPOSE. EXCEPT FOR THE EXPRESS WARRANTY SET FORTH ABOVE, THE COMPANY DOES NOT WARRANT, GUARANTEE, OR MAKE ANY REPRESENTATION REGARDING THE USE OR THE RESULTS OF THE USE OF THE SOFTWARE IN TERMS OF ITS CORRECTNESS, ACCURACY, RELIABILITY, CURRENTNESS, OR OTHERWISE.

IN NO EVENT, SHALL THE COMPANY OR ITS EMPLOYEES, AGENTS, SUPPLIERS, OR CONTRACTORS BE LIABLE FOR ANY INCIDENTAL, INDIRECT, SPECIAL, OR CONSEQUENTIAL DAMAGES ARISING OUT OF OR IN CONNECTION WITH THE LICENSE GRANTED UNDER THIS AGREEMENT, OR FOR LOSS OF USE, LOSS OF DATA, LOSS OF INCOME OR PROFIT, OR OTHER LOSSES, SUSTAINED AS A RESULT OF INJURY TO ANY PERSON, OR LOSS OF OR DAMAGE TO PROPERTY, OR CLAIMS OF THIRD PARTIES, EVEN IF THE COMPANY OR AN AUTHORIZED REPRESENTATIVE OF THE COMPANY HAS BEEN ADVISED OF THE POSSIBILITY OF SUCH DAMAGES. IN NO EVENT SHALL LIABILITY OF THE COMPANY FOR DAMAGES WITH RESPECT TO THE SOFTWARE EXCEED THE AMOUNTS ACTUALLY PAID BY YOU, IF ANY, FOR THE SOFTWARE.

SOME JURISDICTIONS DO NOT ALLOW THE LIMITATION OF IMPLIED WARRANTIES OR LIABILITY FOR INCIDENTAL, INDIRECT, SPECIAL, OR CONSEQUENTIAL DAMAGES, SO THE ABOVE LIMITATIONS MAY NOT ALWAYS APPLY. THE WARRANTIES IN THIS AGREEMENT GIVE YOU SPECIFIC LEGAL RIGHTS AND YOU MAY ALSO HAVE OTHER RIGHTS WHICH VARY IN ACCORDANCE WITH LOCAL LAW.

ACKNOWLEDGMENT

YOU ACKNOWLEDGE THAT YOU HAVE READ THIS AGREEMENT, UNDERSTAND IT, AND AGREE TO BE BOUND BY ITS TERMS AND CONDITIONS. YOU ALSO AGREE THAT THIS AGREEMENT IS THE COMPLETE AND EXCLUSIVE STATEMENT OF THE AGREEMENT BETWEEN YOU AND THE COMPANY AND SUPERSEDES ALL PROPOSALS OR PRIOR AGREEMENTS, ORAL, OR WRITTEN, AND ANY OTHER COMMUNICATIONS BETWEEN YOU AND THE COMPANY OR ANY REPRESENTATIVE OF THE COMPANY RELATING TO THE SUBJECT MATTER OF THIS AGREEMENT.

Should you have any questions concerning this Agreement or if you wish to contact the Company for any reason, please contact in writing at the address below.

Robin Short
Prentice Hall PTR
One Lake Street
Upper Saddle River, New Jersey 07458

About the CD-ROM

The CD-ROM contains the example code associated with each new e-Speak concept. The organization of the CD-ROM is explained in the Introduction. Where appropriate, the chapter introduction page lists the working example directories associated with that chapter. These examples are based on e-Speak A.3.11 and Sun JDK 1.2.2.

The CD-ROM also contains the e-Speak A.3.11 software. Appendix A provides instructions for installing and configuring the software.

Technical Support

Prentice Hall does not offer technical support for any of the programs on this CD-ROM. However, if there is a problem with the CD or it is damaged, you may obtain a replacement copy by sending an email describing the problem to: disc_exchange@prenhall.com